Competing Chinese
Political Visions

Competing Chinese Political Visions

Hong Kong vs. Beijing on Democracy

SONNY SHIU-HING LO

Praeger Security International

 PRAEGER

AN IMPRINT OF ABC-CLIO, LLC
Santa Barbara, California • Denver, Colorado • Oxford, England

Library of Congress Cataloging-in-Publication Data

Lo, Shiu Hing, 1963–
  Competing Chinese political visions : Hong Kong vs. Beijing on democracy / Sonny Shiu-Hing Lo.
     p. cm.
  Includes bibliographical references and index.
   ISBN 978–0–313–36505–8 (hard copy : alk. paper) — 978–0–313–36506–5 (ebook)
1. Democracy—China—Hong Kong. 2. Democratization—China—Hong Kong. 3. Hong Kong (China)—Politics and government. 4. China—Politics and government. I. Title.
JQ1539.5.A91S43   2010
320.95125′090511—dc22   2009050890

ISBN: 978–0–313–36505–8
EISBN: 978–0–313–36506–5

14 13 12 11 10   1 2 3 4 5

This book is also available on the World Wide Web as an eBook.
Visit www.abc-clio.com for details.

Praeger
An Imprint of ABC-CLIO, LLC

ABC-CLIO, LLC
130 Cremona Drive, P.O. Box 1911
Santa Barbara, California 93116-1911

This book is printed on acid-free paper (∞)

Manufactured in the United States of America

I dedicate this book to Winnie, Tracy, and Emily.

Contents

Acknowledgments   ix

Abbreviations   xi

Introduction: Perspectives on Democratization in Hong Kong   1
                and China

Chapter 1   The Political Role of Hong Kong in China's Tiananmen   23
             Tragedy and Legacy

Chapter 2   The Politics of the July 1 March since 2003   44

Chapter 3   From the Debate over Referendum in 2004 to the   61
             Rejection of Reform Package in 2005

Chapter 4   Architects of the Democracy Movement: Martin Lee,   92
             Szeto Wah, George Cautherley, and Anson Chan

Chapter 5   From Democratic Defeat in 2007 District Councils   116
             Elections to Rebound in 2008 Legislative Council
             Elections

Chapter 6   The Hong Kong Democratic Party   140

Chapter 7   Pro-Democracy Parties: Civic Party, League of Social   158
             Democrats, and Association for Democracy and
             People's Livelihood

Chapter 8   Can the Pro-Beijing DAB and Pro-Business Liberal   178
             Party Promote Democratization in Hong Kong?

Chapter 9   The Politics of Co-optation: Beijing, the HKSAR   202
             Government, and Democrats

Conclusion   228

Notes   239

Glossary   271

Bibliography   273

Index   281

Acknowledgments

I am indebted to George Cautherley, Martin Lee, Cyd Ho, Alan Lung, Hilton Cheong-Leen, Fung King-man, Professor Kuan Hsin-chi, Dr. Suzanne Pepper, Professor Joseph Cheng, and Dr. Bruce Kwong for sharing their views with me on Hong Kong. Professor Ming Chan of Stanford University kindly introduced me to Martin Lee so that I could understand his views on democratization. I extend my gratitude to four mainland Chinese officials and a mainland researcher who exchanged their opinions with me on Beijing's policy toward Hong Kong. Indeed, all the errors, interpretations, and arguments in this book are my sole responsibility.

Abbreviations

AD	*Apple Daily*
ADPL	Association for Democracy and People's Livelihood
BLCC	Basic Law Consultative Committee
BLDC	Basic Law Drafting Committee
BPF	Business and Professionals Federation of Hong Kong
CCCD	Citizens' Commission on Constitutional Development
CCP	Chinese Communist Party
CDIC	Central Discipline Inspection Commission
CEPA	Closer Economic Partnership Arrangement
CIA	Central Intelligence Agency
CP	Civic Party
CPPCC	Chinese People's Political Consultative Conference
DAB	Democratic Alliance for Betterment and Progress of Hong Kong
DC	District Councils
DP	Democratic Party
EAC	Electoral Affairs Commission
ExCo	Executive Council
FTU	Federation of Trade Unions
GPPCC	Guangdong People's Political Consultative Conference
HKDF	Hong Kong Democratic Foundation
HKEJ	*Hong Kong Economic Journal*
HKET	*Hong Kong Economic Times*
HKMAO	Hong Kong Macao Affairs Office
HKPA	Hong Kong Progressive Alliance
HKSAR	Hong Kong Special Administrative Region
HYK	Heung Yee Kuk
ICAC	Independent Commission Against Corruption

ICCPR	International Covenant on Civil and Political Rights
KMT	Kuomintang
LegCo	Legislative Council
LP	Liberal Party
MP	*Ming Pao*
NCNA	New China News Agency
NGOs	Non-Governmental Organizations
NPC	National People's Congress
OD	*Oriental Daily*
PLA	People's Liberation Army
PLC	Provisional Legislative Council
POAS	Principal Officials Accountability System
PRC	People's Republic of China
PRD	Pearl River Delta
ROC	Republic of China
RTHK	Radio Television Hong Kong
SARS	Severe Acute Respiratory Syndrome
SCMP	South China Morning Post
SDC	Strategic Development Commission
STD	*Sing Tao Daily*
SUCUHK	Student Union of the Chinese University of Hong Kong
TDN	*Today Daily News* (Toronto Chinese daily)
UDHK	United Democrats of Hong Kong
WJ	*World Journal*
WWP	Wen Wei Po

INTRODUCTION

Perspectives on Democratization in Hong Kong and China

Since the tragedy of the Tiananmen incident in the People's Republic of China (PRC) on June 4, 1989, and particularly after the return of Hong Kong's sovereignty from Britain to the PRC on July 1, 1997, the concept of democracy has actually been separating the hearts and minds of some Hong Kong people from the ruling philosophy of both the central government in Beijing and the government of the Hong Kong Special Administrative Region (HKSAR). The notion of democracy, in the minds of most pro-democracy Hongkongers, entails the direct elections of the chief executive by universal suffrage and of the entire Legislative Council (LegCo). However, this concept of democracy as checks and balances on the chief executive and legislature through direct elections is a Western one in opposition to the mainland Chinese leadership's vision of democracy. For the mainland Chinese leadership, democracy in the socialist PRC has to be procedurally incremental, publicly accountable, and culturally special with Chinese characteristics. Procedurally, the PRC leaders tend to accept a model of democratic reforms that proceed slowly rather than copying any Western model of checks and balances. They regard the gradual improvement of the legal system and the spread of village elections as signs of a Chinese-style of democratization. Hence, the concept of democracy held by the pro-democracy elites in the HKSAR conflicts with that maintained by the PRC leaders. These two divergent visions of democracy—one Western and another Chinese—have been shaping the political development of the HKSAR since July 1, 1997.

PERSPECTIVES ON DEMOCRATIZATION

There are at least six major perspectives for us to comprehend the dynamics of democratization: elite, class, cleavage, geopolitics, political culture, and social movement. The elite perspective focuses on the role of political elites in democratization. If a regime is split into hard-liners opposing political reform and soft-liners supporting it, and yet if the soft-liners prevail over the hard-liners, democratization has an opening through which civil society groups can articulate their interests more freely and political parties can participate in national elections.[1] Indeed, elite political culture plays a critical role in this process of democratic transition. In the event that the dominant elite, or the soft-liner, adopts a liberal-minded and tolerant attitude toward public criticisms and citizen protests, and that it accepts the electoral defeat of the ruling party, a threshold in democratization—the rotation of political party in power— is reached. Yet, if the ruling elites are intolerant of public criticisms and citizen protests and are keen to maintain their political power by all means, they can manipulate election results and refuse to surrender power. Under these circumstances, democratization is protracted, delayed, and perhaps reversed.[2] The role of elites is critical to democratization.

The cases of Hong Kong and the PRC are illuminating the role of elites in democratization. Before Hong Kong's return to the PRC, the British colonial administration led by the governor could be seen as relatively hard-line in its attitude toward political reform until the mid-1980s, when the departing British expatriates sensed the urgency of delegating more political and administrative power to the local Hong Kong Chinese. The increasingly soft-line approach of the British to tackling democratic reform became prominent when Christopher Patten became the last governor, who was determined to democratize Hong Kong to the fullest extent accepted by the PRC. Nevertheless, his bold approach met the PRC opposition and the Chinese government rolled back his electoral reforms injected into the LegCo before Hong Kong's sovereignty change.[3] After the handover, the proportional representation system was adopted in LegCo direct elections so that the ability of democrats to grasp more seats was curbed. The franchise of LegCo functional constituencies, composed of occupational and professional groups, was restricted and not widened to more electorates as what Patten intended to implement.[4] Since PRC officials became the hard-liners prevailing over the soft-line Patten, who departed Hong Kong on the eve of the handover, the door of democratization in Hong Kong was kept ajar. Yet, the local democrats in the HKSAR remain the soft-line elites trying to push the door of democratization open further. As a result, two visions of democracy persist in the HKSAR, one held by the Hong Kong democrats and the other held by

PRC officials responsible for Hong Kong matters. The HKSAR government tends to side with the overlord Beijing and thus becomes hard-line in its attitude toward democratization. At times, critics of the HKSAR government believe that it is more hard-line than PRC officials responsible for Hong Kong matters.[5]

Leo Goodstadt adopts the elite perspective to delineate the origins of the business elite's "distaste for democracy" in Hong Kong.[6] He observed that the British ruling elite in Hong Kong co-opted the business elites and formed an alliance with them. As a result, the business "enjoyed a highly privileged position on the political agenda," while colonial officials "bowed to business pressures and tolerated wholly inadequate self-regulation of the banking and securities industries and extensive monopolistic practices throughout the economy."[7] After Hong Kong's return to the PRC, the business elites have clung to political power through their appointments into various policy-making and consultative bodies and their monopolization of most of the seats in LegCo's functional constituency elections, where the franchise remains relatively narrow. Goodstadt has argued that the business leaders began to participate in Hong Kong's electoral politics, but the obstacle to Hong Kong's democratic development comes from the government and Beijing. As he wrote:

> Repeated claims by Beijing and Hong Kong officials that business candidates could not hope to capture the popular vote had proved ill-founded in Hong Kong as they would be in any other advanced urban society . . . [T]here were still no signs that the leadership, either in Beijing or Hong Kong, was prepared to trust the good sense of the ordinary voter and accept the case for universal suffrage.[8]

According to Goodstadt, the business elites remain distrustful of the politically rational and mature ordinary people. In short, he believes that the coalition of Beijing, the HKSAR government, and some business leaders acts as a hindrance to Hong Kong's democratization.

Sharing Goodstadt's view that the role of the business elite is critical to Hong Kong's political development, Ray Yep has argued that "the business bias in the power structure, limited democracy and a vibrant civil society could only breed suspicion and tension; any government's initiative is now seen as proof of government-business collusion."[9] He observes that the debate in the legislature has become more polemical and class voting is becoming a trend. Under the circumstances in which the public distrusts the government and the business elites, political reform and re-enfranchisement would be imperative for effective governance.[10]

Democratization in the PRC encountered a critical moment of opportunity in May and June 1989 when the hard-line reformers, such as the late

Deng Xiaoping and Premier Li Peng, prevailed over the soft-liner and Chinese Communist Party (CCP) secretary, Zhao Ziyang. The hard-liners in the CCP Politburo decided to suppress the student democrats who protested and stayed on the Tiananmen Square.[11] The violent military crackdown on the student democrats on June 4, 1989, shocked the world, angered the Hong Kong democrats, and had far-reaching repercussions on not only the relations between Hong Kong democrats and the PRC but also democratization in the HKSAR. Those Hong Kong democrats, as will be discussed in Chapter 1, who helped mainland democrats to flee the PRC, have since then been seen as the enemies of the mainland Chinese state. After Hong Kong's return to the PRC on July 1, 1997, the activities of the Hong Kong democrats in support of democratic reforms in the HKSAR have met the staunch resistance from PRC authorities. As long as the PRC is governed by hard-line leaders trying to maintain domestic economic prosperity with minimal democratic changes, and as long as they view the Hong Kong democrats as potentially "subversive" elements supported by foreign countries to change Hong Kong's political system at the expense of Beijing's national security interests, China's hard-liners must prevent the Hong Kong soft-liners from democratizing the HKSAR to the fullest extent of having the direct elections of both the chief executive and the entire legislature. Yet, believing that the politically mature and economically affluent Hong Kong people should be eligible for a fully democratized political system like Western democracies, the Hong Kong democrats are determined to confront Beijing's hard-line leaders. As a result, two visions of democracy are bound to clash, with the PRC hard-liners envisioning a more gradual and limited scope of democratic reforms and the Hong Kong soft-liners retaining the Western ideal of having the direct elections of both the chief executive and the whole legislature.

Another perspective on democratization is class power. The arrival of democracy depends on not only the struggle between various classes but also the state power vis-à-vis social classes and groups. David Potter wrote: "Historically, democratization has been both resisted and pushed forward by the changing dynamics of class relations and different classes pursuing their separate interests. Subordinate classes have usually pushed for democracy, dominant classes nearly always have resisted it."[12] Traditionally, the landlord class has been "the most anti-democratic" because democracy is seen as harmful to its profits and interests.[13] The peasantry and rural workers have an interest in democratization but rarely act in support of it. The urban working class tends to push for democratization through the struggle for union rights and collective bargaining. The bourgeoisie is, however, ambiguous because its orientations depend on whether its members are allying with or independent from the state. Finally, the pro-democracy proclivity of the salaried and professional middle class is ambiguous and contingent upon other classes. As Potter observes, "Where the working class has been comparatively weak, the middle classes have pushed for democratization to improve their positions. Where the working class has been strong, the middle classes may or may not have been as energetic."[14]

In Hong Kong, the landlord class and land developers are powerful forces that often see democracy as an anathema detrimental to their interests of acquiring profits, enjoying low taxes, and accumulating capital easily. While the peasantry and rural working class are weak in the urbanized city of Hong Kong, the bourgeoisie and the salaried/professional middle class are split into a pro-democracy faction and a pro-establishment wing.[15] The working class has traditionally been split into a more pro-democracy faction and a relatively pro-Beijing camp. The ideological cleavage among the classes in the HKSAR shows that the HKSAR is a politically divided society.

The role of the middle class in Hong Kong's democracy movement remains ambiguous. Some of its members are supportive of democracy, notably a majority of lawyers, intellectuals, religious priests, human rights activists, social workers, and teachers. On the other hand, some of them are politically conservative and prefer to see Hong Kong enjoying economic prosperity without necessarily having Western-style democracy. This conservative segment includes mostly civil servants, small business people, accountants, and professionals who increasingly have their business transactions with the PRC and mainland enterprises in Hong Kong. The ambiguity of the middle class in Hong Kong's political development is summed up by sociologist Tai-lok Lui, who observed in 2005 that

If given a choice, the middle class would not choose collective and political action as the most preferred means to voice its grievances. Under normal circumstances, the middle class would choose a form of political action that is less demanding and costly. It would also choose a form of action that would allow for more rational and sophisticated discussion and some space for negotiation in politics ... As a class that has its interests in the *status quo*, the middle class, unless provoked by government's unresponsiveness and top-down action, is unlikely to be convinced to pursue non-institutional political actions as its main political strategy ... The unhappy middle class is still prudent and cautious ... [T]he middle class is unprepared for a major clash with Beijing. It distrusts both the Tung administration and the democrats ... The middle class remains frustrated. But it also finds politics tiring.[16]

In the PRC, the bourgeoisie and the salaried/professional middle class are so far uninterested in Western-style democracy. The bourgeoisie and middle class in mainland China have been generally dependent on the state for their education, economic opportunities, and social welfare. They enjoy the fruits of economic modernization and rapid growth, lacking any interest to clamor for political transformations. On the other hand, the cadre-capitalist class is in general dependent on the state without the political will and economic incentives to fight for democracy.[17] At best, the bourgeoisie and middle class fight for their immediate and parochial interests without the determination to challenge state power on a whole range of issues, such as human rights, democracy, and civil liberties. They are also economically and politically co-opted by the Chinese state at the central level and the provincial governments at the local level. A Marxist scholar argues that a rural bourgeoisie was created by Deng Xiaoping's policy of commercializing the countryside, and that it is composed of the "prosperous commercial farmers and private entrepreneurs."[18] The working class, on the other hand, is so weak that its unions are under the control of the state without much autonomy to fight for the labor rights and interests.[19] The PRC regime is arguably no longer communist or even socialist, but it is ruled by a coalition of the new CCP hard-line elites and the anti-democratic but emergent capitalist class, which benefits much from the Party policy and preferential treatment.

The third perspective is the cleavage approach to comprehending the dynamics of democratization. Political cleavages can involve classes, identity, ethnic groups, policy issues, and, perhaps most importantly, ideology.[20] In the Hong Kong case, identity and ideology are the twin shapers influencing democratization. A recent work that combines identity with ideology to understand Hong Kong's democratization is written by Nick Thomas. He argues that Hong Kong from the 1980s to the 1990s developed into "a distinct and separate political identity."[21] He predicted that Hong Kong would experience "the development of a unique middle path—between the Western liberal-democratic model and the East Asian variant of authoritarianism."[22]

Identity and democratization are intertwined in the HKSAR. Those Hong Kong people who tend to identify themselves as Hong Kong persons are more likely to support and vote for the democratic camp than those who identify themselves as Chinese.[23] An overwhelming majority of the "pan-democrats"—a term used by the media to refer to the alliance of various pro-democracy groups—have a strong sense of belonging in the HKSAR, believing that they should fight for democracy in their homeland regardless of how the motherland views their activities with political suspicions. The Hongkongers who are identifying themselves as Chinese are more likely to support the PRC government and opt for a gradual pace of democratization. In a sense, democratization in the HKSAR is a tug of war between pan-democrats or Hong Kong identifiers on the one hand and pro-Beijing residents who are Chinese identifiers on the other.

Meanwhile, ideology remains crucial in defining the battle lines between the Hong Kong democrats and the PRC, between democrats and the business sector, and among democrats themselves.

The democrats, especially the left-wingers, not only see themselves as the subordinate class being politically suppressed by the dominant classes composed of the HKSAR ruling elite, business class, and PRC officials, but also regard Beijing as an authoritarian regime abandoning communism and socialism for the sake of achieving exploitative capitalism. Ideologically speaking, the Hong Kong democrats are diversified, splitting among themselves into the liberals and the left-wing welfarists. The liberals such as Martin Lee and Emily Lau do not really focus on people's livelihood and social welfare issues, whereas the welfarists such as Lee Cheuk-yan, Raymond Wong, and Frederick Fung attach great importance to the well-being of the poor and the needy. Ideologically, both the HKSAR government and the business sector are politically conservative, opting for a path of gradual, minimal, and incremental processes of political reforms. The business class particularly views democratization as a stimulus to the growth of trade unions, which in its mind would naturally lead to universal suffrage and welfarism harmful to their vested interest of maintaining the economic and political *status quo* in Hong Kong. Hence, ideology and class are intertwined in the politics of democratization in the HKSAR.

In the PRC, the political cleavages in the society embrace ethnic tensions in which some minority groups such as the Uygurs and Tibetans struggle for their right of self-determination in the Hans-dominated Chinese state.[24] Indeed, under the umbrella of the CCP rule, the Hans domination in the Chinese political system is affirmed and solid. The cleavages in the PRC include not only ethnic politics but also social unrest where the have-nots often confront the haves and the ruling elites in local governments, townships, and villages where Beijing and the provincial authorities often fail to rein in the misrule, maladministration, corruption, and organized crime at the grassroots level.[25] The PRC in the 2000s is a superficially "strong" state, but it is actually weak in the sense that ethnic and social unrest at the local grassroots level have exposed the problematic central-local relations in Chinese politics.[26] Social inequality in the PRC is serious and capitalist development is bringing about "an ideological vacuum and a moral desert."[27] Although ideology at the mass level is mainly materialism, the CCP utilizes socialism as a political slogan and tool of controlling the PRC, the co-opted elites, and the official media. While the ideological cleavage between liberalism and conservatism marks the political divide between democrats and pro-government elites in Hong Kong, materialism in the PRC is characterizing the popular culture but the socialist ideology has been relegated into an instrument of political control on the Party elites.

The fourth perspective useful for us to understand democratization in both Hong Kong and China is geopolitics. Geopolitically speaking, Hong Kong is a very small place, economically dependent on its motherland, mainland China, for water, food supply, and tourists. The HKSAR cannot survive without the economic and political support of the PRC. Yet, geo-politically Hong Kong as a cosmopolitan city attracts the attention of for-eign countries, whose nationals and officials are residing in the territory to observe the mainland Chinese and Hong Kong developments. Above all, Hong Kong's international financial status, with its respectable rule of law and a relatively high degree of civil liberties, fits into the Western values of liberalism and capitalism.[28] As an advanced capitalist city-state, Hong Kong's democratic development attracts the attention and political interests of foreign states, notably the United States. The support of the U.S. government for democracy in the HKSAR since its return to the PRC has aroused the political sensitivity of Beijing. In the eyes of Beijing, the United States is trying to foster democratization in the HKSAR with the sinister motive of encouraging a possible spillover effect on mainland China.[29] The superpower struggle between the United States and the PRC provides a broader geopolitical context under which democratization in the HKSAR can be understood. Therefore, democratization in Hong Kong is often a politically sensitive issue in the minds of PRC officials, espe-cially the hard-liners dealing with Hong Kong matters, because they see it as a chess game used by the United States to exert pressure on the main-land, to spread the political "virus" of Western-style democracy, and to subvert the CCP in the long run.

In view of the humiliation of China's Qing dynasty by foreign aggres-sion, and in light of the recent rise of a global China, the current PRC lead-ers are viewing democracy in a very Chinese manner. To them, democracy is not monopolized by the West, especially the United States. Democracy, to the Chinese reform-minded leaders, entails Chinese characteristics: the emphasis on sociopolitical harmony; the use of elections to enhance the accountability of CCP cadres and bureaucrats; the need for government agencies to be monitored internally by the audit commission and anticor-ruption bodies but not by the Western principle of separation of powers; the reactivation of the role of the law-making National People's Congress (NPC) to check government performance; the gradual development of the rule of law; and the partnerships between the state and social groups to resolve disputes and problems.[30] These Chinese characteristics of democ-racy are unique, reflective of the Asian values that cherish the respect for authority hierarchy and harmony, the importance of a "wise and virtuous bureaucratic elite," and the dominant role of the state in social and eco-nomic life.[31] The mind-set of PRC leaders on the concept of democracy is shaped by their historical tradition, cultural values, political socializa-tion, and most importantly their perception of the West trying to impose a Western-style political system onto China. Many ordinary Chinese per-ceive the United States as having the motives of obstructing the PRC's quest for reunification with Taiwan and assisting Japan's military buildup.[32] The Western perception of the PRC as "a threat" to the Western world exacerbates the view of PRC hard-liners that the United States harbors sinister motives by supporting Hong Kong's democratization. Democracy, from the geopolitical perspective and in the minds of the mainland Chinese leaders, cannot be the Western type that has been so alien and hostile to the Chinese.

The fifth perspective on democratization is political culture. Sinologists have long ago examined the evolution of political culture in the PRC.[33] The late Lucian Pye argued that the PRC political culture was paternalistic because citizens treated the political authorities respectfully and obediently.[34] He believed that Chinese politics was characterized by the powerful rulers at the top without accountability to citizens from below. Although Pye saw changes in the Chinese political culture in the Taiwan case during the 1980s, he maintained that the dependency relationships between the rulers and the ruled remained because of citizens' paternalistic attitude toward political authorities.[35] Some scholars have also argued that the Chinese political culture attaches importance more to the concept of good governance than to the Western notion of democracy.[36] Good governance includes such elements as "the balance between the individual and the community, between rights and duties, and between personal happiness and the common welfare of society." [37] In short, political culture in the PRC is by no means conducive to the development of Western-style democracy. However, the late Samuel Huntington argued that although the Confucian political culture was an obstacle to democratization in the PRC, the younger generation would perhaps develop a more liberal-minded and globalized worldview that would propel the mainland's democratic development. As he wrote in 1996:

China's Confucian heritage, with its emphasis on authority, order, hierarchy, and the supremacy of the collectivity over the individual, creates obstacles to democratization. Yet economic growth is creating in South China increasingly high levels of wealth, a dynamic bourgeoisie, accumulations of economic power outside governmental control, and a rapidly expanding middle class. In addition, Chinese people are deeply involved in the outside world in terms of trade, investment, and education. All this creates a social basis for movement toward political pluralism.[38]

Basically, Huntington adopted a modernization theory in predicting the rise of political pluralism resulting from the improvement in education, the emergence of the middle class, and the citizens' changing political outlook.

The psychocultural approach to understanding the mainland Chinese political culture was adopted by Hong Kong scholars such as Siu-kai Lau and Hsin-chi Kuan, who argued that the Hong Kong Chinese have been shaped by their familism and pragmatism and remained ambivalent toward Western democratic values.[39] Their assumption of a largely apolitical Hong Kong Chinese population has been challenged by many scholars, who argue that the local people are by no means apathetic as conventional wisdom assumed.[40] Still, the transformations of the political culture of the Hong Kong people remain to be researched further, partly because of the complexities of the changing elite and mass attitudes, and partly due to the increasing number of mainland immigrants whose political socialization and attitudes have not really been studied.

Michael DeGolyer, an authority in the study of Hong Kong's public opinion and political culture, has found that about 47 to 53 percent of the respondents in his surveys conducted from 2003 to 2009 supported the direct election of the chief executive, and that 17 to 30 percent in the same period strongly supported the idea.[41] In other words, at least 64 to 83 percent of the Hong Kong people support the direct election of the chief executive by universal suffrage. Furthermore, in the May 2009 survey of 1,205 residents, when asked whether the abolition of all LegCo functional constituencies and the election of all legislators from geographical constituencies would make government policies fairer or less fair, 23 percent of the respondents replied it would be "much fairer," 43 percent said "fairer," 13 percent replied that it would "stay the same," 8 percent perceived "less fair," 3 percent said "much less fair," and 11 percent did not know.[42] Clearly, about 68 percent of the respondents felt that the abolition of all functional constituencies and the election of all legislators through direct elections would make government policies fair. If most Hong Kong people are supportive of a broader scope of democratization, the greatest challenge to both the HKSAR government and Beijing is how to meet these demands in the medium and long term, if not simply delaying democratization in order to frustrate the political aspirations of the public. If the political expectations of the Hong Kong people are not met, any economic downturn in the HKSAR, like the Chief Executive Tung Chee-hwa era from July 1997 to March 2005, would perhaps plunge the political system into another crisis of governance because the democratic deficit would easily add fuel to the societal discontent. Democratic reform in the HKSAR is a must to safeguard social and political stability; Hong Kong's political development ideally needs to match its mass political culture and aspirations.

The sixth perspective on democratization is social movement. Although Sinologists have studied environmental movement, the Falun Gong, labor politics, and intellectual activism in the PRC, social movements remain relatively weak in the PRC without the impact of propelling democratization further.[43] The most influential student movement during the Tiananmen tragedy failed to trigger democratization, but its hard-line approach of remaining on the Tiananmen Square arguably provided the excuse for the CCP hard-liners to suppress them and led to the downfall of CCP soft-liner Zhao Ziyang.

In the Hong Kong case, social movements have embraced environmental protection, heritage preservation, town planning, and the opposition to the Victoria Harbor's reclamation plan.[44] While social movement in the HKSAR has indeed improved governmental response to meet some of their demands, it cannot really propel the PRC to allow more political space for the HKSAR to achieve the direct elections of both the chief executive and the entire legislature as soon as possible.

RECENT STUDIES ON HONG KONG'S DEMOCRATIZATION

Some of the recent studies on Hong Kong's democratization have remained politically pessimistic, while other scholars have adopted a more optimistic outlook. Very few argued that democratization in the HKSAR may have positive impacts on the PRC development. Writing in 2007, political scientist Joseph Cheng saw no progress in Hong Kong's democracy because of the opposition from the PRC and the HKSAR government. He wrote:

Ten years after the territory's return to China, there has been no further progress in democracy. In fact interference from Beijing has increased after July 2003 when compared with the initial three years after 1997. The dogmatic insistence on an "executive-led" system of government means that the systemic difficulties in the executive-legislature relationship have not been tackled ... The economy has demonstrated its resilience. But relative international competitiveness has been in decline; and the community's confidence in future development has been eroded. While values are changing, the government's policy programme does not show such awareness. In sum, this may not have been a decade lost, but it was obviously a crucial era in which there was not much to show off.[45]

Cheng appealed to the governments of Hong Kong and the mainland to democratize the HKSAR because, without meeting the public aspirations and changing political values, the capitalist enclave's political stability would not be ensured.

Involving himself in Hong Kong's democracy movement and as a former secretary-general of the pro-democracy Civic Party, Cheng has remained pessimistic toward the future of democratization in the HKSAR. When the democrats grasped 18 of the 30 directly elected seats and 7 of the functional constituency seats in the September 2004 LegCo elections, giving them a total of 25 out of 60 seats in the legislature, Cheng believed that the election results showed both the structural political constraints and "the poor tactical choices by certain democratic parties and politicians."[46] Structurally, the existence of 30 functional constituency seats makes it impossible for the democrats to be a majority in the legislature due to the bias of functional constituencies in favor of pro-establishment and pro-Beijing politicians. Above all, Cheng sees mainland China as the ultimate obstacle to Hong Kong's democratization. He wrote:

[T]he PRC authorities . . . still view their Hong Kong policy within the framework of the united-front strategy. Hence they feel ready to step up their united-front offensive against the pro-democracy movement in the wake of the Legislative Council elections, with the goal of winning over those who can be won over, isolating the hard-liners in the democratic camp, and trying to secure the results of divide and rule. This will pose a severe challenge to the solidarity of the pro-democracy movement . . . The people of Hong Kong realize that unless there is democracy in China, it will be difficult to realize genuine democracy in the HKSAR. The challenge is to keep looking ahead and to keep up efforts to pursue the democratic ideal while upholding the rule of law and the freedoms Hong Kong and its people now enjoy.[47]

Cheng's concept of democracy, as with other pan-democrats, is equivalent to the direct elections of both the chief executive and the entire legislature. He sees the PRC's co-optation of democrats through its united front works as the most damaging one splitting the pan-democratic front. Although Cheng hopes that the people of Hong Kong will continue to strive for democracy, his pessimism is based on a perception of the politically stagnant PRC without much meaningful democratic changes.

Although Cheng appeals to the Hong Kong people to struggle for democracy, he sees Confucian values among the Hong Kong Chinese as another hidden obstacle to political participation. While acknowledging the contributions of Confucian values such as diligence, planning, frugality, self-cultivation, and family ties to the foundation of economic development and social stability, he sees them as the acceptance of the political *status quo*. As Cheng has argued,

The Confucian concept of the "golden mean" allowed moderation and pragmatism to prevail as economic development succeeded in containing and even resolving various social and political contradictions . . . Because the *status quo* is tolerable: economic development, freedom, and the rule of law combine nicely to make an acceptable substitute for democracy while emigration serves as a safety valve . . . Confucianism appeals not only to the dignity of the individual, but also to intellectuals' obligation to sacrifice to preserve dignity for a worthy cause. Now that Hong Kong is a part of China, *zhiguo pintianxia* (governing the country and making it peaceful) should re-emerge as a duty and ideal. Only after members of the Western-educated middle class value democracy enough to sacrifice for it, will the pro-democracy movement maintain its momentum.[48]

Cheng pins his hope on the Western-educated middle class to uphold the ideal of managing the HKSAR affairs in accordance with the political ideal of Confucianism.

Cheng's political caution and pessimism stand out in the recent literature on Hong Kong's democratization, but some of his pessimistic forecasts appear to be shared by other scholars who view the PRC as the most powerful player shaping the political development in the HKSAR.

Joseph Man Chan and Francis Lee have maintained that even though many citizens have been participating in rallies since July 1, 2003, their influence is limited. They have stated:

[T]he pro-democracy rallies in Hong Kong have been influential at least occasionally because of the alliance between the social forces that the movement represents and the institutionalized power that the democrats hold within the legislature. The power of the people should not be mythologized. More importantly, since the democrats' institutionalized power remains highly limited, it remains questionable whether the combination of social forces and institutionalized power can really force the Hong Kong and Chinese governments to democratize to the satisfaction of the public ... If the Chinese government simply will not allow Hong Kong to democratize further at a faster pace, are Hong Kong people ready to employ more radical means and pay higher costs? The answer seems to be no, not because Hong Kong people are economic animals who are concerned with prosperity and stability more than democracy and liberty, but because the current pro-democracy movement in Hong Kong has defined its own worthiness in terms of rationality and peacefulness.[49]

Like Cheng, Chan and Lee regard the pro-democracy movement as having limited impact on the PRC policy toward the HKSAR. They do not see radicalism as the alternative for the democrats. Cheng, Chan, and Lee implicitly adopt a geopolitical perspective to analyze democratization in Hong Kong, which to them is politically dependent on the overlord Beijing.

This power dependent, or geopolitical, perspective is also held by sociologist Sing Ming, who has observed that the mainland's co-optation strategy since the 1980s has facilitated the deeper penetration of the China factor in Hong Kong's democratization.[50] He stresses that the PRC constitutes "the primary constraint" on Hong Kong's democratic development.[51] Comparing Hong Kong with Taiwan and South Korea, Sing concludes that a breakthrough in Hong Kong's democratization would require a hard-line suppression from the PRC authoritarian regime, which secures the support of the local capitalists. If such "suppression" were avoided, the people of Hong Kong would lack the political impetus to push for further democratization. As he wrote:

[T]he huge market potential of China discourages most prominent capitalists from making known their pro-democracy stance, if any, to avoid retaliation from the Chinese government. That, together with an absence of ethnic conflict as that in Taiwan, has resulted in local capitalists offering less support for democratization than their Taiwanese and Korean counterparts. The Chinese government has thus secured a powerful ally in its efforts to restrain Hong Kong's democratic development. Consequently, unless Hong Kong experiences a severe and large-scale suppression of civil liberties or sustained economic hardship, public support for greater democratization will be inadequate to produce a successful democratic breakthrough in Hong Kong in the short and medium term.[52]

Similar to Cheng, Chan, and Lee but perhaps unlike Sing who sees the PRC as the "primary constraint," Suzanne Pepper tends to put her faith on the people of Hong Kong to fight for democracy in the HKSAR. She argues that it is essential for the pan-democrats to mobilize the public to participate in protests, petitions, and parades; nevertheless, the democrats need to address their own organizational and leadership problems so that Hong Kong's democracy movement would become more effective and influential. As she has expounded her views,

Their more immediate challenge is to retain the trust of one million voters, marchers, and volunteers during years without election cycles or major issues to focus public attention on the relevance of the democratic cause. This task must also be pursued by a movement that lacks cohesive leadership, effective organization, adequate funding, theoreticians, historians, an information office, authoritative publications, and regular opportunities for community-wide speechmaking, public education, and debate. At the same time, Beijing and its Hong Kong allies possess more than enough of those resources and are continuing to use them in determined adversarial pursuit, firm in the belief that China's 21st-century timetable for national Chinese Communist Party-led reconstruction is at stake . . . Chinese leaders . . . have mastered the subtle colonial technique of handcrafting safe legislative majorities and can further safeguard results by mobilizing all the relevant resources of their own tradition. The challenge for democratic reformers is to maintain their integrity in a political environment where all the powers that be are working actively to discredit and defeat both the reform cause and its practitioners.[53]

Legislator Margaret Ng agrees with Pepper's view that the organization, strategy, and style of the democrats should be reviewed and improved. Compared with Joseph Cheng, Ng tends to have a far more positive opinion on the contributions of Hong Kong's democracy movement to both the HKSAR and the PRC. She wrote:

The democratic movement has done a great deal in the last decade. It has been under heavy fire and has seen serious setbacks in advancing democracy, but it has held the line. It has upheld the standard and kept the principles clear. This is an important achievement, as evidenced by the number, the quality and diversity of background of the people who have joined in the movement. Democrats' open and fearless resistance has made those in power pause and checked their move, and gone further to justify their action. Surely this has made a difference. Ten years on, it is time for review, reassessment and realignment. It is time for change: not of objective and principle, but of style, strategy, and organization.[54]

Ng appeals to the pro-democracy camp to reach out to the community through various initiatives at the grassroots level, such as "protection of the environment, heritage, urban planning and land use, education and culture, services to the family and the community."[55] Unlike Pepper, Ng is more optimistic toward the creation of leadership in Hong Kong's democracy movement. As Ng argues,

If leadership was a problem for the HKSAR government, it was no less a problem for the democratic movement. Every now and then in history, a leader naturally emerges and takes responsibility. There are too many factors in Hong Kong's circumstances against such a possibility. Hong Kong democrats must consciously create leaders for the task. The good news is that there is no lack of excellent material ... I am more convinced than ever that democratization for Hong Kong is worth fighting for, and no generation ought to have to fight alone. Conviction is not weakened by the difficulty of the task, but strengthened by the knowledge of how necessary it is, not only for the future of Hong Kong, but as a part of China and mankind. Democrats should go and explain to the people at home and abroad what is at stake, in their lifetime.[56]

If Hong Kong's democratization has its impact on the future of the PRC, as Ng asserts, Bob Beatty was the first scholar who elaborated on how the HKSAR can become a model for mainland China's democratic development. Beatty found that although Hong Kong's political elites do not support Asian values, the conservatives were worrying about the impact of democratization on the economy. On the Hong Kong model shaping China, Beatty wrote:

Possibly the largest effect that Hong Kong can have on China in the political realm is establishing within China the precedent of gradual, orderly democratization with a goal. Hong Kong's democratization process since the handover has been orderly and inclusive because of the Basic Law's timetable and the goal of universal suffrage and full democracy. With that plan written into law all politicians can look to the future, strategize, coordinate, and even patiently wait for the time when they can be elected by the people ... If China approaches the idea of democratic political development, it is likely the country would follow the Hong Kong model of a long, gradual process, in which the Chinese Communist Party is in control. But the first step will necessitate that political leaders form a plan for democratization like that contained in the Basic Law.[57]

Beatty was actually the first observer arguing that the PRC can learn from the Hong Kong model of democratization.

As with Ng and Beatty, Alvin So and Ma Ngok tend to adopt a more optimistic view toward Hong Kong's democracy movement. So believes that as long as the pan-democratic flagship, the Democratic Party (DP), persists and as long as elections are held, democratization in the HKSAR cannot be easily rolled back. He wrote:

[I]t seems that a restricted, corporatist democracy will prevail in Hong Kong for at least a few more decades. Yet as long as the Democratic Party is permitted to function, it will play a crucial role in promoting democratization, because of its strong grassroots support at the ballot box. Since the Basic Law stipulates that elections will play a significant role in allocating political power, elections will not be abolished altogether. Thus, while a restricted, corporatist democracy project will survive, it will be under constant challenge from service professionals and the grassroots population. Service professionals will push for pro-labor, pro-welfare policies, defend human rights, and challenge business's and Beijing's dominance in the government. Although democracy may not develop so quickly as it did in Taiwan and South Korea, in time Hong Kong may be neither a capitalist paradise nor a timid Special Administrative Region of the People's Republic.[58]

So implicitly adopts a class perspective to comprehend the momentum of democratization in Hong Kong, believing in the positive role of the middle-class professionals while predicting accurately that the territory is by no means politically "timid" in asserting citizens' demands and grievances.

So's optimism is shared by Ma, who argues that the next stage of Hong Kong's democracy movement will hinge on whether the political actors involved would be able to reach a pact on how democratic reform would proceed. Ma wrote:

From a pessimistic point of view, the first decade after the handover made little progress in democratic institutions—it is a decade of lost opportunities. Moreover, one does not see how in the short run, the priorities of the central government can be changed, and how consensus on reform can be engineered among major political actors. From the optimistic side, the last decade all but confirms Hong Kong people's urge for full democracy. It was an important period of cultural change in terms of building consensus for the desirability and necessity of democracy ... The last ten years have built a consensus towards the direction of universal suffrage: the question is when and how. The task in the next decade is how to build pact-making mechanisms between various stakeholders to solve the questions of how and when.[59]

Partially agreeing with Joseph Cheng's view that the years from 1997 to 2007 were "lost," Ma tends to be more optimistic and sees the prospects of having the political actors make compromises on the issues of how and when universal suffrage will arrive. Ma contends that the HKSAR system is marked by "institutional incongruity" and "strained state-society relations," which explained the governance crisis in the HKSAR.[60] Democratization, according to Ma, provides a solution to address the problems and loopholes in the political system of Hong Kong.

The most explicit use of the bargaining perspective to move Hong Kong's democracy movement to the stage of pact making is the recent work by Larry Diamond. He argues that Hong Kong is already prepared for democracy in terms of per capita income and economic development. The challenge, to Diamond, is the strategies adopted by the democrats. He has advocated a number of strategies if the democrats are keen to achieve a breakthrough in Hong Kong's democratization. First, the pro-democracy forces will be "more effective" if they can form a united and coherent coalition to negotiate with pro-Beijing forces.[61] Second, the moderate segment of the pro-democracy camp should seek compromise with the pro-Beijing side. Third, as with Pepper's argument, Diamond believes that the democrats should continue to demonstrate their capability of mobilizing the public to protest and support for democratization. Fourth, a triangular negotiation between democrats, pro-Beijing forces, and the HKSAR government should be pursued. Fifth, the democrats should aim at the target of how to achieve universal suffrage from 2017 to 2020 onwards. Sixth, they should focus on the concrete options and practical initiatives so that transitional arrangements to full universal suffrage will be reached. Seventh, creative solutions should be combined with public discussions and private negotiations so that the democratic breakthrough will become possible. Overall, Diamond provides a concrete plan for the Hong Kong democrats to follow.

In short, the recent literature on Hong Kong's democratization is diversified. Some tend to be more pessimistic, notably Cheng, Chan, Lee, and Sing, who all tend to see the China factor as the predominant obstacle. Pepper pins her hope on the Hong Kong democrats but is critical of their strategies, leadership, and organization. Ng, however, tends to be more optimistic toward the pan-democratic camp's leadership and its impact on Hong Kong and China. While So sees the tenacity of Hong Kong's democratic space as long as the Basic Law is observed, Ma hopes for the formation of pacts in Hong Kong's democratic development. Diamond puts forward concrete strategies for the democrats to reach such pacts with Beijing, the HKSAR government, and the pro-Beijing forces. Beatty, on the other hand, argues that the Hong Kong model of democratization can serve as a useful reference and lesson for the PRC to emulate.

RECENT STUDIES ON CHINA'S DEMOCRATIZATION

A similar divergence of views can be found in the recent studies of the PRC's democratization. The most optimistic view on China's democratization is the thought-provoking work by Bruce Gilley, who has predicted that the PRC will encounter sudden crises, followed by popular mobilization and violence, the rise of reformers within the regime, and then the formation of a pact that would propel the entire nation-state toward the path of democratic breakthrough.[62] Once the PRC democratization would reach the stage of consolidation, Hong Kong would benefit politically. As Gilley has boldly predicted,

[D]emocratization in China would create an immediate demand for full democratization in Hong Kong and the election of the chief executive [by universal suffrage]. Hong Kong is a virtually self-governing city-state which has been unable to achieve full democracy and whose freedoms and rule of law were constantly being challenged as a result of dictatorship in China, its sovereign after 1997. It is also a city overendowed with the ingredients for a successful democracy—a large well-educated middle class, a tolerant society, successful local elections, strong legal system, a robust free press, and more. Giving it full democracy—a promise Beijing made in the Basic Law—would make it better run and protected, would eliminate a source of criticism of China, and bolster a key entrepot for Asia's economy . . . Fortunately, one might expect that the new government in Beijing will look favorably on such demands. Still, it may well be that the development of democracy may proceed faster in places like Guangzhou and Shanghai, where a people long denied rights embrace them with great vigor, than in Hong Kong, where the post-1997 period revealed a modest political apathy bred by the comforts of colonial rule.[63]

He concludes that Hong Kong's economy "would benefit far more from the spinoffs of a successful democratic transition in China than it would lose as a place with special status within a dictatorial state." [64] In short, China's democratization will be politically and economically beneficial to Hong Kong.

Gilley's forecasts are bold. He assumes that the PRC's democratization would perhaps proceed in a much faster pace than the HKSAR, where some elites are politically conservative and resistant to democracy's arrival. Moreover, his argument is predicated on the prediction that the Hong Kong business elites would accept Beijing's decision to approve democratization in the HKSAR. It is not known whether Hong Kong's politically conservative and cautious capitalist class would really embrace the advent of democracy, which to its members would lead to trade unionism, high tax, and economic downturn. But Gilley's crystal ball will surely stand the test of time, especially when the PRC begins to democratize and deepens political reforms.

Contrary to Gilley, Minxin Pei tends to see the PRC as an "incapacitated state" trapped in a political transition for a much longer period of time than conventional wisdom may assume. He argues that the PRC is a "predatory authoritarian" regime characterized by weak political accountability, pervasive corruption, problematic governance, high social tensions, serious political patronage, fragile opposition, endangered civil liberties, and the absence of the rule of law.[65] Pei contends that short-term economic growth in the PRC has a negative impact on democratization because the ruling elites lack any incentive to embark on political liberalization. The guiding principle of the PRC's ruling elites, to Pei, is to adopt strategies prolonging and ensuring their survival. China, he argues, is displaying all the "pathologies of a trapped transition," including the marginalization of the liberal forces within the CCP and the rise in social inequality alongside the high growth rate.[66]

Pei predicts three scenarios for the PRC's political future. The first would be a difficult choice between "maintaining the deteriorating *status quo* and taking the risks of more radical reforms to restore political accountability and curb decentralized predation."[67] If the reformers or soft-liners prevail over the hard-liners, they would have to mobilize their supporters and trigger an anti-regime uprising. Pei argues that China would be politically stable in this scenario if and only if the reformers within the regime would secure the support of the moderate elements of the societal opposition. The second scenario would be the regime collapse in which social turmoil would bring about the exit of the ruling elite and the downfall of "developmental autocracy."[68] The third scenario would be the devolution of power, leading to not only interregional competition for capital, labor, and markets but also new institutional reforms at the grassroots level. Such reforms may include the refinement of township and village elections. In other words, local innovative governance would tackle some of the problems unleashed by the trapped transition. Pei concludes that "a combination of tactical adaptation, improvisation, luck, and mass apathy may allow the ruling elites to stay in power even as the country is mired in misrule."[69]

Pei's argument that the PRC is located at a trapped transition for a long period of time appears to be far more pessimistic than Gilley. Pei sees regime collapse as only one of the three scenarios for China, with the prolonged transition as the most likely outcome, while Gilley appears to be far more confident about the inevitability of regime collapse in the mainland. The former has not predicted the impact of China's trapped transition on Hong Kong, but the latter affirms the positive consequences of the PRC collapse on the HKSAR.

As a matter of fact, Sinologists have not been able to reach a consensus on the political development and future of the PRC. While some scholars believe that the PRC is on the path toward the development of the rule of law, others warn us that rule by law is actually the norm.[70] Some see the middle class as an agent for political activism and change, but others tend to see it as a dependent political actor without any interest in democracy.[71] Some also see the rise of the Internet as providing a means of activating the civil society, but others regard the spread of the Internet as a sign of political liberalization without democratization.[72] Some scholars identify the use of emails and the Internet by city officials as an indicator of democratization, but others remind us of the regime's repressive policies toward interest groups such as the Catholic Church.[73] The mass media are often under the tight control and surveillance by the CCP, whereas the opposition DP was easily suppressed during the 1990s.[74] While some villagers are keen to take the government to the court for public maladministration, many lawyers are unwilling to take on criminal cases that entail a high degree of political sensitivity and risks.[75] Some scholars see the expansion of village elections as a crucial indicator of democratic reform in China, but others remind us of the complexities in village politics, especially the interrelationships and struggles between the village representatives and village party secretaries, and between the village and the higher-level township government.[76] Although trade unions are supposed to fight for the interests of the working class, they are under the control of the ruling party and have limited functions.[77] While many young people are the pillars of the mainland Chinese society, they tend to be pragmatists rather than idealists yearning for democracy.[78] All these chaotic sociopolitical changes in the PRC have led to a discussion of whether it would follow the path of the Republic of China on Taiwan to democratize the political system, as the late Taiwan President Chiang Ching-kuo did in the late 1980s. Larry Diamond concludes that although Taiwan's democratic breakthrough in the late 1980s was historically unique, the PRC development would likely pursue a different path but the final destination would perhaps be the same. As he predicts,

China today is dramatically different from Taiwan, then and now. Its path and pace of regime transformation will not follow Taiwan's. But many of the political and normative consequences of economic development will be the same. If new generations of Chinese political leaders, technocrats, entrepreneurs, intellectuals, and artists can be vigorously and yet respectfully engaged, the political outcome will, sooner or later, likely be the same as in Taiwan: some form of genuine democracy.[79]

Diamond appears to stick to the modernization theory in the sense that he believes the inevitability of democracy resulting from economic development.[80]

Overall, the PRC's political transformations are chaotic and filled with contradictory tendencies with its final destination remaining unclear and controversial. Although most China specialists have identified tremendous sociopolitical and economic metamorphoses in the PRC, they have divergent views on whether the PRC is heading toward democracy, or whether it remains politically stagnant with uncertain scenarios that will be unfolded.

HONG KONG AS A MODEL SHAPING CHINA'S DEMOCRATIZATION

While most China experts have treated the study of Hong Kong's political development separately from the mainland Chinese context, very few of them have attempted to link the two together in the discussion of democratization. The exceptions are notably Bob Beatty and Bruce Gilley. While the former has argued that the HKSAR can provide useful lessons for the PRC, the latter has propounded that democratization in China must trigger a further push factor for Hong Kong's democracy.

This book is going to argue that the vision of democracy held by most Hong Kong people is far more Westernized than that held by the mainland's political elites. While most Hong Kong people, especially the democrats, are hoping for an idealistic political system in which the chief executive is directly elected by citizens through universal suffrage and the whole legislature is directly elected, the mainland's political elites do not envision such ideal for both the PRC and Hong Kong. This book will build on the argument articulated by Beatty and will show that Hong Kong's style of democracy and democratization has significant implications for the PRC's political development. The implications include participatory, institutional, constitutional, attitudinal, or cultural aspects. In terms of participation, Hong Kong's democrats actively participated in the rescue of mainland democrats after the June 4, 1989, Tiananmen tragedy in which the military was deployed to suppress the dissidents. Hong Kong provided an indispensable channel for mainland dissidents to flee the mainland, and it remains the only place in the PRC that can hold annual candlelight vigils in commemoration of the victims of Tiananmen. This annual event, as will be discussed in the book, has tremendous educative impact on both the Hong Kong people and many mainland visitors to the HKSAR. Hong Kong provides the necessary participatory channel for the Hong Kong and mainland Chinese.

Another important dimension of participation is that the people of Hong Kong, especially the democrats, have remained aggressively active in influencing the PRC policy toward the HKSAR, especially their struggle for the direct election of the chief executive through universal suffrage and of the entire LegCo. As a result of public pressure, the PRC government has to admit that the end point would be universal suffrage in Hong Kong, although it has not really spelled out a concrete timetable. In a sense, the responsiveness of PRC officials responsible for Hong Kong matters has already been enhanced. If governmental responsiveness is an indicator of democracy, such responsiveness on the part of PRC elites can be seen as a democratizing phenomenon resulting from ceaseless public pressure from Hong Kong.

Institutionally speaking, the HKSAR offers institutional experiences for the PRC to emulate, including its respectable anticorruption work, the relatively clean and efficient civil service, the solid rule of law, the media scrutiny of public maladministration, electoral competition among mini-political parties, and the legislative supervision on government policies. Pan Wei believed that the PRC can establish a "consultative rule of law" regime like Hong Kong where the legal system remains vibrant and independent and where the government constantly consults public opinion on government policies.[81] Arguably, institutionalization in the PRC in the aspect of peacefully managing leadership succession is an insufficient condition for democratization.[82] A much fuller scale of institutionaliza-tion in the PRC must entail the invigoration of its anticorruption work, including the improved role of the Central Discipline Inspection Commis-sion (CDIC), the increased autonomy given to the mass media to check public maladministration, more electoral competition at various levels of government, and the empowerment of the law-making NPC to supervise the administration. If "democracy is a good thing" and if the Chinese themselves can map out their own path toward democracy, as Keping Yu has argued, then the Hong Kong model of democracy can be humbly learned by the PRC leaders at the national, provincial, and local levels.[83]

Constitutionally and culturally speaking, the HKSAR can be seen as an experiment in Chinese federalism in which the central government has delegated considerable autonomy, especially financial and economic, to the territory. This experiment in Chinese federalism can constitute a gradual transformation of mainland Chinese political culture that, accord-ing to the late Lucian Pye, develops "the fear of local kingdoms."[84] In other words, the PRC has distrusted "pluralistic decentralization" with independent kingdoms defying the central government's orders and pol-icy directives.[85] Therefore, if the PRC is increasingly accepting the Hong Kong model of operations where small political parties persist, opposition forces thrive, legislative and district-level elections remain competitive without deliberate manipulation by the regime, and citizen protests are commonplace, the mainland leaders would hopefully develop a political culture of tolerating pluralism. The four aspects of Hong Kong's democra-tizing impacts on the mainland—participatory, institutional, constitu-tional, and cultural—cannot be underestimated in the PRC's political interactions with the HKSAR.

CHAPTER 1

The Political Role of Hong Kong in China's Tiananmen Tragedy and Legacy

If Hong Kong under British rule provided a "revolutionary base" for Sun Yat-sen and his supporters to plan their activities of toppling the Qing dynasty,[1] it has become another democratizing base for some Hong Kong Chinese to attempt to transform the PRC from an authoritarian to a democratic regime since the military crackdown on the student democrats on the Tiananmen Square on June 4, 1989. Hong Kong also provided an extremely important base for the local Chinese to rescue the mainland democrats immediately after the Tiananmen incident.

CHAN TAT-CHING AND OPERATION YELLOWBIRD

Operation Yellowbird was a term used by John Shum Kin-fun, an actor in the Hong Kong entertainment circle, to refer to the rescue of mainland Chinese democrats who were suppressed and under the arrest warrant of PRC police and security agents shortly after the June 4 Tiananmen tragedy. The chief organizer of the Operation Yellowbird was Chan Tat-ching, who was seen by the mainland democrats being rescued out of the PRC as a "Hong Kong and Chinese hero" in the history of China. Chan was born in the mainland's Jiangxi province in 1944 and was attacked by the Red Guards in a Guangdong publishing factory during the Cultural Revolution. In 1972, he sneaked into Hong Kong under the British rule and then started his trade and wine businesses through the acquaintances with many members of the underground world.[2] Chan was mysteriously attacked by triad members in Hong Kong in 1996, but he denied that this attack had any political motivation.[3]

Chan revealed the details of the rescue adventures during the twentieth anniversary of the Tiananmen Incident in 2009. According to Chan's personal diary that recorded the rescue events, 133 student democrats were smuggled out of the PRC from June to December 1989. Watching the tragedy in the PRC in June 1989, Chan was totally shocked and psychologically disturbed. He shaved his hair and decided to rescue a few mainland students before the formal inception of Operation Yellowbird.[4] Chan said: "Under the White Terror, the life of the democrats was at stake. Those who have conscience must hope to extend their helping hands. Seeing the exploitation of the weak by the arrogant rascals, I decided to come out and go forward without considering my self-interest. This was the chivalry of Chinese Robin Hood."[5] John Shum looked for Chan through the introduction of his friend, Alan Tang Kwong-wing, also a famous actor in the entertainment scene. As an executive committee member of the Hong Kong Alliance in Support of the Patriotic and Democratic Movement in China, John Shum contacted the other Alliance leaders such as the Reverend Chu Yiu-ming and unionist Lau Chin-shek. Operation Yellowbird was a loosely organized group without hierarchy and fixed memberships. It lasted from June 1989 to June 1997 when Hong Kong approached its return to the PRC. Rescuing altogether almost 300 mainland democrats from the PRC, the core leaders of the Operation clandestinely transported all the related documents and records to overseas countries.

Chan revealed that the rescue operators had a secret name "Li Chenggong," carrying half of a photo of the rescued target, who had to present the other half of the picture to verify himself or herself so that the triad members would implement the plan of helping them flee the mainland.[6] He also unveiled that the son of Zhao Ziyang was recognized by the mainland customs officers, but fortunately the Hainan provincial governor Liang Xiang decided to let Zhao's son leave the PRC. In the case of rescuing Zhao's daughter-in-law and granddaughter, Chan and his brother met the police checkpoint in Hong Kong, but Chan immediately called a phone number given by John Sham for urgent help. The phone number directly reached Governor David Wilson, who then ordered the police to let Chan and his rescue targets go directly to meet the French Consul General in Hong Kong, Jean Pierre Montagne.[7]

The rescue of Chen Yizhe, Zhao's think tank member, was successful. Chen hid in a doctor's home on the Hainan Island. The Hong Kong Alliance in Support of the Patriotic and Democratic Movement in China received the intelligence on Chen and passed it onto Chan Tat-ching, who went to rescue Chen with Ko Sai-cheong. Chan and Ko helped Chen escape by hiding him in a container tanker, where the son of the ship captain held a pistol to protect Chen. In Guangzhou, Chan used a power-ful speedboat to receive both Chen and the captain's son from the tanker.[8] The two escapees were sent to the Alliance, which arranged for them to go to the United Kingdom.

However, four subordinates of Chan died and another was arrested in Operation Yellowbird, including a 33-year-old construction worker, Ng Ho-ming. Ng had a team of ships and speedboats engaging in smuggling activities. He was regarded as a "criminal talent" utilizing *guanxi* with mainland officials effectively, but was imprisoned by the mainland authorities for drug trafficking and smuggling. Two of Chan's four col-leagues who died were Hong Kong men, while the other two were main-landers. Two of them died in a speedboat that crashed with a ship amidst heavy fog, while the other two jumped into the sea and lost their lives when their speedboat overheated and was on fire. Chan gave the family of each dead subordinate HK$500,000 privately, without the Alliance's subsidy or support, because he said solidarity was of paramount impor-tance in his rescue operation.[9]

After Chan's other two subordinates, Lee Lung-hing and Lai Pui-shing, were arrested by the mainland authorities in an abortive attempt to rescue mainland academic Chen Ziming, Chan himself went to the mainland to meet with an official of the Ministry of Public Security. The mainland offi-cial said he understood Chan's action was for the sake of patriotic and humanitarian grounds. Chan offered to abandon his rescue operation on the condition that Lee and Lai would be released. Six months later, the two were released. But the Alliance perceived Chan as "failing to main-tain a firm anti-communist stance."[10]

Although some reports linked the rescue operation with American sup-port, Chan asserted that his work did not have any links with the Central Intelligence Agency (CIA), and that he rejected the American offer to help him emigrate to the United States. However, the American ambassador to the PRC, James Lilley, played a crucial role in issuing visas to some 200 mainland democrats in late May 1989 and quietly lobbied the PRC government to release some dissidents after the June 4 crackdown so that they could go to other countries.[11] In December 1989, Chan ceased his res-cue operation, which was then taken over by the Alliance. On average, each escapee from the mainland required HK$50,000 to HK$100,000, which was used to pay for the rescue operation. After the Alliance man-aged the rescue operation, snakeheads (organizers of the smuggling operation) were utilized as rescue agents, but the scale of the operation was much smaller than the past.

Chan's view of the PRC is perhaps indicative of how some Hong Kong people, if not necessarily the democrats, perceive the mainland's political development. He felt that the Tiananmen incident rescued the PRC because the CCP itself has to ponder the differences between a revolutionary party and a ruling party, and to accept universal values such as democracy and freedom. The tragedy of the Chinese nation is who can topple the PRC. Today, who can replace the PRC? China cannot afford to have chaos. Even the late Zhao Ziyang did not hope for the PRC collapse. He said that the verdict on Tiananmen will be certainly reversed. Perhaps this reversal of verdict is a historical wound and problem that will have to wait for the next generation of PRC leaders to solve.[12]

Chan's role in the Tiananmen tragedy had profound significance in Hong Kong's democracy movement and its political influence on the PRC.

First and foremost, as a Hong Kong citizen with close connections with the triads, Chan has been seen as an underground world's political hero not only for rescuing mainland dissidents out of the PRC from June to December 1989 but also as a fascinating case of interactions with mainland police over Operation Yellowbird. His negotiations with mainland officials represented a daring move that served to confirm the historically complex relations between the ruling regime in China and the underworld. Traditionally, when the secret societies were formed in the Ming dynasty, they aimed at overthrowing the Qing dynasty. Chan and his colleagues did not seek to topple the PRC. But PRC officials eventually admitted that their action was based on humanitarian grounds—a reflection that even police authorities in the mainland sided with the just and bold action of Chan and his peers, who firmly believed that the brutal suppression of mainland democrats was wrong. As the mainland's modernization since the 1980s has opened the door to organized crime activities and since the CCP has been adopting a more hard-line policy toward the suppression of criminal groups,[13] the Ministry of Public Security's treatment of Chan and his colleagues demonstrated the grey area of their political relations, which are actually negotiable contingent upon the changing circumstances.

Second, the operation of Chan and his colleagues symbolized the ways in which Hong Kong triads worked in the mainland. They have been involved in human trafficking, smuggling activities, and the use of powerful speedboats. They utilized *guanxi* effectively in their search for rescue targets, sometimes aided by the generosity of mainland officials, such as the late Hainan Governor Liang Xiang's decision to let the son of Zhao Ziyang leave the mainland. Hong Kong triads did have an auxiliary impact on the PRC's democracy movement, specifically the use of personal relations in the mainland to rescue the democrats and dissidents.

Third, the relations between the Alliance and Chan were special. Although the Alliance's John Shum linked Chan with other Alliance members, Chan's relations with the other Alliance members were by no means close. As Chan revealed, when he negotiated with PRC officials on the release of his two subordinates, some Alliance members suspected that he was hesitant in his anti-communist stance. To Chan, some Alliance members misunderstood him. In the minds of the Alliance, however, Chan might sacrifice the political principle of opposing the PRC regime for the sake of rescuing his colleagues. This difference in mutual perception is understandable. While Chan was an underground hero attaching importance to his tenets of justice and fairness toward his colleagues, the Alliance put its priority over the continuous rescue of mainland dissidents rather than Chan's colleagues who were arrested by the mainland police and security personnel. Hence, while triads were involved in the mainland's democracy movement through the rescue operation, they have not been under the control or direction of Hong Kong's democracy movement. Triads and their members operated independently of the pan-democrats in Hong Kong. The Tiananmen incident provided a rallying point for some of them to group together loosely because they all perceived the violent military crackdown on the mainland democrats as morally unjustifiable.

Although there is no concrete evidence to prove that the CIA had any direct linkage with the Hong Kong triad members in Operation Yellowbird,[14] the involvement of some foreign countries and officials in the rescue of mainland dissidents after the Tiananmen tragedy on June 4, 1989, reinforced the antiforeign sentiment of the top PRC leadership. The PRC leaders, especially the hard-line subordinates in the national security apparatus responsible for Hong Kong and Macao affairs, are often concerned about whether foreign countries and foreigners are involved in mainland, Hong Kong, and Macao politics. These hard-liners have appeared to be heavily influenced by the legacy of the Tiananmen Incident, guarding against any foreign "hands" in fostering domestic unrest in the PRC, Hong Kong, and Macao.

THE ALLIANCE LEADERS

After the Tiananmen incident, the Alliance leaders such as Szeto Wah and Martin Lee were at one time under Hong Kong police protection. Szeto received intimidation calls and the police installed a special detection device in his phone, warding off further threatening calls.[15] According to another leader of the Alliance, Cheung Man-kwong, the police in 1989 urged Szeto and Lee to avoid walking near the sea for fear of their being kidnapped by mainland agents.[16] Martin Lee revealed that after the Tiananmen incident, the Hong Kong police informed him that the People's Liberation Army (PLA) might send agents to "deal with" him, but he believed that the CCP was not the behind-the-scene mastermind.[17] Since Lee was on the top of the mainland's "blacklist," the Hong Kong police provided 24-hour protection for him.[18] The media revelation of all these events during the twentieth anniversary of the June 4 incident not only educated the Hong Kong public but also illustrated the "subversive" activities of the Alliance leaders in the eyes of the PLA in 1989.

Many Hong Kong people strengthened their Chinese identity during the PRC Tiananmen incident. On May 20, 1989, when the PRC Premier Li Peng announced that martial law was implemented in Beijing, 30,000 Hongkongers on the same night went to protest against it in front of Beijing's representative office in Hong Kong, namely the New China News Agency (NCNA, later renamed the Liaison Office after the handover).[19] On May 21, an estimated 600,000 to 1 million Hong Kong people participated in a parade in support of the mainland students, and even the pro-Beijing Federation of Trade Unions (FTU) appealed to its members to join the parade.[20] Some NCNA staff members participated in the protest. On the same day, the pro-Beijing Hong Kong Chinese newspaper *Wen Wei Po* used only four Chinese characters "painful heart and aching mind" in its editorial, while 32 Hong Kong members of the NPC and the Chinese People's Political Consultative Conference (CPPCC) issued a joint declaration to urge the Standing Committees of both the NPC and CPPCC to hold urgent meetings to deal with the crisis.[21] On May 26, about 200,000 Hong Kong people participated in a rally named "the same heart and mind in China and Hong Kong" at the Victoria Park to support the student democrats in Beijing. On May 27, 300,000 citizens participated in a music concert named "Democratic Music and Songs for China," which received public donations of HK$12 million. All the donations were deposited into the Alliance and used to support the mainland democrats. In late May, the former executive member of the Alliance, Gary Cheng Kai-nam, who later in July left the Alliance and joined the pro-Beijing political party Democratic Alliance for Betterment and Progress of Hong Kong (DAB) in the early 1990s, brought HK$500,000 to Beijing's Red Cross.[22] At this moment, it was clear that political participation of Hong Kong people had direct impact on the mainland's democracy movement. On May 28, 1.5 million Hong Kong citizens took to the streets to support the move of all overseas Chinese in the world to support democracy. The parade lasted for eight hours and some citizens shouted the slogans such as "down with Li Peng," "opposing news censorship," and "resisting military control." On June 2, the Alliance sent a delegation to Beijing and said that it would support the mainland students materially and financially. The Alliance participated in political action aiming at opposing the mainland regime and assisting the student democrats in Beijing.

The Alliance's deputy chairman Lee Cheuk-yan brought HK$1 million to Beijing, contacting mainland student leaders and organizers on how to utilize the donations from the people of Hong Kong.[23] Lee's activities could be seen as cross-border participation that aimed at affecting the longevity of the ruling party in the PRC. On June 4, when the military crackdown on the mainland students began, 200,000 Hong Kong people staged a sit-in at the horse-racing course at Happy Valley to oppose the PRC handling of the incident and to commemorate those students killed on the Tiananmen Square. On June 5, hundreds of thousands of Hong Kong people went to the open space outside the NCNA to commemorate those who died on the Square. Some Hong Kong CPPCC members held an emergency meeting to denounce the mainland government's handling of student democrats. It was crystal clear that Hong Kong in May and June 1989 became a "revolutionary" base fostering and supporting the mainland democrats in opposing the PRC government. One day after June 4, many Hong Kong people withdrew their deposits from the Bank of China in Hong Kong and the bank run amounted to HK$50 billion.[24] On the other hand, the Beijing police went to talk to Lee Cheuk-yan, who was frightened, escaped from his hotel, and hid in the British Embassy. The British officials told Lee to return to his hotel because his case would be resolved through diplomatic channels.[25] Lee returned to the hotel and was asked by the mainland police to sign a confession letter saying that he had committed an error by supporting the mainland student movement. After he reluctantly signed the confession letter, Lee was escorted to the airport while the donations he brought to Beijing were all confiscated. The case of Lee's release demonstrated the diplomatic efforts of British officials, but it also proved the cross-border activities of some Hong Kong people to finance and support the mainland democrats—a move that was construed as "subversion" by PRC hard-liners.

After the June 4 tragedy, Sino-British relations over Hong Kong reached an impasse, mainly because of the PRC perception that the British Hong Kong government protected the Alliance and facilitated the escape of many mainland student democrats and dissidents out of China. Former Hong Kong Executive Council member Allen Lee Peng-fei revealed in June 2009 that Governor David Wilson in 1990 asked Lee as a middleman to solve the "problem" of the Alliance. The Alliance was formed in May 1989 by chairman Szeto Wah and other activists such as Vice Chairman Martin Lee, Secretary Albert Ho, and executive committee members Cheung Man-kwong, the Reverend Chu Yiu-ming, Louis Ha, Lee Wing-tat, Yeung Sum, Lee Cheuk-yan, Mak Hoi-wah, John Shum, To Kwan-hang, Kwok Siu-tong, Tsang Kin-shing, Gary Cheng Kai-nam, and Wong Wai-hung.[26] The Alliance has a five-point platform: "releasing democratic elements, reversing the verdict on the 1989 democracy movement, pursuing the responsibility of the massacre, terminating one-party rule and establishing a democratic China." [27] After Governor Wilson's discussion with Allen Lee, the latter met Szeto Wah to probe whether the Alliance would hopefully be disbanded so that the political obstacle to better Sino-British relations would be removed.[28] Szeto refused to do so. In 1998, Chief Executive Tung Chee-hwa met Szeto again and hoped that he would abandon organizing the Alliance activities, but Szeto rejected his request. In 1999, Tung approached Szeto again for the same subject, but the latter remained unmoved. Later, whenever Tung contacted Szeto for any meeting, Szeto simply refused to attend.[29] It is an undeniable fact that Szeto Wah played a critical role in not only maintaining the Alliance's existence but also retaining its political tradition of holding both the annual parade before June 4 and the candlelight vigil on the night of June 4. Otherwise, Hong Kong could not have become the only place on the mainland Chinese soil that can still annually commemorate the Tiananmen tragedy. The civil liberties enjoyed by the Hong Kong people can be attributable to the respectable defiance and consistent position of the Alliance leader Szeto Wah.

However, Szeto's view on Hong Kong's political influence on the mainland is relatively pessimistic. When asked about Hong Kong's role in the PRC democratization, he answered:

Hong Kong does not play a very significant role in China's democratization. The [Hong Kong] tail cannot really move the entire [Chinese] dog. Hong Kong's 7 million people cannot influence the 13 billion mainland citizens. However, Hong Kong is the only place in mainland China where we can commemorate the June 4th. Much of our information can be transferred back to the mainland. If Hong Kong has freedom and if its democracy is not retrogressive, we can present a model for the mainlanders.[30]

Although Szeto sees Hong Kong as having limited impact on China's political metamorphosis, his perception of the HKSAR as presenting a model for the PRC is perhaps widely shared by many Hong Kong people supportive of both democratization in the HKSAR and their motherland. Unlike the PRC hard-liners who harp on the same theme that foreigners participated in the support of the Alliance, Szeto maintained that this perception remains "ludicrous" because the Alliance's donations come from the Hong Kong people and that its finance is transparent.[31]

Apart from Szeto Wah, the Reverend Chu Yiu-ming played a crucial role in the rescue of mainland democrats out of the PRC. According to Chu, each member of the rescue team was vertically responsible to the superior who sent him or her to save the mainland democrats.[32] He said that the people of Hong Kong played a critical role in rescuing many mainland Chinese democrats, some of whom only held the name cards of the Hong Kong contact persons.[33] According to Chu, he helped almost 300 mainland democrats to arrive at Hong Kong. Moreover, the Student Union of the Chinese University of Hong Kong (SUCUHK) tremendously supported the mainland democrats. Even when Chai Ling and Feng Chongde arrived at the boat that helped them flee from the mainland, they told the captain that they were "going to the SUCUHK."[34]

In 2007, Chu helped the formation of a campaign to seek donations so that the overseas Chinese democrats would be able to enjoy the legal rights to return to the PRC.[35] The campaign organizers toyed with the idea that overseas Chinese democrats would perhaps seek to acquire their legal rights to return to the PRC through the international court settlement or through the use of the International Covenant on Civil and Political Rights (ICCPR).[36] If the overseas Chinese democrats pursue this path, it would be similar to those Hong Kong people who are persistently fighting for the double universal suffrage—direct elections of both the chief executive and the entire legislature in conformity with the ICCPR, such as Szeto Wah, Martin Lee, Anson Chan, George Cautherley, and many other democrats.

THE EDUCATIVE IMPACT OF TIANANMEN ON THE YOUNG PEOPLE OF HONG KONG

Although the schools in Hong Kong have tried to depoliticize the Tiananmen incident and most of them avoid discussing its political ramifications, many young people are exposed to the Tiananmen tragedy through the mass media, especially the press and YouTube, so that their memories of Tiananmen cannot fade away easily. A form six student took her initiative to write a 600-word essay to *Ming Pao* on the June 4 tragedy, and she openly disagreed with the argument that China needs "political suppression in order to make the economy touch off." [37] She admitted that her knowledge of the June 1989 tragedy came from various media sources, such as the City Forum on every Sunday at the Victoria Park, *Headline News*, and YouTube. Another 17-year-old Hong Kong student even created "the seeds of the Tiananmen file" under the disguise of a pornographic video and a television program so that 10 mainlanders downloaded the materials within two months.[38] Although his potentially "subversive" activity to change the mind-set of the mainlanders had limited impact, it demonstrates that some young Hongkongers are by no means politically apathetic as conventional wisdom assumes. Moreover, PRC authorities could not easily clamp down on all the politically sensitive Web sites.[39]

All the standard textbooks in Hong Kong schools tend to dilute the Tiananmen incident in 1989.[40] The former education chief Wong Sing-wah in 1994 urged the publishers not to include the Tiananmen incident in the textbooks on the grounds that an event less that 20 years ago remained to be evaluated.[41] The current textbooks merely used terms such as "clearing the Square" and "violent intervention" to talk about the June 1989 event without mentioning the use of tanks and weapons by the PLA.[42] In 2009, 20 years after Tiananmen, critics said that all the textbooks used in Hong Kong's secondary or high schools do not really discuss the event in detail. Because of this intentional depoliticization, the pro-democracy Professional Teachers Union decided to distribute pamphlets, leaflets, and videos to teachers so that at least some of those who are pro-democracy and liberal-minded can educate the young students on a more in-depth picture of the Tiananmen tragedy.

Because of the fact that the Hong Kong mass media remain relatively free, the coverage of the 1989 Tiananmen incident in various Chinese newspapers annually, except for the pro-Beijing *Wen Wei Po* and *Ta Kung Pao*, reminds many Hong Kong people of the repressive nature of the PRC regime and directly or indirectly prompts them to cherish their civil liberties in the HKSAR. The popular circulation and sale of the book on Zhao Ziyang's memoir, *The Reform Journey* (*Gaige Licheng*), in the HKSAR in May and June 2009 provided a crucial educative tool for the pan-democrats to remind the Hong Kong people of the fate of Zhao Ziyang, whose political vision of China as having a more parliamentary system with checks and balances remains unfulfilled.[43] Many Hong Kong democrats share the late Zhao's political vision on China. About 10,000 copies of the book were sold out within one day, breaking the record of the sale of political literature in the HKSAR. Some Hong Kong dailies, such as *Apple Daily, Ming Pao,* and *Sing Tao Daily,* which were keen to boost their daily circulation, carried excerpts from the Zhao book, thereby enhancing the educative impact on the readers who do not buy it.[44] *Ming Pao* highlighted the role of Wen Jiabao, the current premier and the former director of the Party Central Office of Zhao Ziyang, in dissuading Zhao from convening a politburo meeting after the martial law was declared on May 19 because Wen argued that the Office had already been bypassed by Premier Li Peng and other conservative elites.[45] Many mainland tourists in the HKSAR decided to buy the Zhao book. Although most mainlanders visiting the HKSAR hide their political views to avoid any retaliation from mainland officials who identify them, they do express the common interest of rethinking the political ramifications of the Tiananmen tragedy. The civil liberties enjoyed by the Hong Kong people, who have access to books deemed politically "subversive" in the mainland, can open the eyes of the mainland comrades to a whole range of ideas and arguments being suppressed in the PRC.

Another function of the Hong Kong print media is to remind the Chinese in Hong Kong of the views of and encouragement from the overseas Chinese democrats. For example, Yan Jiaqi, who was the political adviser of the late Zhao Ziyang and who eventually went to reside in the United States, maintains that the PRC government should first admit that the Tiananmen incident was "a massacre" rather than "a riot," and that it should begin a review of the official verdict.[46] Yan's hope remains idealistic as long as the CCP remains apprehensive of the impact of totally reversing the official verdict on Tiananmen. But it also represents the ideal shared by many people of Hong Kong, especially those who annually participate in the parade and candlelight vigil in commemoration of the victims of the Tiananmen tragedy. Yan's expectation has much in common with many Hong Kong people, namely the utilization of "the spirit of the rule of law" to resolve a politically sensitive issue.[47]

As with Yan, Wang Juntao, who was imprisoned in October 1989 but allowed to be an exile in the United States in April 1994, praised the efforts of the Hong Kong people to delay the enactment of Article 23 of the Basic Law in mid-2003 as "the people's power."[48] He asserted that because of the internal transformations of the CCP, which has different views on Hong Kong, the HKSAR can surely influence the PRC.[49] He remains cautiously optimistic toward the Hong Kong people's struggle for democracy:

The mainland also hopes that Hong Kong can proceed smoothly because if Hong Kong is good, this is beneficial to the mainland. Moreover, the mainland has face if Hong Kong is good. Therefore political space for Hong Kong exists. However, the Hong Kong people may not fully and skillfully utilize this space because they do not understand the dark side of the mainland's officialdom. Hence, as Mao said, the future is bright, but the path is a zig-zag one.[50]

Furthermore, the pan-democrats in the LegCo are annually determined to put forward Tiananmen-related motions in the HKSAR. In 2009, the LegCo debated the motion of "reversing the verdict of Tiananmen" consecutively for 11 years after the return of Hong Kong to the PRC.[51] Twenty-three members of the pan-democratic faction in the legislature supported the motion; 16 members from the pro-Beijing and pro-establishment camp voted against it; 11 legislators abstained; and 9 were absent.[52] The motion could not be passed because it failed to gain half of the support from each of the two sectors: those legislators directly elected from geographical constituencies and those elected from functional constituencies. Critics accuse the democrats of putting up a political show, but the annual motion debate, albeit failed to be passed every time, has profound symbolic implications. The pan-democrats, some of whom are still the Alliance leaders, are determined to raise public awareness through the motion debate and to force the pro-Beijing legislators to declare their stance. In 2009, interestingly, the pro-Beijing FTU, which had mobilized the public against the martial law in the mainland in May 1989, declared that the Tiananmen was only "a small wave" in the PRC's progressive and rapid transformation from poverty 30 years ago to today's development.[53] This politically opportunistic stance is unsurprising and symbolic of many Hong Kong people who tend to follow those who have political power, status, and influence.

The annual public commemoration of the Tiananmen incident reminds the public of the fact that some pro-government and pro-Beijing elites were formerly supportive of the mainland democrats in June 1989. A case in point was C. Y. Leung, who is an Executive Council (ExCo) member and who is regarded as one of the major contenders for the successor to the current Chief Executive Donald Tsang. Leung used his personal name to participate in a group's signature advertisement against the military crackdown of student democrats in June 1989. He said in 2009 that he did not regret what he had done in 1989.[54]

Most importantly, the pan-democratic legislators' questioning of Chief Executive Donald Tsang in May 2009 forced the HKSAR leader to expose his views, which later prompted him to issue a public apology. In response to Civic Party legislator Margaret Ng's question on whether the chief executive supported the reversal of the PRC verdict on the 1989 Tiananmen incident, Tsang replied:

I understand how the Hong Kong people feel about and see this event. But the incident took place many years ago. During the period, our country made great achievements in every aspect and also brought about Hong Kong's economic prosperity. I believe that the people of Hong Kong can have their objective view of our national development. This is my view. My view can represent the view of the Hong Kong people. Their views also influence my view.[55]

After Tsang made his remarks, the pan-democratic legislators expressed their anger by leaving the legislative chamber. Tsang then apologized to the legislators for saying that his "view can represent the view of the Hong Kong people." Still the democrats were dissatisfied and asked him to apologize to the public for hiding his conscience, "raping public opinion," and misrepresenting the people of Hong Kong.[56] Therefore, the aggressive questioning from the pan-democratic camp in the LegCo's questions and answers session with the chief executive had the consequences of directly forcing Tsang to reveal his political attitude toward the Tiananmen tragedy and indirectly prompting the Hong Kong people to ponder the "truth" behind the 1989 incident. Tsang's careless remarks provided further ammunition for the pan-democrats to mobilize the public to participate in the candlelight vigil and the July 1 parade.[57] Some democrats used Facebook to appeal to their supporters to denounce Tsang's claims.[58] Even the former LegCo President Rita Fan disagreed with Tsang and said that the Tiananmen incident was a "tragedy" in which the Chinese nation would need to consider when the issue should be reassessed.[59] The virtue of Hong Kong's pluralistic society is that once the top leader made politically controversial remarks on the Tiananmen tragedy, political elites ranging from the democrats to pro-Beijing politicians could openly disagree with him without the fear of being retaliated by the authorities.

THE ANNUAL JUNE 4 CANDLELIGHT VIGIL AND ITS POLITICAL SIGNIFICANCE

The annual June 4 candlelight vigil at the Victoria Park has profound implications for Hong Kong politics and the PRC's political development. As a political tradition from 1990 onwards, a parade commemorating the June 4 tragedy must be held several days prior to the candlelight vigil at the Victoria Park, and it usually attracts fewer participants than the candlelight rally. However, the annual parade is a predictive indicator of the number of participants in the ensuing candlelight vigil a few days later.

Table 1.1 shows that the number of parade participants reached an apex in 1990 but it declined with the passage of time. The 2009 parade

Table 1.1

The Number of Participants in the Annual Parade Commemorating June 4

Year	The Alliance Figures	The Police Figures
1990	250,000	100,000
1991	50,000	10,000
1992	10,000	4,000
1993	4,000	3,500
1994	3,500	3,000
1995	2,000	2,750
1996	4,500	2,500
1997	7,000	3,000
1998	2,700	2,000
1999	4,000	2,000–2,500
2000	2,000	No figure released
2001	1,500	No figure released
2002	1,500	No figure released
2003	2,500	No figure released
2004	5,600	3,000
2005	1,400	1,000
2006	1,100	600
2007	1,500	1,000
2008	990	600
2009	8,000	4,700

Source: Ming Pao, June 1, 2009, p. A2.

was significant as it represented the twentieth anniversary, which reminded more Hong Kong people of the June 4 incident. Hence, the number of participants in 2009 was even a bit higher than that in 1997, when many Hong Kong people were concerned about whether their civil liberties would continue in the HKSAR after July 1, 1997. The police figures were consistently lower than the number released by the Alliance, except in 1995 when the police estimate was higher than the Alliance's. The parade in 2009 attracted not only middle-aged citizens whose memories of the Tiananmen had not faded away but also many young people whose political vision of mainland China tends to be more democratic along the line of Western-style checks and balances. Some young people said that their participation was stimulated by the remarks of Chief Executive Donald Tsang, who played down the Tiananmen incident in the PRC history and who said most Hong Kong people agreed with his view that the motherland's progress was far more important than the 1989 saga.

The number of participants in the June 4 candlelight vigil in 2009 was almost the same as that in 1990—proof that many Hong Kong citizens remember the Tiananmen tragedy and hope for a more democratic China (Table 1.2). Arguably, if Hong Kong in the past was a revolutionary base for the mother of the 1911 revolution Sun Yat-sen, it has already become a beacon of democratic aspirations for many Chinese on the mainland Chinese soil since June 1989. The HKSAR enjoys a degree of civil liberties and rule of law unrivaled in any mainland Chinese city. An editorial asserted that the people of Hong Kong should cherish their freedom because the Victoria Park could see hundreds of thousands of candles lit, whereas mainland China's 13 billion citizens had not yet enjoyed such freedom to remember the Tiananmen tragedy.[60] Unlike the PRC, which has remained tense and tight in its security on the Tiananmen Square on June 4 since 1989, the Hong Kong atmosphere has been traditionally punctuated by public sadness, mourning, and the political vision of a fully democratic China.

On the night of June 4, 2009, some Hong Kong parents brought their children to commemorate the Tiananmen tragedy at the Victoria Park. As one of the mothers said, "Today I have to bring my child to participate in a bicycle parade because I hope that he is aware of the historical tragedy that took place 20 years ago, and that he must understand the importance of being a just, conscientious, honest and fair person."[61] Some young students were impressed by the scene of all the sparkling candlelight at the Victoria Park, saying that they hoped to witness the reversal of the official verdict in the future.[62] In many other parts of the world, such as London, Washington, and Toronto, some overseas Chinese commemorate the June 4 tragedy annually. The desire of a more democratic China is arguably a universal value held by citizens in many countries,

Table 1.2

The Number of Participants in the Annual Candlelight Vigil at Victoria Park

Year	The Alliance Figures	The Police Figures
1990	150,000	80,000
1991	100,000	60,000
1992	80,000	28,000
1993	40,000	12,000
1994	40,000	12,000
1995	35,000	16,000
1996	45,000	16,000
1997	55,000	No figure released
1998	40,000	16,000
1999	70,000	No figure released
2000	45,000	No figure released
2001	48,000	No figure released
2002	45,000	No figure released
2003	50,000	No figure released
2004	82,000	48,000
2005	45,000	22,000
2006	44,000	19,000
2007	55,000	27,000
2008	48,000	15,700
2009	150,000	62,800

Source: Sing Tao Daily, June 5, 2009, p. A2.

especially in the HKSAR where the democrats and their staunch supporters hope for a reversal of the official Tiananmen verdict, which is still labeled as a "counter-revolutionary" action instigated by student democrats in 1989.

The annual candlelight vigil, like the July 1 parade organized by the Hong Kong democrats, provides a crucial channel of receiving public donations so that their activities will persist. The amount of public donations on the night of June 4 was HK$439,000 in 1992, HK$330,000 in 1993, HK$480,000 in 1994, HK$569,000 in 1995, HK$742,000 in 1996, HK$1,970,000 in 1997, HK$676,000 in 1998, HK$1,255,000 in 1999, HK$830,000 in 2000, HK$736,000 in 2001, HK$603,000 in 2002, HK$760,000 in 2003, HK$1,125,000 in 2004, HK$640,000 in 2005, HK$617,000 in 2006, HK$826,000 in 2007, HK$683,000 in 2008, and HK$2,100,000 in 2009.[63] Most importantly, in 2009, one donation was made in hundreds of thousands *Renminbi*, an indication that more mainlanders participated in the Hong Kong political tradition. The organizers of the candlelight vigil attached importance to the use of *Putonghua* or Mandarin so that they could communicate easily with the mainland participants. The double functions of the candlelight vigil in receiving ceaseless public donations for future activities and in attracting the political participation of mainlanders cannot be swept under the carpet.

A survey conducted by the Hong Kong Baptist University among 769 students in eight Hong Kong universities in April and May 2009 show that the political culture of Hong Kong students tends to be more critical of the mainland regime than mainland students who study in the HKSAR (Table 1.3). While more Hong Kong students than the mainland counter-parts agreed that the central leadership should be responsible for the June 4 tragedy, the Hong Kong students were more against the use of force in handling the Tiananmen democrats than the mainland opposite numbers. The Hong Kong students were also stronger in their view that the central government should reverse the official verdict on Tiananmen. However, among the mainland students, the majority views were also (1) critical of the central leadership in dealing with the Tiananmen inci-dent, (2) against the use of force, and (3) supportive of the reversal of ver-dict. If this survey result is an indicator of mainland students' political culture, the PRC's political future is perhaps more optimistic than many people may assume. In particular, many mainland students who are exposed to the Hong Kong media and civil liberties may perhaps alter their previously less pro-democracy views. From the survey results on the political culture of mainland students, it can be said that a silent revo-lution transforming the attitudes of mainlanders who study and stay in the HKSAR is underway. This does not mean that the mainland students who study in the HKSAR will necessarily promote democracy in the PRC, especially as many of them tend to favor working in Hong Kong after their graduation. But the point is the HKSAR does have a democra-tizing impact on many mainland students and visitors, whose political culture may be transformed from political indifference to a more pro-democracy political culture.

The transformation of the mainland media coverage of Tiananmen remains inadequate. While the mainland Chinese mass media must shun any report and commentary on the Tiananmen tragedy, the *Global Times* for the first time probed the views of several mainland Chinese academics on the evolution of intellectual thought, including the most sensitive period in the 1980s. The mainstream academic view, according to the *Global Times*, was that the 1980s should be seen carefully, includ-ing its arguments that the Western idealism and sociology were "naïve," that China was undergoing socialist transition, and that the public lacked

Table 1.3

The Different Views of Hong Kong and Mainland University Students on the June 4 Incident

Question/Answer	N = 769	
	Hong Kong Students (%)	Mainland Students (%)
Who should be responsible for the June 4 commemorations?		
1. The central leadership	56	36
2. Students leaders/students	9	22
Do you agree that the central government should use force to disperse the students?		
1. Strongly agree/agree	6.8	12.6
2. Neutral	22.6	40.7
3. Strongly disagree/disagree	70.6	45.1
4. Others	—	1.6
Should the Centre reverse the verdict on Tiananmen?		
1. Strongly agree/agree	48.3	36.9
2. Neutral	46.5	53.1
3. Strongly disagree/disagree	5.2	8
4. Others	—	2

Source: Ming Pao, May 22, 2009, p. A21.

confidence.[64] The unprecedented discussion on the evolution of Chinese intellectual thought in the 1980s, albeit in an English newspaper in the PRC, was perhaps a progressive sign that at least the CCP allowed some space for political discourse, although the academic views tended to be politically correct in upholding the official Party line.

Another silent revolution in the PRC is that more citizens are using the Internet and blogs to express their political views explicitly and implicitly, thus augmenting the political space for discussion although such space is often monitored and limited by the authorities. In early June 2009, many mainlanders utilized the numbers 20 and 64 in their blog discussions.[65] Although some comments were quickly eliminated by the Web site server, the widespread use of the numbers 20 and 64 in some mainland blogs proves that some mainlanders do not forget the Tiananmen tragedy.

On the other hand, the families of the victims of the Tiananmen tragedy have taken action to lobby the PRC government to change its official verdict. In 2009, 128 members of the families of the Tiananmen victims made a declaration through an overseas human rights organization, Human Rights in China, to appeal to the PRC government to reassess the Tiananmen tragedy.[66] Ding Zhilin, a philosophy professor whose son was killed in the tragedy, was interviewed by the Radio Free Asia and said that the Hong Kong people's support of the reversal of official verdict was actually the same as the demand of the families of the victims.[67] She admitted that the families might not be able to achieve their goals in their lifetime, but it remains a distant ideal that is invaluable in the persistent struggle. Ding and other Tiananmen mothers submitted a petition to the NPC in 2008, maintaining that "China has become an airtight iron chamber and all the demands of the people about June 4, all the anguish, lament, and moaning of the victims' relatives and the wounded have been sealed off." [68] If the spirit of the fight for democracy lies more in the process than in the final objective of reversing the official verdict, Ding's spirit of persistent struggle has much in common with many Hong Kong people who are striving for the double direct elections in the HKSAR.

Overall, the PRC authorities treat the anniversary of the Tiananmen incident nervously, illustrating that the mainland regime is by no means confident of its legitimacy, which is strong in the economic performance aspect but remains fragile in the minds of those mainland, Hong Kong, and overseas Chinese who still regard the Tiananmen tragedy as the dark side of the PRC history. Days before the twentieth anniversary of June 4, the mainland police "invited" Bao Tong, the former close adviser of the late Zhao Ziyang, to leave Beijing for fear that his remarks and interactions with the foreign media would have possible boomerang effects on the PRC regime's legitimacy and image.[69] Bao was one of the planners who turned Zhao's memoirs into the book *Gaige Licheng*, which is available in Hong Kong and overseas. On the eve of the twentieth anniversary of Tiananmen, 6,000 Web sites in the mainland were closed down for fear of instigating or inciting public discontent; the Alliance's Web site in Hong Kong could not be accessed by many people because of mainland hackers disrupting its operation; two Tiananmen mothers were forbidden to go out of their homes to commemorate their loved ones; the home of Wang Dan's parents was monitored and guarded; and other dissidents like Chen Ziming and Jiang Yinyong, the doctor who blew the whistle to the foreign media on the situation of the Severe Acute Respiratory Syndrome (SARS) in Beijing in 2003, were under tight surveillance.[70] A veteran CCP member, Du Daozheng, who helped record Zhao Ziyang's memoir, was forced to make a compromise with the government by saying openly that he disagreed with the publication of Zhao's book at a time when the PRC encountered "great difficulties." [71] When the Hong Kong Asia Television (ATV) broadcasted a program on the Tiananmen tragedy on the night of May 23, the Shenzhen Cable TV censored itself and replaced the ATV program with another program on the mainlanders' image of their Hong Kong tour.[72] The ATV program showed the scenes of the military tanks entering the Tiananmen Square on June 4, 1989, of those students who were injured, and of a brave citizen Wang Weilin using his body to prevent the tanks from moving forward. The program also showed the remarks made by student Zhou Duo: "Some people know how to make compromise, but who come out to compromise [with the government] would be seen as traitors and severely denounced, including Wang Dan and Wu'er Kaixi."[73] Zhou also appealed to the people to reflect on "why this just movement failed so dismally."[74] Intentionally or unintentionally, the ATV program appeared to present the facts on the Tiananmen tragedy while utilizing Zhou's comments to prompt the audience to ponder the political implications of the abortive student movement. While the people of Hong Kong could have access to this politically sensitive television program, the mainlanders do not enjoy this luxury.

If legitimacy, as the late political scientist Samuel Huntington reminded us, involves not only performance but also procedural aspects,[75] the PRC government will sooner or later have to confront the issue of toning down or revising the official verdict on Tiananmen so that its procedural legitimacy will be rectified and consolidated in the minds of many mainlanders, Hong Kong people, and overseas Chinese who regard the Tiananmen tragedy as undoubtedly a historical error committed by the PRC government in 1989.

THE HONG KONG COMMEMORATION OF JUNE 4 AND THE OVERSEAS CHINESE DEMOCRATS

An often neglected significance of Hong Kong's annual parade and June 4 candlelight vigil is that they provide a forum for overseas Chinese democrats to reignite and maintain the global hope for democratic improvement in the PRC. The *World Journal* in New York appealed to the PRC government to democratize its political system peacefully without any bloodshed in the future because this is the common aspiration of the overseas Chinese.[76] In June 2009 *Sing Tao Daily* carried extensive coverage of the role and ideals of the famous overseas Chinese democrat Wang Dan, who was arrested by the PRC authorities after Tiananmen and who eventually went to the United States to pursue his graduate studies.[77] Wang hoped to enter the HKSAR in 2009 to commemorate the June 4 anniversary but failed. He eventually went to Taiwan in September 2009 as a lecturer and researcher at the National Chengchi University. Wang hoped that the overseas Chinese democrats will contribute constructively to the development of China's democratization.[78] He also sees Hong Kong as "a political window" having the potential to influence the PRC. As Wang remarked,

After 1989, Hong Kong's influence on the PRC has increased because Hong Kong enjoys the space for the freedom of speech. At present, although Hong Kong is no longer an economic window for the PRC, it can be a window for China's social change ... As long as Hong Kong retains its freedom of speech on the Chinese soil, it can have special significance and influence the motherland's development.[79]

Another former Chinese student leader who is living in Taiwan, Wu'er Kaixi, tried to enter Macao on June 3, 2009, but he was deported back to Taiwan. He said to the Macao customs that he surrendered himself to the Liaison Office, Beijing's representative office in Macao, because he was under the arrest warrant of the PRC government.[80] Like Wu'er Kaixi, another former student activist, Xiang Xiaoji, was denied entry into Hong Kong from New York on June 2, 2009, although Wang and Wu'er nominated Xiang as the representative of the overseas Chinese democrats to try entering the HKSAR to commemorate the June 4 incident.[81]

Chai Ling, a former student leader in the Tiananmen incident, adopted a different tactic to promote the PRC democratic development. She set up the Jenzabar Foundation in the United States to support mainland China's democratization, to support the families of the victims of Tiananmen, and to donate money to those who work for the PRC's political changes. Chai remarked: "After 20 years passed, I feel that it is time for me to come out to declare my support of democracy. This shows that we have not forgotten and will never forget the event. We have to continue to work hard for China's peace and freedom and I hope more people will join us." [82] Being a successful businesswoman in America, Chai has opted for the path of supporting the PRC democratization through financial means—an approach different from Wang and Wu'er. Chai revealed in 2009 that when she was hiding in the PRC for 10 months in 1989 and 1990, about 200 Chinese helped her to flee from the security agents and escape to the United States.[83] According to Chai, 2,000 to 3,000 citizens were killed by the military crackdown during the Tiananmen tragedy.

Xiong Yan, a former student leader in the 1989 Tiananmen incident, could enter Hong Kong in 2009 to participate in the candlelight vigil by using his American passport with a visa granted by the PRC government after numerous rejections.[84] Some observers interpreted the PRC approval of his visa as a sign of loosening the grip over the overseas Chinese participation in the candlelight vigil in Hong Kong. Others speculated that the PRC might be concerned about whether any continuous rejection of the visa application from Xiong, who is an army chaplain, might be seen as an undue hard-line policy toward an American military officer's attempt at visiting the HKSAR.

While some overseas Chinese democrats often try to enter the HKSAR to participate in the June 4 commemoration, the PRC government tends to see their attempted participation as an external intervention in domestic Chinese politics. Compounding the problem of this deep-rooted perception of foreign intervention are the frequent remarks made by American politicians on the Tiananmen tragedy. The Speaker of the U.S. House of Representative, Nancy Pelosi, met 10 overseas Chinese dissidents on June 3, 2009, and then urged President Barack Obama to strengthen the American concern about human rights conditions in China. Secretary of State Hillary Clinton appealed to the PRC government to openly review and reassess the Tiananmen incident, including the number of injuries, deaths, arrests, and disappearances, so that China would learn how to heal from the wounds.[85] In response, Beijing voiced its "strong dissatisfaction" with Clinton's comments, calling them "groundless accusations against the Chinese government."[86] Although Taiwan is consistently regarded by the PRC as an inseparable part of the mainland, its pro-reunification President Ma Ying-jeou also hoped that Beijing would not avoid discussing the Tiananmen tragedy.[87] Since the CCP attaches great importance to face, this deep-rooted Chinese culture is in conflict with the American wish to see the reversal of the official Tiananmen verdict. ("Face" refers to the Chinese term *mianzi*, which means honor in English. Most Chinese attach importance to maintaining their face, without which they believe that their honor and good image are undermined.)

SUMMARY

Hong Kong's role in the Tiananmen incident was extremely important. It provided the financial support of the mainland democrats, provided a channel for some of them to escape from the PRC, and is now entrenching a base to commemorate the tragedy on an annual basis. Hong Kong's democracy is embryonic and does not resemble the West in which the chief executive is directly elected by universal suffrage, but the HKSAR has helped the PRC's "democratic root to grow longer than ever before."[88] Although Hong Kong's political system itself has shown signs of mainlandization,[89] another dialectical tendency is that the Hong Kong style of freedom, political culture, and protest tradition has been seeping into the mainland gradually. In particular, Guangdong province has envisaged many local people and Hong Kong residents resorting to protests to make their grievances heard.[90] If Hong Kong is already part of the PRC, the Hongkong-ization of the mainland is perhaps taking place silently but at a consistent and gradual pace. The mainlanders' political culture, especially those who visit and work in the HKSAR, has been changing slowly to become more like Hong Kong people who cherish their civil liberties and rule of law. The seeds of mainland China's democracy have already been sowed in the HKSAR.

CHAPTER 2

The Politics of the July 1 March since 2003

The July 1 protests against the Tung Chee-hwa administration in 2003 shocked the entire HKSAR government, Beijing, and the people of Hong Kong. Half a million citizens marched on the streets of Hong Kong peacefully and orderly against the maladministration of the Tung regime. Since July 1, 2003, the annual march has become a barometer of the degree of popularity of the HKSAR government and a crucial indicator of the public support of pan-democrats. This is why the central government in Beijing, especially its representative Liaison Office, has been so deeply concerned about the number of protestors on July 1 since 2003, especially on July 1, 2009, when the twentieth anniversary of the June 1989 Tiananmen incident highlighted the importance of both the June 4 candlelight vigil at the Victoria Park and the July 1 march. This chapter focuses on the politics of the annual July 1 march, which has arguably become a Hong Kong–style of democracy versus the far more restrictive way in which the mainland Chinese participate in protests in the PRC.

MODERNIZATION OF MAINLAND POLICING OF SOCIAL PROTESTS: LEARNING FROM HONG KONG?

In the PRC, citizens who dare to take their grievances to the streets are often under the watchful and intimidating eyes of the police. After the Sichuan earthquake on May 12, 2008, some citizens openly demonstrated against the mainland's substandard building structure that might have caused numerous schools to collapse easily during the earthquake. Although they boldly participated in various protests against public maladministration and bureaucratic corruption, the mainland police adopted the policy of monitoring them, persuading them to abandon the protests, and blacklisted the organizers. It can be argued that the mainland way of dealing with these protestors after the Sichuan earthquake has improved substantially since the brutal Tiananmen crackdown of the student demonstrators on June 4, 1989. At least, the police tolerated the Sichuan protestors rather than using violence arbitrarily.

Compared to the police handling of the March 2008 Tibetan unrest in the mainland and the July 2009 Xinjiang unrest where the Tibetans and the Uygurs, respectively, instigated the protests and clashed violently with the police and Hans,[1] the mainland Chinese government has gradually learned to tackle domestic protests more skillfully by (1) minimizing the extent of the use of military force, and (2) containing the spread of the unrest rather than resulting in widespread violent crackdown. If this observation is accurate, there has been a gradual process of modernization of the mainland's way of policing social unrest and citizen protests. The Xinjiang social unrest in the summer of 2009 was quickly curbed and contained, while the mainland government quickly allowed the foreign mass media to cover the incident, unlike the 2008 Tibetan protests, which led to the relatively clumsy and slow response of the PRC government to the foreign media coverage. The Hong Kong media, such as the Television Broadcasting (TVB) reporters, were allowed to interview the Tibetan monks in Lhasa during the 2008 Tibetan unrest, but the interviewees appeared to be far more cautious after the first interviews by the Hong Kong TVB reporters.[2] Apparently, they were under the surveillance and warning from the higher political and religious authorities. However, compared to the Hong Kong style of policing social unrest, the mainland approach remains relatively violent, more prone to authoritarian suppression, and more vulnerable to the use of police discretion. The Hong Kong approach to handling social protests, citizen march, and public parade arguably remains an ideal model for the mainland police to learn and imitate.

One commonality of the mainland policing of the 1989 Tiananmen protests, the 2008 Tibetan unrest, and the 2009 Xinjiang unrest was that PRC authorities have remained concerned about any foreign intervention in instigating the domestic protestors. In the case of mainland officials responsible for the HKSAR, they are often very concerned about (1) the number of protestors on July 1 and, above all, (2) whether foreigners are the behind-the-scene instigators.[3] The vigilant Chinese official attitude toward whether foreigners and foreign countries are involved in domestic social protests is a real one. It is due to the Tiananmen Incident in which foreign countries such as the United States, the United Kingdom, and France did lend their support of the student democrats and dissidents who were under the PRC national security's and police's arrest warrant.

The Tibetan unrest in 2008 was viewed by PRC authorities as being instigated by the Tibetan Youth Congress and the Dalai Lama, while the
Xinjiang unrest in 2009 was seen as being fostered by the overseas Xinjiang
separatists. This Chinese concern about foreign and sinister interventions
remains the defining feature of the PRC perception of large-scale and ethnically sensitive social unrest. With the benefit of hindsight, PRC hard-
liners also viewed the July 1, 2003, protests launched by the people of
Hong Kong as having "black hands" behind the scene. If foreign intervention is seen as politically sinister with the intention of fostering citizens to
threaten the PRC regime and topple the CCP, this mainland perception
has to be taken far more seriously by outside observers than ever before.

Arguably, the mainland style of policing social protests, if not necessarily unrest, should learn from the Hong Kong model. The Hong Kong
style of policing social protests is marked by a relatively high degree of
tolerance by police officers and authorities, whose hard-line action against
protestors can easily be criticized as authoritarian and excessively discre-
tionary. The annual July 1 protests initiated by the democrats have established a political tradition of peaceful demonstration and orderly parade
with minimal confrontation between protestors and police. This tolerant
way of dealing with protests on the part of both the participants and
police has much to be learned by the mainland police and citizens, who
launch protests to make their demands heard by the authorities at village,
township, provincial, and central levels. If the modernization of mainland
policing can constitute an indicator of democratization in the PRC, it
should be taken more seriously by academics and observers in the years
to come. Both the quality and quantity of policing in the mainland have
to be improved, especially the ways in which police at the grassroots level
handle protestors at village, township, provincial, and central levels. The
mainland police appeared to learn gradually from the Hong Kong police,
who managed the Korean farmers' protests during the World Trade
Organization's ministerial meeting in 2005 by using as little force as possible.[4] Before the 2008 Olympics, the mainland police were trained to
use rubber bullets—a progressive sign that any protests might necessitate
a far less violent way of management than the military crackdown of the
Tiananmen protestors in June 1989. In practice, the PRC police should
study the ways in which their counterparts handle the annual July 1 protests in the HKSAR.

THE DYNAMICS OF THE JULY 1 MARCH IN THE HKSAR

On July 1, 2009, the *Apple Daily* adopted its traditional approach since
July 1, 2003, to highlight the need for the citizens to strive for universal
suffrage for the HKSAR. Its front page emphasized that "today we cannot
be left without you on the streets to fight for universal suffrage."[5]

The front page also highlighted the appeal of Martin Lee Chu-ming to "walk for the mainlanders" and the remarks of Anson Chan to ask citizens to "use action in expressing their demands for democratic development, the government's accountability system and the people's livelihood."[6] To facilitate protestors, the *Apple Daily* used a back page to highlight the Chinese words: "Struggling for universal suffrage, No Donald (Tsang)." The popular Chinese newspaper also utilized its inner pages to highlight the appeals of overseas Chinese democrats, notably Wang Dan, who claimed that "the central government in Beijing would be touched by more Hong Kong people taking to the streets."[7] Wang said: "Hong Kong is the only place on the mainland Chinese soil that can release the people's voices." Other pages of the newspaper examined those young people who were concerned more about the preparation of the July 1 march than about their public examination at the high school level. Ethnic minorities, such as Pakistani and Indonesian groups, were determined to fight for their rights to be hired in more civil service positions, which require members of ethnic minorities to not only hold university degrees but also pass the Chinese language examination at the high school level. Nevertheless, most members of ethnic minorities have neither reached the required high Chinese standard nor held university degrees, thus depriving them of the qualifications to join the HKSAR bureaucracy.[8] The *Apple Daily* also appealed to the gay and lesbian community, which has become the pillar of the interest groups participating in the annual July 1 march since mid-2003.

Judging from the reports and commentaries on the *Apple Daily*, they were selected and arranged in such a way as to prepare for full-scale mobilization of citizens to protest on July 1, 2009. Ng Chi-sum, a well-known radio commentator and columnist, wrote that the policy failure of the Tsang administration and the arrest of mainland dissident Liu Xiaobo on the grounds of allegedly inciting subversion by the PRC government provided the "sufficient" reasons for citizens to take to the streets.[9] Liu was one of the key drafters of Charter 8, a manifesto signed by mainland human rights activists to advocate political reform and an end to one-party rule. Days before July 1, the *Apple Daily* began to highlight the heroes, such as lawyer Alan Leong Ka-kit, who succeeded in leading the Hong Kong people to fight for the postponement of enacting the National Security Bill in accordance with Article 23 of the Basic Law, which outlaws subversion, treason, sedition, and secession.[10] Leong insisted in the newspaper interview that the Article 23 debate provided the impetus for him to fight for social justice. Another interview with legislator and protestor "Long Hair" Leung Kwok-hung reminded the newspaper's readers that he became famous after his staunch opposition to the Tung regime in 2003, and that his eventual victory in the 2004 LegCo direct election was attributable to his clear anti-Tung stance.[11]

The *Apple Daily* also carried a report of Anson Chan, who criticized Donald Tsang for "monopolizing power" and the HKSAR government for "conspiring with the business sector." [12] The photo containing Anson Chan showed a group of young people accompanying her. Beside the report on Anson Chan was an interview with the postal union employees, who have been participating in the annual July 1 march since 2003. The postal union spokesman emphasized the educational need for "the torch of July 1st march to be transferred to the sons and daughter[s]" of the younger generation.[13] As a traditional vehicle of the democrats to mobilize their supporters, the *Apple Daily* targeted the younger generation in the July 1, 2009, march.

The forum page of *Ming Pao* tends to intentionally or unintentionally project different views that appear to create an image of the newspaper's neutrality. Sociologist Chan Kin-man criticizes the current HKSAR political system as neither authoritarian nor democratic, but it also lacks the capacity to build up a "truly democratic system." [14] He argued that the HKSAR system should evolve naturally through the introduction of universal suffrage, the growth of political parties, the cultivation of political leadership, and the improvement in the quality of public policy making. Another academic, policy expert Anthony Cheung Bing-leung, questioned whether the July 1 march became a political "ritual" in which the pan-democratic camp competes with the pro-Beijing forces every year.[15] Cheung contended that the July 1 march imposed a political "burden" on the pan-democratic organizers because of the public focus on the number of participants. He asserted that the annual march is by no means "a people's referendum" as some democrats have insisted.[16]

Mobilizing the public to participate in the march, the Civil Human Rights Front used Facebook to appeal to supporters to stay outside the HKSAR government's headquarters on July 2, and to force the Tsang regime to start a dialogue on the issue of universal suffrage.[17] The Front fully mobilized all kinds of interest groups, like civil service unions, human rights activists, young people, gay and lesbian supporters, and ethnic minorities to participate in the July 1 march. The rallying point was the call for universal suffrage, an umbrella concept under which different interests of various groups could be integrated. Before the march, the outbreak of H1N1 prompted the HKSAR government to order the schools to terminate their classes, especially after some schools had found that students were infected with the disease. The secretary for food and health, York Chow, even appealed to the citizens who were sick to avoid participating in the July 1 parade.[18] In response, democrats such as Ronny Tong of the Civic Party (CP) said that the swine flu was not deadly and that citizens who were concerned about the disease could wear masks to protect themselves on July 1.

Although the HKSAR government implemented a series of measures for the sake of minimizing public discontent and hopefully reducing the number of protestors on July 1, 2009, its announcement of rewarding the services of two top officials appeared to anger the public. Notably, the secretary for constitutional and mainland affairs, Stephen Lam, who failed to achieve any breakthrough in political reform proposals and obstructed democratization in the minds of the democrats, was awarded the Golden Bauhinia Medal. Another politically appointed official who also received the Golden Bauhinia Medal was York Chow, whose performance was widely regarded as problematic because of a series of mistakes and maladministration committed by public hospitals. The *Apple Daily* highlighted the fact that these "mediocre officials have been elevated with knighthood." [19]

The HKSAR government tried its best to minimize public discontent and its handling of police grievances was a good example. Weeks before the July 1 protest, the police officers and rank-and-file members complained about the pay trend survey results, which to them collected the "flawed" data of two companies. [20] They were upset by the governmental refusal to implement an independent pay review mechanism for the police. To defuse the crisis, police commissioner Tang King-shing met the disgruntled police officers and insisted that he would take their complaints seriously. Eventually the angry police officers called off their protest march planned for June 28. Supporters of the police argued that the police force is unique and different from other disciplinary services in the HKSAR and that it "should be exempt from any pay cut." [21] Another supporter wrote:

Since the handover, the police force has played a crucial role, maintaining prosperity and stability in Hong Kong . . . Officers spare no effort tackling crimes and providing round-the-clock services to Hong Kong people. They are always ready to perform their duties at any time and anywhere when the situation merits it. Just like medical staff, they have been involved in operations where people's lives could be at risk, for example, the outbreak of severe acute respiratory syndrome, swine flu isolation and the World Trade Organization [ministers] meeting in Hong Kong in 2005. Police officers deserve to receive fair and unbiased, if not preferential, treatment from an accountable and compassionate government. [22]

Originally 5,000 police officers had planned to participate in the June 28 protests, but the intervention from Tang defused the crisis and exerted the pressure on Chief Executive Donald Tsang, the Civil Service Bureau, and the top policy-making ExCo. [23] It was rare to envisage a police commissioner who was determined to stand on the side of his subordinates and rank-and-file staff vis-à-vis the HKSAR leadership. As a commentator noted, "By leading the fight for better pay, Mr. Tang has a personal stake in the negotiations. It will be politically disastrous if he fails to deliver a deal acceptable to his staff. His authority and credibility to lead the police force will be in doubt."[24] Another commentator, Steve Vines, expressed grave reservations about Tang's intention to stay on as the police commissioner while crossing the government line:

In Hong Kong, no one has ever stepped down from the administration on a point of principle but, should this happen, there is every reason to respect such a move. Mr. Tang wants it both ways and has, in effect, been told by the government that it is powerless to prevent him from flouting established practice. He wishes to campaign for a new police pay regime and may well succeed. In that case, matters would move from bad to worse as it would demonstrate that defying accepted norms of behavior in government can be flouted and even rewarded.[25]

Tang appeared to be in a dilemma; on the one hand he was politically sandwiched between the disgruntled colleagues and the administration. But, on the other hand, as a leader of the frequently publicly criticized police force, he had to defuse the internal crisis by acting as the champion of his subordinates. Doing so had the unintended consequence of jeopardizing the principle of collective responsibility at the level of politically appointed officials, who included the police commissioner himself.

About 2,000 police officers were mobilized to control the crowd on July 1, 2009.[26] The July 1 marches contained not only the democratic mobilization of the masses in the afternoon from 3:30 pm onwards but also the pro-Beijing parade in the morning and the march initiated by the victims of the mini-bonds of Lehman Brothers. The pro-Beijing parade was well organized by all the patriotic groups in the HKSAR, such as the Fujian Federation of Associations, the FTU, the Heung Yee Kuk (HYK), and the New Territories Federation of Associations. Their parade was marked by colorful flags and drums. The chief organizers of the parade celebrating the twelfth anniversary of Hong Kong's return to the PRC included the FTU leader Cheng Yiu-tong and the Liaison Office's officials. In his opening speech, Cheng appealed to the people of Hong Kong to express their gratitude to the central government in Beijing for bringing about economic prosperity to the HKSAR. Moreover, the Hong Kong people should thank the PLA and the Foreign Ministry officials for their "love" of Hong Kong. Finally, the Hongkongers, to Cheng, should thank the HKSAR administration for its diligent work to make the "one country, two systems" successful.[27] The celebration at the Hong Kong Stadium began with a PLA performance, lion dancers, and traditional drummers.[28] Attendees included Chief Executive Donald Tsang and the Liaison Office director Peng Qinghua. Although reports claimed that 40,000 citizens participated in the pro-government and pro-Beijing parade, the police estimate was less than 39,000.

As a pluralistic society, the HKSAR naturally envisages anti-democratic groups. On July 1, 2009, some 50 citizens protested on the streets, and they mobilized themselves through the Internet to express their view that the pan-democratic camp did not represent them.[29] The organizer of the group criticized the legislators of the League of Social Democrats, notably Raymond Wong and Leung Kwok-hung, for using "verbal violence" in the LegCo.[30] The group also accused the pan-democrats of not only opposing the government for the sake of opposition but also lacking constructive suggestions to improve the people's livelihood. The birth of such "anti-democratic coalition" reflected the virtue of Hong Kong's pluralistic society where the relatively radical democrats like the League of Social Democrats are constantly monitored by other conservatively minded citizens. Another group seemingly mobilized by the pro-Beijing forces was called the Association for the Protection of Human Dignity, which managed to gather 100 citizens to protest against the pan-democratic camp for "using democracy to make Hong Kong chaotic."[31]

THE POLITICS OF PREDICTING THE NUMBER OF PROTESTORS ON JULY 1

In 2003, both the HKSAR's Chief Executive Office and Beijing, including the Hong Kong Macao Affairs Office (HKMAO) and the Liaison Office, totally misread the degree of public discontent in Hong Kong under the Tung Chee-hwa leadership. The unprecedented protests by 500,000 not only shocked the Beijing authorities but also prompted its representative Liaison Office in the HKSAR to reshuffle its leadership and readjust its policy toward a better understanding of public sentiments in Hong Kong. The July 1 protests in 2003 and 2004 stemmed from massive discontent in the HKSAR, where the Tung administration implemented various reforms alienating many social groups and individual citizens, where the governmental handling of the SARS angered citizens in early 2003, where the concerns about civil liberties erupted after the government attempt at legislating on Article 23 of the Basic Law in mid-2003, and where public fears of the freedom of speech persisted after a few popular radio hosts were reportedly intimidated by mysterious forces in 2004. The two July 1 marches in 2003 and 2004 were heavily mobilized by pro-democracy groups, the *Apple Daily*, and Bishop Joseph Zen. In June 2003, Zen appealed to all 200,000 Catholics to participate in the July 1 protests.[32] In June 2004, he again made a similar appeal: "Participation in the march is a good thing as we can feel more comfortable by doing so. Taking to the streets has already become the only channel of how Hong Kong people can express their opinions."[33] Deeply dissatisfied with the Tung administration and its policies, Bishop Zen's remarks were widely seen as encouraging more Hong Kong people to take to the streets to demonstrate against the government. In June 2005, Zen did not appeal to the Catholics and citizens to join the march, because he said that Hong Kong people were tired and so they should spend more time to accompany family members.[34] But Bishop Zen emphasized that he did not abandon the struggle for having double direct elections in the HKSAR in 2007 and 2008. His withdrawal from making any appeal to citizens in June 2005 might explain partly why the number of protestors on July 1, 2005, declined, but public sentiment in mid-2005 was a far cry from mid-2003 and mid-2004.[35] After Tsang became the chief executive, his popularity rating in mid-2005 was much higher than that of Tung. When asked in June 2005 whether Tsang performed better than Tung, 81 percent of the respondents in a poll conducted by Robert Chung of the University of Hong Kong said Tsang was better.[36] Clearly, public discontent declined considerably by mid-2005.

Since the Article 23 debacle in July 2003, the Liaison Office's officials in the HKSAR have reached out more to various sectors of the society and become more cautious in their public remarks. Whether the Liaison Office in the HKSAR could accurately tap public opinion in the territory has become a yardstick for Beijing's leaders to measure the agency's success and performance. Prior to July 1, 2009, the HKSAR government predicted that there would be over 47,000 demonstrators, a number estimated by the Civil Human Rights Front in 2008.[37] On the other hand, the Liaison Office was very concerned about the size of the democratic protestors on July 1, 2009.

Table 2.1

The Number of Participants in the Annual July 1 March Since 2003

Year	Figures from Civil Human Rights Front	Figures from Police	Estimates from Academics
2003	500,000	350,000	465,500 (Robert Chung)
2004	530,000	200,000	193,500 (Robert Chung)
			140,000–190,000 (Paul Yip)
2005	21,000	17,000	22,000 (Robert Chung)
2006	58,000	28,000	36,000 (Robert Chung)
			25,000–27,000 (Paul Yip)
2007	68,000	20,000	32,000 (Robert Chung)
2008	47,000	15,500	17,500 (Robert Chung)
2009	76,000	28,000	29,000–33,000 (Robert Chung, Joseph Man Chan)
			28,000 (Paul Yip)

Sources: AM730, July 2, 2009, p. 1; *Hong Kong Economic Journal*, July 2, 2009, p. 6.

While the pan-democratic camp's figures tend to overstate the number of participants, the police have the proclivity of underestimating the numbers (Table 2.1). The pan-democratic camp has not developed a systematic way of counting the number of protestors, illustrating the relatively loose nature of its organization. It is natural for the pan-democratic leaders of the July 1 march to overstate the number of participants so as to create a sense of success in mass mobilization. The pro-Beijing camp insisted that the pan-democratic front exaggerated the number of protestors in order to weaken the credibility and legitimacy of the HKSAR government.[38] At the same time, the police count the number of participants in a dubious way. One police officer told the author that it was a practice of the police to lower the number of protestors,[39] mainly because of the calculation problem and perhaps partly due to its bureaucratic tendency of minimizing any negative political impact of citizen protests on the government.

The academic figures and estimates are often controversial. Robert Chung's figures on the 2004 and 2009 marches were seriously questioned, especially the 2009 march in which the author estimated around 58,000 participants.[40] Indeed, the ways in which Chung, Chan, and Yip counted the participants remain controversial. Calculating those who entered the Victoria Park and stayed in the soccer pitches might not give us a full picture of the number of marchers, for some might join along the protest route.

After the march, the pro-Beijing dailies downplayed the number of protestors. *Ta Kung Pao* editorialized that the people of Hong Kong had confidence over the territory because of the backup from the central government. It stressed "the sinister and the ugly" faces of those organizers of the pan-democratic march, which used "the return of administration to the people" and "immediate universal suffrage" as "slogans aiming at repudiating the central government and making Hong Kong chaotic."[41] *Wen Wei Po*'s editorial elaborated on how the pan-democrats wrongly estimated pubic sentiments. It said:

Under the support of the central government and the hard work of the HKSAR administration, Hong Kong succeeded in fending off the shocks from the global financial tsunami, thus stabilizing the society and economy and minimizing public discontent. This made the opposition faction miscalculating themselves and exposing their own lies. On the contrary, the number of those societal sectors that celebrated Hong Kong's return to the motherland was far more than that organized by the opposition faction ... The opposition claimed before the march that there would be 150,000 to 200,000 marchers. After the march, it still exaggerates the number of participants ... This reflects that the opposition is drowned with dizziness, turns a blind eye to the Hong Kong reality and misreads the hearts and minds of the people.[42]

Although the pro-Beijing press downplayed the pro-democracy parade on July 1, the *Sun* and *Oriental Daily* were critical of the HKSAR government. The *Sun* used the headline "Civil Servants were forced to take to the streets" on its front page while the *Oriental Daily* centered on 100,000 people joining the march.[43] In reality, with the exception of the postal union employees and the recreational staff association that carried their banners openly, other civil servants who participated in the march adopted a low profile. Many civil servants, especially those who just enter the bureaucracy, complain about the system of having two three-year contracts before they will be considered for permanent terms.[44] Other complaints of the civil servants included the tremendous workload, the government policy of contracting out various services that undermines their morale, the "low" level of salaries of contractual employees, and the problematic top-level management of some departments such as recreational and welfare services.[45] Both the *Sun* and *Oriental Daily* shared the same editorial, criticizing both the HKSAR government for maladministration and triggering public discontent and the pan-democratic elites for being demagogues and troublemakers who divided the society without any contribution.[46] The editorial implicitly criticized the *Apple Daily* (First Media Group led by pro-democracy businessman Jimmy Lai) for "instigating the fire and achieving the objective of opposing China and turning Hong Kong into chaos."[47] The *Sun* carried a report that ridiculed former chief secretary for administration Anson Chan for being "a democratic grandmother" who was ignored by the pan-democrats.[48] It reminded the readers of Chan's action on July 1, 2007, when she left the marchers to have her hair cut. Clearly, the *Sun* adopted a very critical attitude toward both the government and the pan-democratic front.

This critical coverage of the pan-democratic march was a far cry from the *Apple Daily*, which highlighted on its second page that even an 80-year-old grandmother fought for democracy in Hong Kong for 20 years.[49] She even brought her son to participate in the march. The pro-democracy newspaper carried a poll of 200 participants. It found that 58 percent of them joined the march because of their desire for Hong Kong to have the direct elections of the chief executive and of the entire LegCo; that 24 percent was dissatisfied with the performance of the Tsang administration; that 9 percent protested against the government failure to rescue the economic market; that 5 percent supported the release of mainland dissident Liu Xiaobo by the PRC government; and that 4 percent chose other reasons.[50] An interesting highlight of *Apple Daily* was the remark made by a young lady who felt that

Hong Kong is becoming Macaonized and witnessing the second tier of governing elites sent by the central government. The CCP is entrenching its roots into the HKSAR. It is now more difficult for Hong Kong to have universal suffrage. The only path for the Hong Kong people to struggle for democracy is to take to the streets.[51]

Another report asserted that Beijing would ignore the number of protestors and that it would put forward a conservative political reform proposal by late 2009, thus stimulating a stronger wave of grievances and public protests in the HKSAR.[52] *Apple Daily* was undoubtedly the most crucial mobilization tool of the pan-democratic camp for the annual July 1 march. Its diversified coverage on the demands of ethnic minorities, sex workers, Filipino domestic helpers, the handicap, the youth, pro-animal rights activists, university students, and pro-gay rights workers stood out as the only prominent Chinese newspaper articulating the interests of different strata of the society. An interesting report on the complaints of 100 Pakistanis, who accused the pro-Beijing DAB of betraying them on the promise to improve their educational and career prospects, was noteworthy. Beside this report was a photo showing a citizen who carried a placard to criticize the TVB News for downplaying the June 4 candlelight vigil at the Victoria Park and for deliberately avoiding the coverage on politically sensitive issues.[53] The explicitly pro-democracy and anti-CCP stance of the newspaper could be discerned.

The centralist (neither pro-democratic nor pro-Beijing) Chinese dailies adopted a more independent stance on the demands of the July 1 marchers. The *Hong Kong Economic Times* editorialized that the government should tackle the demands of the pan-democratic camp rather than just taking measures before July 1 to minimize public grievances and reduce the number of protestors.[54] The editorial of *Sing Tao Daily* appealed to the government to communicate with the citizens, whose "rational" demands included the salary dispute over the police force and an increase in the penalty on drunk drivers, who in a number of cases caused the deaths of innocent Hong Kong people.[55] *Ming Pao* editorialized that the systemic weaknesses in the HKSAR called for the government to take political reform seriously, because "the government has responsibilities without any vote" in the legislature, which on the contrary has "votes without responsibilities."[56]

While most observers have focused on the number of participants in the annual pro-democracy march on July 1 since 2003, little attention has been paid to the enormous educative impact on the young generation, especially the Hong Kong and mainland students as well as mainland tourists. One mainland student wrote boldly in the *Apple Daily*:

The July 1st parade is one of the hallmarks of Hong Kong's civil society. When the mainland possesses such imprint of the July 1st parade, it will be a substantial progress in the nation. Taking to the streets is our right, yet this right is so insignificant in the mainland. If a nation cannot even protect the basic right of its citizens, can we still claim that this is a great nation where the people are the master?[57]

As with many Hong Kong democrats, this mainland student openly contended that the Hong Kong vision of democracy represents a model for the PRC because the HKSAR, to him, is by no means an "anti-CCP subversive base" but a reference point for Beijing to take the rule of law and civil liberties more seriously. Another mainland student who studied in the HKSAR wrote to the author: "I am impressed by the people of Hong Kong who fight for democracy in the HKSAR, but in China most citizens are now interested in earning more money." [58] One mainland tourist who witnessed the parade said that she was very "moved" by so many Hong Kong people who enjoyed having civil liberties.[59] In view of the increasing number of mainland tourists visiting the HKSAR, the annual June 4 candlelight vigil and the July 1 protests have constituted influential events that can serve as a rude awakening to the relatively politically apathetic and materialistically minded mainland comrades.

BEIJING'S CONCERN ABOUT THE JULY 1 PROTESTS

The central government in Beijing had a number of concerns about the July 1, 2009, protests. First and foremost, the number of participants did constitute a crucial indicator of the popularity of the Tsang administration.[60] Hence, it was logical to envisage the editorials of *Wen Wei Po* and *Ta Kung Pao* that stressed the much "lower" turnout of the pro-democracy parade than the pro-government celebrations. Beijing originally had estimated 120,000 citizens would participate in the July 1 protests, while the estimates of pan-democrats ranged from 80,000 to 200,000.[61] As it turned out, both Beijing and the pan-democrats were wrong in their predictions. Beijing's think tank and officials responsible for Hong Kong matters tended to neglect the fact that the larger turnout at the June 4 candlelight vigil dampened the desire of citizens to maintain the momentum of public protests on July 1. The pan-democrats underestimated the series of governmental measures, such as distributing more subsidies to citizens and reducing the high salaries of the politically appointed principal officials, which might minimize the extent of public discontent prior to the annual march.[62] Although the economy of Hong Kong prior to the July 1, 2009, parade was affected by the global financial crisis, the consumption level of the Hong Kong people was not seriously undermined.[63] Perhaps thanks to the central government's relaxation on the visits of mainlanders to the HKSAR since mid-2003, the mid-2009 situation was by no means as serious as the atmosphere before the protests by half a million citizens on July 1, 2003. Financial secretary John Tsang in May 2009 put forward HK$110 billion to assist the small and medium enterprises, the middle-lower classes, and the poor. The immediate political objective was to reduce public grievances through economic measures —a strategy that appeared to work well as with the similar situation in Macao where Chief Executive Edmund Ho often relied on the policy of "distributing candies" to appease the anger of the disgruntled citizens.[64]

Beijing's concern about the number of participants was understandable because before July 1 a case involving a mysterious attempt to assassinate Martin Lee was revealed. On July 3, the assassin received the court verdict of being imprisoned for 16 years.[65] Yet, the timing of this mysterious case coincided with the July 1 protest. From a conspiratorial perspective, Beijing could have been concerned about whether the ongoing court case would bring about more protestors, some of whom might misconstrue the attack on Lee as secretly orchestrated by mainland agents. In fact, as Martin Lee said before the July 1 protest, the mainland authorities were surely not the mastermind behind the planned attack.[66] Any mainland official attack on Lee, if publicly discovered, would be condemned internationally and regarded locally as totally an unwise move that would stimulate more people to take to the streets on the annual July 1 protest, for it could be interpreted as a violation of the "one country, two system" principle with a very serious motive from the CCP to "punish" political foes so prominently. Although the mainland officials did not say anything in public about the court case involving the alleged attack on Martin Lee, they might have been privately concerned about the impact of the case on the number of protestors on July 1.

Second, the mainland officials were concerned about the strategies of the pan-democrats from the July 1 protest to their struggle for democratic reform in the near future. Specifically, the mass mobilization was seen as part and parcel of the pan-democratic front's tactic of appealing to more citizens to take to the streets in their fight for universal suffrage in the HKSAR. Some pan-democratic leaders such as Cyd Ho openly admitted that the July 1 protest was merely a "warm-up" campaign leading to a larger-scale mass mobilization in support of the introduction of direct elections to select both the chief executive and the whole LegCo in 2012.[67] Anson Chan revealed in the Radio Television Hong Kong (RTHK) interview that "I hope the government will lead the citizens to rationally discuss the content of political reform models, including the existence of abolition of functional constituencies."[68] She said that the pan-democratic camp would not compromise on the principles of (1) having an orderly and gradual process of reform during the transition in 2012 and 2016 and of (2) achieving the universal suffrage of the chief executive election in 2017 and the direct election of the entire legislature in 2020. Two days after the July 1 march, the democrats held a "lunch box" meeting during which Cyd Ho and Lee Cheuk-yan raised the issues of going to the grassroots level to mobilize public concern about universal suffrage and exerting more pressure on the Tsang administration both inside and outside the legislature to accelerate the pace of democratization.[69] The pan-democratic camp saw the July 1 protest as the inception of its long-term plan to push for democratization in the HKSAR.

Third, Beijing remains vigilant of any foreign intervention and participation in the July 1 protests. While at least eight Kuomintang (KMT) flags
were hoisted by protestors on July 1, Taiwan is ruled by the pro-
reunification KMT and therefore Beijing's degree of political sensitivity
is arguably less than ever before. Above all, Taiwan is regarded by the
PRC as Chinese soil, and it is by no means a foreign country. In practice,
not many foreigners participated in the July 1 protests in 2009, except for
the Filipino domestic helpers, the Asian migrant workers' association,
the Indonesian community, and some non-Chinese Hong Kong residents
working at the RTHK for a long period of time.

Fourth, Beijing attached importance to whether the July 1 protests
might turn violent if pro-democracy supporters clashed with pro-
government marchers. The clash between the victims of the Lehman
Brothers and the police at the Bank of China building appeared to alarm
the central authorities. The scale of such confrontation, lasting for about
20 minutes, was relatively small. Still, the anxiety about any violent confrontation between the police and protestors turned out to be valid.
A group of 120 protestors, who stayed outside the government headquarters after the march, eventually confronted the police who carried
them away from the scene. The protestors included antigovernment activists and pro-Tibetan student Christina Chan Hau-man.[70] Critics of the
government argued that the police deprived the people's right to demonstrate, and that on July 1 the police did not open up enough space, thus
leaving many participants stuck on the streets for a long time under the
scorching sun.[71] After the clash between protestors and the police, *Wen
Wei Po*, which perhaps accurately reflects the position of the Liaison
Office, commented that the police were taking appropriate legal steps to
carry the demonstrators away from the government headquarters.[72] The
pro-Beijing daily also highlighted a report that some citizens got upset
about protestors who clashed violently with the police, and who even
raised the British Hong Kong flag during the parade to "humiliate the
people of Hong Kong."[73]

Indeed, pro-Beijing and conservative commentators believe that the
July 1 march represented a negative action on the part of the Hong Kong
people, whose participation might prompt Beijing's reconsideration of
its Hong Kong policy. As Mary Ma wrote bluntly,

As the heat recedes and cooler minds prevail, it would be in Hong Kong's interest
to ponder whether the sequence of mass protests will have any material impact on
the city's relationship with the central government. Over the years, Beijing
has channeled economic benefits to the SAR through preferential policies. The
most recent example was the yuan deal signed between central banker Zhou
Xiaochuan and the city's monetary chief Joseph Yam Chi-kwong that allows Hong
Kong firms to trade in yuan with firms in Shanghai and four other mainland cities.

Maybe local people should learn to look through the perspective of other stake-holders if they want to better understand the subtle question of mainland-Hong Kong relations which the central government is a key stakeholder. Will Beijing be happy with the never-ending rows in Hong Kong? It's plausible Beijing might even rethink its preferential policies toward Hong Kong in light of its ungrateful people. Those policies enacted over the years have raised the eyebrows of many cities in the mainland.[74]

Ma made a number of questionable assumptions in her argument. First, although mainland cities may be jealous of the privileges enjoyed by Hong Kong under Beijing's protection, this does not necessarily mean that Beijing must rethink its preferential policy toward the HKSAR simply because of the citizen protests on July 1 annually. Arguably, if the annual July 1 parade represents Hong Kong's political tradition, Beijing has to accept this reality and to separate economic issues from the local politics. Second, Ma ignores the fact that as long as Beijing tries to woo Taipei back to the mainland's political orbit through a model similar to, but not neces-sarily the same as, the Hong Kong model, repealing or minimizing the preferential economic policies toward the HKSAR would surely carry the negative connotation that the "one country, two systems" will not work as smoothly as widely expected. Hence, Ma's argument linking the citizen parade on July 1 to Beijing's intention of rethinking its preferential treatment of the HKSAR was unconvincing.

SUMMARY

This chapter argues that the relatively peaceful and orderly ways in which both the protestors and the police handle the annual July 1 pro-tests constitute a model for the mainland police to learn from this sig-nificant political tradition in Hong Kong. The July 1 protests have profound implications for the HKSAR, for they symbolize not simply the existence of civil liberties but also how the people of Hong Kong cherish the concept of democracy as institutional checks and balances and the direct elections of both the chief executive and the entire legisla-ture. Their ideal of having double direct elections may not be easily ful-filled as long as the PRC remains an authoritarian regime fearful of Western-style democratization. Still, this Hong Kong vision is leaving an undeletable imprint that many residents desire a more Western-style political system and a more direct type of democracy. The PRC, however, remains vigilant of Hong Kong's political vision, which to the ruling party constitutes a national security threat and a menace to its monopolistic power. These competing Chinese visions will continue to shape the politics of the pan-democrats vis-à-vis both the HKSAR government and Beijing in the years to come.

With more mainlanders visiting the HKSAR as tourists and some of them residing in the HKSAR, the silent impact of the annual June 4 candlelight vigil and the July 1 protests on their political culture cannot be underestimated. Little research has been conducted on the extent to which the mainlanders who visit and reside in the HKSAR are politically transformed by the annual June 4 candlelight vigil and July 1 protests. Although many mainlanders appear to be materially minded, as with many Hong Kong people, any evolution in their political culture is likely to be a silent revolution.

CHAPTER 3

From the Debate over Referendum in 2004 to the Rejection of Reform Package in 2005

The struggle for democracy on the part of the democrats is long term and protracted. The protests by half a million citizens on July 1, 2003, provided the impetus for the democrats to push the HKSAR government and Beijing to accelerate the pace of democratic reform in the territory. In April 2004, the NPC Standing Committee put the brake on Hong Kong's political reform by ruling out the possibilities of electing the chief executive by universal suffrage in 2007 and of selecting the entire legislature through direct elections in 2008. The democrats were frustrated but even more politically alienated than ever before. The debate over the referendum issue in 2004 and the ensuing rejection of the political reform package initiated by the Donald Tsang administration could be seen as legacies from the triangular wrangling among the democrats, the HKSAR government, and Beijing.

THE DEBATE OVER REFERENDUM

In October 2004, the democrats planned to use the term referendum to exert pressure on the HKSAR government to consult public opinion on democratization. On October 15, Cheung Chiu-hung and 14 democrats seized the opportunity of the absence of some pro-government legislators to suddenly raise the issue of using a referendum in LegCo to decide the direction of political reform in 2007 and 2008. Only five pro-government legislators attended LegCo's political reform subcommittee at that time, prompting the chairman Lui Ming-wah to adopt a delaying tactic until other pro-establishment legislators returned to the meeting room. Eventually the subcommittee decided to postpone the debate over referendum. Later, Cheung again raised the question of referendum in the LegCo's debate, but Ronny Tong thought that it was unwise to use the sensitive term.[1] Tong believed that surveys of all members of the public on their views toward political reform should be conducted. Another legislator, Lee Cheuk-yan, remarked that the crux of the problem was the HKSAR government did not want to use referendum as a means to consult public opinion. Cheung insisted that the pan-democrats should pursue the question of referendum. He contacted other like-minded democrats and groups to adopt a "scientific" way of measuring public views. In response, the Liaison Office's spokesman said that the use of referendum was impractical. An editorial of *Ming Pao* also questioned whether referendum would be counterproductive. It wrote:

There is nothing wrong in principle with holding a referendum to allow people to express their views. However, it is unrealistic to believe it is possible by doing so to reverse the decision to rule out universal suffrage in 2007 and 2008 (which the NPC Standing Committee made when it interpreted some Basic Law provisions) . . . If Beijing agreed that Hong Kong could decide its pace of constitutional development by holding a referendum, it would no longer have misgivings about democracy . . . Yesterday Zhang Xiaoming, a vice chairman of the Hong Kong and Macao Affairs Office, said in Beijing that, in developing its political system, Hong Kong should come to a broadly-based consensus on the basis of the applicable interpretations and decisions of the NPC Standing Committee. He as good as rejected the pro-democracy camp's referendum proposal.[2]

The dominant view in Hong Kong was that if Beijing set the boundary of political reforms in the HKSAR, the pan-democrats should ideally come up with a consensus with the HKSAR government on the pace and scope of political reform. Yet, some hard-line and idealistic democrats remained hopeful of using the referendum to exert pressure on the CCP, which is consistently the hegemonic ruling party in the mainland without the priority given to listen to public opinion.

A former mainland member of the Basic Law Committee, Wang Zhenmin, joined the Hong Kong discourse on referendum. He openly criticized those Hong Kong legislators who advocated the use of referendum to decide the pace and scope of democratization as "disrespecting the Basic Law" and "irresponsible."[3] On the issue of whether the public in Hong Kong could initiate their own referendum, Wang said: "If they like, it is acceptable for them to conduct their research. But it would be unacceptable for such survey in official capacity."[4] Wang appealed to the pan-democrats to maintain their calm attitude because political reform would have to proceed in accordance with the objective circumstances. He implied and warned that if the democrats insisted on what they would like, they would perhaps receive very little in the future. Wang said: "If what you want do not have the required social conditions, and if you still insist on achieving your objective, then you will gain nothing."[5] In response to Wang's arguments, Cheung Chiu-hung maintained:

If the Basic Law does not say that we can do something, then what we can do is disallowed! The Basic Law also does not say we can eat and be human beings! The mainland's legal spirit is a far cry from Hong Kong's. Wang uses the mainland system and imposes it onto Hong Kong. This is a violation of the "one country, two systems."[6]

Cheung and legislator Albert Cheng King-hon added that the referendum proposed by pan-democrats would neither be legally binding nor bypass the Basic Law. Pro-democracy legislator Audrey Eu argued that referendum would only be used as a way of understanding public opinion. Martin Lee revealed that during the drafting process of the Basic Law in February 1989, the second draft of the Basic Law did mention that all Hong Kong citizens would vote for the methods of electing both the chief executive and the LegCo. He added that if referendum in Hong Kong was once accepted by the CCP, then Wang Zhenmin was wrong in saying that referendum violated the Basic Law.

Echoing Wang's remarks, Tam Yiu-chung of the DAB said that referendum represented a Taiwan-style action that would be a blow to Hong Kong as well as time-consuming. ExCo member C. Y. Leung maintained that since the HKSAR is part of the PRC, the people of Hong Kong cannot arbitrarily put forward any referendum. The chairman of the pro-Beijing think tank, the Hong Kong Policy Research Institute, Yip Kwok-wah, compared using referendum to playing with fire because it would exert a "tremendous moral pressure" on both the HKSAR government and Beijing.[7]

The most important remark made by PRC officials on the question of referendum was actually made by Zhu Yucheng, the director of the PRC State Council's Hong Kong and Macao Research Center. Zhu said that some Hong Kong people raised the idea of referendum after Taiwan had stirred up the issue of using a referendum to decide its political future, and after the NPC Standing Committee had made a decision on Hong Kong's political system. He asked: "Is this action of some Hong Kong people challenging the central governments authority? You can judge it yourself."[8] Zhu's viewpoint represented Beijing's worry because the authority of the PRC's political center was challenged not only by Taiwan's separatist movement but also by the Hong Kong democrats. As with Zhu, the deputy secretary of the NPC, Qiao Xiaoyang, agreed that referendum actually challenged the central government because the NPC Standing Committee had already vetoed double direct elections in Hong Kong in 2007 and 2008.[9]

Interestingly, one democrat who preferred to be anonymous told the mass media that the idea of referendum actually did not represent the view of the "mainstream" democrats, but it was triggered by independent democrat Cheung Chiu-hung.[10] He admitted that referendum was related to the political development of Taiwan and that it did not necessarily gain public support. Hence, some democrats perhaps shared the view of Zhu but did not wish to openly oppose Cheung's idea of referendum for the sake of maintaining an image of unity among the pan-democrats.

On October 29, when legislator Leung Kwok-hung tried to use a private member's bill to raise the issue of referendum, the secretary for constitutional affairs, Stephen Lam, replied that private members' bills cannot really touch upon governmental operations and the political system.[11] He tried to use Article 74 of the Basic Law to force pan-democrats to accept the requirement that any private member's bill affecting the political system would have to acquire the written approval of the chief executive. The use of Article 74 by Stephen Lam showed the inbuilt executive-led nature of the Hong Kong polity. In response to Lam's argument, democratic legislator Margaret Ng contended that whether the issue of referendum touches upon the political system and governmental operation would be decided first by the LegCo president. Lam reiterated that any political reform proposal would need to cross three hurdles in the Basic Law: obtain the approval of two-thirds of the legislators, the consent of the chief executive, and Beijing's endorsement.[12] Clearly, Lam relied on the Basic Law's executive-led stipulations to warn the democrats of the implications of using referendum to shape Hong Kong's political system.

On November 1, 2004, Chief Executive Tung met the pan-democrats and discussed the issues of political reform and referendum. He told the mass media after the meeting that since the NPC Standing Committee made its decision on the 2007 and 2008 universal suffrage, the government would not conduct a referendum.[13] Nor did he approve of any organization using referendum. During the meeting, Tung reiterated his stance and an official maintained that any referendum would violate the Basic Law.[14] In response to Tung's position, the pan-democrats tried to project a united stance. Cheung Chiu-hung hoped that social groups would implement their referendum rather than allowing the 25 pan-democratic legislators to shoulder the burden. Ronny Tong said Tung merely put up his political show and citizens would decide themselves whether referendum would be impracticable. Emily Lau insisted that many Hong Kong people remained supportive of universal suffrage and referendum by expressing their views through protests. While Cheung appeared to step back on his initiative, Tong changed his earlier softer stance and Lau was wedded to the belief that public opinion was on the side of the pan-democrats.

The relatively liberal-minded patriotic elites also viewed the pan-democratic idea of using referendum as unrealistic. Allen Lee, the Hong Kong NPC member, criticized the democrats for "day dreaming and wasting their political capacity."[15] He said that the 2004 situation was different from the 2003 uproar against the government's attempt at legislating on Article 23 of the Basic Law. Lee argued that, as with Tung and many pro-establishment elites, the pan-democrats should accept the reality of the NPC Standing Committee's decision to veto double direct elections in both 2007 and 2008. He took the democrats to task and accused them of "preventing the earth from moving."[16] In fact, the proposal for holding a referendum divided the Hong Kong elites into two groups: the idealists, who still believed that public opinion could pressure Beijing as with the situation in mid-2003, and the realists, who tended to see confrontation with the central government as unnecessary and excessive.

On November 29, 2004, the LegCo voted against the motion initiated by Cheung Chiu-hung on referendum. The motion demanded that the government should use a referendum to decide the directions of political reform in 2007 and 2008; nevertheless, it was supported by only 20 legislators and rejected by 31 colleagues, with 3 legislators abstaining from voting.[17] Legislator Chim Pui-chung, who abstained from voting, appealed to the democrats to devote more time to discuss unjust and livelihood issues. Several democrats either abstained or were absent. Those who abstained included Mandy Tam Heung-man and Joseph Lee Kwok-lun, while the absentees were Lau Chin-shek, Albert Ho, and Kwok Ka-kay. Yang Wenchang, the commissioner of the Ministry of Foreign Affairs of the PRC government in Hong Kong, said prior to the legislative debate that the people of Hong Kong should calm down because referendum was "a very serious matter."[18] The mainland legal expert and former Basic Law Drafting Committee member Xiao Weiyun argued that the people of Hong Kong were merely "residents" and therefore they did not really enjoy the right to have "a citizen referendum."[19] To Xiao, the people of Hong Kong are only residents in the HKSAR under Chinese sovereignty, and they are by no means citizens.[20] Stephen Lam did not comment on Xiao's provocative argument but mentioned that because the Basic Law did not touch upon the issue of referendum, the HKSAR government did not want to add anything into the existing constitutional operation. On the other hand, the Civil Human Rights Front planned to hold a referendum at the grassroots level. Academics such as Robert Chung, Kenneth Chan, Chan Kin-man, and Wilson Wong participated in a project exploring the feasibility of holding a referendum in the HKSAR.[21] However, such referendum conducted by social groups without any government involvement meant that it would be politically futile.

The visions on sovereignty are very different between Beijing and the Hong Kong democrats. For Beijing, the people of Hong Kong simply do not have the right of self-determination through the use of any referendum because the HKSAR sovereignty belongs to the PRC. For the idealistic democrats, the people of Hong Kong possess their own sovereignty and can use referendum to shape their political development. Sandwiched between Beijing and the democrats, the HKSAR government must side with the central authorities. As the Central Policy Unit director Lau Siu-kai asserted, those people who advocated the use of referendum actually brought about "troubles and chaos" to the motherland.[22]

THE POLITICAL REFORM PROPOSALS IN 2005

On October 19, 2005, the Hong Kong government released its political reform plan on the methods of electing the chief executive in 2007 and the LegCo in 2008. The plan was endorsed by the PRC President Hu Jintao.[23] According to the political blueprint, in 2007, the Election Committee that would select the chief executive would be increased from 800 to 1,600 members of which 300 would come from commercial and monetary sectors, 300 from the industrial sector, 300 from labor, social services, and religious sectors, and 700 from the political circle.[24] The chief executive candidates would need to secure at least 200 nominations. If there were only one candidate, an election would still be held. Finally, the chief executive would not be allowed to have political party background. With regard to the formation of the LegCo in 2008, its members would be increased from 60 to 70, half of which would come from geographical constituencies, and half from functional constituencies. The five new functional constituency seats would be elected from some 500 members of the 18 District Councils (DC). Moreover, the existing stipulation that allowed for 12 legislators to be permanent Hong Kong residents holding foreign citizenship would remain unchanged. The procedures for the political reform plan would go through three stages: the approval of LegCo, the chief executive, and Beijing within 12 months; the amendment of the bill on the chief executive election by January 2006; and then the completion of revising the LegCo Ordinance by 2007.

At the same time, the Strategic Development Commission (SDC) established by Chief Executive Tsang to study political reform issues explored the feasibility and acceptability of the two houses model for Hong Kong —a lower house directly elected by citizens and an upper house parallel to the British House of Lords.[25] The Business and Professionals Federation of Hong Kong supported the idea of using a bicameral system for the HKSAR. It proposed that all directly elected legislators would constitute the lower chamber, while the upper chamber would comprise those representatives elected from functional constituencies. Bills approved by the lower chamber would be considered by the upper chamber. The HKSAR government in October 2005 attempted to project an image of adopting a progressive approach to handling political reform, exploring various options for Hong Kong.

According to the government's survey conducted by the Polytechnic University, about 55 percent of the respondents supported its political reform proposals. When asked whether they agreed that the LegCo should increase the number of seats to 70, 79 percent of 1,225 respondents said they agreed, 13 percent disagreed, and 8 percent gave other answers.[26] When asked whether they agreed that the new functional constituency seats would come from DC, 49 percent agreed with the idea, 33 percent disagreed, and 18 percent gave other answers. When asked further whether they agreed with the idea that the new functional constituency seats would be returned from the election among all DC members, 60 percent agreed, 30 percent disagreed, and 10 percent gave other answers. When asked whether they accepted changes in the method for the selection of both the chief executive and the LegCo even though Hong Kong would not have double direct elections in 2007 and 2008, 75 percent agreed with the idea, 11 percent disagreed, and 14 percent gave other answers. Finally, when asked whether they supported the overall government reform proposal, 55 percent said they supported, 22 percent did not support, and 23 percent gave other answers. Critics said that the phrasing of some of the questions in the survey was misleading and that the respondents were not given sufficient reform options.[27]

According to Annex I and Annex II of the Basic Law, any political reform plan has to acquire the two-thirds support of the legislators, and therefore the government in 2005 required at least 40 votes in the 60-member legislature to have its proposals passed. Immediately after the revelation of the political reform plan, 25 pan-democratic legislators opposed it while 28 pro-establishment elites expressed their support.[28] The chief secretary for administration Rafael Hui Si-yan appealed to all parties for support because "the government's proposals were by no means an empty slogan."[29] It was reported that the HKSAR government would lobby for support from seven pan-democratic legislators, including Mandy Tam, Kwok Kar-kay, Joseph Lee, Frederick Fung, Albert Cheng, Chan Wai-yip, and Lau Chin-shek.

The American Consul General in Hong Kong, James Cunningham, said that the political reform proposals could be more progressive. The British Consul General in the HKSAR, Stephen Bradley, stated that although the reform plan could not satisfy those who wished to have double direct elections in 2007 and 2008, it was moving in the right direction.[30] Clearly, the American position tended to be more enthusiastic toward

Hong Kong's democratic reform than the very moderate position of the British government.

The pan-democratic camp criticized the reform plan on several fronts. Martin Lee said that it failed to achieve democracy in the HKSAR. Democratic Party (DP) Chairman Lee Wing-tat asserted that the government failed to satisfy the four major demands of his party, namely, a clear timetable and road map for universal suffrage, the abolition of the appointed system, the need to transform the corporate votes in LegCo elections to individual votes, and the necessity of expanding the electoral base of the Election Committee selecting the chief executive.[31] Other democrats such as Audrey Eu and Lee Cheuk-yan criticized the plan for DC as maintaining "a small circle election."[32] While the government would have to submit the whole plan to the LegCo for a vote in December, the pan-democrats were determined to oppose it.

In reality, the plan for DC members who would be able to vote for the chief executive was actually beneficial to the DP and the pro-Beijing DAB. In 2005, the DP grasped 87 seats in all the 529 District Council positions; the DAB captured 83 seats; the pro-business Liberal Party (LP) got 26 seats; the Association for Democracy and People's Livelihood (ADPL) received 23 seats; and the Frontier led by Emily Lau got 12 seats.[33] Although the electoral method of electing DC members to the legislature was unclear in the government reform plan, the DP and the DAB as the two largest parties would stand a better chance than other parties to elect their legislators. Still, the hard-line stance of the pan-democratic camp meant that the government's moderate reform proposal would very likely be rejected.

In a bid to drum up political support, Chief Executive Tsang made use of his visit to the United States in late October 2005 to promote his reform blueprint. He admitted that the U.S. Secretary of State Condoleezza Rice hoped to envisage a faster progress of democratic reform in the HKSAR. He met Congressmen Henry Hyde, Tom Lantos, and James Leach.[34] Tsang told the public that the democrats had no grounds to reject his reform plan because of three main factors.[35] First, his package was progressive as the number of both LegCo members and the members of the Election Committee selecting the chief executive would increase. Moreover, DC members would be able to elect their representatives to the legislature. Second, public opinion supported his reform package. Third, rejecting his reform plan would mean a stagnant progress in democratization, affecting the morale of all sides, and postponing the reform agenda to 2012.[36] While Tsang was accurate in all three points, he shunned the demands of democrats for a clear timetable for the universal suffrage of both the chief executive and LegCo. Hence, his reform concessions could not bridge the expectation gap between democrats and the government.

On November 3, 2005, a group of academics from the Chinese University of Hong Kong released their survey results that showed almost 60 percent of the respondents supported the government's reform package, thus unintentionally exerting invisible pressure on the democrats who tried to reject the reform plan. When asked whether they accepted Tsang's reform package, 58.8 percent of the 1,006 respondents supported it, 23.6 percent rejected it, 9.7 percent partly accepted but partly rejected it, 3.4 had no opinion, and 4.4 percent did not know.[37] One of the academics who conducted the survey, Chan Kin-man, warned that "we cannot underestimate the number of participants in the parade in December. The government should not dream that its reform plan would be passed by the legislature without amending a word."[38] The survey also found that 65 percent of the respondents hoped there would be a clear timetable for Hong Kong to have universal suffrage. In response to this demand, DP chairman Lee Wig-tat requested that the HKSAR government delay the LegCo's discussion of the reform plan until February 2006.[39] Unfortunately, neither the LP nor the DAB supported this position. James Tien of the LP said that even if the central government laid out a timetable, it would be very safe and the Hong Kong people would be disappointed. Tam Yiu-chung of the DAB believed that the question of timetable should be discussed in the SDC and that Hong Kong could not decide it unilaterally. At this moment, unless the Tsang administration postponed the vote on political reform, its reform plan would likely be rejected in the legislature.

On the timing of universal suffrage, the survey showed that public opinion was divided. When asked which year they would favor double direct elections, 34.8 percent chose 2012, 34.2 said 2007 and 2008, 18.1 percent pointed to the years beyond 2012, 6.9 percent said it was difficult to say, and 6.1 replied that there should not be any concrete timetable.[40] Clearly, the opinions of citizens remained diverse and there appeared to be no mainstream public view in November 2005.

In November 2005, a window of opportunity was opened for political bargaining between democrats and Beijing, and between democrats and the HKSAR government. Lee Wing-tat of the DP openly said that he would be willing to visit Beijing to reach a compromise on political reform, and that the democrats would be satisfied if there was a sincerity to implement universal suffrage.[41] He said that PRC officials did contact pro-democracy legislators Ronny Tong and Emily Lau; nevertheless, Beijing's policy of selectively consulting with some democrats and excluding others meant that Lee's proposal was not seriously heard by the central government.

Interestingly, Ronny Tong appeared to soften his tone by advocating the idea that he would meet Chief Executive Tsang after his visit to Europe.[42] Tong also said that he would very likely oppose the reform plan if there was no timetable of abolishing the appointed seats in DC.[43]

He maintained that in order to achieve substantial progress in democracy, both the democrats and the government should sit down to discuss mutual concessions. Tong appealed to the democrats to first put aside the demand for having a timetable for universal suffrage because Beijing had the final say on the timetable.[44] Tong's surprisingly softer stance was resisted by other democrats. Cheung Man-kwong of the DP said that the timetable issue could not be abandoned. Even Frederick Fung of the ADPL believed that the government should take the initiative to discuss political reform with the democrats rather than the democrats seeking the administration to discuss a model for concessions.[45] While Tong appeared to be the soft-liner within the democratic camp, others tended to stick to the tenet of pushing Beijing and the HKSAR government for a timetable of universal suffrage.

The democrats adopted the strategy of visiting overseas countries to solicit international support. Martin Lee, Ronny Tong, Margaret Ng, Sin Chung-kai, and Kwok Kar-kay went to visit Europe and the United States. They met European Union officials, such as Eneko Landaburu and Joao Vale De Almeida, and American Secretary of State Condoleezza Rice.[46] Although the European Union and the United States supported Hong Kong's democratization, the efforts of the democrats to internationalize the issue of political reform were seen as politically unacceptable to Beijing, which adopts a vigilant attitude toward any foreign intervention in the PRC's "domestic" affairs.[47] The visit by the democrats to the United States followed Chief Executive Tsang's visit to the U.S. Congress in late October—a tug-of-war between the two sides over the battle of democratization.

MASS MOBILIZATION AGAINST THE POLITICAL REFORM BLUEPRINT IN DECEMBER 2005

Two days before the democrats mobilized their supporters to take to the streets to support the double direct elections, the deputy secretary of the NPC Standing Committee, Qiao Xiaoyang, went to Shenzhen to listen to the views of the Hong Kong people on political reform. The choice of Shenzhen was political, symbolizing the fact that political reform in the HKSAR would have to be approved by the central government, which possesses the sovereignty over Hong Kong. Of the 25 Hong Kong people who expressed their opinions in the meeting with Qiao, only 6 of them were the democrats.[48] Qiao appealed to the Hong Kong people for support of the HKSAR government's political reform plan. He urged the Hong Kong democrats to abandon the principle of linking the reform plan with a timetable for universal suffrage. Finally, Qiao was worried that, if the Hong Kong people continued to dispute over political reform, which to him should proceed orderly, social harmony would be affected.

Emily Lau, who spoke out in the meeting, maintained that Beijing did not allow Hong Kong to have universal suffrage, while other democrats demanded a clear timetable and road map for democratization. The bone of contention was the timetable of double direct elections in which Beijing refused to make concessions while the democrats insisted on finalizing a clear blueprint.

On December 4, 2005, the pan-democrats mobilized hundreds of thousands of supporters to demand that the HKSAR government implement double direct elections as soon as possible. One day before the parade, Cardinal Joseph Zen appealed to the Hong Kong people to take to the streets to support democratization—a move parallel to his appeal to the citizens to protest against the Tung administration on July 1, 2003.[49] The Civil Human Rights Front claimed that 250,000 citizens participated in the December 2005 parade, but the police gave an estimate of only 63,000.[50] Academic Paul Yip estimated 72,400 participated in the parade, whereas *Ming Pao* and a satellite photo expert gave the figure of 92,000.[51] Martin Lee visited the United States and returned to Hong Kong, saying that he would consider resigning from LegCo or launching a hunger strike if the Tsang reform blueprint were passed in the legislature.[52] He felt that while the United States and Europe expressed their interest in Hong Kong's democratization, the British government was more indifferent. In fact, the American government said that while the pace of democratization should be decided by the Hong Kong people, it hoped that Beijing would put forward a timetable for universal suffrage.[53] Lee also criticized Chief Executive Donald Tsang's and Qiao Xiaoyang's appeal that political reform should be separated from the timetable of universal suffrage in the HKSAR. In the mind of Martin Lee, chief executive Donald Tsang tried a political gamble by pushing the political reform plan through the Legislative Council. In short, Tsang would like to see whether his reform plan would be approved by the legislature.

A poll of 560 protestors on December 4 showed that 57 percent of them demanded that the Tsang regime should put forward a concrete timetable for Hong Kong's universal suffrage to select the chief executive and the entire legislature.[54] Twenty percent of them were against the Tsang reform plan, and 19 percent wanted the government to accelerate the pace of democratization. When asked whether they were satisfied with Donald Tsang's handling of the political reform issue, 61 percent said they were dissatisfied; 28 percent was very dissatisfied; 7 percent had no opinion; and only 5 percent was satisfied. The protestors did give a mandate to the pan-democratic legislators to reject the Tsang reform blueprint.

In response to the massive number of protestors, the PRC government was indifferent. A former Basic Law Committee member, Xu Chongde, openly said that "truth" did not stem from a large number of people participating in a parade, and that the people of Hong Kong should be "more rational."[55] He even compared Hong Kong's universal suffrage to a marriage in which the couple decides when they should get married. Premier Wen Jiabao was on a visit to France during the Hong Kong debate over democratization. He appealed to the people of Hong Kong to promote democratic development in line with the Basic Law and the resolutions of the NPC Standing Committee.[56] Wen admitted that he had not caught up with Hong Kong's development but reiterated the need for Hong Kong to approach democratic reforms in an orderly and a gradual manner. It appeared that the power holders on the PRC policy toward the HKSAR in December 2005 remained firmly in the hands of the elites in the NPC Standing Committee and the HKMAO, such as Qiao Xiaoyang and Liao Hui.

Former senior civil servants such as Anson Chan and Lily Yam joined the pan-democratic camp's call for a faster pace of democratization in the HKSAR. Chan said that she would participate in the protest on December 4 in her own capacity. She agreed with Chief Executive Tsang's view that the people of Hong Kong were at political crossroads, but Chan hoped that she would be able to witness Hong Kong's realization of democracy in her lifetime.[57] Hence, she decided to join the protest for democracy and universal suffrage. Another former secretary for environment and food security, Lily Yam, firmly believed that the people of Hong Kong were mature enough to directly elect their chief executive. She criticized the Tsang administration for failing to put forward a timetable for universal suffrage and for handling political reform in a perfunctory manner.[58]

Anson Chan's decision to join the December 2005 parade in support of democratic reform was widely seen as her ambition to participate in Hong Kong politics in the future. One day after she partook in the protest, Chan went to the United Kingdom, and it was speculated that she might consult some of her friends, like Chris Patten and Lydia Dunn, on whether and how she should participate in Hong Kong politics.[59] The PRC officials have never trusted Chan, thinking that she was groomed by the British administration in Hong Kong, that she should have cooperated with the former Chief Executive Tung, and that she was "utilized" by foreigners to influence Hong Kong politics.[60] This PRC perspective was shared by many pro-Beijing elites in Hong Kong as they tended to adopt "a conspiracy theory" to view Chan and her motivation.[61] They were worried that Chan would compete in the chief executive election. Interestingly, Albert Cheng King-hon, a member of the democratic camp, also believed that Chan's move was backed up by "some people" as she used a "special channel" to participate in the parade on December 4.[62]

The rumors about Chan's intention of running for the chief executive election existed in the political circle for some time. When the nomination period for the first HKSAR chief executive election was held in

December 1996, Chan, as the most senior civil servant, asked her subordinates whether she would have a chance of winning the election if she participated.[63] Later, after Chief Executive Tung wished to change the governor's residence into a museum, she told an official that "why is there a need to change its purpose? Who knows whether the second Chief Executive would live there?"[64] In late 2000, the anti-Tung sentiment in the HKSAR became more prominent than ever before due to his controversial reform policies. At that time, rumors were rife that Chan had the ambition to become the future chief executive. In September 2000, the former vice premier of the PRC government, Qian Qichen, invited Chan to Beijing, where Qian and HKMAO director Liao Hui criticized her in a closed-door meeting for not supporting Tung.[65] After Chan returned to the HKSAR, she decided to resign from her position as the chief secretary for administration.

Anson Chan remains a baffling problem to PRC officials responsible for Hong Kong affairs. On the one hand, they see Chan as an ambitious democrat who is "utilized" by foreigners and foreign countries. On the other hand, they find it difficult to co-opt her. Chan also distrusts PRC authorities, whose criticisms of her relations with Tung in September 2000 sowed the seeds of mutual antagonism. Viewed by the Hong Kong media as "the conscience" for Hong Kong, Anson Chan sees herself as doing nothing wrong during her service in the HKSAR government under Tung's leadership. Chan understood that the cronies and political loyalists surrounding Tung made her look disloyal and "troublesome" in the eyes of Beijing. Although the Anson Chan core group that discusses political reform alternatives includes Allen Lee, the Hong Kong NPC member and a middleman between her and Beijing, the damaged relationship between Chan and Beijing cannot easily be repaired.

After the December 4 parade, Chief Executive Tsang agreed to amend his political reform proposals while admitting that the people of Hong Kong remained "patriotic."[66] However, he insisted that the political reform proposals should be separated from the timetable for universal suffrage. His position avoided violating Beijing's bottom line of tolerance, which was to shun the timetable for Hong Kong to have universal suffrage to select the chief executive and the entire legislature. To Beijing, democratizing Hong Kong fully would run the risk of making the HKSAR system akin to Taiwan's Western-style polity in which an independent chief executive like the former Taiwan President Chen Shui-bian would have the possibility of being directly elected. Failing to trust the people of Hong Kong, who in Beijing's view may vote for a leader defiant of its interests and wishes, the central government must adopt a delaying tactic in handling the issue of double direct elections in the HKSAR.

In response to the public protest on December 4, the HKSAR government considered the possibility of abolishing the appointed seats in DC. However, the business sector and pro-Beijing forces argued that the government should not make concessions to the democrats.[67] They insisted that even if the government made concessions, the pan-democrats would still reject the political reform plan on the grounds that a timetable for universal suffrage was nonexistent. The government became a political sandwich between the democrats on the one hand and the conservative-minded business and pro-Beijing forces on the other.

Shortly after the July 1, 2005, protest, Beijing appeared to float some ideas on political reform to the democrats through third parties in order to test whether they would accept its top-down proposals. Ronny Tong of the CP revealed in early December 2005 that after the July 1 parade, he felt that Beijing's attitude was actually more relaxed than the HKSAR government on political reform. Tong disclosed that in November he sent a letter to Beijing and suggested that the central government should promise to allow Hong Kong to have universal suffrage in 2012.[68] Then Tong received a message from Beijing, suggesting that the central government would only promise Hong Kong to have universal suffrage in the future. Indeed, Beijing appeared to test the reactions of the democrats such as Tong rather than really sitting down with them to have a negotiated outcome. Two days later, Tong received another message from his Beijing contact that the central government would promise to allow the HKSAR to have universal suffrage in 2017, but he replied that it would be too long because Donald Tsang and some mainland Chinese leaders would step down by that time. However, the Liaison Office on December 8, 2005, quickly rejected the rumor that Beijing would allow the HKSAR to have universal suffrage in 2017.[69] It said that the central government did not make any decision on a timetable for Hong Kong's democratization.

Beijing was apprehensive of any American intervention in Hong Kong's political reform. When the U.S. Congress issued a report in 2004 to criticize the PRC handling of Hong Kong matters, such as the NPC Standing Committee's decision to veto double direct elections in 2007 and 2008, and the mysterious political intimidation of a few Hong Kong democrats, the PRC Foreign Ministry immediately accused the American government of meddling in its domestic affairs.[70] Shortly after the Hong Kong people's protest for democratization on December 4, 2005, the U.S. government urged that Beijing should quickly delineate a timetable for Hong Kong's political reform. Two days later, the PRC Foreign Ministry asserted that "the United States arbitrarily commented on the HKSAR affairs and this was inappropriate. The HKSAR affairs belong to China's domestic matter and we cannot allow any other country's intervention."[71]

On December 19, the HKSAR government decided to make concessions by proposing a gradual decrease in the number of appointed

DC members. In 2008, the number of appointees in DC would be reduced by one-third. Another two-thirds would be curbed in 2011 and 2015. This government's concession would be implemented on the condition that its reform plan would be passed by the LegCo. The pan-democrats were uninterested in the minimal concessions and remained hard-line in their position. At the same time, the Tsang administration could not make bolder concessions due to the opposition from the LP and the DAB, which both felt that the reform plan would excessively benefit the democrats.[72]

On December 22, Tsang's reform proposals were rejected by 24 pan-democratic legislators, were supported by 34 pro-establishment colleagues, and failed to get the approval of a minimum of 40 votes from the 60-member LegCo. Democrat Lau Chin-shek abstained, whereas President Rita Fan did not vote.[73] One day before the vote, Chief Executive Tsang made a last-minute effort to acquire the support of democrats Mandy Tam, Frederick Fung, and Lee Cheuk-yan, apart from Joseph Lee and Albert Cheng King-hon who were also targets of government lobbying.[74] According to Mandy Tam, a democratic "professional" was lobbied hard by the government, which originally did not target for lobbying six independent democrats (Tam, Kwok Kar-kay, Joseph Lee, Chan Wai-yip, Albert Cheng, and Lau Chin-shek).[75] The Chinese press speculated that the "professional" was referred to Ronny Tong, who told the government that he would try to get more votes for the Tsang reform package.[76] But after the professional was severely criticized by democratic colleagues and changed political posture, according to Tam, the HKSAR government started to lobby the democrats hard one week before the vote.[77] However, the lobbying effort was too little and too late.

Chief Executive Tsang was disappointed with the reaction from the democrats, treating the LegCo vote as an immediate setback shortly after he succeeded Chief Executive Tung, who submitted his resignation to Beijing on March 10, 2005. Tsang remarked:

We did not fail, but we did not succeed. It was still a glorious defeat. Hong Kong people are tired of discussions on constitutional development. It is not even among the top 10 issues of public concern. I'll focus more on economic issues. I had a dream to sped up and make substantial changes to the mutual trust between the pro-democracy camp and Beijing. Maybe I was too rushed, maybe a few months in the political agenda is too short. I had thought the political environment had changed slightly, but that was just a wish on my part.[78]

Several factors account for the failure of Tsang's reform plan. His concessions could not satisfy the demands of the pan-democrats and they were too little, too late. Tsang also refused to postpone the vote in the LegCo—a miscalculation on his part because he regarded the vote as a political gamble. If Tsang adopted Lee Wing-tat's suggestion that the vote be delayed to February 2006, more time could be used for bargaining with the democrats. Even worse, Rafael Hui did not appear to lobby the democrats effectively; he said in the Wanchai District Council in November 2005 that universal suffrage would scare the middle class away from Hong Kong because the pro-democracy welfarists would come to power under a full-fledged democratic system.[79] Tsang's rigidity and Hui's unskillful promotion of the reform blueprint almost guaranteed that it would likely be rejected by the democratic legislators.

The LP and the DAB refused to accept drastic concessions from the HKSAR government on the abolition of appointed DC members because they had the vested interests, especially the LP, which was still in the learning and embryonic stage of electoral participation. One month before the LegCo vote, Selina Chow expressed the LP's dissatisfaction with the democrats. She remarked that the pan-democratic camp was "dishonest" and "tried to look for stepping stone to save face" after realizing that it would be impossible to achieve double direct elections in 2007 and 2008.[80] Chow accused the democrats of sticking "dishonestly" to the "moral high ground" of having "a rose garden filled with universal suffrage." [81] To the LP, the pan-democrats kept on retaining their maximal demands under the circumstances that it would be virtually impossible to achieve such demands.

For Beijing, democratization in the HKSAR could not lead the territory to become another Taiwan. Chief Executive Tsang told American reporter Fred Hiatt that the "foremost fear" of PRC leaders was that the HKSAR would seek independence and become "another Taiwan." [82] Tsang's remarks could be traced back to Zhu Yucheng's reaction in October 2004 to the issue of referendum raised by Hong Kong legislator Cheung Chiu-hung and other democrats. As mentioned before, Zhu questioned whether the Hong Kong democrats challenged Beijing's authority as with the Taiwan independence movement. Beijing's mentality in 2004 and 2005 was to guard against the possibility that Hong Kong's democratization would bring about separatist tendencies.

The HKMAO under Liao Hui gave Chief Executive Tsang sufficient autonomy to make concessions and compromise with the pan-democrats, but it failed to exert sufficient pressure on the Tsang regime so that a political breakthrough could have been achieved. The PRC officials let the HKSAR government deal with the revised reform proposals without really understanding the bottom line of the democrats. If the HKMAO and the Liaison Office acted more effectively as crucial players, they could have provided more inputs into the Tsang regime on the content of the revised reform proposals. Instead, both agencies appeared to give "a high degree of autonomy" to Chief Executive Tsang, whose timetable of getting his reform plan passed by LegCo was tight and rigid. If political bargaining constitutes an indispensable element in politics, such bargaining between the Tsang administration and the democrats was definitely insufficient. After the July 1, 2003, protest in the HKSAR, Beijing's agencies responsible for Hong Kong affairs, especially the Liaison Office, moderated their stance by listening more widely to the people of Hong Kong, but they failed to accurately tap the opinions of the pan-democrats. In short, while the failure of the reform proposal was largely attributable to the insufficient bargaining, Beijing lacked decisive intervention that could have been conducive to an easier tacit agreement between the Tsang regime and the democrats. Indeed, the legacy of the June 4 tragedy in 1989 was haunting the relations between Beijing and the Hong Kong democrats. Beijing in 2005 still saw some Hong Kong democrats as "subversive" elements trying to topple the CCP in 1989. This led to the persistent lack of dialogue and legacy of mutual distrust. As a result, the 2005 reform plan was mainly decentralized to the HKSAR government, especially the minimal bargaining between Tsang and pan-democrats, even though the central government did approve the reform package.

In the final analysis, the pan-democrats themselves shouldered the political baggage of their success in delaying the legislation on Article 23 of the Basic Law in July 2003. None of the democratic legislators was willing to be the "traitor" deviating from the pan-democratic line, except for Lau Chin-shek whose political stance and activities changed prominently after the PRC attempts at co-opting him intensified. Although chief secretary Rafael Hui criticized Martin Lee and Bishop (now Cardinal) Joseph Zen for being the "black hands" behind the democratic camp's rejection of the reform package, Zen replied that Hui should "take it easy" because he just adhered to his principles.[83] Zen said he was not a lawmaker, but he praised the legislators for acting "responsibly" by voting down the reform plan. Zen appealed to Chief Executive Tsang to follow Anson Chan's suggestion that there should be double direct elections in 2012. In fact, as early as November 2005, Bishop Zen and the Reverend Chu Yiu-ming met the core leaders of the pan-democrats and appealed to them to oppose Tsang's reform plan.[84] Zen was quoted by Margaret Ng as saying that "We have to go up to the mountain top. If the path of going there is blocked, we can go up slowly and patiently. But we cannot take the path that can never lead us to the top."[85] Meeting the democrats, Chu asserted that the pan-democratic front should stick to the principle of having a timetable of universal suffrage.

After meeting Zen and Chu, Audrey Eu appeared to adopt a hard-line attitude, saying that the Tsang reform plan was like a "distorted path" ignoring a timetable and cheating the democrats like "three year old children."[86] On November 7 Bishop Zen appealed to the Catholics to join the protest on December 4 "to continue the miracle in the debate over Article 23," to call for the NPC Standing Committee to reverse its veto on Hong Kong's universal suffrage in 2007 and 2008, and to push Beijing to set up a timetable for Hong Kong's universal suffrage.[87] Bishop Zen, Martin Lee, and even Chu might be significant behind the scene. All the pro-democracy legislators, except for Lau Chin-shek, had a nostalgic feeling on their solidarity in successfully opposing the national security legislation in 2003. Hence, the rejection of the 2005 political reform plan could be seen as a legacy resulting from a multiplicity of factors, including Tsang's hurried nature of getting his package passed by LegCo, the deep mutual distrust between Beijing and pan-democrats, the failure of PRC officials to give sufficient input into the content of Tsang's concessions, and the political baggage of the pan-democrats after their success in postponing the legislation on Article 23 of the Basic Law.

Objectively speaking, the pan-democrats scored a Pyrrhic victory. Prior to the LegCo vote, a survey conducted by the Chinese University of Hong Kong's public policy study center showed that actually 49.9 percent of the 924 respondents supported the government's reform plan, while 28.9 percent opposed it.[88] If this result was accurate, the veto of the pan-democrats against the reform plan ran against the wishes of many Hong Kong people. Moreover, when asked whether they agreed that the reform plan should be rejected if there was no timetable for universal suffrage, 39 percent disagreed, 17.3 strongly disagreed, 26.4 percent agreed, 8.6 percent strongly agreed, and 8.7 found it difficult to say.[89] Clearly, many Hong Kong people are politically moderates and hoped that the pan-democrats in 2005 would accept the moderate reform proposals. When asked who would have to shoulder the responsibility of rejecting the reform plan, 28.7 percent said the democratic camp, 23.4 percent pointed to the HKSAR government, 20.4 percent thought that the central government in Beijing would have to be responsible, and 15.5 percent gave other answers. Hence, the rejection of the reform plan resulted in the public perception that the three main parties—the democrats, the government, and Beijing—were all responsible, but the democrats appeared to fail to win the hearts and minds of many moderate Hong Kong people.

After the rejection of the Tsang reform plan, Li Wah-ming of the DP publicly expressed his regret, saying that both the democratic camp and the PRC lacked trust.[90] He speculated that the relationships between democrats and Beijing would surely be undermined, and that he might not be able to meet President Hu Jintao in his lifetime. Li added that the Article 45 Concern Group, which was the target of the PRC's co-optation, actually "lost a lot of marks in the eyes of the central government."[91] Li's regret was not shared by some democrats. Immediately after the LegCo vote, an advertisement on the *South China Morning Post* praised the action of the democrats as "a victory of the people, a victory for democracy" and it appealed to the readers to send Short Message Service (SMS) messages to the government in support of the demand that the chief executive should request Beijing prepare a timetable for universal suffrage.[92] The advertisement campaign was launched by barrister Wong Hin-lee, who was close to Martin Lee and who could garner the signatures from not only the 24 legislators rejecting the reform plan but also other core supporters of the pan-democrats, such as Anson Chan, the Reverend Chu Yiu-ming, barrister Denis Chang Khen-lee, Bishop Zen, Louis Ha, and businessman Jimmy Lai.[93] Even the Hong Kong NPC member Allen Lee had his name on the advertisement, although some democrats such as Lau Chin-shek, Albert Cheng, Yeung Sum, and Li Wah-ming revealed that they were not aware of their names on the advertisement.[94]

The pro-Beijing press, *Wen Wei Po*, has labeled the pan-democrats as the "opposition faction" since December 2005. After the rejection of Tsang's reform plan, the chief executive went to Beijing to report on Hong Kong's development. Premier Wen Jiabao told Tsang that the "deep-rooted contradictions and problems" persisted in the HKSAR.[95] While Beijing saw the pan-democrats as anti-PRC, the latter refused to soften its resistant attitude toward Tsang's reform package.

THE STRUGGLE FOR DEMOCRATIZATION SINCE DECEMBER 2005

The relationships between the democrats and the HKSAR government turned sour immediately after the rejection of Tsang's reform plan. The chief secretary Rafael Hui referred to the democrats as an "opposition faction."[96] Tsang openly demonstrated his policy of "distinguishing the relatives from those who are not" by visiting the DAB headquarters and attending the party's Central Standing Committee meeting. Hui went to Dongguan to attend the DAB camp on its directions and future development. All these moves illustrated a political standoff between the government and the pan-democrats.

In April 2006, the former Basic Law Committee member Wang Zhenmin remarked that Article 23 of the Basic Law should be enacted before the HKSAR would have the direct elections of the chief executive and the entire legislature through universal suffrage.[97] His comment triggered widespread criticisms in the HKSAR. Later, PRC officials persuaded him not to visit the HKSAR in June for fear that his comments and answers on any Article 23-related questions would trigger public protests before the July 1 protest in 2006. Clearly, PRC authorities learned to be more sensitive toward the Hong Kong people's questions on universal suffrage.

In September 2006, the pan-democrats began a fund-raising campaign to initiate "a public referendum," but the organizers needed to look for places for voting stations.[98] The number of voting booths was discussed among the organizers, but it was not known how many voting stations would enhance the credibility of the "referendum," which would not be legally binding at all. Objectively speaking, such referendum did not have any political impact but at most carried the educative function of allowing more people to be aware of the issue and prospects of double direct elections in the HKSAR.

In December 2007 the pan-democrats mobilized the public and coordinated with some overseas Chinese to support democratic reform in the HKSAR. An advertisement on *Apple Daily* in December 2007 included a variety of overseas Chinese groups supportive of democracy in Hong Kong.[99] They included the Alliance of Hong Kong Chinese in the United States (New York), the Tiananmen Memorial Foundation (New York), the Federation of Overseas Hong Kong Chinese (Washington), the Association of Overseas Hong Kong Chinese for Democracy and Human Rights in Boston, the Long March for Democracy Fund in Boston, the Boston Macao Chinese Club, the Foundation for Chinese Democracy in San Francisco, the Vancouver Society in Support of Democratic Movement, the Toronto Association for Democracy in China, the Canada–Hong Kong Link in Toronto, the Movement for Democracy in China (Calgary), and the Democracy China in Ottawa. All these groups not only appealed to the Hong Kong people to vote for the LegCo by-election candidate, Anson Chan, but they also said that the HKSAR had the danger of becoming "mainlandized" due to the government's prosecution of Szeto Wah for attending the People's Radio program. Organizers of the People's Radio, such as democrats Tsang Kin-shing and Leung Kwok-hung, were regarded as using illicit airwaves for broadcasting their program without any formal government approval. The surge of the overseas Hong Kong Chinese and mainland Chinese groups in support of Szeto Wah, Anson Chan, and universal suffrage aimed at providing the impetus for Hong Kong people to back up the momentum of democratization.

DECISION OF THE NPC STANDING COMMITTEE AND REACTIONS FROM DEMOCRATS

On December 12, 2007, Chief Executive Tsang submitted a report to Beijing, seeking the decision of the NPC Standing Committee on the methods of electing the chief executive and the LegCo in 2012.[100] The report said that over half of the surveyed citizens supported double direct elections in 2012, but this finding was only for Beijing's reference.[101] On December 29, 2007, the NPC Standing Committee announced its decision on Hong Kong's political reform. First, with regard to the chief executive election, its method can be amended in 2012 but the possibility of direct election through universal suffrage is ruled out.[102] Second, in 2017, the chief executive election can implement the method of direct election through universal suffrage. Third, such universal suffrage would need a broadly representative Election

Committee, whose composition can follow the current chief executive election and which will retain the nomination procedures to select chief executive candidates. Fourth, with regard to LegCo election, its method can be amended in 2012 but direct election of the whole legislature through universal suffrage is ruled out. Fifth, in 2012, the current proportion—50 percent returned from functional constituencies and 50 percent from direct elections in geographical constituencies—will be maintained, while the procedures of bills and motions will also be unchanged. Sixth, after the chief executive is directly elected by universal suffrage, the LegCo election method will be able to implement direct elections through universal suffrage.

The NPC Standing Committee's decision opened the door to the likelihood of electing the chief executive by universal suffrage in 2017. To the HKSAR government, the earliest possible year of envisaging the chief executive directly elected by universal suffrage would be 2017 and that of having the whole LegCo directly elected by universal suffrage would be 2020. Five hours immediately after the NPC Standing Committee's decision of vetoing the double direct elections of the chief executive and the whole legislature in 2012, the pan-democrats mobilized 800 supporters to protest against the decision. Martin Lee continued the hunger strike launched by the DP until January 13, 2009. He expressed his frustrations after listening to the seminar hosted by the deputy secretary of the NPC Standing Committee, Qiao Xiaoyang. Lee said he no longer trusted the central government in Beijing.

In January 2008, pro-democracy legislator Chan Wai-yip put forward a motion criticizing the government for deviating from public opinion and urging it to implement the direct elections of both the chief executive and the entire legislature no later than 2012.[103] During the motion debate, LP chairman James Tien appealed to the democrats to establish a trustful relationship with Beijing.[104] The question of trust is very important, but some democrats such as Martin Lee have maintained that they do open the door to have dialogue with Beijing, which, however, distrusts them. The crux of the problem is the Tiananmen legacy in which Beijing and the Liaison Office officials are concerned that any direct dialogue with the democrats would be tantamount to a formal recognition of the pan-democratic camp—a move that would also hurt the image of the DAB as the most influential middleman between the Hong Kong people and Beijing.[105]

Five other democrats amended Chan Wai-yip's motion, including Yeung Sum of the DP, Lee Cheuk-yan of the Confederation of Trade Unions, Alan Leong and Ronny Tong of the CP, and Leung Kwok-hung of the League of Social Democrats. But all the motions and amended ones were defeated by pro-government legislators. In response to three amended motions, Anson Chan and Frederick Fung of the ADPL abstained from voting.[106] Anson Chan said that while she opposed the interpretation of the NPC Standing Committee on Hong Kong's pace of democratic reform, any attempt by the government to revive the 2005 political reform blueprint would be unacceptable.

In response to the demand of the democrats that LegCo's functional constituencies should be abolished in the future, Jasper Tsang of the DAB interpreted the PRC stance as being open-minded. He believed that the central government would allow the chief executive to be directly elected by universal suffrage, but the Election Committee screening the candidates would set a higher threshold.[107] Tsang claimed that he himself would prefer an election without threshold inside the Election Committee, meaning that candidates who receive a certain number of nominations within the Election Committee would be able to stand in the chief executive elections. Tsang's views here contained two parts: his perception of Beijing's position and his own ideal. His perception of the central government's stance is actually accurate because as long as the central government can control the screening process to root out politically undesirable candidates, those politically acceptable candidates would be voted on by all the people of Hong Kong. Tsang's ideal, however, remains remote as it is similar to the pan-democratic camp's position. Hence, Tsang presented two visions of the chief executive elections: one acceptable to Beijing and the other "ideal" shared by him and the pan-democrats.

Echoing Tsang's views, DAB deputy chairman Ip Kwok-him said that Beijing would accept a chief executive directly elected by the Hong Kong people, but the elected candidate must not confront the central government. He added that the threshold of screening out candidates could be explored further and was negotiable. Ip said that the Tsang administration would not have to spell out the final model of the chief executive election because this task should be left to Tsang's successor. Ip's remarks were important because if the Tsang administration adopts a timetable for universal suffrage, it could easily argue that such a blueprint would deprive the new chief executive of the political space to map out Hong Kong's reform directions in the long run. This argument, to the democrats, is only a pretext to postpone democratization indefinitely in the HKSAR.

REACHING POLITICAL COMPROMISE IN THE STRATEGIC DEVELOPMENT COMMISSION?

To deal with the legacy of the decision reached by the NPC Standing Committee and to appease the anger of the pan-democrats, the HKSAR government utilized the SDC as a forum to hammer out options for political reform in the HKSAR. When the SDC was set up to deal with the directions of political reform, Martin Lee questioned whether the Tsang administration actually preempted the LegCo to discuss Hong Kong's democratization. According to Lee, the Basic Law empowers the LegCo to question the government, which needs to send officials to answer questions from legislators. Hence, the LegCo is "the highest power organ representing the citizens and playing the constitutional role of supervising the government's performance and policies, but the government often regards the defiant legislators as 'troublemakers.'"[108] In the minds of Lee, the SDC was only a consultative body but it lacked any constitutional status. He questioned whether Stephen Lam used the SDC to pre-empt or usurp the role of LegCo. Furthermore, the SDC did not meet frequently and its meetings were closed to the public. Without any transparency, the SDC, to Lee, was an attempt by the government to bypass the legislature.

The HKSAR government tried to co-opt the democrats by using the SDC, but democrat Albert Cheng withdrew from the SDC and believed that his participation was politically futile.[109] He felt that the democrats and citizens wished to have a clear timetable for universal suffrage, while Lee Cheuk-yan said that the government should lay out a timetable first before examining a road map for political reform. The Tsang administration avoided discussing the timetable for fear of exceeding Beijing's bottom line of political tolerance.[110] The varying assumptions held by the pan-democrats and the government made any political compromise relatively difficult.

Lo Chi-kin, a former democrat whose views have become far more conservative and pro-administration since the return of Hong Kong's sovereignty to the PRC, criticized the democrats for being radical and idealistic without elevating their own standards.[111] What Lo implied was that the democrats should grasp the available political space in the HKSAR, such as joining the SDC, to articulate the interests of the citizens and to prove that they are constructive oppositionists. In reality, Lo's criticisms reflect the common perception among some pragmatic Hong Kong people. But the inability of the pro-democracy parties to grasp political power represents a structural defect in Hong Kong's semidemocratic system in which they are destined to be oppositionists. The formation of the SDC and its subgroup on political reform did, as Martin Lee argued, represent another institutional mechanism that preempted the LegCo in designing solutions for political reform in the HKSAR.

Martin Lee's observation turned out to be accurate; the task of the SDC's political reform committee was to keep the discussions going so that the media attention could be diverted from LegCo. In November 2005, political sociologist Sing Ming suggested in the SDC meeting that the HKSAR could consider implementing a bicameral system in which the lower house composed of all directly elected members would be more powerful than the upper house, which would comprise members elected from functional constituencies.[112] Although the bicameral system appears to satisfy the demands of the business sector, which does not want to witness the abolition of functional constituencies, it has been rejected by most democrats because they see it as a preservation of the executive-led government and business interests, which can easily check the influence of the democratic camp. Ronny Tong of the CP, Lee Wing-tat of the DP, and Lee Cheuk-yan all argued that the bicameral system actually showed the government's intention of retaining functional constituencies and that it "violated" the Basic Law.[113] Another argument against the bicameral model is that Beijing does not wish to amend the Basic Law considerably in order to accommodate this new system, which might trigger lawsuits initiated by the democrats.[114] Beijing has actually remained tight-lipped on its attitude toward the bicameral model, but the possibility of encountering lawsuits would be a real one. When Donald Tsang's reform proposal was put forward to the LegCo for a vote, a citizen began a lawsuit to challenge the legality of increasing the number of seats in the legislature from 60 to 70.[115] Albert Ho of the DP once considered the possibility of a legal challenge to the government on the reform plan in which DC members would select the chief executive, although the CP said political disputes should not be resolved through the judicial channel.[116]

Arguably, it was very difficult for the SDC to bridge the gap between the democrats and the government partly due to the existence of hard-line democrats in the political reform committee and partly because of the constraints of the Basic Law. The HKSAR government insisted that political reform would have to conform to four principles in the Basic Law: "the orderly and gradual process," "the practical circumstances," "the need to take care of the interests of all social strata," and "the benefits to capitalist economic development." [117] These four principles assume the need to maintain LegCo functional constituencies without which capitalist development and other social interests cannot be easily protected. Compounding this inbuilt conservatism of the parameters of political discussion is the presence of several hard-line democrats, notably Lee Cheuk-yan and Lee Wing-tat. Lee Cheuk-yan said that the SDC was useless and it was better for the people to take to the streets.[118] Lee Wing-tat threatened that if the SDC could not achieve anything, the pan-democrats would resign from the commission. As Basic Law Committee member and SDC member Albert Chen remarked, "It is difficult to reach a compromise because some pro-democracy legislators in the committee are quite hard-line." [119]

In March 2006, when the government put forward a discussion paper in the SDC political reform committee, it had bias against the welfare system in the West. The government document said universal suffrage would lead to welfarism, which in turn would affect the investment environment in the HKSAR.[120] The political prejudice of the HKSAR government was based on its lack of understanding of the operation and nature of Western welfare states. Canada, for example, can be seen as a welfare state with universal suffrage, but there is no evidence to show that its investment environment has been affected by universal suffrage. The investment environment of a nation-state or city-state depends on a variety of factors, such as its tax system, investment incentives, government policies, and natural resources. It is a biased assumption of the HKSAR government, as with the business sector, to maintain that universal suffrage must give rise to welfarism, which in turn undermines the investment conditions. In the first place, universal suffrage does not necessarily bring about welfarism; the former may bring about a more balanced political system in which labor interests can be better protected in a business-dominated polity. Second, even if universal suffrage might bring about welfarism in the HKSAR, the lower-class citizens would enjoy better benefits and class contradictions between the rich and the poor would be narrowed, thus minimizing the incidence of social conflicts, confrontations and instability. Third, welfarism is by no means a sufficient condition that undermines investment environment because other factors are at play. The simplistic view of the HKSAR government, and its think tank Central Policy Unit, reflected a remarkable degree of conservatism and ignorance on the complex relations between universal suffrage, welfare states, and investment conditions. No wonder the democrats in the SDC political reform group regarded the government's arguments on universal suffrage, welfarism, and investment conditions as far-fetched and an excuse to delay the implementation of double direct elections in the HKSAR.[121]

Objectively speaking, the HKSAR government and the business sector are deeply concerned about trade unionism resulting from the implementation of universal suffrage, but they shy away from mentioning it for fear of antagonizing the independent (neither pro-Beijing nor pro-Taiwan) and pro-Beijing trade unions in the HKSAR. The case of Canada is valid as its trade unions are so influential that strikes by workers are commonplace every year. Trade unions, in the eyes of the conservative Hong Kong government and its business elites, constitute a real threat to their political power and status. Interestingly, the HKSAR government avoided mentioning trade unionism for the sake of avoiding strong backlash from independent and pro-Beijing unions. In particular, the FTU leader Cheng Yiu-tong has been co-opted into the ExCo and the government does not want to antagonize the FTU because of its anxiety over trade unionism in Hong Kong.

Chief Executive Tsang appointed 30 members of the SDC's political reform committee in February 2008, but only five came from the pan-democratic camp. They included Audrey Eu of the CP, Lee Wing-tat of the DP, Law Chi-kong of the DP, Lee Cheuk-yan of the Confederation of Trade Unions, and Tam Kwok-kiu of the ADPL.[122] Since the pro-establishment elites dominated the committee, the outnumbered pan-democrats must reject any mainstream view reached in the meetings. Three Basic Law Committee members were appointed, including Maria Tam, Albert Chen, and Lau Nai-keung. The mandate of the SDC political reform committee was to discuss the electoral arrangements in 2012. Because the electoral arrangements in 2017 and 2020 would belong to the work of the next government of the HKSAR, the committee did not study them. Still, the pan-democrats participated in the committee meetings and discussions. Therefore, it can be argued that they were moderate and willing to explore limited options within a restricted political space. Lee Wing-tat said that he did not expect the committee to achieve any real breakthrough because of its underrepresentation of the pan-democrats who were so popularly supported by the Hong Kong people. Political analyst Sung Lap-kung accurately pointed out that the role of pan-democrats in the SDC political reform committee was merely "a political vase." [123]

In February 2008, the SDC's political reform committee attempted to discuss the method of selecting the chief executive in 2012. The government suggested that the Election Committee's membership could be increased from 800 to a larger number—a move back to the Tsang reform plan even though it did not propose 1,600 members in the 2012 Election Committee. Other questions raised by the government were old ones, such as whether the four sectors in the Election Committee should be revamped, whether the electoral base should be widened from corporate votes to individual votes, and whether the nomination threshold for the chief executive candidates should be increased or decreased. [124] The SDC tried to heal the political wounds left from the democratic camp's rejection of Tsang's reform plan. From another perspective, it returned to all the old questions that failed to be resolved by both the democrats and the Tsang administration in December 2005.

In April 2008, the SDC political reform committee tried to reach a compromise that the number of LegCo seats in 2012 would be increased by 10. [125] For the five new seats to be returned from functional constituencies, the government refloated the idea of allowing DC to select the five new legislators. The democrats in the SDC, such as Lee Wing-tat, accepted an increase in the number of legislators in exchange for having all DC members elect the five new LegCo members. Lee said the DP would oppose any move by the government to retain appointed seats in DC. However, some pro-establishment elites in the SDC opposed the government proposal on the grounds that it would change the current political "ecology" and that it would be harmful to party development. [126] Some SDC members suggested that the five new members from functional constituencies should come from the underrepresented sectors, such as women, small and medium enterprises, and the Chinese medicine profession. The government proposed that other sectors might also be considered, including youth, family workers, creative sector members, and the mainland Chinese enterprises in the HKSAR.

Can the SDC provide a forum for political bargaining and compromise between the democrats and the government? Two factors hamper its prospects: (1) the dominance of pro-establishment elites, and (2) the perception of pan-democrats such as Martin Lee that it aims at usurping the LegCo role. *Ming Pao* also editorialized and argued that the SDC makeup was similar to the Basic Law Consultative Committee (BLCC) in the late 1980s:

Clearly, owing to political realities, the makeup of the Commission is at variance with the government's original design—that it should comprise mainly middle-of-the-roaders and include both left-wingers and right-wingers ... The Chief Executive was worried that, as LegCo was divided and its right wing and left wing were unlikely to compromise with each other, their discussions of a roadmap for universal suffrage might be too stormy to prove fruitful. Therefore, the government came up with the idea of putting key figures from the two camps on the Commission and appointing a number of people in whom both camps would have faith (academics, senior journalists, retired officials and veteran politicians) to the body. It intended that Commission members should have intensive consultations at which the two cams would feel compelled to compromise and come to a consensus. The government would then sell the consensus to the central government. Overwhelmingly dominating the SDC, would left-wingers be prepared to compromise with democrats? Democrats would feel in the minority. In the 1980s, only 10 democrats sat on the 180-member BLCC, but 89 of its members were from the business community. After the latter had jointly put forward a plan for slow-paced democratization, democrats had no option but to take to the streets. They founded a 190-member group with supporters who did not sit on the BLCC. They came up with a plan for quick-paced democratization and kept organizing mass movements to promote it. As a result, the BLCC became a talking shop. Now the Commission may follow the way the BLCC went more than a decade ago. Unless the government makes sure that the Commission will operate as it originally planned and serve as a forum where political groups may have rational discussions and reach consensus, Hong Kong will see many more street demonstrations.[127]

The editorial raised two issues that deserve our attention. First, the SDC remains to be dominated by the business sector and pro-government elites, and hence the pan-democrats had a strong sense of powerlessness, unlike their performance in elections where citizens empowered them by voting for their representation in LegCo. This structural defect created a strong sense of political alienation, which could be expressed through protests and demonstrations as with the December 4, 2005, parade. Second, the Hong Kong style of democratic consultation is to use the numerical majority of pro-government elites to dominate the minority of pro-democracy elites—a phenomenon attributable to the PRC style of consultation of Hong Kong people over the content of the Basic Law. As long as these two features mark the Hong Kong or increasingly mainland style of democratic consultation, political compromise between the democrats and the government/business/Beijing coalition will remain difficult.

In January 2009, Chief Executive Tsang announced that due to Hong Kong's economic downturn in the midst of the global financial crisis, the public consultation on the methods of the elections for the chief executive and the LegCo in 2012 would be postponed to late 2009.[128] Tsang stressed that the delay in public consultation would not affect the timetable of having double direct elections in 2017 and 2020. The pan-democratic camp expressed its disappointment with the deliberate procrastination. From the angle of the interactive dynamics between economics and politics, the Tsang administration obviously attached importance more to the economic crisis than to the issue of democratic reform. The mentality of economics in command had much in common with the ruling philosophy of the mainland Chinese authorities, who tend to see economic growth and prosperity as far more significant than how to make the CCP more accountable to the public than before.

An editorial in *Sing Tao Daily* interpreted Tsang's move as an attempt to mobilize all the residents' energies to tackle the financial crisis while buying more time to study how to reform the political system later.[129] A more accurate interpretation is that the Tsang regime grasped the economic crisis as an opportunity to not only unify the people of Hong Kong, who must overwhelmingly support the economics-in-command philosophy, but also win their hearts and minds so that they would eventually back up the government's political reform proposals later. In other words, social unity was the hidden objective of Tsang's focus on the economic crisis. Subsequently, social solidarity would hopefully generate harmony and consensus that would be translated into political support for the reform blueprints prepared by the government. The political calculations of the Tsang administration were more strategic than the Tung regime, which put forward a series of reforms without priorities and which insisted on reform programs that antagonized various sectors of the society.[130]

The HKSAR government tried to use the political reform discussion to enhance social cohesion in such a way that democratization would be beneficial to economic development. As secretary for constitutional and mainland affairs Stephen Lam said in September 2008, the purpose of political reform would be to bring "the system to the proper track."[131] He also hoped that "Hong Kong's democratic development would provide clear directions so that the political discourse would focus on social, economic, and livelihood agendas."[132] In other words, democratic reform can be a means to an end, hopefully improving the people's livelihood and economic performance. This assumption was altered once the global financial crisis deepened in late 2008. It can be said that prior to the global financial tsunami, the HKSAR government viewed democratization as being beneficial to both the society and economy, but the onset of the economic crisis changed its equation and turned the priority back to economics in command.

PROSPECTS OF DEMOCRATIZATION

In April 2008, DP chairman Albert Ho warned the HKSAR government that if the 2012 political reform proposals were put forward without mentioning "an ultimate universal suffrage model" for Hong Kong, his party would vote against it in LegCo.[133] This position remained to be held by the pan-democratic camp, including Anson Chan and George Cautherley in the summer of 2009. For the democrats, the HKSAR government should not adopt a delaying tactic in mapping out a timetable and an ultimate model for universal suffrage. Yet, the HKSAR government must shy away from doing so without fully consulting Beijing and acquiring its approval in the first place.

Jasper Tsang of the DAB predicted in 2009 that if the pan-democratic camp insisted on maintaining its "moral high ground," namely having its ideal political model to be adopted in 2012, then the deadlock between the democrats and government would not be easily broken.[134] He envisaged that both the HKSAR government and pro-establishment forces would not be confident enough to accept the scenario that the democratic camp would grasp political power through the election of the chief executive by universal suffrage in 2017. As a result, Tsang predicted that pro-establishment elites and the HKSAR government would adopt a more conservative approach to handling political reform in 2012, thus increasing the difficulties of a negotiated outcome with the democratic camp.

In August 2009, Raymond Wong from the League of Social Democrats challenged the other pro-democracy parties by putting forward a bold proposal. He proposed that one of the pan-democratic legislators resign from each of the five geographical constituencies, thus forcing the government to hold by-elections during which universal suffrage would be the critical issue raised by all pro-democracy candidates. If the pro-democracy candidates won the by-elections and if the votes supportive of them were more than the number of votes cast for pro-government forces, then the HKSAR government would have to abide by the electoral result and to recognize the need for universal suffrage. In other words, Wong proposed an idea of having by-elections for the LegCo as a form of referendum in the HKSAR. Szeto Wah of the DP quickly supported Wong's idea and named five democrats to resign from their geographical constituencies, namely Emily Lau, Alan Leong, Raymond Wong,

Lee Cheuk-yan, and Cyd Ho. But Hong Kong NPC member Allen Lee Peng-fei criticized Wong's proposal as being "unconstructive," being not legally binding, and sending a wrong message to Beijing.[135] Cyd Ho cautiously warned that if some of the five democrats were defeated, the pan-democrats would lose control of at least 20 seats in LegCo. Wong's idea was bold and creative, but Beijing may see it as a challenge to its authority because the issue of universal suffrage is different from a referendum.[136]

In November 2009, the HKSAR government published a consultative document on political reform.[137] It proposed that the LegCo in 2012 would increase its members from 60 to 70. Among the proposed ten additional seats, five would be directly elected by citizens through geographical constituencies, and five would be elected by all the directly elected members of District Councils. Moreover, in 2012, the 800-member Election Committee selecting the chief executive would be expanded to 1,200 members. Viewing the government's reform proposals as "retrogressive," the League of Social Democrats led by Raymond Wong, Leung Kwok-hung, and Chan Wai-yip insisted that one democrat should resign from each of the five geographical constituencies. DP member Szeto Wah, who originally supported the League's proposal of resignation from LegCo, eventually reversed his position because he felt that the veto power of the democrats in the legislature should not be endangered by the resignation plan. In November 2009, the Civic Party was supportive of the League's resignation blueprint, but member Ronny Tong openly rejected it. Martin Lee of the DP, who had originally supported the League's bold plan, changed his position and said that the veto power of all the democratic legislators would be critical to Hong Kong's democracy movement. Szeto Wah also publicly revealed that Martin Lee had cooperated with other democrats, like Anson Chan and Jimmy Lai, to lobby for his support of the League's resignation plan. Clearly, the core leaders of the pro-democracy camp had opinion differences over the resignation proposal.

In December 2009, the Democratic Party held a meeting in which 81 percent of its members voted against the proposal of having five pro-democracy legislators resign from five geographical constituencies. Yet, the Democratic Party allowed its members to campaign in their own individual capacities for other democrats who would resign and who would run for the by-elections. Martin Lee expressed his disappointment with the party's decision. His final position change revealed the opinion difference with Szeto Wah. Meanwhile, the Civic Party held its executive committee meeting and reaffirmed its support of the resignation plan. An electoral alliance between the Civic Party and the League of Social Democrats was formed. The Young Turks and hard-liners within the Civic Party not only opted for the more radical path of action initiated by the League of Social Democrats, but they also claimed that a new democracy movement should be launched. Both parties set up a committee to study the details of the resignation plan. The entire debate illustrated the bitter power struggle among the pro-democracy parties for the leadership in Hong Kong's democracy movement.

SUMMARY

The debate over whether the HKSAR should hold a referendum to decide the future directions of democratic reform demonstrates the fundamental differences in the two political visions. The pan-democrats, especially the radical and idealistic ones, regard the use of referendum as an accurate and the most democratic form of determining the directions of democratization in the future. The PRC authorities tend to see the people of Hong Kong as subjects with political rights granted by the central government. Hence, the argument that the people of Hong Kong are "residents" rather than citizens with the right of self-determination remains alive in the minds of Beijing's hard-liners responsible for Hong Kong affairs. Another consideration of Beijing is that any referendum in Hong Kong may propel the HKSAR into another Taiwan, where a full-fledged Western-style democracy with the rotation of political party in power would perhaps produce an independent-minded chief executive defiant and disrespectful of Beijing's interests and wishes. Ultimately, the CCP is reluctant to surrender or delegate real political power to the people of Hong Kong, who cannot be fully trusted by Beijing after almost 155 years of British colonial rule and after Hong Kong's political role in the 1989 Tiananmen incident.

The rejection of the Tsang reform plan in December 2005 was natural, because it was an extension of the political confrontation between the democrats and the HKSAR government, and between the democrats and Beijing after the July 1 protests and the abortive national security bill in 2003. Yet, the gulf between the democrats on the one hand and the HKSAR government and Beijing on the other persists. A multiplicity of factors explained why the Tsang reform package was vetoed by the democrats: the Tiananmen legacy, the July 1, 2003, protests, the national security bill, Beijing's fear of the Taiwanization of Hong Kong, Tsang's hurried way of handling his reform package without postponing the LegCo vote, the opposition of LP and DAB to concessions made by the government, and the nostalgic solidarity of the pan-democrats. Some, if not necessarily all, of these factors will likely shape and haunt the progress of democratization in the HKSAR in the years to come.

CHAPTER 4

Architects of the Democracy Movement: Martin Lee, Szeto Wah, George Cautherley, and Anson Chan

The leaders and architects of the Hong Kong democracy movement include the mainstream leaders such as Martin Lee, Szeto Wah, Albert Ho, Emily Lau, Lee Wing-tat, and Lee Cheuk-yan; nevertheless, the mass media in the HKSAR have neglected those planners and organizers behind the scene. These planners and organizers are often the political unknowns, but they do contribute tremendously to Hong Kong's democracy movement. This chapter discusses only four of the well-known architects of the Hong Kong democracy movement, namely, Martin Lee and Szeto Wah of the DP, George Cautherley of the Hong Kong Democratic Foundation (HKDF), and former chief secretary for administration Anson Chan Fang On-sang. Their roles in and views of the Hong Kong democracy movement will be examined. It does not mean that other leaders of the democracy movement are insignificant.

Martin Lee's political career was similar to Szeto Wah as they have been the champions of social justice, human rights, and democracy in both mainland China and Hong Kong, especially after the June 4 tragedy. George Cautherley is playing a crucial role behind the scenes of Hong Kong's democracy movement. Anson Chan was a former senior civil servant who has become a key player in the local democracy movement. These four figures have a major commonality: the belief that double direct elections of the chief executive and the entire legislature should be the ultimate objective of democratization in Hong Kong.

THE PRC DEMOCRATIZATION AND HONG KONG'S
SPECIAL ROLE

Most Hong Kong democrats are holding the view that the PRC democratization is speeding up through intra-CCP reforms, and that the Hong Kong model of democracy can and will serve as a useful stimulus for the mainland to undertake and deepen political reforms. This increasingly popular view is held by the former leader of the Civil Human Rights Front, Richard Tsoi Yiu-cheong, who revealed in his visit to Toronto in June 2009 that the HKSAR can become a "bridgehead for mainland China's democratization."[1] The idea of using the HKSAR as a "bridgehead" to spread the spirit and practice of democracy to the mainland is exactly the most fearful concern in the minds of the mainland hard-line officials responsible for Hong Kong matters. One of them told the author that this bridgehead concept would facilitate foreign intervention in an attempt to transform the mainland political system.[2]

The PRC's political development is conforming to the wishes of the pan-democrats in the HKSAR, namely a gradual transformation of the CCP. President Hu Jintao renewed calls for improved democracy within the CCP on the eve of the ruling party's eighty-eighth birthday. He said in late June 2009 that "intra-party democracy" must be promoted and mechanisms must be reformed to better supervise the CCP.[3] Hu also remarked: "We must converge the wisdom and strength of the Party to the utmost level, we must fully inspire the creativity and vigor of the Party."[4] During the annual NPC meeting in March 2009, NPC chair Wu Bangguo said that the PRC would not copy Western-style democracy. In July 2009, government officials who made errors would be penalized, and they would not be transferred to work in another agency at the same level for at least a year—a move aimed at responding to criticisms that some officials responsible for the mismanagement of the SARS crisis and coal mine disasters were transferred horizontally to other positions without demotion. Internal supervision (*jiandu*) is a mainland Chinese concept aimed at enhancing checks and balances on the CCP and the government, but it falls short of the separation of powers in the West where the judiciary, executive, and legislature check against each other.

The PRC democratization under President Hu is marked by several characteristics of internal supervision. First and foremost, anticorruption work is enhanced as the CDIC has been empowered to investigate corruption within the CCP and at different levels of the government. Second, the Audit Commission remains assertive in exposing public maladministration, financial mismanagement, and budgeting problems of various governmental agencies. Third, the accountability system of government officials has been introduced since July 2009 to increase the transparency of deploying officials and demoting those who fail to perform up to the public expectations. Fourth, intra-CCP democracy is emphasized so that the CCP Central Committee has internal voting mechanisms to root out those top party members who are unpopular and to confer legitimacy upon those who are popular. Fifth, the mainland police have been increasingly modernized and trained in such a way as to control domestic social unrest in a minimally violent manner, as the case of the July 2009 Xinjiang unrest showed. Although critics of the mainland police easily point to their use of force in cracking down social unrest and citizen protests, their attempts at minimizing the use of force have been neglected. Sixth, some relatively assertive print media, notably the *Southern Metropolitan Daily*, have been politically tolerated to provide a degree of supervision on the CCP as long as its critical reports and coverage do not constitute a menace to the dominance and authority of the ruling party. Seventh, PRC officials have been forced by the changing political circumstances to respond to the questions and criticisms from not only local elites and media inside the mainland but also the Hong Kong and foreign reporters in a far more open manner. The annual NPC meeting is now witnessing more aggressive questions from Hong Kong and foreign reporters. Even the mainland-controlled Phoenix commented that the annual fanfare in Beijing should envisage a bolder effort by the local media to focus on concrete policy issues rather than just chasing the political stars for sensational stories.[5] Although views on the quality of mainland media varies, PRC officials have been hard-pressed to deal with the more assertive Hong Kong and foreign reporters in a more transparent way than ever before. If governmental responsiveness remains an indicator of democracy, it has been improving gradually in the PRC.

MARTIN LEE AND HIS IDEA OF DEMOCRATIC HONG KONG

Martin Lee is the most prestigious and the most internationally recognized Hong Kong democrat in the eyes of foreign countries and reporters. He was born in Guangdong province in 1938 and his father was a KMT general fighting against the Japanese. In 1949, Lee and his father, who disliked the KMT's corruption and did not leave the mainland for Taiwan, went to Hong Kong.[6] In 1956, Lee was admitted to the University of Hong Kong to study English literature and philosophy. After graduation he studied law at Lincoln's Inn in London and became a barrister. Lee was appointed to Queen's Counsel in 1979 and Senior Counsel in 1997, was Honorary Bencher of Lincoln's Inn in 2000, and was the chairman of the Hong Kong Bar Association from 1980 to 1983.[7] In 1983, Lee and Allen Lee Peng-fei joined the young talents group to visit Beijing, and they met the Chinese leader Deng Xiaoping. Beijing began to notice Lee's legal expertise. In 1985, he was elected to the LegCo through the legal functional constituency. Lee served as a member of the Basic Law Drafting

Committee (BLDC), a body appointed by Beijing to draft Hong Kong's post-1997 constitution, until his expulsion after the Tiananmen tragedy. In 1990, he became the chairman of the United Democrats of Hong Kong (UDHK). In 1991, he was directly elected to the LegCo. In 1994, the UDHK merged with another democratic group named Meeting Point into the DP and Lee became the founding chairman. After Hong Kong's return to the PRC on July 1, 1997, Beijing abolished the LegCo elected by the Hong Kong people in 1995 and replaced it with the Provisional Legislative Council (PLC), a body that had been established in January 1997. The PLC had many members defeated in the 1995 LegCo election and its legitimacy problem was serious.[8] Lee and many democrats, who were excluded from the PLC, returned to the LegCo in 1998, and they won almost two-thirds of the votes cast in direct elections. Because of the structural arrangements of LegCo with functional constituency members elected from a restricted franchise and biased in favor of the business and pro-Beijing elites, the democrats got only one-third of the total number of seats in LegCo. Lee was reelected to the LegCo in 2000 and 2004. In November 2002, Lee stepped down from the position of the DP chairman. In September 2005, Lee visited Guangdong for the first time in 16 years together with other pro-democracy legislators.

Lee was internationally recognized, and therefore his struggle for democracy in Hong Kong does have worldwide support. In 1995, the 350,000-member American Bar Association awarded him the 1995 International Human Rights Award "in recognition of extraordinary contributions to human rights, the rule of law, and the promotion of justice."[9] In 1996, the Liberal International, which represented 70 political parties in the world, awarded him the Prize for Freedom at the World Council of Liberals meeting. In 1997, the U.S. National Endowment for Democracy presented Lee its Democracy Award at a ceremony at Capitol Hill. In 1998, the Claremont Institute in Los Angeles gave the Statesmanship Award to him. In January 2000, the European People's Party and European Democrats in the European Parliament named Lee as the first non-European recipient of the Schuman Medal, while the University of Toronto honored him as the Goodman Fellow. In the same year, he had an audience with U.S. President Bill Clinton in the White House.[10] In November 2004, Rutgers College conferred upon Lee the Brennan Human Rights Award. Given Lee's international status and respectability, some hard-line and xenophobic PRC officials view him as a "tool" for foreign countries, but they ignore that many international countries do support further democratic development in the HKSAR.

Lee's role in Hong Kong's democracy movement has been controversial. In 2004, he and Yeung Sum ran in a party ticket and appealed urgently to the voters for support by claiming that they would be defeated. The DP voters flocked to vote for his list, but the end result was that another independent democrat, Cyd Ho, failed to be elected. She was narrowly defeated by the DAB candidate Choy So-yuk. Critics of Martin Lee were dissatisfied with his campaign strategy.[11] In October 2007, he said publicly that foreign countries could use the 2008 Olympics Games to exert pressure on China to improve its human rights and democratic development.[12] His view was severely criticized by the pro-Beijing press and elites in the HKSAR. They labeled him as a "traitor" without appreciating the fact that Lee is a classical liberal seeing human rights and democracy as universal values. Lee said that 95 essays criticized him in one day alone and that "the event demonstrated to the Hong Kong people the horrified extent of the CCP's control over the freedom of speech."[13] Lee's supporters said that the critics misunderstood his argument and blew up the issue deliberately for the sake of discrediting him. For the democrats, Lee has remained highly respectable although his decisions might be sometimes controversial. For Beijing, especially the hardliners, Lee remains a defiant Hong Kong democrat who forms an alliance with foreign countries to exert pressure on the PRC and the Hong Kong government.

Martin Lee can be regarded as a staunch liberal idealist whose lobbying activities in foreign countries are bound to clash with the traditional Chinese emphasis on face. Traditionally, the Chinese in general have disliked the revelation of their family or domestic problems in public, because doing so would constitute a loss of their face.[14] To the PRC and the HKSAR government, Lee's lobbying activities in foreign countries have made the "one country, two systems" model look bad. In 1997, Chief Executive Tung Chee-hwa implicitly criticized Lee for "bad-mouthing" Hong Kong.[15] To Lee, however, his visits to foreign countries only allowed them to understand Hong Kong's democratic development in a deeper way. In short, Lee's liberalism is destined to clash with the traditional Chinese culture of conservatism.

Lee's decision to step down from the LegCo election was influenced by his son, who asked him not to run again in 2008.[16] He also told the mass media that the DP would have to rely on the younger generation rather than on him. The 70-year-old Lee said that even if he participated in the 2008 elections, some citizens might not vote for him, and therefore it was necessary for him to provide more opportunities for the second tier of leadership to develop.[17] Lee revealed that during the DP observations of Taiwan's presidential election in March 2008, he already expressed his wish of stepping down to Albert Ho, who asked him to reconsider.[18] Lee admitted that after he stepped down, his chances of meeting the top leaders of foreign countries would be reduced, but he would continue to visit foreign countries so they could understand the political and democratic development of the HKSAR. After he stepped down from legislative election, Lee tried to persuade Anson Chan to participate in LegCo's direct elections on the Hong Kong Island,[19] but Chan eventually decided to opt out of the electoral contest and paved the way for more young blood in the pan-democracy camp to replace them.

In May 2008, Lee publicly praised PRC Premier Wen Jiabao for leadership in the rescue of the victims of the Sichuan earthquake. Lee's commentary raised the concern of Professor Ong Yew Kim, a Chinese legal expert. Ong appealed to the left-wingers and right-wingers in Hong Kong and the PRC to take Lee's stance seriously because Lee, to Ong, is by no means unpatriotic.[20] Ong observed that Martin Lee is actually patriotic as he has been influenced by his late father who was a KMT general. Ong thought that Lee suffered from being criticized as a "running dog for the West." Ong distinguished Martin Lee from those anti-communist Hong Kong hard-liners who said that the Sichuan earthquake represented "a punishment by the heaven" on the PRC. Ong asked the people of Hong Kong and Beijing authorities to notice that Martin Lee regarded Wen as the "people's premier," and that he hoped China would be democratic. Hence, as Ong argues, Martin Lee is by no means anti-China. Ong's essay in support of Lee was significant because none of the pro-Beijing legal experts in the HKSAR made such positive comments before.

When Martin Lee stepped down from legislative elections, his political foes judged him too harshly and displayed a lack of political acumen. Gary Cheng Kai-nam, the former disgraced DAB member who was imprisoned for misusing his political influence for personal gains, argued that Lee shouldered "the political baggage of fighting for democracy" in Hong Kong and thus he "entered a political tunnel without creativity."[21] Lee's political foes, namely the former DAB leaders such as Jasper Tsang and the late Ma Lik, did not really show any political creativity in developing any new democratic blueprint for the HKSAR. Nor do other patriotic leaders show any innovation in proposing how to narrow the huge gap between the PRC perspective and the Hong Kong people's vision of a more democratic HKSAR. Cheng's negative assessment of Martin Lee perhaps reflected the deep-rooted bias of some pro-Beijing elites in the HKSAR.

In fact, Martin Lee was once rumored to be a candidate for the secretary for justice in the HKSAR, for he did help some pro-Beijing workers in the 1960s when he was a young lawyer in Hong Kong under British rule. At that time, the colonial police penetrated working-class meetings and organizations to monitor left-wing activities.[22] Lee's action of assisting the pro-Beijing workers was regarded as one of the reasons why he was appointed to the BLDC in the mid-1980s. After the June 4 tragedy, Lee and Szeto Wah withdrew from the BLDC, but Beijing did not say it approved their withdrawal and instead removed the two's titles as BLDC members.[23] Because of Lee and Szeto Wah's belief that the PRC suppression of the student democrats on Tiananmen Square was incorrect and unjust, they have become the "permanent opposition" in Hong Kong.[24] Ann Yu, a political commentator, concluded that Martin Lee has actually been fighting for justice in both Hong Kong and the PRC—an action ignored by his pro-Beijing but politically opportunistic critics. Ann wrote:

Ten years after Hong Kong's return to mainland China, Martin Lee and Szeto Wah have remained their own ways while the Hong Kong society in general looks to the north . . . Some people say that they both are the hard-liners in the democratic camp and the communications between Beijing and Hong Kong would have been better without them . . . The society's view that Martin Lee and Szeto Wah are the obstacle to better communication with the central government is very superficial and simplistic . . . The answer is very simple. Both of them want to have the reversal of the official verdict on Tiananmen and the universal suffrage to select the Hong Kong Chief Executive and the entire legislature. They do not want to have themselves reversing the verdict and to become the Chief Executive after universal suffrage. Perhaps in the secular world, where some people attach importance to gain one elected seat or to be an official, they think that Martin Lee and Szeto Wah must follow them to pursue political benefits. But they cannot expect that both of them actually have a much higher level of social justice in their minds . . . In Hong Kong where the city is rapidly mainlandized, Martin Lee's position and attitude must turn against himself and must be stupid in the eyes of some people. Indeed, in a Special Administrative Region where we have already become an industrialized society, very few people are acting stupidly like Martin Lee and Szeto Wah. In fact, what both of them have been doing [is] not beneficial to themselves; they cannot become officials. Nor do they become rich and meet the top Chinese leaders. But what they are thinking is another type, the type that belongs to the interests of the general public and citizens.[25]

Ann's positive but objective evaluation of Lee and Szeto is important because both of them have been fighting for social justice and democracy in Hong Kong and the PRC. Their vision of democracy in Hong Kong and mainland China is a just and democratic one, an ideal shared by many Hong Kong and overseas Chinese. Both of them are by no means the politically opportunistic elites in the HKSAR. Their political vision of democracy and justice for Hong Kong and mainland China is respectable.

Lee is dissatisfied with the way in which the PRC government fails to put forward a clear timetable for Hong Kong to have double direct elections of both the chief executive and the entire LegCo. He wrote:

China took control of our political development through an unsolicited "interpretation" of our constitution in April 2004, thereby giving itself the unilateral right to decide when it would be appropriate for Hong Kong to have democracy, and it has become abundantly clear that the Chinese leaders want to keep control over our electoral system until they are sure that the pro-Beijing parties will win all elections. In 1990, when the Basic Law was promulgated, they thought it would happen 10 years from the handover date, that is 2007. In 2004, they decided that

that would not happen so soon. So they unilaterally declared in April 2004 that Hong Kong would not have democracy in 2007 without specifying when we would have it. Then Hong Kong people turned to 2012 as the appropriate date. But Beijing once more dashed their aspirations in December 2007 and decided that Hong Kong would only be allowed to elect the Chief Executive by universal suffrage in 2017, and the entire legislature in 2020. But even then, there is no guarantee at all that such elections by universal suffrage would be in accordance with international standards.[26]

In the minds of Lee, democracy means the direct elections for the chief executive and the entire LegCo—a firm position and definition held by him since the mid-1980s. He firmly believes that the PRC government has been adopting a delaying tactic to postpone the arrival of democracy in the HKSAR.

Lee appeals to the mainland Chinese leaders to accelerate the development of democracy in China and Hong Kong. He argued that the late Deng Xiaoping actually wanted to envision democracy in the PRC.

Deng's economic loosening in effect got rid of Communism in China by bringing in a market economy that has lifted millions out of poverty. But Deng wanted the fruits of democracy without the tree, and he left in place the Communist political controls that even he and his family had previously been victimized by. What China urgently needs now is a good example to follow: an open political system with reforms to the rule of law and other key areas to sustain the opening of the market. For the time being, Chinese leaders obviously fear such a system.[27]

Lee hopes that mainland China after the 2008 Olympics will continue to democratize its political system, protect human rights, and improve the rule of law while allowing Hong Kong to have "genuine democracy." [28] When China democratizes and Hong Kong becomes truly democratic, "that would really be something worth cheering, not only for the Chinese people, but the people of all the five continents." [29] Martin Lee is actually a classical liberal who firmly believes in the rule of law, the protection of civil liberties and human rights, and the universal value of having direct elections of both the chief executive and the entire legislature. At the same time, he perceives himself as a Hong Kong Chinese. Unfortunately, without an in-depth understanding of Martin Lee's liberal and universal values as well as his self-identity, the PRC officials, especially those hard-line ideologues, see him as an agent utilized by the Western nation-states to "subvert" the Chinese political systems.

Martin Lee has a close friendship with Jimmy Lai, who supported Anson Chan to participate in the by-election held for the LegCo in December 2007.[30] Lai is regarded as a media tycoon behind the pan-democratic camp in Hong Kong, for his *Apple Daily* covers the democrats positively before local elections and has mobilized citizens to protest against the HKSAR government on every July 1 since 2003. Lai reportedly also rejected the Tsang reform plan in 2005, and he tried but failed to encourage Anson Chan to run in the 2008 LegCo elections. As a friend of Lai, Martin Lee introduced Bishop Zen to him after the June 4 tragedy, thus forming a triangular political friendship since then. Three of them share the common aspiration of promoting double direct elections in the HKSAR.

Lee's perception of foreign help in Hong Kong's democratization and his concept of patriotism have rarely been understood by many Hong Kong people and Beijing's hard-liners. He argues that foreign countries have "a humanitarian responsibility" to ensure that Beijing sticks to the promises in the Sino-British Joint Declaration, an internationally binding agreement reached between the United Kingdom and the PRC govern- ments.[31] Lee stressed that before the Sino-British Joint Declaration was signed, both governments went out to lobby for public and international support while many foreign countries said that they believed the prom- ises in the agreement would be followed. After July 1, 2003, the PRC's intervention in Hong Kong has increased, according to Lee. At present, the principle of "Hong Kong people ruling Hong Kong" is turned into "Beijing people ruling Hong Kong." [32] Hence, foreign countries have the humanitarian obligation to observe the implementation of the Joint Decla- ration. On patriotism, Lee argued:

Why do they say that I am unpatriotic? Was Sun Yat-sen patriotic? Why did they look for foreign countries to support the Sino-British Joint Declaration at that time? Now if things go wrong, why can't I go to look for the foreign countries? They often say that if things go wrong, you can speak out. Was it acceptable to them when I spoke out during the Sino-British Joint Declaration? Yet, now when I speak out, it is unacceptable to them. This is absolutely illogical.[33]

As a barrister, Lee adheres to the legalistic argument that as long as the Sino-British Joint Declaration is an international and legally binding agreement, it is legitimate for him to explain to foreign countries what is happening in the HKSAR.

Martin Lee's legacy will be felt in Hong Kong's democracy movement in the years to come. His role symbolizes not only the highly respectable status of a pro-democracy barrister, but also the international recognition from foreign countries, statesmen, and human rights organizations. His personal charisma has earned him the trust and massive support from the people of Hong Kong, especially his staunch supporters from the pan-democratic camp. His impeccable legalistic arguments and consistent political logic have made some of the pro-Beijing elites fearful and yet respectful of him. It is perhaps difficult to look for Lee's replacement in the short run, although the CP has a number of prestigious lawyers, such as Alan Leong, Ronny Tong, Audrey Eu, and Margaret Ng. Martin Lee's encouraging remarks to the democrats in March 2008 when he decided to step down from LegCo elections will remain an important legacy: "democracy is still unsuccessful and comrades have to work harder."[34] He regrets that his "democratic dream has not yet been realized."[35] Lee also humbly said: "I have never mentioned I am the father of democracy, but I am only a democracy uncle."[36] The unfinished democracy movement led by Martin Lee, and Szeto Wah, is going to be a serious and daunting challenge to the younger generations of pan-democrats in the HKSAR.

SZETO WAH AND HIS POLITICAL PHILOSOPHY

Any discussion of Martin Lee's role in Hong Kong's democracy movement without Szeto Wah is incomplete. Szeto's role in the 1989 Tiananmen tragedy was critical, as discussed before, because he was the Alliance chairman assisting the mainland democrats to escape from the PRC after the violent crackdown. Like Lee, Szeto is equally identifying himself as a Chinese. Unlike Martin Lee who received his legal education in London and who has been frequently interviewed by foreign media and politicians, Szeto Wah was educated in Hong Kong. Unlike Martin Lee who was born in the mainland, Szeto was born in Hong Kong in 1931.[37] In 1950 Szeto graduated from Queen's College. Two years later he graduated from the Grantham Teachers' College. From 1960 to 1966, Szeto became chief editor of a children's newspaper. From 1961 to 1992 he was a school principal in Kwuntong district. Since 1974, Szeto has been the president, deputy president, and then the chairman of the board of directors in the Professional Teachers Union. From 1985 to 2004 he was a member of the LegCo. In 1985, Szeto entered the legislature through the educational functional constituency. In 1986, both Szeto and Martin Lee were appointed to the BLDC, and they were expelled from the committee after the June 4 incident. From 1989 to the present, Szeto remains the chairman of the Alliance for the Promotion of Patriotic and Democratic Movement in China. In 1990 he was a founding member of the UDHK and later helped the establishment of the DP. From 1990 to 1992 he was the secretary general of the Confederation of Trade Unions. Szeto received a number of international awards for his human rights activities, including the 1989 Outstanding Contribution to China's Democracy Award from the Chinese Democratic Education Foundation.[38]

The most prominent feature of Szeto's political philosophy is his belief that patriotism and the love for democracy are by no means incompatible.[39] His argument is directed at PRC officials and pro-Beijing Hong Kong elites who label the democrats as "unpatriotic." Szeto elaborated on his argument:

As a matter of fact, Hong Kong's water comes from Dongjiang and Hong Kong Chinese are the sons and daughters of the Yellow River. At present, an overwhelming majority of those Hong Kong people who call for "a return of the administration to the people" have also grown up by drinking the Dongjiang water, and their bodies are filled with the blood of the offspring of the Yellow River. They are all patriotic. Take a look at the 1989 democracy movement. A million of people took to the streets several times and this showed their spirit of loving the nation. But they also love democracy. On July 1, 2003 half a million people went onto the streets and again demonstrated their love of democracy. Loving the country and loving democracy are not antagonistic but united. A true patriot must support democracy. A true democrat must love the nation.[40]

Szeto has argued that the HKSAR government should stick to four principles in its governance: (1) conveying to Beijing clearly the demand for democracy on the part of the Hong Kong people; (2) explaining to the central government that "the demand for a return of the administration to the people" is not tantamount to any "pro-Hong Kong independence movement"; (3) ensuring that economic rebound cannot solve political problems and that democratization can guarantee economic prosperity; and (4) clarifying to the public the content of the government's communications with Beijing, especially the views of the central government. His arguments are clear: Beijing–Hong Kong relations have to reflect the aspirations of the Hong Kong people; the Hong Kong people are both patriotic and pro-democracy; democracy is beneficial to Hong Kong's economy; and the interactions between the Hong Kong government and Beijing must be transparent. So far, it seems that the HKSAR government since July 1, 1997, has failed to meet Szeto's four principles. The pro-democracy demands of the Hong Kong people remain to be unfulfilled; they are regarded as "unpatriotic" and "pro-Hong Kong independence" by Beijing's hard-line officials; democracy is seen by Beijing, the Hong Kong government, and business elites as detrimental to the economy; and the government's discussions with Beijing remain secretive.

As with Martin Lee who believes in the universality of democratic values such as human rights, universal suffrage, and freedom, Szeto holds the view that democracy is "a mandate whose tide cannot be turned against."[41] He even asserts that those rulers who "embrace democracy will have their prospects prosper, but those who resist it will be toppled."[42] He appealed to the Tsang administration to embrace the tide of democratization.

Szeto also rejects the suggestion that he should withdraw from the DP so as to break the deadlock in the relationships between the party and Beijing. The reason is that, to Szeto, the Alliance has other executive committee members who are legislators, such as Andrew Cheng, Albert Ho, Cheung Man-kwong, Lee Cheuk-yan, and Leung Yiu-chung. Szeto defends that those who asked him to quit the DP have not read the party platform in which the reversal of the official verdict on Tiananmen is stated clearly. He thinks that the idea of persuading him to leave the DP is a "conspiracy" aimed at splitting the pan-democratic camp.[43] Nor does Szeto find it necessary to go to the mainland silently for the sake of communicating with PRC authorities—a move that he sees as lacking any transparency and open dialogue.

Similar to Martin Lee, Szeto appeals to the younger generation of the Hong Kong people to struggle for democracy in the future. He believes that "the democratic path is long, zig-zag and difficult." [44] The people of Hong Kong, to Szeto, should be united in their struggle for democracy and should make progress in their attempt at "returning the administration to the people." He realizes that the path of democratization in both Hong Kong and mainland China will be a long one. Szeto revealed that during the drafting process of the Basic Law in the latter half of the 1980s, PRC officials did not really understand Hong Kong's development and the importance of democracy. One mainland Chinese drafter asked Szeto whether democracy and universal suffrage would bring about the triads to power in Hong Kong, and whether triad elements would control the elections.[45] Szeto laughed bitterly at his remark but firmly believed that the PRC elites did not understand Hong Kong at that time. The abortive attempt by the Hong Kong government to legislate on Article 23 of the Basic Law in mid-2003, to Szeto, was due to the victory of the "people's power" in Hong Kong.[46] On the prospects of democracy in the HKSAR and the PRC, Szeto said:

I started teaching in 1952. The students in the early years were more mature and they are now over 60 years old. The question that I do not ask is: "Will I be able to see universal suffrage one day?" Instead, my question is: "How many of my students will see universal suffrage one day?" I hope to see my students in the parades supportive of democracy and universal suffrage. I told those students who were taught by me in these forty years: If you feel that I am a good teacher and a good principal, and that I did teach you to know some knowledge and reasons, then please join me in the December 4, 2005 protest for the double direct elections in the HKSAR. This will be the best dinner from my students expressing their gratitude to their teachers. In the past, I have never attended your thanking-the-teacher banquet.[47]

Obviously, Szeto mobilizes his students and supporters to participate in parades and protests for universal suffrage in the HKSAR. He does not entertain the hope that democracy will arrive in both Hong Kong and China in his lifetime, but, as with Martin Lee, he expects the younger generation of the Hong Kong people to continue striving for their political ideals. During a visit to Toronto in April 2009, Szeto predicted that the reversal of the Tiananmen verdict would occur in 2022.[48]

In the final analysis, Szeto Wah cherishes the importance of retaining the diversity in the pro-democracy camp. When the PRC leader Zeng Qinghong visited the HKSAR in September 2005, "Long Hair" Leung Kwok-hung shouted slogans during the banquet. Szeto said that he fully supported Leung's action because different people have different ways of expressing their ideas and dissent. He also remarked: "How can we ask everyone to imitate 'Long Hair'? Why can't we ask 'Long Hair' to learn from other democrats?"[49] What Szeto meant was that Leung had his own way of political expression, which cannot be imposed on any others. He also supports any democrat to begin a dialogue with PRC officials, such as Zeng, on the condition that a firm stance to fight for democracy is maintained. Yet, he thought that Zeng's visit to the HKSAR in 2005 was a political show because he could reach out more actively to the democrats.[50] In short, Szeto remains a democrat of principles in the fight for democratization in the HKSAR.

THE ROLE OF GEORGE CAUTHERLEY IN HONG KONG'S DEMOCRACY MOVEMENT

George Cautherley, one of the key founders of the think tank HKDF together with former legislator Jimmy McGregor, was born in Hong Kong during the Japanese occupation in 1942. He belongs to the fifth generation of his family that has lived and worked in China. After being educated in the United Kingdom, he returned to Hong Kong in 1964 to pursue a career in marketing and distributing medical devices to pharmaceuticals and health-care professionals in China and other international markets. Having a strong sense of belonging in Hong Kong, Cautherley decided to stay in the HKSAR after July 1, 1997. He thought that he would adapt well to the changing circumstances. In 2006, he was awarded an Honorary Doctorate in Business Administration by the Edinburgh Napier University. On the Queen's Birthday Honour List in 2008, Cautherley was made Officer of the Order of the British Empire for his "tireless" work for "the causes of democratic and public policy development in Hong Kong."[51] Very few observers had attached importance to him until a report revealed that he donated HK$250,000 to Anson Chan's campaign for her directly elected seat in the LegCo in 2007.

Cautherley holds the view that the PRC political system is changing gradually. He told the author that the intraparty democracy in the mainland would lead to a "diffusion process" in other provinces.[52] But this diffusion would take at least a decade. In the long term, Cautherley believes, democracy will take place in the mainland. In the mind of Cautherley, it is unclear who are the ultimate decision makers in the PRC policy toward Hong Kong. He believes that the Liaison Office has its own agendas, but whether Hu Jintao and Wen Jiabao have the final say in the PRC development is uncertain. He doubts whether a group of ruling families may be behind the scene of the PRC power structure. Chinese politics, to Cautherley, is like a black box full of mysteries.[53]

He believed that the lower turnout of the July 1 protests in 2009 would "give the HKSAR government some confidence" while the pan-democrats would need to have some "soul searching."[54] Cautherley felt that the lower number of participants in the July 1, 2009, march was due to the decline of political parties in the HKSAR. He believed that the people of Hong Kong lost confidence and trust in political parties and thus abandoned participation in the annual march. Political parties, to Cautherley, are introverted and lack resources as well as infrastructure. However, he said, the June 4 candlelight vigil had nothing to do with political parties partly because of the perceived Chinese identity of the participants and also partly due to the Tiananmen "massacre," which created strong emotional attachment in the minds of those who strongly identified themselves as Chinese.[55]

Cautherley is critical of the way in which the HKSAR government handles political reform. He feels that the HKSAR government fails to see its role in forging consensus in the politically divided society. The government, to him, should be something more than just a messenger or a middleman bridging the gap between the business sector and the democrats; it should be a "consensus-builder."[56] Failing this task and "abdicating its responsibility," the HKSAR government's role is now taken over by the Citizens' Commission on Constitutional Development (CCCD), a think tank that was formed by Anson Chan and that, to Cautherley, can become a consensus maker reaching out to have dialogue with all political groups.[57] What the HKSAR needs sorely is quality leadership, which involves political visions at the top level and political party development with better policies to alter the existing "equation" of Hong Kong politics.[58]

Cautherley as a successful entrepreneur regards his "engagement with the business elite as extremely difficult" because it is much larger and diverse.[59] The power elite in the business sector, to him, focuses on the chambers of commerce, which are unwilling to share, not to mention surrender, political power with other forces. Compounding the impasse is the reluctance of the HKSAR government to "part with political power."[60] Yet, if the central government in Beijing sends any message on how to deal with political power, the business elite will change. The crux of the problem is how the pan-democrats can lobby Beijing and get their political reform ideas upward to the political center in the mainland. The CCCD can hopefully play the role of articulating its views to Beijing, Cautherley hopes, because one of the key members is Allen Lee Peng-fei, a Hong Kong NPC member. Pro-democracy parties like the DP, the CP, and others participate in the CCCD's political reform discussions. Yet, these parties lack resources and coordination.

To plug the loopholes of the democracy movement, Cautherley has taken the initiatives to introduce a number of organizational reforms. First and foremost, he was a donor supportive of Anson Chan's electoral campaign. By supporting Chan, he took the risk of being labeled as a foreigner providing support for Chan's election, especially in the eyes of some PRC officials who may not fully understand that Cautherley himself has a very strong Hong Kong origin and identity. Second, Cautherley was instrumental in the formation of the Community Television, which has a studio in Wanchai and which produces programs supportive of the democracy movement and democratic education. In a sense, the Community TV initiative was Cautherley's effort at dealing with Hong Kong's media censorship. Third, he provides the necessary policy advice and research support for the pan-democrats. Together with the HKDF, which regularly organizes seminars to discuss political, economic, and social issues, Cautherley was one of the founders of the newly created Professional Commons, which is composed of young intellectuals and professionals who were the Election Committee members supportive of CP member Alan Leong to compete with Donald Tsang in the 2007 chief executive election. In practice, Cautherley foresees the necessary generational change in Hong Kong's democracy movement, and so he gradually fostered activities to groom the younger generation of leaders. Fourth, in 2009 he planned to form an association for all the pro-democracy think tanks in 2009, but the Synergy Net led by Executive Councilor Anthony Cheung appeared to be less interested in his effort at avoiding duplication in research work. Fifth, Cautherley in 2008 went to India with CP members Margaret Ng and Kenneth Chan to study how non-governmental organizations (NGOs) organized their activities. He also expresses an interest in supporting some young Hong Kong people to be interns in foreign NGOs in the future. Overall, Cautherley is playing the role of being a communicator, coordinator, policy planner, financial supporter, and behind-the-scenes organizer of Hong Kong's democracy movement.

Earlier than any other political group, Cautherley proposed several options for Hong Kong's democratic reform from 2011 to 2010. Entitled "Constitutional Development, 2011–2020: Possible Scenarios for Discussion," his paper proposes that the chief executive election in 2012 would envisage two changes: (1) the elimination of corporate voting in the Election Committee and expansion in the electorate by extending the franchise to either corporate directors or office-bearers or to occupational employees who hold licenses or qualifications in the functional constituencies. In 2012, the Election Committee for the Chief Executive can retain the 800 members or increase the size to 1,200 members through the addition of DC members. In 2017, the chief executive would be selected by universal suffrage. Candidates would have to receive the required number of nominations (nominations from 8 percent to 10 percent of members) from the Nomination Committee.[61] Moreover, there should be no requirement to achieve any quota of nominations from any specific sector of the Nomination Committee.

His ideal model of LegCo reform is a three-step evolution from 2012 to 2016, and then to 2020. In 2012, the corporate voting in functional constituencies would be eliminated and their electorate would be expanded by transferring the votes from corporate electors to its directors, partners, or office-bearers as individuals. The corporate directors, partners, and office-bearers would have to be registered with their Companies Registry, the Business Registration Office, and the Societies Ordinance, respectively. Alternatively, in 2012, the functional constituency voters would include any eligible voter "who works in an occupation that falls within a functional constituency with corporate voting who requires a license or qualification in order to carry out their job."[62] Another option in 2012 would be the consolidation of existing functional constituencies into a number of multiseat functional constituencies, with the total number of functional seats being maintained at 30. In 2016, two changes would be needed: (1) further consolidation of the multiseat functional constituencies into four multiseat constituencies in line of the four sectors (commercial/industrial/monetary; professional; labor/grassroots/religious; and political circle/Hong Kong members to the NPC and the CPPCC) used to delineate the Election Committee for the Chief Executive. In 2020, Cautherley's proposal envisions a fully directly elected LegCo through universal suffrage. One option includes 60 or 70 or 80 seats, which would be elected from geographical constituencies on a "first past the post" voting system. The second option would see half of the seats returned from 5 multiseat geographical constituencies on a party list voting system where the voters choose the ranking of candidates on any list, while the other half would be returned from a single territory-wide geographical constituency on a party list voting system where the voters choose the ranking of the candidates on any list. The third option would retain half of the 60 seats returned from 5 multiseat geographical constituencies on a party list voting system where the voters rank the candidates on any list, whereas the other half would be composed of 30 seats in which 18 would be returned from 18 DC constituencies on a party list voting system where the voters rank the candidates on any list, and 12 returned from a single territory-wide geographical constituency on a party list voting system where the voters rank the candidates on any list. The Cautherley model of political reform emerged as the first one immediately after the July 1 protests with regard to how Hong Kong's political system should be reformed in the future.

ANSON CHAN AND HER IDEA OF DEMOCRATIC HONG KONG

Anson Chan is the most prominent former senior civil servant who has transformed from a government elite to a pro-democracy activist. Chan joined the Hong Kong government in 1962 as an administrative officer. In 1993 she became the first Chinese and first woman to become the chief secretary, a position she continued until her retirement in late April 2001.

Chan is keen to envisage stronger checks and balances on the government.[63] Groomed by the British administration to be a senior civil servant straddling July 1, 1997, Chan was never trusted by the pro-Beijing elites and PRC officials in the HKSAR under the Tung leadership. PRC officials such as Liao Hui in September 2000 criticized her and the Hong Kong civil servants for not supporting the chief executive.[64] When she participated in the December 4, 2005, protest in support for double direct elections in the HKSAR, PRC officials were concerned about the possibility that she would run in the chief executive elections. They were curious about the supporters behind Chan's moves, including whether the DP and the Article 45 Concern Group were the behind-the-scenes "instigators." [65]

In December 2007, Chan participated in the LegCo by-election on the Hong Kong Island. The by-election was held after the death of the former DAB chairman Ma Lik. She got 175,874 votes and defeated another former senior civil servant Regina Ip, who obtained 137,550 votes.[66] While Anson Chan was supported by the entire pan-democratic camp, Regina Ip was backed by the DAB, FTU, LP, and most importantly the Liaison Office.[67] The pro-Chan campaign team clashed with the Regina camp, leading to cases of intimidation, abuse in the use of loudspeakers, and brawls involving campaign members from the two sides.[68] About 52 percent of the registered voters on the Hong Kong Island cast their ballots—a relatively high level of local participation.[69] While *Apple Daily* published a special issue in support of Chan on election day by claiming that her chance was at stake and thus attracting Chan's supporters to go to the polls, Regina Ip acquired the assistance of pro-Beijing forces, which used emails and text messages to mobilize voters to support Ip and to stress her ability to communicate with the central government.[70] In fact, Ip's percentage of votes obtained was higher than that acquired by the late Ma Lik and the list composed of Rita Fan in 2004 (see Table 4.1). No wonder Ip felt that she was elected.[71]

The democrats were keen to help Chan win the by-election because they did not perform well in the November 2007 DC elections.[72] They emphasized to the voters that Chan was in great danger of being defeated if they did not come out to vote for her. On the voting day, many students were mobilized by the pro-Beijing forces to conduct exit polls to see how voters supported the two main candidates—Chan and Ip—and then they

Table 4.1

The Number of Votes in the 2007 By-Elections and the 2004 Legislative Direct Elections in the Hong Kong Island

Year	Votes for Pro-Establishment Forces	Votes for Pan-Democratic Camp
2004	DAB Ma Lik's list and Rita Fan's list 140,320 (39.6%)	Yeung Sum's list, Tsang Kin-shing's list, Audrey Eu's list 210,945 (59.6%)
2007	Regina Ip 137,550 (42.7%)	Anson Chan 175,874 (54.6%)

Source: Ming Pao, December 4, 2007, p. A15.

reported their findings to the pro-Ip campaign headquarters.[73] The *Apple Daily* carried commentaries to fully support Anson Chan and appealed to the voters to vote for her prior to the voting day.[74] It also showed a headline reminding the voters that "non-voting, abstention will be the same as supporting Mrs. Ip," while emphasizing Chan's remark that "I need every vote."[75] The explicit political tone of *Apple Daily* in support of Chan was unprecedented.

The electoral battle between Anson Chan and Regina Ip had special implications for Hong Kong politics and democratization. For the first time in Hong Kong's political development, two former senior civil servants who were educated and groomed in the territory under British rule, turned out to be politicians seeking voters' support. It meant that even former senior civil servants, who gained their fame and popularity in the eyes of the public, realized the importance of grasping the votes of the people to make the government more accountable in LegCo. Chan was a popular senior civil servant, while Ip discredited herself during the difficult task of promoting the national security bill to the Hong Kong people from 2002 to mid-2003. While Chan joined the pro-democracy camp to fight for democracy in the HKSAR, Ip sided with the patriotic front to adopt a gradualist approach to democratic reform. Chan was seen as a pro-British "ambitious" politician in the eyes of PRC officials, especially those xenophobic hard-liners, but Ip was regarded as a pro-Beijing loyalist who tried her best to sell the national security bill to the public. Chan criticized Ip for "lacking independent judgment" in the election campaign,[76] but Ip argued that the question of universal suffrage in the HKSAR would need "political compromise" and that Chan stuck to the "moral high ground" of supporting universal suffrage.[77] While Chan joins the pan-democrats to fight for the democratic ideals, Ip becomes a realist siding with those who hold political power and influence. The paths chosen by the two former senior civil servants are very different, meaning that democratization in the HKSAR is divided into the democratic idealists and pro-Beijing realists. Both camps have varying political assumptions and objectives. Chan assumes that democracy is a difficult path on which she and the democrats have to struggle, but the objective is to bring about democracy and accountability to the HKSAR. Ip, however, assumes that democracy must need political compromises, and her objective is to maximize her influence through the adoption of a pro-Beijing policy line. Although Ip says that she is by no means "pro-royalist," her political orientations tend to be a mixture of realism and opportunism. Anson Chan, however, changes her political philosophy from being a loyal senior civil servant with a relatively independent conscience to being an idealistic democrat determined to jettison political opportunism.

After entering the LegCo, Anson Chan's influence was limited, and later she decided not to run in the 2008 LegCo election. When she became a legislator, Chan criticized her former colleague Stephen Lam for doing nothing on the restriction of exit polls on the voting day because such polls were frequently utilized by pro-Beijing forces to understand the voting behavior of citizens and then reported to the headquarters for mobilization strategies. Chan said angrily in the legislature that she regretted promoting and grooming Lam in the past.[78] The HKSAR government used the excuse of avoiding interference with academic and independent research to adopt a noninterventionist policy toward exit polls on the voting day. This foot-dragging policy continued to favor pro-Beijing groups to use exit polls as tools for mobilization during the legislative and district elections. In the LegCo, Chan played the role of monitoring the government, but the pro-Beijing elites pursued her by digging out her bank loans and mortgages in the past.[79] Under the circumstances in which Chan's influence was curbed, and believing that her withdrawal from electoral politics would pave the way for more young blood in the pan-democratic camp to climb up the political ladder, Anson Chan decided in July 2008 that she would not participate in LegCo elections in September.[80]

Prior to Chan's decision of not running as an incumbent in the 2008 LegCo elections, she and her supporters formed a think tank to engage in political reform discussions and planning activities. On June 17, 2008, Chan held a press conference to announce the establishment of the CCCD, which aimed at not only engaging public discussion on social and political issues, but also encouraging the citizens to shape the future of the government system. Members of the CCCD included barrister Dennis Kwok Wing-hang, DP member Stanley Ng Wing-fai, Senior Counsel Gladys Li, Professor Johannes Chan, George Cautherley, and former deputy secretary for economic services Elizabeth Bosher.[81] The CCCD followed from Chan's creation of her core group in 2006 when the think tank involved Allen Lee Peng-fei, Christine Loh, Lily Yam, and Chandran

Nair.[82] While the core group made presentations to the SDC on its views toward democratic reform, the CCCD is acting as a vehicle for the democrats and the public to explore how the HKSAR can move toward the goal of achieving the election of the chief executive by universal suffrage and the direct election of the entire legislature. The CCCD declared that it would try to ensure the 2012 electoral arrangements would put forward a road map for universal suffrage in both 2017 (for the chief executive election) and 2020 (for the LegCo elections).[83] Anson Chan stressed that the CCCD was not formed for the sake of her electoral participation, and that its birth was due to her perception of the slow progress and limited public outreach of the SDC's political reform committee.

Chan's think tanks like the core group and the CCCD aroused the suspicions of PRC authorities, who think that she may become a tool for foreigners to influence the HKSAR development. This mainland Chinese perception is understandable but mostly inaccurate. Although Chan's core group and the CCCD have the participation of non-Chinese, both George Cautherley and Elizabeth Bosher strongly identify themselves as Hong Kong persons residing in Hong Kong for many years. George Cautherley donated HK$300,000 to Chan's electoral campaign during the 2007 LegCo by-election. Chan gained financial support from a wide spectrum, including HK$250,000 from Heng Seng Bank's honorary director Lee Kwok-wai, HK$65,000 from the DP, HK$50,000 from Ronny Tong and his wife, and HK$15,000 from commentator Leung Man-to.[84] Many Hong Kong people who support Anson Chan have a strong sense of belonging in Hong Kong. Hence, the PRC perception that Chan often gets foreign political and economic support and that she becomes an agent of foreign countries to intervene in Hong Kong politics is undoubtedly hard-line, biased, and xenophobic.

Critics say that Chan's role in Hong Kong's democracy movement is limited because her participation in electoral politics alone could change neither the system nor its political development.[85] While this argument is valid, it turns a blind eye to the fact that Anson Chan's electoral participation and her current think tank activities have tremendous impact on those moderate Hong Kong people. Anson Chan's electoral participation could prompt many civil servants to rethink their role in their careers and future. Many civil servants in the HKSAR did not undergo training in political science, democracy, and human rights. Traditionally they have viewed public criticisms as a huge administrative burden. Many of them see the democrats in LegCo and DC as "troublemakers" making their work more difficult than before. Chan's sudden participation in elections and her changing role as a legislator prompted them to rethink whether civil servants' roles and perspectives are actually one-sided without fully taking into account different arguments, especially from the side where the democratic legislators monitor governmental performance.

Chan's changing role as a think tank director also prompts civil servants, and many citizens who support her, to rethink Hong Kong's political system in the future. If Lily Yam and Elizabeth Bosher as the former senior bureaucrats also joined the Anson Chan core group, it meant that Chan's political metamorphosis acted as a stimulus to encourage some former civil servants to reassess their roles after their retirements or departures from the government. Hence, Chan's electoral participation and her current role in the CCCD have educative impact on some Hong Kong people, especially civil servants who have traditionally lacked a political culture of embracing public criticisms, democracy, and accountability.

A positive but perhaps an accurate view of Anson Chan's contributions to Hong Kong was articulated by Cheung Man-yee, the former director of the RTHK. Cheung argued that Chan's participation in the LegCo by-election aimed to show Beijing that she did have the support of public opinion in Hong Kong.[86] Cheung wrote:

Anson Chan must face the international world. Can we say that the Western world is her shield? She is the darling of the international mass media. Under the circumstances in which "the China threat" is popular, the Western media must be happy to meet and see a challenging "Hong Kong conscience." This cannot be controlled by both Donald Tsang and the PRC side. Also, Mrs. Chan has to show that she can use her capability and influence to force the Chinese side to cooperate with her, and that she is not using confrontations. Furthermore, she can enhance the compromise and coordination with the democratic faction. Some people still hate Mrs. Chan and think that she is "a chess left by the British." In fact, this view is very outdated and the time of putting a label or a hat on someone has long gone.[87]

Cheung's interpretation of Anson Chan as a bridge between Beijing and the pan-democrats is perhaps in conformity with what Chan has in her mind. Although PRC authorities still view Chan as "a chess" utilized by Western countries, they are interested in the CCCD's work and research outcome. Yet, the prospects of Chan-Beijing communications seems to depend on the work of intermediaries, like Hong Kong NPC member Allen Lee, and on whether Beijing's officials will be able to put aside their misperception of Chan as a "chess" used by foreigners and foreign countries to exert pressure on the PRC to democratize the HKSAR. As long as Beijing and Chan have a huge communication gap, the hope of using the CCCD to garner public views on Hong Kong's democratization and then channel their opinions to Beijing would likely encounter political obstacles.

In an interview with the *Asiaweek* in the summer of 2008, Anson Chan revealed her political philosophy that has rarely been understood by the people of Hong Kong, let alone the hard-liners in Beijing. First and foremost, Chan believed that the HKSAR government is not sufficiently tolerant.[88] As a former senior civil servant, Chan actually understands all the inherent problems of the government. She said that the government responded "tardily" to many issues raised by the hard-working pro-democracy legislators, such as inflation, fuel tax, and the sudden creation of political assistants and undersecretaries. Chan thinks that the HKSAR government attaches importance to the use of "political cosmetics," and that good governance requires legislative scrutiny of the government.[89] Chan reacted negatively to the idea of creating a new batch of political assistants and undersecretaries, who to her represented an "executive-hegemonic" system favoring the friends and loyal supporters of the Tsang administration.[90] She believes that Chief Executive Tsang's policy of "distinguishing the relatives from those who are not" represents political intolerance. According to Chan, the government should be "transparent," but the HKSAR administration under Tsang's leadership lacks transparency and tolerance.

Chan has strong opinions on the accountability system adopted by Chief Executive Tung and expanded by his successor Donald Tsang. To Chan, the accountability system implemented in mid-2002 curbed the role and influence of the chief secretary for administration.[91] She questions whether the chief secretary can coordinate various government departments—a role that she assumed when she was the chief secretary. Chan is critical of Tsang, who she thinks should understand the bureaucracy as he also worked as a senior civil servant for a long time. What Chan implies is that Tsang's expansion of the accountability system through the creation of undersecretaries and political assistants actually curbs the role of civil servants. As a result, the chief executive who is not directly elected by citizens through universal suffrage can centralize his or her powers easily, while the politically appointed principal officials reduce the power and influence of senior civil servants, who, according to Chan, has expertise, knowledge, and experience in running the government. Chan bemoans the birth and growth of the accountability system in Hong Kong as the development of a spoils system without democracy.

On her attitude toward Beijing, Chan openly admits that she knows some Hong Kong people bad-mouth her in front of PRC officials and leaders, who do not communicate with her for the sake of understanding the situation.[92] Chan says that her principle is to communicate with Beijing, but she hopes the central government does not listen to the views of only some people. The crux of the problem, to Chan, does not lie with the democrats in Hong Kong. She just sticks to her core values without siding with those who are powerful and influential, and she is working for the interests of Hong Kong without any self-interests.[93] Chan believes that Beijing does not understand her as she is a woman of principles.[94] By implication, Chan might refer to her policy disagreement with Chief Executive Tung in the past, when she spoke her mind without the need to be a yes-woman obeying whatever the superior might think and say. After Chan's electoral victory, Beijing remained unwilling to communicate with her for fear that such dialogue would give credit to the democratic camp.[95] Above all, Beijing's communication with Anson Chan would have the unintended consequence of sidelining pro-Beijing forces in the HKSAR. The politics of communication and Beijing's perception of a zero-sum game in any direct dialogue with Chan are the fundamental obstacles to the prospects of their improved relationships.

In the final analysis, Chan is a moderate and principled democrat. She criticized Raymond Wong's act of hurling bananas at Chief Executive Tsang as "shocking" and putting up a political show before the public.[96] She believes that the struggle for democracy is not necessarily inside the legislature and that achieving it outside, like protests and parade, is feasible.[97] In short, Chan's political vision has much in common with many other democrats, namely the double direct elections of both the chief executive and the entire legislature. Her concept of a satisfactory political system is one in which democracy is entrenched, transparency is observed, tolerance is respected, and legislative scrutiny is necessary to improve governmental performance. Anson Chan can be seen as a liberal-minded democrat who fully understands the inherent problems of governmental secrecy and intolerance.

SUMMARY

It is unfair to overstate the contributions of any leader in Hong Kong's democracy movement because a multiplicity of leaders persists. However, the main architects of the democracy movement in Hong Kong include Martin Lee, Szeto Wah, George Cautherley, Anson Chan, and many other younger leaders such as Albert Ho and Sin Chung-kai. Szeto can be seen as a principled hard-liner in Hong Kong's democracy movement, and he played a critical role in rescuing the mainland democrats from the PRC. His chair position in the Alliance remains significant, educating the younger generation and mainlanders on the Tiananmen tragedy. Martin Lee, on the other hand, provides a model for many young democrats who are lawyers and professionals, because he remains a principled democrat and legal professional respected by not only many Hong Kong people but also foreign countries, leaders, officials, and mass media. While Martin Lee and Szeto Wah contributed significantly to Hong Kong's democracy movement from the 1980s to the 2000s, their work is now picked up by the younger generation of the pan-democrats. Cautherley is playing the behind-the-scenes role as an organizer, fund-raiser, coordinator, and think-tank member. His role as the brainchild of the Hong Kong democracy movement hidden from the public eye is arguably a significant one. Anson Chan understands the meaningful role of being an organizer of Hong Kong's democracy movement, thus fading away from electoral politics and opting for a new path in generating ideas, options, and solutions for Hong Kong's democratization in the years to come. As "the conscience for Hong Kong," Chan's new role in providing alternatives and solutions to Hong Kong's democratic impasse has special meanings for both Hong Kong and China, which should ideally seek compromises on their very different visions of democracy.

CHAPTER 5

From Democratic Defeat in 2007 District Councils Elections to Rebound in 2008 Legislative Council Elections

The Hong Kong style of democracy is characterized by fierce competition at both the LegCo and district level—a phenomenon unseen in mainland China.[1] When the battle for the Tsang reform plan ended in 2005, the pro-Beijing forces had already prepared for a retaliation of their defeat in the 2003 DC elections and launched a full-scale mobilization campaign prior to the 2007 DC elections. The victory of pro-Beijing forces in the 2007 DC elections sent a warning signal to the pan-democrats, who then had a political comeback during the 2008 LegCo elections, when a younger generation of democrats replaced the elder leaders such as Martin Lee and Anson Chan. This chapter focuses on the Hong Kong style of democracy by analyzing the two elections after the return of Hong Kong to the PRC: the 2007 DC elections and the 2008 LegCo elections.

RESULTS OF THE 2007 DISTRICT COUNCILS ELECTIONS

The 2007 DC elections can be seen as a significant electoral victory of the DAB, which grasped only 62 seats in the 2003 DC elections but which captured 115 seats of the total 405 directly elected seats in all the 18 districts during the November 2007 DC elections (see Table 5.1). Out of 405 seats, 41 candidates were automatically elected without any opponent, leaving 364 seats up for grabs by a total of 866 candidates.

In the 2003 DC elections, the DAB defeat by the DP was widely attributable to the immediate impact of the July 1 protest against the Tung administration. The DAB fielded 206 candidates but only 62 won in 2003. Largely due to the widespread public dissatisfaction with the government, the pro-establishment DAB was punished by the voters going to the polls. The DP nominated 120 candidates but succeeded in gaining 95 seats in the 2003 DC elections. However, four years later, the DP only managed to get 59 seats—a reverse of the result compared to the DAB's significant improvement in the 2007 DC elections. The DP performance in 2007 was much worse than its result in the 1999 DC elections, when the party captured 86 seats and slightly outperformed the DAB.

The voter turnout in the 2007 DC elections was only 38 percent, a slight decline in percentage compared to the 2003 figure (see Table 5.2). Although the number of voters in 2007 was 1,140,000 compared with 1,066,373 voters going to the polls in 2003, the small increase did not favor the democrats. Usually, voters in DC elections attach more importance to the candidates' constituency work at the grassroots level. Except for the 2003 DC elections during which some voters were affected by the negative image of the DAB, which was allying with the unpopular Tung regime, voters often judge the candidates in terms of the diligence of their district work, their qualifications and appeals, and whether they can really fight for the interests of residents.

The DAB's success in gaining 115 seats in the 18 DC was attributable to several factors. First and foremost, shortly after the 2003 DC elections, the DAB headquarters and party branches in 18 districts persuaded many of the defeated party candidates to stay working in the same constituencies, preparing a political comeback for the 2007 elections. This strategy worked well because 20 of the 28 candidates who lost in the 2003 elections were elected in 2007—a success rate of 71 percent (see Table 5.3). Chung Kong-mo, who defeated an independent democrat replacing James To of the DP, had actually been paid HK$20,000 per month by the DAB continuously for eight years before he could capture the DC seat in 2007.[2] Chung was only one good example of how the DAB groomed district activists to prepare for their local elections and of the extent to which the party spent considerable financial resources in creating successful local politicians.

Second, the DAB candidates were very diligent in their constituency work. One candidate in Wanchai went out to the street to interact with residents three days per week continuously from 2006 to 2007.[3] Many other DAB candidates acted in a similar way, contacting new immigrants, visiting the homes of voters several times before the elections, helping the elderly, and winning the hearts and minds of their constituents. The DAB arranged all sorts of short-term tours for residents, including one-day tours in the HKSAR, economy tours to visit the mainland, and residents' banquets during holidays.[4] Other pro-Beijing organizations organized

Table 5.1

The Number of Seats Captured by Political Parties in District Councils Elections, 1999–2007

Parties	1999		2003		2007		Total Number of votes
	No. of Nominated Candidates	No. of Elected Candidates	No. of Nominated Candidates	No. of Elected Candidates	No. of Nominated Candidates	No. of Elected Candidates	
DAB	176	83	206	62	177	115	292,925
DP	173	86	120	95	108	59	173,968
LP	34	15	25	12	56	14	50,569
CP	—	—	—	—	41	8	50,216
ADPL	32	19	37	25	37	17	52,386
LSD	—	—	—	—	30	6	33,317
SPI	—	—	—	—	4	2	3,152
The Frontier	9	4	14	7	3	15	18,406

Sources: Ming Pao, November 20, 2007, p. A15; *Sing Tao Daily*, November 20, 2007, p. B5; and *Today Daily News*, November 19, 2007, p. C 4.
Note: DAB stands for the Democratic Alliance for Betterment and Progress of Hong Kong; DP for the Democratic Party; LP for the Liberal Party; CP for the Civic Party; ADPL for the Association for Democracy and People's Livelihood; LSD for the League of Social Democrats; and SPI for the Savantas Policy Institute led by Regina Ip. The Frontier was led by legislator Emily Lau.

Table 5.2

Voter Turnout and the Number of Voters in District Councils Elections, 1982–2007

Year	Number of Voters	Voter Turnout (%)
1982	342,764	38.9
1985	476,558	37.5
1988	424,201	30.3
1991	423,923	32.5
1994	639,548	33.1
1999	816,503	35.82
2003	1,066,373	44.1
2007	1,140,000	38

Source: Ming Pao, November 19, 2007, p. A16.

computer, accounting, and bookkeeping classes for residents so as to win the hearts and the minds of the populace. The DAB even targeted ethnic minorities such as the local Indians, organizing the Young Indian Friends Group to help them learn various languages, including English and Chinese.[5] Conducting endless electioneering work during both the election and non-election time, and gathering the phone numbers and addresses of many residents through these activities, the DAB actually planted considerable "iron votes" without technically violating the election law.

Third, many DAB candidates were young and their educated and youthful looks did appeal to many younger voters. Some young candidates explicitly said that they saw the DAB as having far more political opportunities to climb up the ladder in the future. With the implementation and expansion of the political appointee system, or the Principal Officials Accountability System (POAS), a few young DAB members like Chan Hak-kan and Greg So Kam-leung were selected to serve the Chief Executive Office and the POAS, respectively. As a result, many young DAB candidates saw Chan's experience as a model for them to imitate. In other words, the DAB's succession planning and its policy of promoting the young people to the top leadership and recommending them to the POAS team provided a positive impetus for its young candidates in DC elections. DAB veteran politician Chan Kam-lam successfully groomed a younger candidate, Chan Pak-li, to replace him in the 2007 elections. Above all, 56 percent of the DAB candidates under 40 years old were elected—a satisfactory result for the party.

Fourth, the DAB implemented large-scale publicity in the subway stations and strategically mobilized citizens and its supporters in each of the 18 districts to register as voters. In particular, the DAB targeted the elderly to mobilize them to register as voters and then arranged buses to transport them to the polling stations on voting day. The DAB mobilization tactics were unrivaled; the pan-democrats were loosely organized and failed to mobilize citizens to register as voters in a way as comprehensive as the DAB.

Fifth, the DAB enjoyed the financial and logistical support of the Liaison Office and of the FTU. The PRC officials and agents in the HKSAR did considerable coordination and planning work for DAB candidates in every DC election, thus contributing to the DAB victory.[6] As early as April 2006, the FTU trained 40 young members and activists to prepare for their possible candidacy and campaign assistance work in the 2007 DC elections.[7] In the 2007 DC elections, the FTU acted as an essential auxiliary organization supportive of its friendly party, the DAB, by mobilizing its volunteers and members in electioneering work.

Sixth, the DAB conducted extensive penetrative work at the district level, capturing the Mutual Aid Committees and Owners Corporations of many buildings and thus securing the vehicles of political mobilization before the 2007 DC elections.[8] A case in point was the defeat of DP candidate Fong Lai-man in Tuen Mun. Fong had obtained the support of many housing committees shortly after the 2003 DC elections, but later the DAB infiltrated into many of them and eroded her support considerably.[9] Meanwhile, a crisis consciousness developed among the DAB incumbents and 96 percent of them were reelected, showing the success of their preparatory work. Both incumbents and new candidates were assisted by the electoral strategy of penetrating various housing committees and elderly centers so that the DAB's "iron votes" could be ensured.

Last but not least, the most critical factor leading to the DAB defeat in the 2003 DC elections, namely the unpopularity of the government and the DAB's close relationship with the regime, no longer existed in 2007. The Donald Tsang administration had a relatively high degree of popularity, thereby solving the image problem of the DAB. In terms of the number of votes received by the DAB, it got 250,000 votes in 2003, but the figure rose to 292,000 votes in 2007.

The pan-democratic camp performed poorly in the 2007 DC elections. The DP merely captured 59 of the 405 directly elected seats in the 18 districts, a drastic reduction from the 95 seats it had obtained in 2003. The CP got only 8 candidates elected with a success rate of 19 percent. Its young member Tanya Chan Shuk-chong defeated incumbent Lam Man-kit of the LP by 116 votes in the Peak district on the Hong Kong Island. But its legislator Mandy Tam was defeated in Wong Tai Sin district. The League of Social Democrats captured 6 seats with a success rate of 20 percent. The Frontier performed poorly by maintaining only three seats with a success rate of 20 percent, a significant reduction of four seats compared to the 2003 election result. The ADPL performed unsatisfactorily, reducing its number of seats from 25 in 2003 to 17 in 2007. The success

Table 5.3

The Performance of the Democratic Alliance for Betterment and Progress of Hong Kong in the 2007 District Council Elections

	Number of Candidates	Number of Elected Candidates	Success Rate (%)
Total	177	115	65
Incumbents	67	63	94
Defeated in 2004	28	20	71
New candidates	62	21	34
Candidates under 40 years old	63	35	56

Source: Ming Pao, November 20, 2007, p. A15.

rate of nominated candidates of the ADPL declined from 68 percent in 2003 to 46 percent in 2007. Other individual pan-democrats were defeated, notably Richard Tsoi Yiu-cheong of the Civil Human Rights Front. He was defeated by independent candidate Pong Oi-lan by 180 votes in Shatin district, demonstrating the significant decline in the July 1, 2003, factor during the 2007 DC elections.

Because of the DP's poor performance, its chairman, Albert Ho, offered to resign but his party colleagues persuaded him to stay on. However, election strategist Lee Wing-tat shouldered the responsibility of the election result and resigned from the position. Lee pointed out that 23 incumbent DP candidates were defeated mainly because they were indolent in constituency work.[10] He appealed to James To, the DP legislator, to work harder. To did not even participate in the 2007 DC elections in Kowloon West, leading to widespread criticism that he abandoned the voters. To supported independent democrat Lai Lai-ha to compete with DAB member Chung Kong-mo. But Chung won an easy victory due to his diligent work in the constituency for almost 10 years.[11] Critics of To said that his indolence led to the belief that he would likely be defeated by Chung. Hence, to save face, To did not run in the election and supported a political unknown who actually had little chance to defeat Chung.[12]

Other important DP candidates were defeated, notably Cheung Yin-tang and Chan Kar-wai. Chan was beaten by the pro-Beijing academic and legal expert Priscilla Leung Mei-fun.[13] Cheung's defeat by a young and new DAB candidate Yiu Kwok-wai resulted in a phenomenon that the DP had no elected member working in the critical Tin Shui Wai district where many lower-class citizens are residing and where the DP can forge a closer link with ordinary citizens at the grassroots level. Yiu had been groomed by the DAB to target Cheung as early as 2004, but Cheung was

not politically alert to the DAB plan and his lack of district work contributed to his "surprise" defeat. Another DP veteran in Shatin district,
Ho Shuk-ping, was also defeated by the young and new DAB candidate,
24-year-old Yeung Man-yui, who revealed that he had spent considerable
time to interact with the elderly people in the constituency. Clearly, the
DAB strategically targeted the DP candidates, some of whom did not
really raise their political sensitivity of being ousted by young and new
DAB foes. No wonder an editorial appealed to the DP to review its election
result critically, because "the DP cannot rely on the old assets and yet lack
constituency work." [14] It also ridiculed the trend of "gerontocracy" within
the pro-democracy camp and hoped that the democrats would undergo a
genuine period of rejuvenation. [15]

After the electoral defeat, the DP held a meeting in December 2007 to
review the election strategy. Eleven reformers, including Chan King-ming,
drafted a paper listing eight areas of necessary reforms: (1) the rejuvenation of the leadership; (2) a ban on legislators who would be simultaneously District Council members after 2011; (3) the reestablishment of a
party school to train cadres; (4) the formation of a district development
strategy committee; (5) the need to change election strategy every four
years; (6) the improvement in resources and central-local branches relations; (7) the consolidation of cooperation with people who are not in the
democratic camp; and (8) the strengthening in the study of youth attitudes. [16] The DP leaders who attended the meeting, including Albert Ho,
legislators, and representatives of party branches, listened to the views of
the reformers. Chan King-ming bemoaned the fact that the DP did not
have any innovative image during the 2007 DC elections, except for the
support of double direct elections. Martin Lee warned that the DP might
have to prepare for the worst-case scenario in the 2008 LegCo elections,
and that the pan-democrats might only get a total of 20 seats in the
60-member legislature. [17] Overall, the DP's Young Turks wished to implement new reforms to rejuvenate the party.

Ronny Tong of the CP admitted that his party was unhappy with the
election result and would conduct a review of its performance. However,
Tsang Kwok-fung of the CP put up an impressive performance. He was
defeated by DAB incumbent Lee Kwok-ying in the Tai Po district, but the
1,192 votes he obtained represented a respectable outcome given his first
attempt to run in the election. [18] The victory of Tanya Chan Shuk-chong
in the Peak was critical to the CP, for she would later partner with legislator Audrey Eu to compete in the 2008 LegCo elections. In December 2007,
the CP's party branch in Kowloon East conducted a review and the branch
chairman, Alan Leong, wrote publicly:

The Kowloon East district branch of the CP just held a meeting for evaluating
our performance in the DC elections. Although none of the 7 candidates fielded

by the branch succeeded in getting elected. We are all in very good spirit. We know that for a new party of just over a year old, there is still a long way to go before we can win the hearts and full trust of *kaifongs* (residents). Given our limitations, we consider ourselves not having done too badly. In Ping Shek and Sau Mau Pin, for instance, which are two constituencies used to be firmly controlled by conservative forces, the CP has secured respectively 33% and 40% of the votes cast. In absolute numbers, we have obtained a total of about 11,200 votes in the 7 constituencies. The trust reposed in us as evidenced by these votes provides us with the best platform from which the party could launch other initiatives for better serving the interests of the *kaifongs*. We are determined to build on what we have and strive to earn the confidence of the electorate by tangible deliverables ... The elections have also provided an excellent opportunity for team building. Through working closely together for the elections during the last 6 months to a year, members have a much enhanced understanding of one another. We now know more not only about our own members but also their wives, children and families. The branch has come out of the elections more united and better spirited than ever.[19]

As a new party without any experience in elections, Leong's assessment of the CP performance was a progressive step toward its improvement in electoral contests in the future.

It was noteworthy that democratic independent Ho Wai-to was defeated by DAB candidate Kwok Pit-chun. In September 2004, Ho was arrested by the Dongguan police for soliciting prostitution in the mainland. It was believed that he was politically framed and persecuted, although the mass media and pro-Beijing forces portrayed Ho as committing the "crime." Ho was released in early 2005 and returned to Hong Kong, but he withdrew from the DP and then ran in the 2007 DC election. While Ho defeated Kwok of the DAB in the 2003 DC elections, Kwok gained 3,357 votes and defeated him (2,715 votes) quite easily in the 2007 DC elections. The result showed that Ho's image was tarnished by his scandal and that Kwok remained very strong in Kwun Tong's Shun Tin district where the DAB constituency services for residents persisted despite Kwok's defeat in 2003.[20] Kwok was fully assisted by the FTU, which mobilized staff members and volunteers to participate in his election campaign. While Kwok had a 50-member campaign team, Ho had only 10 members. Although Ho managed to get the support from DP member Li Wah-ming, Kwok secured the DAB star Chan Yuen-han to lobby for the support from residents.[21] On voting day, a heckler remained aggressive toward Ho, staying near him and shouting that Ho went to the mainland to solicit prostitution. This reminder led to a rebuttal from a female voter in support of Ho, saying that "all men look for prostitutes."[22] Although Ho continued to lobby for the support from residents, the heckler's action could constitute an electoral harassment reminding the voters of Ho's scandal and image problem.

Some democrats were severely criticized for failing to deal with the 2007 DC elections seriously. Cyd Ho and her Civic Act-Up performed well in the 2003 DC elections, especially in the Wanchai district, but she as the leader of the group did not even compete in the 2007 DC elections. In 2003, Cyd Ho went to challenge Ip Kwok-him of the DAB in the Kwun Lung constituency on the Hong Kong Island. She defeated Ip narrowly by 64 votes. However, Cyd lost her interest in the District Council affairs, thinking that they were too parochial and therefore deciding not to compete in the 2007 DC elections.[23] Ip returned to run in 2007 and had an easy victory with 2,702 votes against two political unknowns, one named Ho Loyi who gained only 315 votes and the other Leung Kim-kam who managed to get merely 165 votes.[24] The decision of Cyd Ho not to run in the 2007 DC elections tarnished her image. Although she was later reelected to LegCo through direct elections on the Hong Kong Island constituency in 2008, some critics still remember her abandonment of the 2007 DC elections. With the benefit of hindsight, her decision to not run in the 2007 DC elections was strategic as she targeted the upper-level LegCo, but still she had failed to groom any successor to maintain her hard-won seat in the Kwun Lung constituency.

Although the DP performed poorly, it still constituted a formidable force, beating many DAB and LP candidates. Table 5.4 shows that in 56 constituencies where the DP candidates competed with DAB counterparts, 33 DP candidates won and 21 DAB candidates were victorious. The result showed that the DP candidates still showed a strong showing when they confronted DAB competitors. The DAB was much stronger than all other small parties in the HKSAR, including the CP, ADPL, League of Social Democrats (LSD), the Frontier, and the LP. The weakest party that could not compete with the DAB was the CP, whose candidates lacked training, experience, strategy, and any mentorship. The pro-business LP did not appear to be strong at all; its candidates were destined to be defeated by the DAB.

Apart from the unsatisfactory performance of the DP, another devastating defeat in the pan-democratic camp was the ADPL, which was traditionally based in Shumshuipo but which lost eight seats in the 2007 DC elections. Frederick Fung was narrowly elected by only 85 votes in his own constituency. Fung's competitor, Fan Kwok-wai of the DAB, had a strong showing by gaining 700 more votes compared to the 2003 DC elections. Fan's performance surprised Fung, who was saddened by the defeat of several ADPL veterans, such as Leung Lai, Ng Po-shan, and Leung Kam-to. Fung told the media that the DAB had already penetrated many housing estates' committees. At least 400 households in the Shumshuipo district moved out, leading to the influx of new residents who spoke Mandarin and whose political loyalty did not lie with the ADPL.[25] Many of the mainland immigrants who had come to Hong Kong before

Table 5.4

The Performance of Political Parties in Constituencies Where They Competed with Each Other in the 2007 District Councils Elections

Parties in Competition	Number of Constituencies	Results
DAB against DP	56	DP 33 elected DAB 21 elected
DAB against CP	15	DAB 14 elected CP 1 elected
DAB against ADPL	22	DAB 14 elected ADPL 8 elected
DAB against LSD	15	DAB 9 elected LSD 3 elected
DAB against Frontier	8	DAB 5 elected Frontier 2 elected
LP against DP	17	DP 11 elected LP 3 elected
LP against CP	7	CP 3 elected LP 2 elected
LP against ADPL	3	LP 1 elected ADPL 1 elected
LP against DAB	19	DAB 10 elected LP none elected

Note: There might be other candidates running in these constituencies.
Source: Sing Tao Daily, November 20, 2007, p. B4.

2000 could vote in the 2007 DC elections after they obtained Hong Kong identity cards, which are granted to those who reside in the HKSAR continuously for seven years.[26] In fact, urban redevelopment in the Shumshuipo and Shek Kip Mei areas favored the DAB, whose financial resources and diligent grassroots-level work meant that many new residents might have to rely on its work to protect their interests and then become the sources of pro-Beijing votes in DC elections. Saddened by the ADPL performance, Frederick Fung resigned from his position as the party chairman.[27]

TRIADS AND DC ELECTIONS

The 2007 DC elections were marred by violence and triad involvement.[28] Two days before the voting day, a village head named Ku Wah-keung distributed campaign leaflets for two candidates, but then he was attacked by two gangsters and had his finger cut off violently. Ku has been a village head in

Yuen Long's Sung Ching new village since 1995. In 1997 he and his wife were violently attacked by a gangster holding a knife. In the 2007 DC elections, he lobbied for LP candidate Wong Pak-yan in Shap Pat Heung (Eighteen Village) North while simultaneously being a campaign manager for incumbent Lam Tim-fok in Shap Pat Heung South.[29] In response, the police in Yuen Long investigated the incident. Some villagers reported to the police that they were intimidated and asked to vote for a particular candidate. In the HKSAR, village heads are powerful and influential in certifying who lives in the village, approving who can build small houses, understanding the government's land development plan, and interacting with land developers directly on land requisition. Hence, many villagers, especially triad members, wish to become village heads. Traditionally, village elections have remained fiercely competitive in the New Territories, where village candidates utilize personal networks, clan mobilization, and triad influence to get elected in village-level and DC elections.

In response to the violence, police commissioner Tang King-shing said that the event was by no means normal and that his colleagues attached great importance to it. The police arrested a 36-year-old suspect. It was reported that the suspect arrested by the police was a triad member who became active prior to the election.[30] Two triads, namely the 14K and Wo Shing Wo, were competing against each other in Yuen Long.[31] In order to deter electoral violence, the police disrupted a banquet involving a triad official and deployed three constables to guard each voting station in Yuen Long district on the voting day. Reacting to the police crackdown, some triad members expressed their anger by setting two shops and several wooden carts on fire.[32] Clearly, the triad concerned made a "security declaration" to the police force, saying that its members were unhappy about the police action.[33]

POWER AND RESOURCES OF DISTRICT COUNCILS

Although the government vows to enhance the responsibilities and resources of DC, they remain consultative bodies and their limited powers perpetuate the sense of political powerlessness on the part of their elected members. Wu Chi-wai of the DP, who got 4,300 votes and was elected in the 2007 DC elections, said that the constituencies of DC are very small but the government often delays its response to the demands of councilors. As a result, he feels politically frustrated and the resources for the council have been wasted.[34] An editorial in *Ming Pao* also appealed to the HKSAR government to enhance the power of DC, abolish the appointed seats made to each of the 18 Councils after the elections, and empower the Council members so that they would be able to work more effectively for the people's livelihood.[35] The suggestion here is that the more powerful DC would attract more professionals and educated candidates to participate in elections, thus realizing the principle of allowing Hong Kong citizens to manage their own affairs.[36] In fact, barrister Ronny Tong of the CP also suggested that the number of District Council members should be reduced by half and that their salaries should be increased to HK$30,000 so as to attract local talent to participate in DC elections.[37]

After the elections, the HKSAR government has empowered DC by allowing them to manage public libraries, entertainment centers and arenas, and sports facilities, and to decide the fees charged to citizens using district swimming pools. Moreover, the government slightly increased its subsidies to DC, such as the allocation of HK$3 billion for "small projects" in various districts and the rise in each councilor's subsidy from HK$17,000 to HK$18,000 per month.[38] The chief executive would also attend an annual meeting with all the DC members so as to improve the links between the government at the top and DC at the grassroots level.[39] Finally, the government planned that high-level officials, including the politically appointed secretaries, would attend DC meetings so as to empower the councils.

Still, the status and image of some District Council members have been tarnished by various scandals involving their misuse of public money. The problematic integrity of DC members includes all political parties, but it seems that coincidentally the pan-democratic parties appear to be most affected and commonly pursued by the Independent Commission Against Corruption (ICAC).[40] DP members Fung King-man and Lau Ting-bong were arrested in January 2006, together with independent Council member Luk Wai-kong, for "deceiving rental subsidies."[41] Fung was later convicted. Another case involved independent democrat Ng Chung-tak, who was imprisoned immediately for 18 months for squeezing HK$114,000 subsidies from the District Council for personal use.[42] The court judge also criticized Ng for exploiting his assistant because he did not pay the assistant a monthly amount that he reported to the Council.

POLITICAL APPOINTEES AND INTERNAL RIVALRIES IN DISTRICT COUNCILS

In the wake of the election, the HKSAR government appointed 102 DC members to 18 districts. Of the 102 appointees, 28 (27 percent) came from the pro-establishment camp, including 13 members from the DAB, 13 from the LP, and 2 from the FTU. In 2003, only 8 LP members were appointed, but the number increased to 13 in 2007. Yeung Sum of the DP criticized such appointments as political patronage, but the government responded to his criticism and asserted that the appointees were selected from various occupational sectors, such as education, social work, and business.[43] However, Wong Sing-chi of the DP severely criticized the

government for appointing some members who had been defeated in pre-
vious DC elections.[44] Lee Wing-tat of the DP said that this government
move aimed at balancing the influence of the democrats and preventing
them from grasping any DC chair in the upcoming internal elections of
the chairpersons in all 18 councils.

In January 2008, DC members elected the chairs and deputy chairs of
each of the 18 districts, but the democrats were utterly defeated and
failed to occupy any chair positions. Although the role of chairs and
deputy chairs are more symbolic than substantial, they do have the
influence to decide the priority of agendas in DC meetings and can
attend the higher-level District Management Committees, which coordinates with government departments and hammer out policy priorities in
the allocation of resources to all districts. In Table 5.5, 7 of the 18 chairs
were from the DAB. The LP got two chair positions. Moreover, the DAB
grasped 5 deputy chairs while the pro-democracy ADPL merely
obtained the deputy chairmanship in Shumshuipo. It was reported that
Tam Kwok-kiu of the ADPL was at loggerheads with the DP member
Man Tak-chuen, who turned to support appointee Chan Tung as the
chair. Although DP chair Albert Ho called Man and expressed his dissatisfaction with the latter's decision, the damaged relations between
the DP's party branch in Shumshuipo and the ADPL became irrepa-
rable.[45] The DP's party branch in the Northern district was so unhappy
with the appointee system that it boycotted the election of the chair and
deputy chair.[46] In fact, 6 of the 18 chairs were appointees, indicating that
the appointee system did have an impact on balancing the influence of
the democrats in DC.

THE DEMOCRATIC REBOUND IN THE 2008 LEGISLATIVE COUNCIL ELECTIONS

Although there were widespread predictions that the pan-democrats
would perform unsatisfactorily in the upcoming 2008 LegCo elections
because of their poor showing in the 2007 DC elections, the 2008 election
results showed that they managed to grasp 19 seats in direct elections
and 4 seats in functional constituency elections (see Table 5.6). With a total
number of 23 seats, the pan-democrats can vote against government initiatives in putting forward any political reform plan, such as the 2005
abortive Tsang reform blueprint. Although the pro-Beijing *Wen Wei Po*
claimed that the DAB garnered 13 seats in the 60-member legislature,
the claim was a bit over-stated because it appeared to count other allies
of the DAB, such as Cheung Hok-ming and Regina Ip.[47]

Table 5.6 shows that the pan-democrats actually became increasingly
influential in terms of its number of legislators in the 60-member chamber
from 1999 to 2008. Its number actually rose from 19 in 1999 to 21 in 2000

Table 5.5

The Distribution of Chairs and Deputy Chairs in the 18 District Councils after the 2007 Elections

District	Chair	Background	Deputy Chairs	Background
Central	Chan Tak-chor	LP	Chan Chit-kwei	Independent
Eastern	Ting Yuk-chu	Appointed	Chung Shu-kan	DAB
Southern	Ma Yuet-ha	Independent	Chu Hing-hung	Independent
Wanchai	Suen Kai-cheong	DAB	Ng Kam-chun	Independent
Kowloon City	Wong Kwok-keung	Appointed	Lau Wai-wing	Independent
Yau Tsim Mong	Chung Kwong-mo	DAB	Leung Wai-kuen	Independent
Shumshuipo	Chan Tung	Appointed	Tam Kwok-kiu	ADPL
Wong Tai Sin	Lee Tak-hong	DAB	Wong Kam-chi	Independent
Kwun Tong	Chan Chun-bun	Appointed	So Lai-chun	Independent
Tai Po	Cheung Hok-ming	Appointed DAB	Man Chun-fai	Ex-officio
Tuen Mun	Lau Wong-fat	Ex-officio and LP	Leung Kin-man	DAB
Yuen Long	Leung Chi-cheung	DAB	Tang Yan-chor	Ex-officio
Northern	So Sai-ch	DAB	Hau Chi-keung	Ex-officio
Sai Kung	Ng Si-fook	DAB	Wan Yuet-kau	DAB
Shatin	Wai Kwok-hung	Civil Power*	Thomas Pang	DAB
Tsuen Wan	Chow Hau-ching	Appointed	Chung Wai-ping	Ex-officio
Kwai Ching	Tang Kwok-kwong	Ex-officio	Mak Mei-kuen	Independent
Island	Lam Wai-keung	Ex-officio	Chow Chuen-heung	DAB

*Civil Power is a district group formed by DAB member Lau Kong-wah in the Shatin district with the objective of securing the supporters of voters for his legislative elections.
Note: Ex-officio refers to those chairpersons of the 27 Rural Committees, and they must have seats in the District Councils located in the New Territories. The Civil Power is led by DAB member Lau Kong-wah in the Shatin district.
Source: Ming Pao, January 11, 2008, p. A15.

and to 23 in 2004, and the 2004 figure was actually maintained in 2008. Arguably, without the functional constituencies that have traditionally retained the seats for pro-government forces, the entire LegCo could have been captured by a democratic majority easily. The proportion of total number of legislative seats obtained by the pan-democrats has been much

Table 5.6

The Legislative Council Elections Results from 1999 to 2008

Parties	1998			2000			2004		2008	
	GCa	FC	EC	GC	FC	EC	GC	FC	GC	FC
Pro-government camp										
DAB/FTU	5	3	3	6	4	1	9	3	8	3
HKPA	—	2	2	1	1	2	—	—	—	—
LP	—	8	—	—	8	—	2	8	—	7
Non-democratic Independents	1	12	3	1	12	3	1	12	3	16
Pro-democracy camp										
DPb	8	4	—	9	3	—	7	2	7	1
ADPL	—	—	—	1	—	—	1	—	1	1
Frontier	2	—	—	2	—	—	1	1	1	—
ACC/CP	—	—	—	—	—	—	1	1	4	1
Pro-democracy Independents	4	1	—	4	2	—	6	4	6	1

Parties	1998		2000				2004		2008		
Total	20	30	10	24	30	6	30	30	30	30	30

[a]GC: geographical constituencies; FC: functional constituencies; EC: Electoral College or Committee.
[b]The areas under "pro-democracy camp" represent the gains of the pro-democracy forces.

Sources: Sing Tao Daily, September 8, 2008, p. B4; and Joseph Y. S. Cheng, "Hong Kong's Democrats Stumble," *Journal of Democracy*, vol. 16, no. 1 (January 2005), p. 140.

Note: DAB represents the Democratic Alliance for Betterment and Progress of Hong Kong; FTU—Federation of Trade Unions; HKPA—Hong Kong Progressive Alliance; LP—Liberal Party; DP—Democratic Party; ADPL—Association for Democracy and People's Livelihood; ACC—Article 45 Concern Group, which later became the Civic Party (CP). Pro-democracy independents include the Hong Kong Confederation of Trade Unions (CTU) led by Lee Cheuk-yan and also the Neighborhood and Worker's Service Center led by Leung Yiu-chung.

less than that obtained by them in direct elections. Table 5.7 shows that in 1998, the democrats received almost 66 percent of the votes in direct elections but they captured only 31.6 percent of the total seats in the legislature, a gap of 34 percent. The gap became narrower in 2000, and increasingly in 2004 and 2008 as the pro-Beijing forces became stronger in direct elections. Still, in 2008, the democrats got 58 percent of the votes in direct elections but only got 38 percent of the total seats in the legislature. Hence, the democrats actually remain the most popular forces in Hong Kong's direct elections, but the existence of functional constituencies reduces their ability to capture a proportional number of total seats in the legislature.

The politically artificial constraint on the ability of democrats to capture political power is evident. Still, the democrats target obtaining at least 20 seats in the 60-member legislature so as to check the government's political reform bill. As Annex 2 of the Basic Law states, any amendment on the methods of forming the legislature after 2007 needs to cross three hurdles: two-thirds majority support of the legislature, the approval of the chief executive, and the endorsement of the NPC Standing Committee. The democrats still hold the power to vote against any amendment they deem as unsatisfactory, thus exercising its negative veto, as with the case of the abortive 2005 Tsang reform plan demonstrated. Because of the institutional mechanism laid down by the Basic Law, the tug of war between the democrats and pro-government forces is destined to be tense and serious not only during legislative elections but also inside the law-making chamber.

Legislative elections are critical to Hong Kong's politics and democratization. Apart from the need for the democrats to control at least

Table 5.7

The Proportion of Direct Elections Votes and of Total Legislative Seats Captured by Pro-Democracy Forces

Year	Voters	Turnout (%)	Percentage of Total Votes (a)	Total Number of Seats	Percentage of Total Seats (b)	Difference in Percent (a) – (b)
2008	1,524,249	45.2	58	23	38.3	19.7
2004	1,784,406	55.64	61.34	23	38.3	23
2000	1,331,080	43.57	61.87	19	31.6	30.27
1998	1,489,705	53.29	65.94	19	31.6	34.34

Sources: Ming Pao, September 8, 2008, p. A12; *Sing Tao Daily*, September 9, 2008, p. B4; and Suzanne Pepper, *Keeping Democracy at Bay: Hong Kong and the Challenge of Chinese Political Reform* (Lanham, MD: Rowman & Littlefield, 2008), p. 379.

one-third of the LegCo seats, the election result represents a barometer of the popularity of pro-government and pro-democracy camps. The task of the DAB/FTU coalition is to check the ability of the democrats to capture more directly elected seats, while functional constituencies are critical to the checks and balances on the democrats within the legislature. Therefore, the PRC authorities and the HKSAR government have no incentive to abolish functional constituencies, at least in the foreseeable future. No wonder the NPC Standing Committee's interpretation of the Basic Law in April 2004 stressed that in 2008 "the ratio between members returned by functional constituencies and members returned by geographical constituencies through direct elections, who shall respectively occupy half of the seats, is to remain unchanged. The procedures for voting on bills and motions in the LegCo are to remain unchanged." [48] Annex 2 of the Basic Law states that bills initiated by the government need the approval of over half of the legislators, while bills and motions initiated by individual legislators need the majority approval of colleagues from each of the two sectors: those elected from geographical constituencies and those returned from functional constituencies. This mechanism can check the power of the pro-democracy legislators who wish to initiate bills and motions contrary to the whims of the HKSAR government or Beijing.

The 2008 LegCo elections were significant in several aspects. First and foremost, the democrats envisaged generational changes. With the stepping down of Martin Lee from direct elections, young DP member Kam Nai-wai managed to be elected on the Hong Kong Island, together with democratic independent Cyd Ho who had abandoned the 2007 DC elections. Many other democratic parties had generational transformations, such as Audrey Eu's young partner Tanya Chan who had won in the 2007 DC elections in the Peak constituency. Another newly elected democrat was Raymond Wong, who was directly elected in Kowloon West and whose criticisms of the CP list led by Claudia Mo worsened the relations between Wong's LSD and Mo's CP. During the election campaign, Wong fiercely attacked the DAB and his criticisms became a popular video clip in YouTube.[49] Finally, former democratic unionist Lau Chin-shek was defeated in Kowloon West, partly because he lacked constituency work and partly because his political orientations appeared to be diluted in view of the PRC's co-optation efforts at wooing him. Although Lau tried his best to mobilize voters to support him in the days before the election, his appeals and efforts became too little, too late.[50]

Second, generational changes could also be seen in the pro-Beijing camp. The DAB veteran Lau Kong-wai managed to be directly elected alongside with the young Gary Chan Hak-kan in the New Territories East constituency. Moreover, Starry Lee Wai-ling of the DAB was for the first time directly elected to the legislative chamber in the Kowloon

West constituency. The FTU veteran Chan Yuen-han was deliberately ranked second to the first candidate, Wong Kwok-kin. Wong was elected, but the DAB list failed to get Chan reelected.

Third, the DAB actually made a strategic error by merging Choy So-yuk with Jasper Tsang to run in the Hong Kong Island. While Tsang was elected, his party list failed to bring Choy into the legislature. If the DAB was split into two lists to compete in the Hong Kong Island, Choy's chance could have been better. Even worse, because the DAB supported pro-Beijing independent Regina Ip to compete with pro-democracy and former chief secretary Anson Chan during the by-election held for the LegCo in 2007, some of the pro-DAB votes in 2008 shifted to support Ip rather than the Tsang list. Furthermore, the DAB support of Ip in the 2007 by-election disappointed its member Chung Shu-kan, who worked hard at the district level, who wishes to be a legislator, but who was persuaded to let Ip compete with Anson Chan. Chung was not only upset but was ranked number three in the DAB list after Jasper Tsang and Choy So-yuk. This meant that Chung's chance of being elected as a legislator in 2008 was almost zero. As a result, Chung wished to withdraw from the DAB but he was persuaded not to do so.[51] Furthermore, the electoral competition between the DAB list led by Jasper Tsang and independent Regina Ip favored independent democrat Cyd Ho, whose victory was anticipated by a pubic opinion survey at the University of Hong Kong.[52] The conservative, timid, and problematic ways in which the DAB dealt with its strategy in the Hong Kong Island constituency in 2008 left much to be desired.

Fourth, the defeat of LP chair James Tien and veteran Selina Chow in direct elections sounded an alarm bell to the pro-business party and signaled a setback in promoting business participation in Hong Kong's democratization. Tien gained 28,875 votes and failed to be reelected in the New Territories East, while Chow obtained 21,570 votes and also failed to return to the legislature. Critics believe that the LP lacked constituency work and it did not appear to acquire the full support of the rural advisory body, HYK, whose mass mobilization could have helped the two LP heavyweights. Instead, the HYK supported Cheung Hok-ming to run in a DAB ticket led by Tam Yiu-chung. Both Tam and Cheung were elected, thus depriving the chance of Chow to be elected in the New Territories West constituency. Tien's defeat could also be attributable to the competition with independent but charismatic Pong Oi-lan, who garnered 20,455 votes in the New Territories East for the first time she ran in direct elections. Overall, the LP's fiasco in direct elections sent an ominous signal to Hong Kong's democratization. If the business leaders like Tien and Chow were defeated in direct elections, other business elites would see universal suffrage as a threat to their status, influence, and power.

Democratization in the HKSAR would need to calm the fears of not only Beijing but also the business sector. Beijing and the HKSAR government, which is bound to look to the north for final decisions, are reluctant to accept a faster pace and wider scope of democratization in the HKSAR unless three conditions would be met. First, the pro-Beijing forces led by DAB and FTU can perform well in direct elections and even grasp more directly elected seats than all the pan-democrats. Second, the business elites can develop their confidence in direct elections and do not see universal suffrage as a menace to their interests. Third, the democrats can really be checked by the pro-establishment camp so that they cannot capture a majority in the legislature. The last condition— democrats failing to grasp a majority—is fulfilled so long as functional constituencies are maintained. If functional constituencies were abolished, there would be a realistic possibility that the democrats would capture the legislative majority. How to replace functional constituencies by any other electoral methods that can safeguard the elections and interests of the business elites and pro-Beijing forces remain a baffling problem, which is, however, politically unacceptable to most democrats. Some business elites have suggested the adoption of a bicameral system for the HKSAR where a second chamber can be made up of business elites and occupational representatives while the first chamber can be fully directly elected.[53] Moreover, the second chamber may have the power of "special veto."[54] The balance of power between the two chambers will have to be worked out carefully. Otherwise the democrats may regard the bicameral model as a perpetuation of the current functional constituencies. From the perspective of minimizing any amendment to the Basic Law, the bicameral model is complicated and may necessitate more legalistic and technical amendments than what the business elites who advocate it may assume.

Two noteworthy events took place in the 2008 LegCo elections. The first was an accusation made by James Tien shortly after his defeat that the Liaison Office interfered with the elections. He claimed that the Liaison Office did not support him and Selina Chow, but it backed up independent candidate Priscilla Leung Mei-fun who was eventually directly elected. The involvement of the Liaison Office in Hong Kong's electoral politics is not new, for the agency regularly has staff members coordinating candidates in the pro-Beijing camp and providing logistical support as well as planning work. One candidate in the health functional constituency, namely Ho Pak-leung, was reportedly gaining the support and lobbying efforts from the Liaison Office.[55] An editorial in *Ming Pao* appealed to the Liaison Office to refrain from intervening in Hong Kong's elections.[56] However, it is often neglected that the participation of the Liaison Office in Hong Kong's elections, both legislative and district levels, belong to a constitutional convention in the HKSAR.[57]

Another controversial issue in the 2008 LegCo elections focused on public opinion polls. It was an open secret that many pro-Beijing candidates and forces utilized research organizations as a means to conduct exit polls outside the voting stations on the election day of both the 2007 DC elections and the LegCo by-election in Hong Kong Island in 2008. The students conducting the polls reported the findings, especially the voting decisions of the voters, immediately to the headquarters of pro-Beijing organizations, which in turn provided the updated information to the DAB and FTU for mass mobilization so as to maximize the chance of electoral victory of their candidates.[58] The pro-democracy legislators took the complaint about the misuse of exit polls to the government. In response, the Electoral Affairs Commission (EAC), which handles electoral matters and complaints, eventually tightened the guidelines governing exit polls. The new guidelines stated that any organization and individual have the right to freely collect election data, but they have to apply to the EAC for such research at least 10 days before the voting day. Furthermore, the researchers conducting the exit polls outside the voting stations will have to carry identification saying that they do not represent the government. The mass media cannot release the election results before the election; otherwise they will be "reprimanded severely."[59] The EAC's amendment of the guidelines was criticized by some democrats as minimal because they are by no means legally binding. The impact on any organization using exit polls for the political objective of mass mobilization was negligible.

Robert Chung of the University of Hong Kong, who conducted exit polls during Hong Kong's elections since the 1980s, announced in late August 2008 that he would release the exit polls results at noon, in the afternoon at 5 pm, and at night at 9 pm and 11 pm.[60] Chung's announcement angered some local academics and many critics, who said that his move would still provide a golden opportunity for pro-Beijing and pro-government forces to utilize polls for political ends.[61] The EAC responded to Chung's move in a very weak manner, only repeating that the mass media's reports of exit polls results would be severely reprimanded. When Chung held a press conference to explain his moves, democrat Emily Lau and the CP campaign team suddenly attended it and took note of his remarks.[62] Anson Chan, Audrey Eu of the CP, and Sin Chung-kai of the DP criticized the EAC for adopting a noninterventionist policy toward exit polls.[63] At the same time, political scientist Li Pang-kwong criticized Chung and said that he should release the data at 9 pm so as to minimize any impact on the misuse of polls results by both the media and any political groups.[64] An editorial in *Ming Pao* also criticized Chung for making an error of judgment and appealed to him to rectify his own mistake.[65] Under a barrage of public criticisms, Chung decided to release the data once and for all at 8 pm.[66] His fluctuating decision and minor concession alienated some democrats, who held a press conference to appeal to all the voters not to answer any question from researchers conducting the exit polls on the voting day.[67] The entire saga demonstrated Chung's error of judgment and the EAC's basically *laissez faire* policy toward exit polls.

The EAC's noninterventionist policy toward exit polls was harmful to the fairness of elections, while Chung's rigidity led to the inaccuracy of exit polls after they were severely criticized by politicians and after many citizens refused to answer questions from pollsters on voting day.[68] Chung himself said after the election that he would perhaps terminate exit polls research four years later.[69] Ultimately, the EAC should review its noninterventionist policy toward exit polls. As an editorial stated,

Table 5.8

The Restrictions on Exit Polls During Elections in Different Countries

Nation	Banned Period before Voting Day	Exit Polls	Penalty on Any Violation
Albania	5 days before voting day	Banned	Fines
Australia	No banned period	No restriction	Nil
Bulgaria	14 days before voting day	Banned	Fines
Canada	Banned on voting day	Banned	Nil
Czechoslovakia	7 days before voting day	Banned	Nil
France	On voting day	Banned	Fines
India	No banned period	No restriction	Nil
Italy	15 days before voting day	Banned	Nil
Peru	15 days before voting day	Banned	Fines
Russia	5 days before voting day	Banned	Nil
Singapore	Banned in the entire election	Banned	Fines and Imprisonment
South Africa	No banned period	Banned	Nil
Sweden	Voluntarily stopped one day before voting day	Cannot release data before the voting stations are closed	Nil
United Kingdom	No banned period	Cannot release data before the voting stations are closed	Nil
United States	No banned period	No restriction	Nil

Source: Sing Tao Daily, March 14, 2008, p. B5.

The EAC should shoulder the responsibility of not being responsive and failing to attach importance to the controversies over exit polls. After the DC elections last year, some people raised the issue of exit polls being utilized as a tool for electoral mobilization. The authorities concerned should pay attention to this. But after review and discussion, both the government and the EAC decided not to regulate exit polls. Eventually, the situation deteriorated. After this election, the EAC should review thoroughly the electoral arrangements, including the regulations on exit polls and the functions and operations of the polls, so that elections would be fair and just.[70]

In a commentary, Ronny Tong of the CP compared the noninterventionist policy toward exit polls in Hong Kong with other countries (see Table 5.8). As a matter of fact, many Western democracies, such as Canada, France, Italy, and Russia, banned exit polls, whereas Sweden and the United Kingdom have restrictions on the timing of the release of such polls. Hence, the Hong Kong EAC's noninterventionist policy toward exit polls fails to be in conformity with the global trend. Tong revealed that during the 2007 DC elections, Tsang Kwok-fung of the CP was defeated by Lee Kwok-ying of the DAB in Tai Po partly because of the DAB mobilization of citizens in the last two hours of the voting period and partly because Lee made use of such exit polls as a vehicle to tap the voters' behavior and trends.[71]

SUMMARY

Unlike Taiwan where the opposition Democratic Progressive Party began to obtain elected seats from city and county councils from the 1980s to the 1990s and then encircled the ruling KMT by winning more directly elected seats in the Legislative Yuan, the Hong Kong political opposition tended to capture considerable votes first in the legislature. In the HKSAR, the democratic camp remains influential in the legislative elections because it could garner about 60 percent of the votes in direct elections. Frightened by the strong showing of the democrats, Beijing and the pro-government forces in the HKSAR have to maintain functional constituencies, mobilize the DAB/FTU to check them in direct elections, and delay the pace of democratic reforms as long as possible. In the HKSAR, although the democrats have not performed impressively in DC elections, DC remain advisory and lack political power and substantial financial resources. Still, most political parties assume that, by capturing as many votes as possible in each of the 18 DC, they can entrench their power base securely at the district level and build up the electoral support for their candidates in LegCo's direct elections. This assumption is particularly held by the DAB and FTU because of their strong financial resources and manpower. On the contrary, the lack of financial resources and manpower means that the pan-democrats tend to rely on political stars, ideological appeals, and comprehensive policy platforms to acquire the votes from citizens during the LegCo direct elections. The democrats leave the task of diligent constituency work to their district activists, who actually face a formidable task to compete with the DAB and FTU. Partly because of the lack of resources and partly because of the limited powers of DC, some democrats at the district level find it difficult to maintain their elected positions and power base. Critics can easily point to the lack of leadership and organization on the part of the democrats, but they often fail to appreciate the fact that the pro-democracy camp is facing an uphill battle to compete with the pro-Beijing DAB and FTU, which are both enjoying the full financial and logistical support of Beijing and its representative Liaison Office in the HKSAR. In a sense, the pan-democrats have to compete with "the state machinery"—an impossible task for them to win the battle.[72] The fact that the democrats could still garner almost 60 percent of the votes in direct elections was arguably an impressive result amidst the tremendous political constraints.

The phenomenon that the DAB and FTU have to compete with the relatively strong democratic camp is a situation drastically different from the CCP in the PRC. The CCP in the mainland has been enjoying hegemony and political power to such an extent that it is often unchallenged in local elections. At best, some independent candidates run in village elections to challenge CCP-backed candidates. Still, in terms of political learning, the DAB and FTU have been adapting to Hong Kong's pluralistic setting and improving their electoral gains with the passage of time. This improvement in their electoral performance and their coexistence with the democratic opposition has significant implications for the mainland. If the PRC were to implement democratic and electoral reforms further, the CCP would have to learn from the Hong Kong case in allowing more political space for any opposing groups and candidates to participate in mainland elections. In other words, the Hong Kong model of political tolerance and electoral contests can be tested in the PRC, especially if the CCP decides to liberalize the political system and allow more electoral competition at the village, township, and county levels in the future. In short, the Hong Kong experience can provide a useful lesson for the PRC's long process of democratization.

CHAPTER 6

The Hong Kong Democratic Party

Critics of Hong Kong's political parties refer to the lack of leadership, resources, research capability, and above all the failure to grasp political power as the reasons for their underdevelopment.[1] The structural deficiency of Hong Kong's semidemocratic political system is arguably characterized by the absence of any party in power, not even reaching the critical democratizing threshold of rotating the political party in power as mentioned by political scientist Samuel Huntington.[2] The impossibility of coming to power means that political parties must lack sufficient financial resources to grow, and their leadership problem is perpetuated. Businesspeople are not interested in funding political parties, which to them are weak and relatively unnecessary in Hong Kong's already business-dominated political system. Although some businesspeople make their donations to the pro-business LP and pro-Beijing DAB, many of them see donations to the pan-democratic parties as carrying the political risk of antagonizing the PRC government and the Liaison Office. With the exceptions of the LP and the DAB, which enjoy the financial resources from big business and Beijing, respectively, all the pan-democratic parties have financial problems. Businesspeople who are willing to support the pan-democratic parties financially prefer to be low profile without being identified by the Liaison Office and PRC officials dealing with Hong Kong matters. The pan-democratic parties, and the LP, remain cadre or small parties in the HKSAR.

The DP, which was formed in October 1994, remains the flagship in the democratic camp. As of November 2008, it only had 688 members.[3] The party is bound to be a political opponent because of the structural setup of the LegCo in which members returned from functional constituencies must check those returned from direct elections. Above all, Tsang's policy of favoring his own friends and supporters means that the government is biased against the DP. Szeto Wah of the DP Central Standing Committee urged Chief Executive Tsang to "attach importance to those who have merit and distance himself from the cronies."[4]

THE POLITICS OF SUCCESSION PLANNING

After the DP's unimpressive performance in the September 2004 LegCo elections, the party planned to groom a new and younger tier of leaders, but there was dissatisfaction among some party members. One member said: "Even in China, Jiang Zemin had to step down, but Yeung Sum of our party does not. Also, if you take a look at the DAB, its young people have lots of opportunities to climb up the political ladder. The DAB has a comprehensive plan to groom them."[5]

When Martin Lee decided not to run in the 2008 LegCo election and mentioned that the DP could let the CP take the leadership of the democratic camp, his comments raised the eyebrows of some DP members.[6] To some DP members, Lee's announcement of not running dealt the party a blow. Adding salt to the wound was his suggestion that the DP could cooperate with the emergent CP. DP member Mak Hoi-wah said that Lee's comments hurt the feelings of DP members. In response, Lee emotionally said that the DP members should not distinguish themselves from the like-minded CP. Lee defended that a father must not let his son suffer, implying that he himself was protective of the DP. Still, some DP members viewed Lee's remark in the mass media as going a bit too far. Even the deputy chairman of the CP, Albert Lai, said that Lee's remarks might be embarrassing to the DP members who contributed much to the party's development.[7] Lee's positive comment on the potential role of the CP to lead the pan-democratic camp could be traced back to his idea that, when Anson Chan participated in the by-election held for the LegCo's Hong Kong Island constituency, he did not exclude the possibility of a merger between the DP and CP.[8]

Lee's decision to step down from legislative elections opened the door for not only leadership succession but also more young party members to fight for democracy in the HKSAR in the long run. Critics of Lee and Szeto Wah say that their rigid position has been "an obstacle" to Hong Kong's democratization and that Lee's departure from electoral politics was perhaps a good sign for the party to ponder new ideas and ways of moving forward. An editorial of *Ming Pao* said,

In the past, Martin Lee and Szeto Wah were located at a special historical time span, especially the June 4th incident. In addition, their personal capacity and conditions created their status as the Godfathers of the democratic camp. This background enables them to acquire the support of public opinion to deal with

Beijing in the democratizing tug-of-war. But to some extent this may also hamper the progress of democratization . . . The diligent work of Martin Lee and Szeto Wah in Hong Kong's democratization is absolutely confirmed and their contribution must be included in historical record. The new democratic camp does not have any historical burden. Without charismatic leadership, its members will have to retain Hong Kong's core values while at the same time considering the agendas of establishing new horizons, new thinking, and new methods to catch the pulse of Hong Kong and to construct a dynamic relationship with the central government. It is also time for the central government to adopt a more open-minded acumen to tolerate the Hong Kong democrats so as to create a consensual and harmonious society.[9]

Although *Ming Pao* has been adopting a political stance much closer to Beijing than the pre-1997 era, its comments on Lee's and Szeto's fading role in Hong Kong's democracy are valid, especially the insight that Lee's departure from electoral politics forces the new generation of democrats to ponder any new strategies of coping with Beijing and Hong Kong's democratization.

In May 2008, in order to avoid the DP's internal struggle, Sin Chung-kai decided to let Kam Nai-wai run for the direct election on the Hong Kong Island. Sin announced that he withdrew from the party's internal election mechanism. In March 2008, Martin Lee decided not to run for the LegCo elections on the Hong Kong Island constituency. He then supported Sin to abandon the information technology functional constituency, where Sin was elected to the LegCo, and to replace him.[10] Sin intended to shift to the Hong Kong Island, but the DP's Hong Kong Island branch felt that Martin Lee's personal whims should not override its collective discussions. It was reported that the party branch members even planned to veto Sin's attempt at running in the Hong Kong Island during the branch meeting in mid-May.[11] Other DP leaders such as Albert Ho, Tik Chi-yuen, Lee Wing-tat, and Cheung Man-kwong understood the importance of retaining the morale of the Hong Kong Island branch. At the party's members meeting in March 2008, it was decided tentatively that there would be two lists running in the Hong Kong Island, with one led by Sin Chung-kai and Lai Chi-keung. But this decision would have to be ratified and confirmed by the party branch meeting in mid-May. Seeing that Martin Lee stepped down and his change of constituency not only affected the chance of Kam Nai-wai but also prompted the opposition from the Hong Kong Island branch, Sin decided not to run in the internal election. The 47-year-old Sin was one year younger than Kam, and his temporary withdrawal from both the functional and geographical constituency elections in 2008 meant that he would serve the DP in another way in the short run. The decision of Sin was important in two aspects: Martin Lee's personal wish could not override the intention and decisions of the Hong Kong Island branch, and his strategic withdrawal aimed at maintaining party unity, especially on the Hong Kong Island where Lai Chi-keung, who later wanted to run on two separate party lists but was not allowed to do so, decided to quit the party. Originally, the media speculated that Kam's low popularity rate would not help him win a seat in the September 2008 LegCo election.[12] But as it turned out, he could win and thereby demonstrated the bold but very farsighted decision of Sin Chung-kai, who gave Kam the chance to climb up the political ladder.

Preparing for the DC elections in the future, the DP has combined the three tactical aspects of training, assessment, and selection so that its members will be able to compete with the DAB in district-level elections. The DP's Party School principal Yeung Sum said that the party used the three mechanisms so as to dilute the negative image of having mentors or "big brothers" who have traditionally cultivated their friends and followers to enhance influence and prestige in a particular district constituency. This "big brother" system, to Yeung, contributes to the development of personal rule within the DP—a phenomenon criticized by party members and outsiders.[13]

Yeung revealed that with the stepping down of veterans such as Martin Lee, Sin Chung-kai, and himself, the Party School has more manpower while inviting friendly academics such as Johnny Lau, Ivan Choi Chi-keung, and Chan Kin-man to deliver lectures and train party members. The first batch of trainees had 30 party members. He said the Party School would assess the participation, performance, and attendance of the DP DC members and district developmental directors. These data would be presented to the DP Election Committee, which would also evaluate the Party School attendees on their social activities and efforts to seek public donations.

Succession politics inside the DP came to a head in December 2008 when the young blood led by lawyer Andrew Cheng tried to challenge the party elders in the DP leadership elections. Cheng said before the elections that he and the younger members did not want to see the party being led by the elders for a long time, that the central leadership should be rejuvenated, that the DP should aggressively and directly recruit young members from university campuses, that the party center should communicate with the party branches monthly, and that the center should allocate more financial resources to all the branches. Clearly, Cheng and his supporters hoped for a party renewal and a proper adjustment in the party's central-local relations. However, Cheng garnered 132 votes in his election for the deputy chair position and was defeated by Sin Chung-kai (205 votes) and Emily Lau (228 votes), who joined the DP after the merger with the Frontier (see Table 6.1). It was speculated that Cheng's votes came from the reformists or the Young Turks within the DP.[14] Cheng said he would consider participation in the election again if there were an additional deputy chair position in the future. Most DP

Table 6.1

The Eighth Central Committee Election of the Democratic Party

---

Chairman:

Albert Ho (elected with 288 confidence votes; 15 no-confidence votes; 6 abstained)

Deputy Chairs (two persons):

Emily Lau (elected with 228 votes)

Sin Chung-kai (elected with 205 votes)

Andrew Cheng (defeated with 132 votes)

Committee Members (27 elected):

Three members from the former Frontier

23 members from the DP (such as Tik Chi-yuen, James To, Wong Sing-chi, Wu Chi-wai, Yeung Sum, Chan Shu-ying, Chiang Yuet-lan, Fung Wai-kwong, Lee Wing-tat, Lee Kin-yin, Ng Wing-fai, Andrew Cheng Choi Yu-lung, and Li Wah-ming)

Source: Ming Pao, December 15, 2008, p. A18.

members thought that Sin was more pragmatic and could communicate with the government. Although Cheng got 267 votes in becoming a Central Committee member, his 132 votes for his bid for the deputy chair position reflected the necessity of electing Emily Lau as the deputy chairperson. As one DP member said, after the merger with the Frontier, DP members knew how to give "face" to Emily Lau and her former colleagues in the Frontier.[15] Indeed, the DP remains to be dominated by males; female Central Committee members such as Chan Shu-ying and Chiang Yuet-lan lack the personal charisma and sharp political image compared to Emily Lau, whose election to the deputy position was understandable. To guarantee that Emily Lau was elected, chairman Albert Ho presented his "cabinet members' list" prior to the election. The list was composed of Ho, Emily Lau, Sin Chung-kai, Cheung Yin-tang, and Tsui Hon-kwong. Under the circumstances in which the party elders expressed their preferences, and the "big brother" culture remained alive, many DP members opted for the list suggested by the "mainstream faction."[16] After his defeat, Cheng maintained that he would not change his policy stance and would continue to engage his colleagues like Sin in internal policy debates.

In comparison with the DAB, the DP is keen to promote younger people to participate in party work. Choi Yu-lung, a 22-year-old graduate student at the City University of Hong Kong, was elected to the Central

Committee with 155 votes, and he was recruited by Martin Lee to work as a legislator's research assistant.[17] After the September 2008 LegCo elections, Albert Ho decided to recruit more young professionals with law degrees into the party. He acted as a mentor or big brother to select Hui Chi-fung, a 26-year-old research director in the DP, as his running mate in the LegCo elections.[18]

PARTY MEMBERS' INTEGRITY AND PERSECUTION

Because the DP is the most important flagship of the pan-democratic camp, the integrity of its members is often in the media spotlight. The case of Ho Wai-to was a good example showing the importance of the integrity of DP members. In September 2004, Ho was arrested by the mainland police for soliciting prostitution in Dongguan, and he was sent to a detention center for reeducation for five months. It was speculated that the sudden arrest of Ho was a deliberate move by the mainland authorities to blacken the image of the DP during the September 2004 LegCo elections. The detention not only damaged his reputation as a District Council member but also raised the question whether he had personal integrity problems or he had been framed by PRC authorities in Dongguan.[19] The DAB members severely criticized Ho and grasped the opportunity to tarnish the DP image. After the Hong Kong government secured the early release of Ho from the mainland detention center, Ho and his supporters held a press conference and insisted that he "did not do anything harmful to public interest." [20] Ho also said that he was innocent and that he signed a confession letter because of the mainland police's pressure. Ho decided to quit the DP for fear that his scandal would undermine the party's image. He complained that the detention center mistreated him and his health conditions were seriously affected. In response to Ho's complaint, DAB member Chan Kam-lam wrote to the Dongguan police and sought their clarifications.[21] The mainland police replied to Ho's criticisms, insisted that they did not make any mistake, and displayed photos showing his naked body taken in a room.[22] Interestingly, the Hong Kong Chinese press appeared to treat Ho as having integrity problems and surely soliciting prostitution.[23] The Hong Kong NPC member, Allen Lee, openly criticized the DP for allowing Ho Wai-to to hold a press conference when he was back in Hong Kong, because Lee had acted as an intermediary assisting the DP to rescue Ho.[24] Because of the coincidence of Ho's arrest with the September 2004 LegCo elections, and because of the suspicious nature of how mainland police gathered evidence, the Ho case remains a mystery and the possibility of persecuting him for deliberate political purposes cannot be ruled out.

Other DP members were the target of persecution. Fung King-man, a DP District Council member in Kowloon Tong, was convicted by the court of misappropriating her subsidies from the Kowloon City District Council. Fung complained to the author that she was not only a target of political persecution by pro-Beijing forces but also a victim of the DP's internal personnel problems.[25] Another example was Wong Sing-chi. After the 2008 LegCo elections, although Wong of the DP was directly elected, a group of citizens pursued him and criticized him for misrepresenting his own profile in the campaign leaflet, which said Wong was a registered social worker. The group said that Wong was not a registered social worker at the time of the election campaign. It went so far as to file an application to the ICAC.[26] The saga illustrated the fierce struggle between Wong and his political foes. Martin Lee has admitted in public that the HKSAR government and the Liaison Office "persecuted" the DP, but he is cautiously optimistic toward the DP's future because the party's grassroots and constituency work remains strong.[27]

THE PARTY'S INFILTRATION BY MYSTERIOUS FORCES

In early 2006 the DP was plagued by mysterious infiltration from outside. It revealed the DP's internal dispute and aroused the question of whether outsiders might penetrate into the party and stir up troubles from within. A special committee was set up to investigate 31 new members recommended by the New Territories East's party branch to see whether there were perpetrators.[28] The suspicion that the party branch became a "base" for outsiders to penetrate the DP and to reveal its internal disputes to the media affected Chan King-ming, the New Territories branch chairman and the DP's deputy chair.[29] Because of the fact that Chan recommended 32 new members to join the party, other DP members suspected that he had the ambition of toppling the DP chair Lee Wing-tat. However, some party members suspected that Lee utilized the excuse of Beijing's intervention to purge his opponents in the DP. Plagued by internal struggle, the DP's senior leaders appealed to all members for unity, especially in light of the rise of the CP.

The DP's party branch in the New Territories East reacted to the rumors and charges of infiltration in a negative manner. Party branch chair Chan King-ming and nine members whose background and activities were investigated by the party center, such as veterans Kong Kwok-chuen and Gary Fan Kwok-wai and young members like Kwan Wing-yip and Yam Kai-pong, held a press conference to clarify the 34 new members who attempted to join the party.[30] The party center argued that some new members who had interactions with the mainland did not report to the DP's central authorities, and that a few of them might receive financial support from the PRC. The party center suspected the background of a few new members who did not have contact telephone numbers. It looked into the new members, some of whom were not aware of the need to pay membership fees. The party branch responded to the charges, explaining that the new members were young and did not want their parents to know they had joined the DP, and therefore they kept their telephone numbers confidential. Five new members came from a friend of a DP District Council member, and he simply paid for the membership fees of all his family members. Yet, the party branch did not respond to the charge of some members having communication with the mainland and allegedly receiving financial gains. Chan King-ming complained that the DP set a target of increasing its members from 600 in 2006 to 1,000 in the near future, and that the party branch's diligent work was unnecessarily politicized and its image unfairly tarnished.[31]

The DP chairman Lee Wing-tat pointed his accusing finger to the mass media for deliberately blowing up his party's internal "problems." Lee said he told the mass media there were only two party members who suspected that PRC authorities tried to bribe them in exchange for political defection. Overall, the issue of infiltration dealt a severe blow to the New Territories East's party branch because it worked hard to expand its members at the cost of undermining its own image. The branch's senior members who were investigated joined the party for 7 to 12 years. The inability of the DP's party center to contain the spread of the rumors and internal dispute undermined its image. In fact, the party branch's members were dissatisfied with the way in which Lee handled the incident by talking to the mass media prior to any internal investigation.[32] The party's policy committee members such as Cheung Yin-tang, Szeto Wah, and Martin Lee met the Chinese reporters before the investigation, thus fueling some degree of mistrust between the party center and its branch in the New Territories East. The lesson from the infiltration saga was that the DP's party center will have to handle any similar charges of infiltration in a more sensitive and low-key manner in the future.

The communications between DP members and the mainland constitute a challenge to the party center on how to handle this sensitive issue, particularly as the distrust between party leaders and Beijing persists. During the infiltration scare, it was revealed that Lee Wai-man, the party branch's executive committee member in the New Territories East, went to visit the mainland with another DP member. Lee said he had already reported his visit to party branch chairman Chan King-ming.[33] The party center suspected that the party branch had the secret motive of recruiting new members so that Lee Wing-tat's position as the chairman would be challenged. However, the party branch members suspected that the party center wished to purge its new members from the New Territories East. The entire dispute demonstrates not only a political legacy of deep mutual distrust between DP leaders and the PRC, but also an internal mistrust between the party center and it branch.

In response to the danger of infiltration, the DP tightened the processes and requirements of applicants to be party members. In April 2006, the DP Central Standing Committee lengthened the transition period of becoming a basic party member from the need to observe his or her performance for 6 months to 24 months.[34] A basic party member can have the right to elect the party chairperson. The DP deputy chair Albert Ho said in 2006 that due to the increasing interactions between Beijing and the party members after 2003, it was necessary to improve the mechanism of applying for full party membership. However, a member of the Central Standing Committee, Kwan Wing-yip, said that the new mechanism would affect new members who would like to participate in DC elections. Ho replied that the plan would have a degree of flexibility, but the idea was to have a deeper understanding of the new party members during the longer observation period.

In June 2006, the DP Web site was attacked by hackers twice and the party's membership list was leaked out to the mass media.[35] The blog that contained the DP's membership list appeared to look for those hidden party members who joined the DP but were afraid that their political status could be leaked out. The 311-member list on the blog included names such as chairman Lee Wing-tat, deputy chairman Chan King-ming, Martin Lee, Yeung Sum, and those who withdrew from the party, like Anthony Cheung, Chan Wai-yip, and Lau Chin-shek. The incident concerning any secret members' list could be traced back to the CP's demand in May 2006, when it tried to use the Company Ordinance to look for the DAB's membership list, especially those hidden party members.[36] But the CP's plan unintentionally affected the DP, which had secret party members hiding their identity in public. Some academics, journalists, and businesspeople who joined the DP did not want to reveal their identity, and therefore the DP at one point refused to unveil its membership list and even threatened to resort to judicial review if they were required by the Company Ordinance to do so.[37] In response to the DP reaction, Chan Kam-lam of the DAB said: "Political parties are not triads, which are afraid of being known. If people who join the party do not want to reveal their identity, they should not join it and should better become invisible at all."[38] The DP's delay in disclosing its memberships sparked severe criticisms from pro-Beijing commentators.[39] Anyway, the hacker's attacks on the DP Web site appeared to target the secret memberships of the party.

The DP members remain the target of vicious criticisms, if not necessarily persecution, from pro-Beijing forces. Many of them compete fiercely with DAB candidates in LegCo and DC elections. Even after the elections, shouting matches and legal struggles between members of the two parties persist. In October 2004, when James To was found misusing public money and failing to report to LegCo on his personal property, the DAB members in the DC in Yaumati, Tsimshastui, and Mong Kok districts aggressively pursued him and asked him to resign from the District Council. Although the democrats in the Council prevented the DAB members from doing so, the incident was highlighted by the mass media and dealt a severe blow to To's image.[40] In February 2008, Andrew Cheng of the DP and three lawyers sued DAB member Ho Sau-mo for libel in a campaign leaflet distributed by Ho during the 2007 District Council elections.[41] In February 2009, when Andrew Cheng was found speeding twice but did not attend the court hearing, pro-Beijing FTU legislator Wong Kwok-hing criticized him for lacking public credibility and asked Cheng to resign from his position as a member of LegCo's transport committee.[42]

THE INTERNAL SELECTION MECHANISM AND PARTY STRIFE

Despite the row between the DP party center and its branch in the New Territories East in 2006, the DP remains the most internally democratically operated party in the HKSAR. Still, internal strife within the DP persists because of the fierce struggle among members who are nominated to run in local elections. The party's internal democracy was seen in its special members meeting held in March 2008 to decide tentative lists for candidates in the five LegCo geographical constituencies—Hong Kong Island, Kowloon East, Kowloon West, New Territories East, and New Territories West. About 100 members attended the meeting and voted for the suggested number of lists and names of candidates in the five constituencies (Table 6.2), but the final decisions would be made by the party branches. Hence, centralism was the first step followed by a decentralization of decisions to the level of party branches. The recommended lists and names of candidates from the center had to be endorsed by the party branches—a democratic way of deciding the best candidates and number of lists to run in each geographical constituency.

Occasionally, some DP members who disagree with the decisions of the party center or branch withdraw from the party. A good example was Lai Chi-keung, who withdrew from the party after the party branch refused to allow him to lead a separate list to compete in the 2008 LegCo elections. Lai's withdrawal could be traced back to the 2004 LegCo election in Hong Kong Island, where he was ranked the third candidate in the DP list and was defeated. Lai put the blame on Kam Nai-wai and said that Kam did not assist him fully.[43] In May 2008, Lai was disappointed at his defeat by Sin Chung-kai in the DP's internal selection of candidates in the September elections. In July, Lai decided to quit the party to run in the September elections as an independent. His application to withdraw from the DP was approved by the party center, which exercised the discretion to deal with his request although the normal period of withdrawal application needs two months' prior notice.[44] Apart from Lai, another example was Angela Leung On-kei, who withdrew from the DP after it rejected her wish to be nominated to run in the 1999 DC elections in the Eastern district.[45] The proportional representation (list) system adopted in Hong Kong's LegCo elections did force some party members to struggle internally with their colleagues so that they could be ranked higher on the party list. If they were ranked lower and often defeated, the possibility of their withdrawal from the party would be higher unless their party discipline were consistently strong.

At the level of DC, the DP's internal selection and nomination mechanism is sometimes so controversial that it brings about the withdrawal of a few party members. Three months prior to the November 2007 DC elections, Ho Chi-wing, a DP member and district director in Fan Ling, withdrew from the party.[46] Joining the DP in 2004, Ho angrily told the mass media that a new member Law Sai-yan suddenly participated in the district affairs in 2006 because of *guanxi* or personal networks. In July, the DP election committee decided to nominate Law to compete in the November elections. Ho said that the residents in the district were cheated because they needed time to adjust to the work of a new member. Moreover, the DP strategy would affect coordination work with the CP. Ho even went so far as to accuse the party of cultivating patron-client relations with the Northern Livelihood Promotion Society, which was supported by the DP to apply for funding from the Northern District Council. After the Society received the funding support, the DP hired Law to work as a temporary staff member.[47] Ho held a press conference to severely criticize the DP for favoritism and clientelism. But the DP party branch convener, Shum Wing-kan, also held a press briefing simultaneously and argued that Ho lacked performance in the district.

Table 6.2

The Suggestions from the DP's Special Members Meeting on the 2008 Legislative Council Elections

Geographical Constituency	Number of Lists Recommended	Suggested Leaders of the Lists
Hong Kong Island	Not more than 2 lists	Kam Nai-wai
Kowloon East	2	Li Wah-ming and Wu Chi-wai
Kowloon West	Not more than 2 lists	James To
New Territories East	2	Andrew Cheng and Wong Sing-chi
New Territories West	3	Albert Ho, Lee Wing-tat, and Cheung Yin-tang

Source: Ming Pao, March 31, 2008, p. A11.

According to Shum, it was natural for the DP election committee to select Law rather than Ho to run for the November election. In response to the party's internal dispute, Albert Ho said that the party center had already followed up the Ho case, and that Ho did not pass the selection criteria of district work, party solidarity, cooperative ability, and the chance of electoral success.[48] Ho added that if some party members were dissatisfied with the party center's nominations and that they decided to withdraw, it was a natural phenomenon. Clearly, some DP members did not have a strong degree of party discipline and tended to disobey the DP center's nominations of candidates to run in DC elections.

MANAGING INTERNAL DISPUTES

How to manage internal disputes has become a challenge to the DP since its establishment. Since the merger between the UDHK and the Meeting Point into the DP, the DP was for some time plagued by the legacy of the merger. Because of the fact that the Meeting Point had moderate democrats such as Anthony Cheung and Yeung Sum, the DP's development from its formation to Yeung's stepping down as the DP chair in November 2004 was characterized by internal disputes. The origins of such disputes were partly because of personality conflicts and partly because of policy lines. Immediately after the return of Hong Kong to the PRC, the DP was plagued by internal struggle between the Young Turks and Meeting Point moderates such as Anthony Cheung. In 1998, Lau Chin-shek who was supported by the Young Turks defeated Anthony Cheung to become the DP vice chairman. To Cheung, the DP failed to switch its policy line to focus on the middle class, which remained the pillar of DP votes throughout the 1990s.[49] However, Young Turks such as Chan Wai-yip and To Kwan-hang (both are now members of the LSD) maintained that the DP policy line should appeal to not only middle class but also the middle-lower and working classes. Cheung disagreed with their argument because he believed that the DP should not be another ADPL, which remains a Shumshuipo-based political party fighting for the interests of the lower-class citizens. Cheung's middle-class background as an academic was different from that of veterans Chan Wai-yip and To Kwan-hang, who fought for their political careers from the grassroots level. In October 2004, Cheung decided to quit the DP and set up his own new think tank named the Synergy Net. His decision to withdraw from the DP affected the future of some former Meeting Point members who were also DP members, such as Lo Chi-kin, Luk Shun-tim, and Fung Wai-kwong.[50] There were fears that the DP would be split, but fortunately the former Meeting Point members such as Li Wah-ming and Yeung Sum remained loyal to the party. As a result of the departure of Cheung, Chan, and To, the DP's possible internal split was avoided.

In November 2004, DP chairman Yeung Sum decided not to run for the party chair position because he shouldered the responsibility for the party's unsatisfactory performance in the 2004 LegCo elections. Actually, the defeat of independent democrat Cyd Ho in the Hong Kong Island was not Yeung's responsibility, as Martin Lee said, because Lee himself appealed to the voters urgently for support and thus affected the number of votes obtained by Ho. Moreover, the sudden arrest of Ho Wai-to in Dongguan did affect the party image, especially for the Kowloon East constituency where young member Wu Chi-wai failed to be elected and to replace the position of party veteran Szeto Wah.[51] Yeung was under tremendous pressure after he became the chairman of the DP in 2002. When Yeung was elected as the chair without any opponent, Young Turks Chan Wai-yip withdrew from the party to express his discontent.[52] However, Yeung's stepping down did terminate a possible wave of withdrawal of party members amidst Anthony Cheung's firm decision to leave the DP.[53] After 2002, Yeung actually implemented a moderate line by keeping the communication channel with the HKSAR government open. However, he felt uncomfortable with the DP LegCo election results in 2004 and offered to resign immediately on the night of September 12. His party colleagues stopped him from doing so until a week later when Yeung announced his decision. As with Martin Lee, Yeung was critical of both the HKSAR government and Beijing for "suppressing" the DP.[54] He complained that the Liaison Office did not even contact him during his two years of chairmanship. The Liaison Office's united front work failed dismally due to its favoritism toward the pro-Beijing elites in the HKSAR, but it missed a golden opportunity to begin a dialogue with moderate Yeung. Summing up his experience, Yeung sighed: "We were seen by the British as anti-colonial, but we do not expect that the Chinese government has been viewed as anti-China. Both the British and the Chinese governments regard us as alien."[55]

Yeung's successor was Lee Wing-tat, who had been defeated in the 2000 LegCo elections and spent considerable time managing party affairs. Some party members said that Lee became more mature and humble after his defeat in the 2000 legislative elections.[56] After Lee became the DP chair in December 2004, he reminded himself of the need to exhibit his integrity in private and public life.[57] Lee revealed that after the protests by half a million residents on July 1, 2003, the communications between the DP members and mainlanders increased significantly. He did not know the official titles of these mainlanders, who according to Lee had contacts with the central government. He hoped that the DP's interactions with these mainlanders would change from private to public so that they would be able to discuss issues of common concerns. Lee responded to the personal and financial scandals affecting Ho Wai-to and James To, respectively, with four administrative measures. Lee set up a committee led by Law Chi-kong and Tik Chi-yuen to implement financial reform; urged the party center to clarify and delineate rules governing the use of public funds on the part of legislators and DC members; invited staff members of the ICAC to educate all party members on ethical issues; and required all party members to report to the party center on their activities.[58] Lee appealed to all party members to learn from the model of Szeto Wah, who was a respectable party whip dealing with internal discipline.

The DP learned a bitter lesson after the unsatisfactory performance in the September 2004 LegCo elections. The DP legislators began to modify the mentorship or big brother scheme slightly by cultivating a younger party member to assist with their legislative work, to meet high-level officials and businesspeople, and to participate in press conferences so as to increase their public exposure.[59] Yeung Sum, for example, acted as a legislative mentor grooming Fung Wai-kwong to gain more political experience at the district level. Although Fung was poorly prepared and defeated in the 2003 DC elections, he continued to learn from Yeung's experience and to improve his district work in the Southern district.

Still, Lee Wing-tat inherited a party with internal problems and disputes. Apart from Anthony Cheung who left the party, other party members intended to quit the DP. They included Kwai Ching DP District Council chair Chow Yik-hei, who eventually decided to stay in the party after Lee's persuasion. However, critics of Chow said that he no longer belonged to the democratic camp because of his opportunistic shifts.[60] Because of the scandal involving Fung King-man and Lau Ting-bong, who were allegedly deceiving subsidies from the Kowloon City District Council, DP members Lam Kin-man and Au Ka-sing also intended to withdraw from the party. Moreover, DP members Fong Chun-bong from the Shatin district and Lau Tak-cheong from the northern district left the DP, whose image after the September 2004 LegCo elections reached its nadir. Fong and Lau used the excuse of conducting business in the PRC to claim that they found it inconvenient to stay in the party.[61] No wonder Sin Chung-kai remarked that the DP in 2006 became "a mini-political party testing whether its party members can deal with the difficult challenges."[62]

Despite the DP's internal problems and external crises, it has maintained constituency work effectively at the grassroots level. The DP fought for the interests of citizens by holding press briefings, lobbying officials, and monitoring the government through legislative work. In March 2006, the DP held a press conference where chair Lee Wing-tat and Albert Ho supported the building of the Hong Kong government's new headquarters in the open space near the Tamar military base, but the party raised five conditions for the government to fulfill. They included the need to lower the height of the government buildings, to retain the old headquarters in the Central district, to increase the area for leisure and recreation at the new headquarters, to allow citizens' access to the Victoria Harbor, and to set up a fund to educate the public on how to protect the harbor.[63] In April 2006, the DP mobilized citizens to email Sarah Liu, the secretary for environment, transport, and land, because it lobbied the government to set up safety fences that would protect citizens waiting for the light transit train on the railway platform.[64] In August 2006, the DP launched a signature campaign on the streets to collect the signatures from citizens to oppose any attempt by the government to introduce the General Sales Tax (GST).[65] Because of widespread public opposition, including the DP and the pro-business LP, the government shelved the plan to implement GST in late October 2006.[66]

MERGER WITH THE FRONTIER AND COOPERATION WITH DEMOCRATIC PARTIES

In 2008, the DP merged with the Frontier, which had been a party led by Emily Lau. The party rose to prominence in 1996 as it was formed and when Emily Lau remained a political star in Hong Kong under British rule. With the fading of her popularity after the handover, and the ability of the small party to retain only three seats in the 2007 DC elections, the Frontier's future was doomed. Some members of the Frontier hoped that the party would become a formal political party, but most members did not want to participate in local elections. In 2008, Lau described the Frontier not as a party but as a pressure or political group. With about 100 members, the Frontier eventually in 2008 decided to merge with the DP. Those members who wanted to join the DP could do so, while those who refused could remain in the pressure group. After the merger of the Frontier with the DP, the former no longer functions as an effective pressure group because its activities were minimal and the media simply ignored its existence.

The rise and fall of the Frontier demonstrated the weaknesses of Hong Kong's mini-political parties. The Frontier was a *de facto* political party, although its members perceived it as more a pressure group because it did participate in LegCo and DC elections. When the mini-party was set up in early 1996, its influence was considerable because of the participation of other democrats, such as Lau Chin-shek, Lee Cheuk-yan, Cyd Ho, and former senior civil servant Elizabeth Wong Chin Kay-lim. In 1998, Cyd Ho ran in the LegCo election in a list together with Emily Lau, but Ho later ran as an independent candidate without any affiliation with the Frontier. In the 2000 LegCo election, Emily Lau and Richard Tsoi ran together in a party list, but Tsoi was defeated while Lau was elected. Before the 2008 LegCo election, Lau admitted that her political life might reach the end, and that she would like to assist the mainland lawyers in the future. In September 2008, Lau was narrowly elected to LegCo and her political future would be at stake. The Frontier's merger with the DP may actually prolong Lau's political life and survival. After Lau joined the DP, foreign media and officials often meet her, and hence she replaces Martin Lee as the DP spokesperson dealing with foreigners.[67] With only Emily Lau providing the rallying point for most members, the 100-member Frontier was doomed to be a temporary mini-party.

The merger of the DP and Frontier could strengthen the pro-democracy forces and signaled the political realignment of democrats. Internally, the DP saw the rise of the CP as a threat, while the Frontier regarded its poor performance in the 2008 LegCo elections as a death knell. In 2002, DP member To Kwan-hang left the DP and joined the Frontier, whose ideological orientation at that time was more pro-grassroots and pro-welfare. Later To left the Frontier and participated in Raymond Wong's and Chan Wai-yip's LSD. But the Frontier, which had 79 members when it was formed in August 1996, did not have much progress in membership recruitment, electoral performance, and livelihood issues by 2008. Hence, the amalgamation of the Frontier and DP was a marriage of convenience facilitating Lau's longevity, providing more political space for the existing Frontier members, and consolidating the declining DP.

Yet, some Frontier members opposed the merger with the DP—a reflection of the diversity and pluralism in the pro-democracy camp. On November 23, 2008, when the Frontier's executive committee members voted for the merger issue, 34 votes supported the amalgamation move, and 15 votes opposed and abstained. According to the Frontier's constitution, whether the party should be dissolved would require a support of four-fifths of all the votes. Only 41 of the 54 votes approved of the idea.[68] The vote indicated the opposition of some Frontier members to the merger and their determination to maintain the group. They were concerned that, after the merger, members of the Frontier would be marginalized.[69] It was rumored that Chan King-ming of the DP did not welcome Richard Tsoi of the Frontier to join the party.[70] Personality issues appeared to surface in the politics of the merger between the DP and the Frontier.

Prior to the 2007 chief executive election, the DP cooperated with the CP in nominating candidate Alan Leong of the CP to compete in the election.[71] They tried to garner the support of at least 100 members of the Election Committee to nominate Leong. At one time, the DP tried to support its chairman Lee Wing-tat to run for the chief executive election.[72] In March 2008, when Martin Lee stepped down from legislative elections and suggested that the 300-member CP might lead the pan-democratic camp, his comment triggered the uneasy feeling among some DP members and leaders. Cheung Man-kwong of the DP revealed that he got used to hearing Lee's "special views," implying that Lee as a charismatic and strong leader must have his own views regardless of how other party members might think.[73] Cheung added that since the DP and CP had different power bases, their merger might not be conducive to the consolidation of the democracy movement. Albert Ho added that Martin Lee often held the view that "the democratic development in general is more influential than the DP's interests."[74] Both Cheung and Ho made valid observations that could explain why Lee hoped for the democracy movement to be led by the CP, which includes many barristers with the similar occupational background as with Lee.

In practice, the CP is not keen to merge with the DP. The CP appeals to the professionals and middle class for support, whereas the DP tends to be more middle-lower class and more pro-livelihood in its policies. When Martin Lee proposed that the CP could lead the democracy movement, CP chair Audrey Eu said that the struggle for democracy would not be a matter of one particular party, and that the space for both DP and CP to cooperate was much larger than their amalgamation.[75] Clearly, the CP wished to maintain its own character.

Sometimes the DP has tensions with other democrats because of opinion differences over policy issues. A case in point was the dissatisfaction of some pro-democracy legislators, such as Lee Cheuk-yan, with the DP's support of the government proposal of allocating HK$90 billion to the Mandatory Provident Fund.[76] Lee, Cyd Ho, Frederick Fung, and Leung Yiu-chung argued that the vote should be postponed so that government subsidies could be given to the bank accounts of individuals rather than allowing them to receive the fund by the age of 65. The DP argued that there was no reason to reject the entire government plan and that its members disagreed with Lee. Because of policy differences, Lee and his supporters left LegCo's meeting chamber when a vote was called for, whereas three members of the LSD simply voted against the government plan.

SUMMARY

It is easy to criticize the DP for its failure to maintain party unity, to improve the integrity of its members, and to transform its mode of operation from the "big brother system" to a mentorship scheme with the upward mobility of rank-and-file members. Nevertheless, critics fail to appreciate the fact that the DP has been operating in an extremely hostile political environment. As a mini-political party in the HKSAR, the DP withstands the external crises in which outside forces constantly attempt to find fault at the party and penetrate into its operations. Compounding the external threat is the emergence of new pro-democracy forces, such as the CP, which constitutes a menace to the unity of DP members. Yet, the DP as a small and an elitist party has been adapting flexibly to the unfavorable external circumstances and internal disputes. The DP suffered only temporary setbacks during difficult times, but it has bounced back resiliently in legislative elections. With the rise of the CP, the DP adapted quickly to the possible loss of pan-democratic leadership by amalgamating with the Frontier.[77] The DP also adapted to electoral setbacks by reorganizing the party after DC elections, by renewing the party through new waves of recruitment, and by electing new leaders at the top echelon. The DP responded to scandals involving party members in a calm manner, weathering the storm and tackling the media criticisms in an open manner. Overall, critics of the DP have swept under the carpet the tenacity and, above all, the adaptability of the DP to the malicious external political conditions and the internal personnel struggle. Critics have also neglected the fact that the DP as a small and underfunded party has continued to gain a high level of public support and a large number of votes disproportionately far exceeding its size, manpower, and resources. From this perspective, the DP remains the flagship of Hong Kong's democracy movement.

CHAPTER 7

Pro-Democracy Parties: Civic Party, League of Social Democrats, and Association for Democracy and People's Livelihood

The rise of the CP in April 2006 and the birth of the LSD in July 2006 represented a significant political realignment in Hong Kong's democracy movement. With the decline in the DP's popularity and its scandals highlighted by the mass media, many pro-democracy elites decided to set up other "stoves" to fight for democracy in the HKSAR. On the other hand, the ADPL has become a relatively old mini-party operating mainly in the Shumshuipo district. Its poor performance in the 2007 DC elections prompted Frederick Fung to step down as the chair and to rethink the party's strategy and directions for the future. This chapter analyzes the development of the three pro-democracy mini-parties in the HKSAR: the CP, LSD, and ADPL.

EMERGENCE OF THE CIVIC PARTY

The CP's origin was the opposition of a group of barristers, such as Ronny Tong, Audrey Eu, Margaret Ng, and Alan Leong, to the Tung administration's attempt at legislating on Article 23 of the Basic Law in 2002 and 2003. The group later evolved into the Article 45 Concern Group, which expressed its views on the methods of selecting the chief executive in the future. In December 2005, the Article 45 Concern Group expanded to include new members, including academics and professionals.

Its intention was to form a new political party. These academics and professionals were Kuan Hsin-chi, Kenneth Chan Ka-lok, Joseph Chan Cho-wai, Albert Lai, Claudia Mo, Tsang Kwok-fung, and Mark Williams.[1] Ronny Tong told the mass media that when he was elected to the LegCo in 2004, he had the idea of uniting more professionals so as to struggle for democracy.

The CP was formed at a ripe time when the DP failed to obtain more votes from the middle-class citizens, and when the Article 45 Concern Group's opposition to Article 23 of the Basic Law in 2003 and the NPC Standing Committee's interpretation of the Basic Law in April 2004 won the support of many professionals. The editorial of *Ming Pao* argued that the CP's formation would rejuvenate the pan-democracy camp, compensate for the aging DP's weaknesses, tap the support of the middle class, and even stimulate the business to participate in Hong Kong politics. As it said,

It would speed up the pro-democracy camp's regeneration. Democrats are a major force in Hong Kong politics. In the past they on average snatched 60 percent of the vote. The biggest pro-democracy group is the DP, which controls nine LegCo seats. However, the party has few up-and-coming young members, and it has great difficulty recruiting members and obtaining donations. There are clear signs of its aging ... The rising Article 45 Concern Group may make up for the DP's weaknesses ... [T]he new party might, by engaging the DP in constructive competition, also help promote the pro-democracy camp's regeneration ... It would urge political parties to set greater store by the support of middle-class citizens. The Article 45 Concern Group's professional image sits quite well with middle-class citizens. If it becomes a political party and goes all out to take part in direct elections, more middle-class professionals will go to the polls and stand in elections. Then, the pro-democracy camp may tread two political lines—one catering to the grassroots, and the other, the middle class ... It would stimulate people from the business community to participate in politics.[2]

Indeed, the rise of the CP can plug the loopholes of the DP, notably the aging problem and its appeals to middle-lower classes. The CP tends to appeal to the middle-class professionals rather than the lower-class citizens. Led by professionals, lawyers, and academics, the CP is a typical middle-class party. It has been criticized for lacking sufficient interest in issues affecting the people's livelihood.[3] The CP member Cheung Chiu-hung even said that the CP was not a grassroots-level party because labeling it in this way would affect the businesses' willingness to donate money to the organization.[4] He stressed that the CP's support of improving social security for the elderly, disabled, and single parents did not mean that the CP was a "socialist" party.[5]

It is debatable whether the CP can really encourage and stimulate business participation in politics. Traditionally, the big business in Hong Kong

has been politically spoiled by both the colonial and post-1997 governments. Relying on personal lobbying and personal networks as well as
political appointments into key policy-making and consultative bodies,
most business elites have found electoral participation time consuming
and economically unrewarding. A businessman named Ku Ming-kwan,
who was viewed as "an electronic tycoon," said in June 2006 that
although he toyed with the idea of donating money to the CP, he eventually refrained from doing so because he questioned whether a lawyer in
the CP was involved in a case of "obstructing justice." [6] There was no evidence to substantiate his claim, but Ku's hesitant attitude in making donations to the CP demonstrated that he was concerned about not only the
quality of the party but also the professional conduct of its core members.
In fact, the CP secures the support of some business elites. Paul Zimmerman, for instance, supports the CP through the introduction of environmental activist Christine Loh.[7] However, the extent to which the local
Chinese businesspeople support the CP is unclear as the CP remains relatively new.

On the other hand, some lower-class citizens perceive the CP as a "rich"
party filled with lawyers and professionals. As such, the CP found it not
easy to secure donations from ordinary citizens on the streets. The
amount of donations that the CP received from street-level citizens was
much less than that of the other pro-democracy parties.[8] Citizens' class
perception of the CP affects its efforts at securing donations at the street
level, although its core leaders can acquire the financial support from
like-minded barristers and lawyers relatively easily.

After the September 2008 LegCo elections, the CP's financial situation
was tight. The party had about HK$900,000 left, and yet it needed
HK$300,000 monthly to sustain its work at the headquarters and three
party branches. Hence, the CP secretary-general Kenneth Chan, who
replaced Joseph Cheng Yu-shek in 2008, revealed that the party began to
conduct fund-raising campaigns through film shows.[9] Another way in
which the CP reduced its expenditures was to consider using mobile offices rather than fixed offices in constituencies so that its members would
interact easily with citizens through vehicles. In 2008 the CP used a film
show for its fund-raising campaign, an event that brought about
HK$1 million to the party.[10] Unlike the DP in which a financial mecha-
nism requires local party members at the district level to submit a certain
amount of their monthly stipends to the party headquarters, the CP does
not institute this central-local financial structure and instead relies on
fund-raising campaigns.

In terms of the CP membership, it has a "secret" membership list that
includes judges, professionals, and academics. A report said that the CP
members include a few judges, prompting the concern of critics about
the political neutrality of a minority of court judges.[11] However, some

court judges did express their political views, as demonstrated by the controversy over the interpretation of the Basic Law by the NPC Standing Committee in mid-1999 on the right of abode of mainland Chinese.[12] As long as their court judgments do not carry political bias, the participation of some court judges in the membership of any pro-democracy party is by no means a serious concern.

However, a minority of CP members includes non-Chinese, and this may arouse the sensitivity of Beijing's hard-line officials responsible for Hong Kong affairs. One former assistant political advisor of Governor Christopher Patten, John Shannon, joined the 155-member CP in May 2006.[13] Audrey Eu of the CP said that the party could not refuse Shannon's membership application as he fit into the criteria of being a CP member and that she was not afraid of the party being infiltrated by any possible British spy.[14] In fact, the CP Web site was attacked by mysterious hackers,[15] who could perhaps be regarded as the genuine spies targeting at the pro-democracy party.

Because the CP is led by a group of barristers, its leadership nature is unique, and the withdrawal of Mandy Tam from the party in June 2009 demonstrated this problem. Tam complained that although she paid attention to district and constituency affairs, the CP neglected the people's livelihood.[16] Being defeated in the November 2007 DC election, Tam lacked the CP support to conduct constituency work. She felt politically isolated and thereby withdrew from the party. She also implied that the barristers who led the CP appeared to have a communication gap with her. Hence, class differences loomed large in the CP and explained why the more pro-grassroots Tam decided to leave the CP.

Mandy Tam discussed with the DP the possibility of joining the democratic flagship, but she needed more time to consider the issue.[17] One former democrat, Kai Ting-kong, who withdrew from the CP to join the DAB, commented on Tam's departure from the CP: "Tam's move again proves that the CP attaches far more importance to political struggle than livelihood issues."[18] After Tam left the CP, she formed a group "Caring about Hong Kong" under which a suborganization with 12 members named "Caring about China" was established.[19] The Caring China group aims at implementing the spirit of the May 4 movement in China, holding seminars and exhibitions to understand the PRC development and reforms, and organizing activities to commemorate the June 4 tragedy.

Before Tam left the CP, there were signs of internal class differences within the party. Cheung Chiu-hung, who was defeated in the September 2008 LegCo direct elections in the New Territories West, appeared to distance himself from the CP in November when he formed a district group to help the poor and the needy in the constituency.[20] He secured the support of some social workers who had assisted him during the LegCo elections. Cheung admitted that he had opinion differences with the CP, notably his personal opposition to any further reduction of profit tax and salary tax. He felt that the tax rate in the HKSAR was already low and hence his pro-grassroots ideology was at odds with the CP.

One interesting distinction between the CP and the DP is the former's position on the Tiananmen tragedy. The CP leaders and members are less rigid on how they view the Tiananmen incident. They do not have the political baggage of the DP whose core leaders such as Martin Lee, Szeto Wah, and Albert Ho were all deeply involved in the Hong Kong Alliance in Support of the Patriotic and Democratic Movement in China. The CP chairman Kuan Hsin-chi openly criticized some democrats for their "obsession" with the Tiananmen tragedy.[21] He defended the CP's silence on the Tiananmen issue, saying that "since the 1990s, the democracy movement up until today has had some real problems. To put it nicely, there's been a delay or a stalling. To put it more harshly, there's been a turnaround, a crisis."[22] The CP grew out of a deep conviction of fighting for Hong Kong's civil liberties and judicial independence, and its focus is naturally different from that of the DP.

Ideologically speaking, the CP can be seen as a middle-of-the-road party, neither adopting a conservative right-wing ideology nor upholding a socialist line. Alan Leong of the CP responded to the societal discussion on whether it is a right-wing or left-wing party in the following way:

Many ideas in the CP platform actually conform to the rights and benefits of citizens. But we also protect business interests, such as a fair judicial system and fair market competition. In fact, on issues concerning the harbor reclamation and urban planning, we have communicated frankly with the business community . . . In the past the Article 45 Concern Group opposed the abolition of the tax on property inheritance . . . Private accumulation of property can even exacerbate the degree of wealth concentration and it is not beneficial to market competition. Maintaining the property inheritance tax can conform with the principle of a *laissez faire* economy . . . The CP promotes the principle of pluralistic competition.[23]

As mentioned before, the CP leaders do not like to see any label of leftism on their party, for doing so would scare away some businesspeople who financially support the party. Hence, Alan Leong himself avoided confronting the issue of leftism versus rightism, but he instead emphasized the party's convergence of interests with the business sector.

Organizationally speaking, the CP remains an elitist mini-party whose objective is to grasp political power by winning more seats in mainly the LegCo elections. The CP has a 17-member executive committee in which the chairperson is responsible for managing party affairs internally, while the party leader is representing the CP's position inside the LegCo.[24] Two deputy chairs are responsible for the internal and external affairs of the party, whereas the secretary-general deals with party discipline. Moreover, the treasurer copes with financial and legal matters, and the chief director handles party headquarters, the newspaper A45, and the A45 radio channel. Five policy branch chairs are responsible for political and economic policy areas, while another five district branch chairs have to coordinate the affairs in the five geographical constituencies of the LegCo. The executive committee in 2006 was elected by the 20 core members of the Article 45 Concern Group. The executive committee members serve two years and are now elected at the annual meeting of the CP members.

Audrey Eu said that even if the CP members had communications with Beijing, the one-way communication was unhealthy because the central authorities appeared to just collect the views from its party members without genuine dialogue and discussions.[25] Eu thought that, although the CP had six votes in the LegCo, it did not intend to be the largest party in the legislature. Nor did the CP discuss with the DP the possibility of a merger. She hoped that the CP would expand its work at the grassroots level and encourage more citizens to join the party. Usually, it takes six months to observe the performance of a new CP member—a mechanism beneficial to both the member concerned and the CP. Eu herself does not want the CP to focus on the middle class alone, but a party that can appeal to social justice across the societal strata.

After the CP was formed, the party made two important contributions to Hong Kong's democracy movement. The first was to mobilize its members, such as Kuan Hsin-chi, Joseph Cheng, Kenneth Chan, To Yiu-ming, Paul Zimmerman, and Chan Ching-liu, to compete in the elections of the members of the Election Committee that would select the chief executive in March 2007.[26] Some CP members were elected to the Election Committee, like Kuan Hsin-chi, Kenneth Chan, and Joseph Cheng. The CP cooperated successfully with other members of the pan-democratic camp, including Chan King-ming of the DP, independent democrat Michael DeGolyer, and Eliza Lee and Chan Kin-man of the Democratic Development Network. They formed a united front to contact the eligible voters in the higher education subsector. A total of 156 pan-democrats were nominated to run for the 708 representatives of various subsectors in the Election Committee.[27] The fact that Alan Leong, who later ran for the chief executive elections, could secure 132 nominations out of the 800-member Election Committee demonstrated the unprecedented political success of the pan-democrats, including the CP, in the selection of Election Committee members.

Although Alan Leong was defeated in the March 2007 chief executive election by getting 123 votes while Donald Tsang was elected with 649 votes, the CP and its democratic allies succeeded in presenting an image of a moderate but loyal opposition in the HKSAR.[28] Critics of Leong argued that he should not participate in a "small circle election" without any chance of winning but entailing the unintended consequence of legitimizing the election. These critics included Raymond Wong, Albert

Chan Wai-yip, and Leung Kwok-hung who were later the core leaders of the LSD. However, Alan Leong succeeded in engaging Tsang to debate on concrete policy issues and raising public awareness of a whole range of issues, such as education, economy, double direct elections, the policy toward the poor and the elderly, environmental protection, and poverty. The pan-democrats also succeeded in raising HK$3 million for Leong to conduct his campaign.[29] Leong's competition in the chief executive election was unprecedented in the HKSAR as he was affiliated with a political party, the CP. In a nutshell, the contributions of the CP were to project an image of a loyal opposition and improve the quality of the debate during the 2007 chief executive election.

Finally, a crucial contribution of the CP is to monitor the government inside the legislature. For example, the CP severely criticized the Tsang administration for failing to consult the environmental and transport implications of the new government headquarters near the Tamar military base.[30] The party argued that the data released by the administration were incomplete, especially the expenditure on the new government headquarters. The way in which the CP opposed the government's incomplete plan raised the alarm of the Tsang administration, which was forced to provide more data and explain its blueprint to the public.

EMERGENCE OF THE LEAGUE OF SOCIAL DEMOCRATS

Ideologically, the LSD is the most radical, pro-democratic, and yet socialist among all the political parties in the HKSAR. The LSD is punctuated by strong personalities, notably Raymond Wong Yuk-man, Leung Kwok-hung, and Albert Chan Wai-yip. While Albert Chan was a former DP member and withdrew from the democratic flagship partly because of his grassroots approach to tackling policy debates and partly because of his personality clashes with other DP colleagues, both Wong and Leung have been traditionally the vocal critics of the HKSAR government. Three of them are the LSD legislators, and their speeches and criticisms of the government can be seen on YouTube, which provides an effective means for the LSD to appeal to voters. LSD leader Raymond Wong has admitted explicitly that the new party's ideology adopts a socialist or "left-wing" line. As he claimed, "The CP and the DP are both parties located at the middle but tilting toward the right. The DAB changes from the left-wing to a big right-wing party. The FTU is left-wing but it is often controlled by the DAB. We hold the real flag of being left-wing."[31] Wong's remarks provide an accurate ideological spectrum of political parties in the HKSAR.

Since mid-2006, when the LSD was formed, its platform has remained very clear: it opposes small circle elections, supports the reunification of the mainland and Taiwan, calls for the PRC government to release the facts on the bloody crackdown on Tiananmen Square in June 1989, and advocates a public policy of wealth redistribution.[32] Its preparatory committee that founded the LSD included 35 members of whom 2 were legislators (Albert Chan and Leung Kwok-hung), 6 DC members, and 20 social activists. When the LSD was founded, about 100 young people in their twenties joined the party. Their participation illustrated the personal appeal of core leaders such as Raymond Wong and Leung Kwok-hung. Wong said that the party would set up a school to train the young members on political theory, speech making, district work, and public policy research.[33] It aims at grasping more seats not only in the legislature but also at the DC level.

The LSD claims to support socialist democracy and direct participation of citizens in managing their affairs.[34] In 2009, it has 1,000 members and 20 offices. Although the party nominated 30 candidates to compete in the 2007 DC elections, only 6 of them were elected. Still, for many LSD candidates who were defeated and who faced DAB counterparts, they managed to get 30 percent of the total vote in the constituencies—a good performance for the LSD's political unknowns participating in local elections for the first time.[35] Given more time, the LSD would likely be able to develop into a full-fledged political party with more elected DC members in the future.

Although the LSD lacked electoral experience in the 2007 DC elections, Wong was elected to the legislature in 2008 together with Albert Chan and Leung Kwok-hung. The LSD members have to learn how to campaign and win in district-level elections. In June 2009, Kwai Si-kit of the LSD participated in the Wanchai District Council by-election and was defeated by DAB member Chung Kar-man.[36] He sought the support of the DP and the CP, but the two parties refused, especially the CP, which said that it would support "candidates with the same ideals."[37] Obviously, Raymond Wong's severe criticisms of the CP in the 2008 LegCo direct elections angered the CP leaders, who regarded the LSD as a radical and competitive enemy. The fierce competition between the LSD and the CP in the 2008 LegCo elections had the unintended consequence of affecting the ability of LSD to fully mobilize the pan-democratic camp in the 2009 by-election held for the Wanchai District Council.

THE ROLE OF RAYMOND WONG

Raymond Wong, a popular political commentator in Hong Kong during the 1990s, left Commercial Radio in 2004 after a row with the radio station's authorities. His fierce criticisms of the HKSAR government and pro-Beijing politicians in his ATV program earned him a reputation and respect in the minds of many Hong Kong people. After Wong was elected to the LegCo, he has resorted to verbal attacks and once hurled bananas at the chief executive in 2008. Critics and pro-Beijing commentators severely criticized Wong's action as "uncivilized," but he remains to be supported by many citizens.

Wong was born in mainland China in 1952, where his father was a landlord.[38] Land reform in the PRC prompted his family to migrate to Hong Kong where Wong's father, who was staunchly anti-communist, passed away in 1988. The person most influential on Wong was the former triad boss Heung Chin, as admitted by Wong himself.[39] Wong was a good friend of the son of Heung Chin, namely Heung Wah-bor. There is no evidence to show that Wong participated in any triad activities, but his background and critical character earned him the nickname "rascal academic."[40] After Heung Chin was deported by the British Hong Kong government to Taiwan on the grounds that he was "not welcome," Wong in 1970 was sent by his late father to live in Heung's family home in Taiwan and to pursue his studies there. Later Wong returned to Hong Kong and completed his graduate studies at the Chu Hai College. After graduation, Wong worked as a reporter for several Hong Kong Chinese newspapers. From 1988 to 1992, Wong taught at the Chu Hai College's department of journalism and communication. In 1993, Wong co-hosted his popular ATV talk show with Albert Cheng King-hon. The program's critical approach to the PRC handling of Hong Kong led to tremendous pressure on ATV, which eventually had to terminate the program. In 1996, Wong opened his newspaper, *Mad Dog Daily*, but suffered a serious loss of HK$15 million. Wong revealed that, after he was dismissed by Commercial Radio in 2003, he opened a restaurant and was intimidated in March 2004 by mainland security agents and Hong Kong triad members.[41] Wong was afraid that his wife might be the victim of underground and political intimidations. DP legislator Albert Ho revealed in June 2004 that both Albert Cheng and Raymond Wong reported to the police about continuous harassment and pressure from triad bosses, who told the two popular commentators that the PRC's national security apparatus said they should be silent.[42] The message was clear: Wong and Cheng's personal safety would be exchanged for their political self-moderation. Wong's wife also revealed that some people did not want to envisage Wong's presence before the September 2004 LegCo elections. If triads in Hong Kong rescued mainland democrats in 1989, they also threatened some outspoken democrats in the HKSAR.

On October 1, 2006, Wong formed the LSD together with Leung Kwok-hung and Chan Wai-yip. In late 2007, the media reported that the League's office in Tsimshatsui district was possessed by a member of the triad, Sun Yee On.[43] Wong responded to such charge and maintained that his friend who owned the League's property did not commit any crime at that time, and that the LSD was concerned about the minorities in society, including those former prisoners released from jail. In 2008, Wong participated in the LegCo direct elections and was elected with 37,553 votes in the Kowloon West constituency. Because of the fact that Wong was severely critical of a candidate of the CP, Claudia Mo, the relationships between the CP and the LSD plunged into a nadir.

In October 2008, when Chief Executive Tsang delivered his policy address in the LegCo, Wong stood up angrily and accused Tsang's report of lacking any substantial policy measure to help the poor and the needy. Chan Wai-yip joined Wong and shouted that LegCo President Jasper Tsang was actually a member of the CCP.[44] Jasper Tsang said that their action obstructed the progress of the meeting and that they should leave the chamber if their action continued. Angered by Jasper Tsang's remarks, Wong continued to criticize Donald Tsang for ignoring the poor and the elderly. In response, Jasper Tsang ordered the security guards to expel Wong from the meeting room. Leung Kwok-hung was also angered by Tsang's decision and shouted whether the LegCo president was actually a member of the CCP in Hong Kong.[45] Angered by the president's order, Wong threw three bananas at the chief executive but missed the target. Chan Wai-yip left the room but shouted: "I strongly protest against the lack of HK$1,000 fruits subsidy to the elderly people who are humiliated by this policy. It is an insult to the elderly in a society that is so affluent and that cannot even afford to subsidize each of them by HK$1,000."[46] Anson Chan on October 20, 2008, criticized Wong's action as "wrong and disrespectful" of the political system.[47] Wong retorted by accusing Chan of suddenly turning into a democrat after working for the British Hong Kong government for many years. He maintained that the LSD merely fought for the interests of the lower classes and minorities. Although the LegCo received many complaints about Wong's action in the chamber, over 60 percent of the written and verbal comments received by LegCo supported him.

RADICALISM OF "LONG HAIR" LEUNG KWOK-HUNG

Another prominent and radical member of the LSD is "Long Hair" Leung Kwok-hung. Leung often resorts to the use of street protests, the burning of car tires, the confrontation with police, and the shouting of slogans inside the legislature to make his demands heard. In September 2005, when PRC Vice President Zeng Qinghong visited the HKSAR and met with the community leaders, including the pan-democrats, Leung and his supporter Ku Si-yiu tried to plunge into the security line outside the meeting room by using a wooden coffin.[48] Their purpose was to demand that the PRC government should return the confiscated home return permits to the Alliance leaders and members, that it should build up democracy, and that it should allow Hong Kong to have double direct elections as soon as possible. The police confiscated the wooden coffin.

When Leung attended a dinner hosted by Chief Executive Tsang for Vice President Zeng, he shouted his slogans in both Putonghua and Cantonese: "reversing the verdict on June 4th, returning the administration to the people, and terminating one-party dictatorship."[49] The security guards had little choice but to invite him to leave the dining room. Leung wore a coat with the words "reversing the verdict on June 4th," but security guards succeeded in persuading Leung to take it off.

After Leung was elected to LegCo in September 2004, he continued to show his politically defiant attitude toward political authorities. During the swearing-in ceremony in LegCo, Leung deliberately raised his middle finger and critics accused him of not only putting on a political show but also using inappropriate moves to disrespect the rule of law in the HKSAR.[50] His philosophy of defying political authorities through action is not easily accepted by many Hong Kong people who cherish political moderation. Indeed, Leung's behavior provided a golden opportunity for his political foes, such as Lau Kong-wah of the DAB, to accuse him of "insulting the public and women."[51] Acting defiantly, Leung invited Lau to debate with him and said he would apologize in public if Lau could persuade him that he was wrong.

Leung's pan-democratic colleagues sometimes distance themselves from his radical behavior for fear of antagonizing the moderate voters in the HKSAR. After Leung raised his middle finger in the legislature, Sin Chung-kai of the DP said that his party demanded an apology from Leung. Audrey Eu of the Article 45 Concern Group remarked that Leung should apologize because he should respect both himself and the public.[52] But Leung did gain the support of some democrats. Chan Wai-yip said that the situation did not reach the stage of asking him to apologize, while Lee Cheuk-yan remarked that Leung's action "did not intentionally insult the public but represented an action of imitation."[53] The response of voters was divided, with some criticizing his "uncivilized" behavior and some praising his action. One voter said that the incident was actually insignificant but blown up by the mass media and Leung's political foes because his action was similar to those legislators who slept during LegCo's meetings.[54]

The most provocative move by Leung was his attempt to add several phrases into his oath of office in the LegCo. He tried to amend the oath by adding the phrases: "being loyal to the Chinese people and Hong Kong citizens to fight for democracy, justice, human rights, and freedom."[55] The HKSAR government was alarmed because Leung's amendment challenged Beijing's political bottom line of tolerance. The Liaison Office's deputy director, Li Gang, said that "if someone insists on amending the oath, this is a violation of the law and he is not qualified to be a legislator."[56] The NPC Standing Committee's deputy secretary, Qiao Xiaoyang, criticized Leung for not following the regulation. Leung even applied to the High Court for judicial review, but the High Court rejected his application. The court said that the oath of office was a seriously written regulation that legislators would have to follow. The HKSAR government's secretary for justice warned that if Leung insisted on amending the oath, the most serious consequence would be his loss of the elected seat.[57] On the day of the swearing-in ceremony of legislators, Leung changed his tactics by adding phrases at the end of the oath, namely, "Long live democracy, long live for the people, people to the people, opposition to small circle election, selection of the Chief Executive by universal suffrage, and election of the entire LegCo by universal suffrage."[58] Leung said that his supporters persuaded him to moderate the tactics so that he could struggle for democracy inside the LegCo. Wearing his T-shirt with the picture of his favorite Cuban revolutionary hero, Che Guevara, and with the Chinese slogan "reversing the June 4th verdict, returning the administration to the people," Leung finished reading his prolonged swearing-in statement without violating any law.[59] Leung is by no means an anarchist, but he is constantly determined to challenge the regime's bottom line of political tolerance.

Leung's radicalism is often criticized by his critics, but they ignore his political philosophy of not only challenging the regime's authority but also protecting individual rights. In August 2005, Leung applied to the High Court for judicial review and argued that the government's administrative order on secret surveillance should be repealed.[60] According to the HKSAR government, it could empower departments to conduct surveillance on citizens and the data obtained, after the consent of the secretary for security, could be shared with the mainland police and national security agency.[61] Leung contended that he was the target of the government's secret surveillance for many years. The police, to Leung, kept a close eye on him and his office, phones, and home were all bugged. He revealed that in 1998, he noticed that a person followed him and later appeared in his court case. Leung also complained that he once canceled a street protest, but before he informed the police of his decision, they had asked him whether the protest would be canceled. Leung argued that the government's secret surveillance on citizens actually violated Article 30 of the Basic Law, which says that citizens should enjoy the freedom of and secrecy of communications.

Leung often challenges the regime authority in such a way that he was frequently convicted. In 1979, he was jailed for a month because of illegal protest outside the PRC New China News Agency in Hong Kong.[62] In August 1998, he was fined and ordered by the court to observe his behavior after setting a coffin on fire to protest against PRC President Jiang Zemin's visit to Hong Kong. Two months later, he was imprisoned for two weeks for shouting inside the LegCo when Chief Executive Tung delivered the policy address. In 1999, Leung was fined HK$3,000 for showing a damaged HKSAR flag and a vandalized PRC flag. In October 2000, he was jailed for seven days because he shouted slogans inside the LegCo and forced the meeting to terminate. In May 2001, he was fined for coloring the HKSAR flag during a protest against police power. In February 2002, he was required to observe his behavior for three months after violating the public order ordinance to stage a protest without police approval. In January 2009, Leung was ordered to do 120 hours of social service work after he and To Kwan-hang clashed with the police and burnt car tires in protest against the visit of Qiao Xiaoyang, the NPC Standing Committee's deputy secretary, to the HKSAR.[63] Naturally, many critics of Leung regard him as a political "troublemaker."

As a radical democrat, Leung is bound to be politically excluded by the PRC authorities. After the earthquake that plunged Sichuan province into crisis in the summer of 2008, 19 Hong Kong legislators paid a visit to the province to inspect the serious damage. But when Leung, who wore a T-shirt claiming the Tiananmen verdict should be reversed, was on his way to the Hong Kong Chek Lap Kok airport, he was informed that the authorities had not issued him a home return permit to visit the mainland.[64] The mainland authorities explained that Leung tried to achieve political objectives that were not in conformity with the purpose of the legislators' visit. Chief Executive Tsang refused to comment on the issue by saying that it was an internal affair of the mainland. The LegCo president, Rita Fan, said that she was overoptimistic toward the visit and had to apologize to Leung for any inconvenience that might cause him. Leung said that the mainland's decision was a retrogressive step in democratic development and that he did not wish to initiate any radical action in the PRC except for seeking to understand whether bureaucratic corruption caused the collapse of so many schools during the earthquake. With the benefit of hindsight, Leung had earlier revealed his intentions of investigating corruption in the mainland and requesting that the PRC government allow freedom of press and of speech.[65] His clear intentions aroused the concern of PRC authorities who must bar him from entering the mainland.

POLITICAL SYMBOLISM OF LSD'S VERBAL AND PHYSICAL PROTEST

One of the most provocative collective actions involving verbal and physical protests staged by Raymond Wong, Leung Kwok-hung, and Albert Chan was in February and March 2009. After Wong hurled three bananas at Chief Executive Tsang but missed the target, the pro-Beijing press and politicians grasped the opportunity to launch a fierce attack at the LSD legislators. In February 2009, the financial secretary John Tsang delivered his budget speech in the LegCo. Prior to John Tsang's speech,

Wong raised a banner claiming that the government had millions of financial reserves but it ignored the plight of the poor. When Tsang delivered his speech, Wong went up to him, tried to snatch his script, pushed down his cup of water, and later hurled a plastic banana at the financial secretary when he was escorted away by LegCo's security guards. While Albert Chan was shouting in support of Wong, Leung left the chamber but then returned at once to walk near John Tsang. Leung showed Tsang a broken rice bowl and the LSD pamphlet and complained that many citizens were unemployed.[66] In response, President Jasper Tsang terminated the meeting and ordered the three LSD members be expelled from the chamber. Leung at once hurled a banana at John Tsang but almost hit the secretary for justice, Wong Yan-lung, who sat beside John Tsang. After the incident, Wong defended their action by saying that no one was hurt and that reporters would get used to the LSD's action of violating the rules of conduct in the LegCo. Albert Chan argued that it was the government lacking respect because the current system disrespected the citizens. Leung added that he did not want to put up a show but only expressed how citizens felt during the global financial crisis. Immediately after the event, 30 legislators signed a declaration regretting and reprimanding the behavior of three LSD legislators. The chief secretary for administration, Henry Tang, wrote a letter to express his regret over the behavior of LSD legislators, who to him "publicly ignore order."[67] Tang added: "Hong Kong's society generally agrees that any protest has to be conducted peacefully . . . and it does not condone action in violation of this consensus, especially the behavior of disrupting the normal proceedings of the meeting of the LegCo."[68] John Tsang echoed Tang's view and added that "the rude language and behavior are incomprehensible."[69] The ExCo's convener Leung Chun-ying criticized the three LSD members of "being too radical, damaging social serenity, stability, order, and they should be reprimanded."[70] Interestingly, Albert Ho of the DP declared that the LSD behavior was "unacceptable," while Audrey Eu of the CP said the party "did not identify with" the LSD action. At once, the LSD was politically ostracized.

In the wake of the LSD's verbal and physical protest inside the LegCo, most legislators decided to amend the rules of conduct in the chamber. The DP and CP supported the move of amending the existing rules of conduct.[71] Independent democrat Cyd Ho said she supported the action of the LSD as long as there was no physical contact between them and the government officials in LegCo.[72] She argued that the existing legislature was dominated by the DAB and the pro-establishment elites, and therefore "fair discussion" could not be conducted.

In March 2009, both Raymond Wong and Leung Kwok-hung used foul language in the Finance Committee meetings. A senior civil servant who attended the meeting, Ling Hon-ho, said Leung used foul language that must be shunned by parents.[73] Finance Committee chairwoman Emily Lau had to terminate the meeting and appealed to legislators to refrain from using improper language. The three LSD legislators surrounded Ling and argued whether the term used by Leung was really foul language.[74] In another Finance Committee meeting, Albert Chan repeated the term used by both Wong and Leung, and Emily Lau ordered him to be expelled. In response, Chan criticized Lau of being "dictatorial."[75] Lau insisted that legislators should not use terms that, in accordance with Article 41 of LegCo Standing Order, are "aggressive" and "insulting."[76]

While the verbal and physical action, if not necessarily abuse, initiated by the three LSD members made them less popular in public opinion polls than ever before, their behavior represents political symbolism with significant implications. A poll conducted by the University of Hong Kong in April 2009 showed that the popularity of Albert Chan, Leung Kwok-hung, and Raymond Wong dropped considerably, especially Wong whose image was affected by his relatively radical action inside the legislature.[77] Yet, political scientist Lowell Dittmer had long reminded us that symbols, colors, gestures, and slogans can represent political roles, beliefs, and meanings.[78] The relatively radical action of Wong, Leung, and Chan in the Hong Kong LegCo has at least several political meanings, including their beliefs and special roles in the local democracy movement.

First and foremost, the three LSD legislators are by no means anarchists. Nor do they advocate any revolutionary action as with Che Guevara. In fact, Leung Kwok-hung since his reelection to LegCo in 2008 has moderated his radical action, which is now assumed by the newly elected Wong. Chan had a track record of legally challenging the regime, as with his decision of applying to the court in April 2005 for judicial review of the years of office of the chief executive who replaced Tung Chee-hwa.[79] All three LSD legislators are attempting to challenge the regime's bottom line of political tolerance inside the legislature. In a relatively moderate mass political culture in which many citizens, especially middle-class members, see radical action as unacceptable, the three LSD legislators are bound to moderate their behavior after radical moves undermine their popularity.

Second, ideologically three of them are in conformity with the left-wing and lower-class orientations of the LSD. They fight for the interests of the poor and the needy, and their political support lies with the lower-class and working-class citizens. The three LSD legislators share a premise, namely the HKSAR government has been allying with big business to exploit the lower-class citizens. This Marxist perspective is held by the LSD, whose ideology is politically unacceptable to not only the HKSAR government but also the PRC, which is ironically far more capitalist than ever before. The three LSD members are critical Marxists in the sense that they adopt a critical stance on bureaucratic corruption in the mainland, the Tiananmen tragedy, and the lack of human rights and democracy in the PRC. The reason why the Hong Kong media and pro-Beijing forces portray the three LSD legislators negatively is that the mainstream media are increasingly pro-PRC and politically cautious. Meanwhile, the DAB and FTU are by no means critical Marxists. The DAB co-opts some pro-Beijing business elites while steering a middle-lower class approach to winning the hearts and minds of the populace. The FTU is more pro-workers, but its ideology lacks the critical perspective that distinguishes the LSD from the pro-Beijing forces.

Third, the LSD is ideologically at odds with other pro-democracy parties. While the CP is focusing on the support of the middle class, the LSD is a middle-lower and lower-class party rather than being interested merely in middle-class professionals. Unlike the DP, which is a very moderate loyal opposition within the legislature, the LSD deviates from the moderate line of the DP and seeks to challenge all the political authorities. The three LSD legislators believe that whatever the "radical" action they take, it is far more moderate than the Taiwan opposition from the 1980s to the present, when legislators sometimes fought against themselves inside the Legislative Yuan. Critics of the LSD, such as legislator Priscilla Leung, have argued that there is a danger of Taiwanization of the Hong Kong legislature, meaning that the verbal and physical action employed by the LSD has become more similar to Taiwan's radical oppositionists.[80] Yet, the reality is that the LSD is a relatively defiant loyal opposition in LegCo. The LSD is arguably a loyal opposition in the sense that its core leaders and members are determined to fight for the interests of the poor and the needy inside the legislature. They do not seek to topple the Hong Kong political system. But they remain defiant as they find the ruling coalition composed of the government elites, DAB, FTU, and the pro-business LP as disgraceful.

Fourth, the LSD's street protests outside the LegCo mean that it remains a party utilizing both institutional and unconventional tactics to make the demands of citizens known. Leung's street protests are well known but detested by most police constables dealing with him and his supporters. Although other democrats such as the DP and CP do not identify themselves with the LSD's radical politics, especially the LSD's verbal and physical actions in LegCo, the diversified ways in which the pan-democrats adopt their strategies in lobbying, opposing, and reprimanding the government create a wide ideological spectrum for voters to choose them in elections. Hence, while critics see the LSD as a "deviant" group that may politically split the democrats, it can also be regarded as an indispensable political opposition that combines critical Marxism curiously with the liberal objective of achieving the direct elections of both the chief executive through universal suffrage and the entire LegCo.

DECLINE OF THE ASSOCIATION FOR DEMOCRACY AND PEOPLE'S LIVELIHOOD

The rise of the LSD has been accompanied by the decline of the ADPL. Founded in 1984, the ADPL has been traditionally influential in its power base, the Shumshuipo district. The most glorious years of the ADPL were in 1994 and 1995, when the party had 4 elected legislators, 9 elected urban and regional councilors, and 28 elected District Boards members.[81] The party suffered a setback in 1998 when all of its four candidates running for the LegCo were defeated, while the number of DC members was only maintained at 14. The ADPL relied too heavily on Frederick Fung, who decided to resign from the chair position after its failure to retain 25 DC seats in 2007. He promised a review of the party's future directions. The ADPL has considered the alternative of returning to a pressure group rather than being a political party. Actually, this consideration is superficial. As long as the ADPL nominates its members to run in LegCo and DC elections, it intends to grasp political power and thus can be seen as a political party. Unless the ADPL does not nominate any candidate to run in DC elections and instead focuses on district livelihood issues, it would remain a mini-political party.

The ADPL's decline in the 2007 DC elections was attributable to two main factors. First, the DAB and FTU spent a long time span and sufficient resources to penetrate the ADPL power base, thus depriving the ADPL of more voters than Fung and his colleagues expected. Second, since mid-2003 Fung has sided with the pan-democrats in such a politically close manner that many voters see him and the ADPL as the same as other pro-democracy forces. In other words, the uniqueness of the ADPL was diluted from mid-2003 to 2007. Fung's stepping down from the chair position could be seen as a positive sign of opening the door to party renewal.

According to the ADPL's alternatives, it may expand the number of elected representatives at the district levels, attract more people to join the group so as to improve its image, merge with a political party, and co-opt more legislators.[82] But Fung added: "If the directions fail and we cannot manage politics well, the ADPL would return to be a pressure group by focusing on livelihood issues and avoiding politics."[83] Fung's view of politics appears to be relatively narrow and he distinguishes it from livelihood matters, but both can be intertwined in that the fight for the people's livelihood has to go through political channels and institutions. What Fung meant was that the ADPL would have to avoid those sensitive issues like universal suffrage, referendum, and the Tiananmen incident. As one critic of the ADPL wrote:

Hong Kong's livelihood issues cannot be separated from the political boundaries. The government dominates the distribution of societal resources, but the undemocratic system generates a trend of the collusion between the government and business. Any group seeking to improve livelihood issues must touch upon the political arena so as to maximize the chance of redistributing resources. Unless the ADPL wants to be marginalized, the avoidance from politics would not only become unhelpful to livelihood matters but also pave the way for suicide.[84]

While Fung might be accurate in delineating the future options for the ADPL, it will likely remain a district-based mini-party. Meanwhile, the ADPL leaders are in their mid-forties and would have at least a decade of political life. Provided that the ADPL can retain these core members, such as Liu Shing-lee and Tam Kwok-kiu, and recruit young members, its political future would not be as pessimistic as being portrayed in the Hong Kong Chinese press.

Critics say that the ADPL has been fluctuating from the pro-Beijing to pro-democracy lines, thus making its political position ambiguous. In Hong Kong's late transition period from the British sovereignty to the Chinese Special Administrative Region, the ADPL led by Frederick Fung and Liu Shing-lee accepted the PRC arrangement of abolishing the last colonial legislature and replacing it with the PLC dominated by the pro-Beijing elites.[85] Fung and Liu became the PLC members, but both were utterly defeated in the 1998 LegCo elections. Clearly, the ADPL was punished by pro-democracy voters for its excessively pro-Beijing line. The ADPL's support of the PLC alienated other pro-democracy parties and groups. After the debate over Article 23 of the Basic Law in early July 2003, the ADPL shifted to the pan-democratic camp and yet alienated PRC authorities. After the 2007 DC election setback, Fung's ADPL began to consider a third path, but whether it would drift back to the pro-PRC line remains to be seen. Basically, from 1997 to 2007 the ADPL failed to maintain a politically consistent direction, unintentionally hurting the party's image in the minds of voters. In terms of class background, the ADPL is similar to the LSD in that both are middle-lower class and lower-class parties. Yet, in its attitude toward Beijing, the ADPL has been oscillating since 1997, whereas the LSD has been consistently anti-PRC.

Wong On-yin, a critic of the ADPL, compares the party with trade unionist Lau Chin-shek, who has drifted gradually from the support of democracy in Hong Kong and China to a more pro-Beijing line in the 2000s. Interestingly, Wong used the example of the ADPL to appeal to Lau not to follow the ADPL line before the September 2008 LegCo elections. Wong wrote:

Ten years ago the ADPL adopted the line of the so-called fighting and discussing simultaneously. The pro-Beijing elites ridiculed this line as "opportunistic democrats." What was the result? Originally the ADPL had 4 seats in the last colonial legislature, but its 4 legislators went to join the PLC, which later became a political vase in enacting several bad laws for the HKSAR. In the 1998 legislative elections, all four former ADPL legislators were defeated. Only Frederick Fung returned to the Legislative Council in 2000. Since then the ADPL has become a marginalized party.[86]

Wong argued that before the 2008 LegCo election, Lau Chin-shek still had a chance of being reelected. Although Lau later was defeated, Wong's argument that the pan-democratic camp had a "triad culture" was noteworthy. He argued that some democrats saw Lau's deviation from the pan-democratic line as a defection to the PRC side and that this was the hallmark of their "triad culture."[87] Wong's argument was indeed debatable, but his criticisms leveled at the ADPL's opportunistic drift toward the PRC during the handover period were valid. If the ADPL cannot map out its policy toward both Beijing and the pan-democratic camp, any further oscillation between the two sides would likely repeat the ADPL's past experiences in elections: voters punished them for being excessively pro-Beijing in 1998 and for being blindly pro-democracy in 2007.

Finally, the ADPL lacks party discipline. In September 2009, when social worker and ADPL member Cheung Kwok-chu was elected to the LegCo, he said he would not necessarily follow the ADPL line in his voting behavior. Frederick Fung accommodated Cheung's wishes and said that since Cheung represented his social workers' union, he would be exempted by the ADPL to follow the party line. But Fung added that on issues in which the social workers' union and their sector do not have any position, Cheung's stance should be the same as the ADPL. It was understandable why the ADPL dealt with Cheung's voting behavior in a flexible way, but it also illustrated the weakness of the ADPL discipline, which can be overridden by the elected legislator's union interests.

SUMMARY

While the CP and LSD are relatively new pro-democracy mini-parties in the HKSAR, the ADPL has experienced a decline after two decades of development. The birth of the CP and LSD filled in the gap left by the DP, whose internal and external difficulties during the mid-2000s led to the emergence of professionals and activists keen to set up other organizations to fight for democracy in the HKSAR. Furthermore, the middle-lower class orientations of the DP could not satisfy the aspirations of some middle-class professionals and the lower-class citizens. As a result, the emergence of the CP could tap the middle-class market, whereas the LSD targets at the middle-lower class and especially the lower-class citizens. The proliferation of pro-democracy mini-parties has not really weakened the local democracy movement. Instead, different small parties can focus on specific social classes, thus compensating the weaknesses of the aging DP, which remains the target of political persecution by both the HKSAR regime and Beijing's national security agents in Hong Kong. The decline of the ADPL is understandable because of the growing influence and improved organization of the DAB on the one hand and of the party's oscillating political orientations toward Beijing and the pan-democratic camp on the other.

The radicalism of the LSD has important political implications for Hong Kong's politics and democracy movement. Its radicalism marks the existence of critical Marxism, which is also mingled with the socialist ideology and the liberal objective of supporting the direct elections of the chief executive through universal suffrage and of the entire legislature. Raymond Wong, Leung Kwok-hung, and Albert Chan are playing a crucial role in Hong Kong's democracy movement because they are constantly challenging the bottom line of political tolerance by the HKSAR government and Beijing. Arguably, they are the democratic socialists in the HKSAR. Their vision of democracy and justice remains very different from the PRC authorities, who are keen to maintain political authoritarianism and social paternalism in the mainland. Nevertheless, the vision of democracy, in the minds of Wong, Leung, and Chan, is the Western one with double direct elections as soon as possible. Their vision of social justice is socialist; namely there should not be any collusion between the government and business, and the redistribution of wealth in favor of the poor and the needy would be necessary. It is rare to find so few dedicated and yet enthusiastic as well as principled democratic socialists on mainland Chinese soil.

CHAPTER 8

Can the Pro-Beijing DAB and Pro-Business Liberal Party Promote Democratization in Hong Kong?

The DAB can promote democratization in the HKSAR by consolidating its role in electoral politics, by lobbying Beijing for the protection of Hong Kong's interests, and by displaying its tolerance of other political foes, namely the pro-democracy parties. In the first two aspects, the DAB has performed well, but its leaders and core members sometimes display a relatively intolerant attitude toward pro-democracy parties. Such intolerance, as shown in verbal attacks, is understandable because of the competitive nature of Hong Kong politics. But ideally, if the DAB leaders can articulate the interests of the pan-democratic camp, which has problems in its relations and dialogue with Beijing, the DAB's positive role in Hong Kong's democratization can be enhanced. Furthermore, if the DAB attitude toward other democratic parties is more tolerant and helpful, it can arguably have a neglected demonstration effect on the CCP in the mainland. In the PRC, the CCP remains a hegemonic and the largest party without any challenge from any opposition party. Arguably, if the DAB in the HKSAR can coexist with the pan-democratic parties and display a far more tolerant attitude toward its political opponents, the CCP can learn from the DAB experience. Needless to say, the size of the DAB is no match with the CCP. Yet, as a very small mass party in the HKSAR, the DAB's invisible influence on the CCP has often been neglected by observers.

The pro-business LP remains in the stage of political learning because most business elites are uninterested in electoral participation. They have traditionally enjoyed political influence and power through colonial and postcolonial appointments into various policy-making and consultative committees without the urgency of participating in electoral politics. The LP, as will be discussed below, has various weaknesses that have to be addressed if it is expected to contribute to Hong Kong's democratization. In brief, although the DAB and LP are by no means identifying themselves with the democratic camp, they can contribute to Hong Kong's democratization through their active electoral participation.

DAB ELECTORAL PERFORMANCE AND MERGER WITH THE HONG KONG PROGRESSIVE ALLIANCE

The DAB was formed by 56 founding members in July 1992.[1] By July 2009, the DAB had 12,844 members of whom 13 were legislators, 132 DC members, 9 Hong Kong NPC members, and 32 CPPCC members. The DAB has 18 party branches in the HKSAR, with each branch having a chairperson, a monthly paid district director responsible for organizing the party at the district level, a few district work assistants, and a number of executive committee members. The top policy-making body of the DAB is the 50-member Central Committee. Candidates for the Central Committee have to compete for votes among party members, but some committee members had the problem of absenteeism in Central Committee meetings. The DAB is led by a chairperson (Tam Yiu-chung from 2007 to the present, the late Ma Lik from 2003 to 2007, and Jasper Tsang from 1992 to 2003), four deputy chairs, a secretary, a deputy secretary, and a treasurer.[2] The platform of the DAB is to uphold the banner of "loving the nation and loving Hong Kong," "democratic participation," "building Hong Kong," and "wholeheartedly serving the HKSAR."[3] Its share of the total votes in LegCo direct elections from 1998 to 2008 ranged from 25 to 30 percent of the total votes (see Table 8.1). Although its public

Table 8.1

The DAB Share of Total Votes in the Legislative Council Direct Elections, 1998–2008

Year	Votes got by DAB	Total Votes Cast	No. of Elected Candidates	Percentage of Total Votes
2008	433,684	1,515,479	9	28.61
2004	454,827	1,769,911	9	25.7
2000	391,718	1,319,694	8	29.68
1998	373,428	1,480,240	5	25.22

Source: See www.dab.org.hk (accessed: August 13, 2009).

support appeared to decline slightly after the Article 23 debate in 2003 and during the 2004 LegCo elections, the DAB rebound could be seen in the 2008 LegCo elections. Overall, the DAD succeeded in grasping more directly elected seats and about 29 percent of the votes with the passage of time, and thereby it fulfills the function of checking the influence of the pan-democrats in direct elections.

The DAB merger with the 300-member Hong Kong Progressive Alliance (HKPA) took place in early 2005 after a negotiated settlement. At that time the DAB had 1,800 members and needed to broaden its united front umbrella to include more members from the society, especially business-people.[4] According to the deal, the HKPA expected that after the merger, one-third of the members of the new DAB's Central Committee would be HKPA members.[5] Moreover, some key HKPA leaders such as Maria Tam, Lau Hon-chuen, and Yeung Suen-sai would play a crucial role in the new DAB leadership. But some local-level members of the HKPA were dissatisfied and said they might withdraw from the new DAB after the merger. The reason was that they were worried about the likelihood of the HKPA being swallowed by the new DAB, just like the Meeting Point's merger with the pro-democracy flagship UDHK into the DP in the early 1990s. In comparing the HKPA with the Meeting Point, the anxiety of some HKPA members was understandable. In fact, after the merger and with the recruitment of more young members, the aging HKPA members are no longer important in the continuously growing DAB.

The HKPA represented a small business party that failed to perform well in direct elections, and thus its merger with the DAB was a marriage of convenience aimed at prolonging its survival by tapping into the DAB's strength. The HKPA was founded in July 1994 by a group of patriotic businesspeople such as Lau Hon-chuen, Wan Ka-shuen, and Yeung Suen-sai. Three months later, HKPA chair Lau visited Beijing and met PRC President Jiang Zemin, who hoped that the party would continue to "work hard for the long-term and important task of maintaining Hong Kong's prosperity and achieving the success of 'one country, two systems.'"[6] In May 1997, the HKPA merged with the pro-business Liberal Democratic Federation led by former member of the ExCo Maria Tam. In 1998, the HKPA succeeded in capturing six LegCo seats through the Electoral College and functional constituencies. In 2000, HKPA member Choy So-yuk left the party and joined the DAB, but the HKPA managed to maintain four seats in the legislature. Yet, in the 2004 LegCo elections, none of the HKPA members was elected, thus sounding its death knell. Lacking political stars, organization, and leadership, the HKPA opted for the amalgamation with the DAB to prolong the longevity of the declining party. The merger was also a deliberate political move that would enhance the DAB influence on the Election Committee that would select the chief executive in 2007.[7]

SUCCESSION PLANNING AND THE STRATEGY OF WINNING THE HEARTS AND MINDS OF HONG KONG PEOPLE

The DAB, which became the largest political party in the LegCo after the September 2004 legislative elections, planned to train a second tier of leaders. Three new young DAB members could enter the LegCo after September 2004, stimulating the party morale and planning to groom new party members who would follow their mentors in the legislature.[8] The party aimed at strengthening its "patriotic, popular, and professional" aspects.[9] Starting in 2005, the DAB began to recruit more professionals into the party, notably businesswoman Chiang Lai-wan.[10] The DAB also targeted the training of district branch organizer Chung Kong-mo and accountant Starry Lee Wai-ling in the future, while Jasper Tsang himself acted as a mentor for both of them. Before Lee was elected as a legislator in 2008, she had been appointed to the government's think tank Central Policy Unit as a part-time member and became a rising star in the Kowloon City District Council.[11] When Jasper Tsang participated in the 2004 LegCo elections, both Lee and Chung were on Tsang's party list. With the benefit of hindsight, given the successful election of Starry Lee into the LegCo in 2008 and the election of Chung into the Tsimshatsui District Council in 2007, the DAB succession planning proceeded smoothly. At present, DAB deputy chair Cheung Kwok-kwan is a young lawyer whose political mentor was the late Ma Lik.[12] Cheung was given lots of opportunities to represent the DAB as a spokesman in various public forums, gaining considerable experience in public speaking and political commentaries. In the minds of many moderate but politically pragmatic Hong Kong people, they prefer to join the DAB so that their political prospects can be far more encouraging than participating in those "anti-PRC" parties as the DP and the CP.

The DAB plan of training its young members stands out among all political parties in Hong Kong because of its sufficient financial resources. In April 2008, the DAB continued with its plan of recruiting more young members. There were 1,100 members affiliated with the "young DAB," an organization that trains political talents to be politicians, government appointees, and party researchers.[13] It sent 30 young members to study politics and public administration at Cambridge University. Another six member delegation of the DAB visited Texas and Ohio and learned how the DP and Republican Party campaigned during the American presidential elections.[14] At the same time, the DAB mobilized its professionals to study Hong Kong's urban planning and heath-care funding so as to enhance their communications with the local professional organizations.[15] In March 2008, 153 professionals joined the DAB as members, and they came from sectors such as information technology, environment, insurance, and accountancy.[16] The party opened a blog for professional members to discuss various issues, including mainland–Hong Kong relations and cross-border business cooperation. The objective was to broaden the social network and win the hearts and minds of more professionals in Hong Kong. In April 2009, the DAB instituted an internal selection of 18 deputy policy spokespersons among 50 candidates.[17] Jasper Tsang was invited as the adjudicator and he gave comments on the performance of the candidates. Therefore, the DAB's internal organization has injected the ingredient of competition so as to select its young leaders on the basis of merit.

Like the DP, the DAB trains young members by using the mentorship scheme in which the "big brothers" or "sisters" impart their political and electoral experience onto the young members. The former DAB deputy chair, So Kam-leung, said that the "big brother" system had its virtue of training political talents.[18] He pointed to the lack of job security on the part of some DAB members who lost in local elections. The DAB injected considerable resources to continue employing those defeated candidates so that they would have a better chance of winning the next elections. Except for the DAB, no political parties in the HKSAR can afford to pay 18 district organizers in 18 districts monthly and continuously for several years prior to each round of DC elections so that the party's power base can be deeply entrenched. In this aspect, the DAB's infiltration into the grassroots level is perhaps parallel to the CCP's tactics of mass mobilization and political penetration.

Starting in early 2006, the DAB has an external committee dealing with foreign diplomats in the HKSAR. Its committee chairman, Lam Kwong-yu, revealed that he and the party interacted more closely with foreigners, listened to their views and questions on Hong Kong, and exchanged opinions on issues of common concern.[19] Not surprisingly, the PRC officials responsible for Hong Kong matters can also better understand the views of foreign diplomats indirectly through their intensive interactions with the DAB.

Financially, the DAB is undoubtedly the most affluent political party in the HKSAR due to its strong support from patriotic businesspeople and organizations, not to mention the logistical and hidden support provided by the Liaison Office. In Table 8.2, the DAB's financial reserves were the strongest compared to the DP and even the pro-business LP. While the LP secured considerable financial donations in 1993–1994 and 2003–2004, its income tended to fluctuate from 1994 to 2003. The DP's financial donations were the strongest in 1997–1998, when some Hong Kong people were perhaps most concerned about their civil liberties in the HKSAR. The DP's financial reserves declined considerably after 1999, perhaps a reflection of the party's internal and external crises. Yet, the DAB's financial income has risen continuously since 1992—a testimony to the growing pro-Beijing party and its financial donors.

Table 8.2

The Financial Reserves of the Democratic Alliance for Betterment and Progress of Hong Kong, Liberal Party, and Democratic Party, 1992–2005

	HK$ million		
Year	DAB	LP	DP
1992–1993	5.25	N/A[a]	N/A
1993–1994	10	21.39	N/A
1994–1995	12.59	12.28	5.93
1995–1996	18.59	9	14.52
1996–1997	15.27	8.49	12.21
1997–1998	21.4	11.5	16.65
1998–1999	26.37	12.5	12.33
1999–2000	29.36	15.31	7.34
2000–2001	33.94	9.78	5.51
2001–2002	25.46	9.79	5.73
2002–2003	25.54	9.68	5.14
2003–2004	30.11	21.98	7.36
2004–2005	39.45	N/A	7.45

[a]N/A: Data were not available.
Source: *Ming Pao*, June 13, 2006, p. A18.

Although the DAB tries to extend its united front tentacles to other pro-Beijing forces, notably the rural advisory body Heung Yee Kuk (HYK), their relations are sometimes tense and conflict-ridden. A case in point was the DAB decision of supporting its deputy chair Ip Kwok-him to run for the DC functional constituency election held for the LegCo in July 2008. Its decision led to the anger of some HYK members, who severely and openly criticized the DAB in a HYK meeting. HYK member Tang Ho-nian argued that the DAB in the first place should not nominate Ip to compete with HYK chair Lau Wong-fat in the DC constituency.[20] Some HYK members, such as Kan Ping-chee, even asked HYK deputy chair Cheung Hok-ming, who teamed up with DAB chair Tam Yiu-chung to run in LegCo's direct elections, to leave the HYK.[21] Later, HYK deputy chair Lam Wai-keung ran in the DC functional constituency as an independent while Cheung continued to cooperate with DAB chair Tam Yiu-chung to run in the geographical constituency elections in the New Territories West. Lam was defeated by Ip, but Cheung was elected together with Tam. The election result showed that Lam Wai-keung was forced to run as an independent in order to let Cheung follow the DAB party list led by Tam.

This compromise appeared to satisfy the DAB, but some pro-Lam HYK members saw the DAB-HYK coalition as not only a marriage of political convenience but also an imposed solution orchestrated by the DAB and endorsed by the HYK chair Lau Wong-fat.

The DAB's support of independent candidate Regina Ip to compete with pro-democracy Anson Chan in the by-election held for the LegCo in 2007 entailed an unforeseen consequence leading to the failure of its candidate Choy So-yuk to be reelected in the 2008 LegCo direct elections on the Hong Kong Island. The DAB backed up Ip at the costs of frustrating its diligent party branch chair Chung Shu-kan on the Hong Kong Island and considerably reducing Choy's votes in 2008. Chung wished to run in the 2007 by-election, but his intention was suppressed by the DAB decision to support Ip. In 2008, the DAB list led by Jasper Tsang and Choy got 60,417 votes, whereas pro-Beijing independent Ip captured 61,073 votes, thus leading to Choy's inability to get sufficient votes to be elected.[22] After her defeat, Choy was reluctant to admit publicly that the DAB support of Ip in 2007 affected her chance of being reelected in 2008. But she emphasized that the DAB votes on the Hong Kong Island declined from 74,659 in 2004 to 60,417 votes, a loss of 14,000 votes, of which many shifted to become votes for other candidates, especially Regina Ip.

An important political weakness of the DAB is that its position on democracy in the HKSAR is contingent on the PRC attitude and policy. In this aspect, the DAB lacks autonomy vis-à-vis Beijing. After the NPC Standing Committee vetoed double direct election for the chief executive in Hong Kong in 2007 and the LegCo in 2008, DAB chair Tam Yiu-chung went so far as to assert that "the pan-democratic camp would gradually disappear, because the concept of democracy is now outdated. The only camps left will be the pro-establishment and opposition factions."[23] Tam's personal view is more conservative than the former DAB chair Jasper Tsang, who admitted that the possibility of "confirming a timetable for universal suffrage in Hong Kong would generate a 'third way' of political party development."[24] Critics of Tam said that the NPC Standing Committee actually opened the door for the HKSAR to have the possibility of directly electing the chief executive through universal suffrage in 2017 and directly electing the whole legislature in 2020. Hence, the DAB has to prepare for constructive solutions and blueprints rather than constantly adopting a politically passive and evasive attitude toward democratization.

Another problem of the DAB is that its task is to support the HKSAR government. If the HKSAR government were unpopular, as with the case of the Tung Chee-hwa administration, the DAB's popularity would be easily affected. After the massive protests against the Tung administration on July 1, 2003, and July 1, 2004, the DAB has begun to develop a more autonomous policy stance so as to project an image of not blindly following the policies and position of the HKSAR government. Still, the voting behavior of DAB legislators shows that they are destined to support the administration, especially if the pan-democratic camp is united to oppose government bills and policies.[25]

FIGHTING FOR THE PEOPLE'S LIVELIHOOD

To win the hearts and minds of the Hong Kong people, the DAB has been engaging in district work extensively, articulating the interests of the poor and the needy and supervising the government. In November 2007, it appealed to the government to allocate HK$240 billion to soothe the difficulties of the poor and the needy.[26] The DAB opposed any increase in the fares charged to vehicles and cars going through the cross-harbor tunnel in the Western district.[27] To cope with the global financial crisis in late 2008, the DAB suggested that the government and the business sector should implement a HK$5 billion lottery scheme that would stimulate each citizen who spent HK$300 to enter the lottery for the possibility of getting various benefits and gifts, such as free transportation, apartment units, and vehicles.[28] In May 2008, the DAB held a candlelight vigil to commemorate the victims of the Sichuan province's earthquake.[29] It accepted monthly donations of HK$333 from each Hong Kong household that participated in the 12-month relief scheme for the earthquake victims.[30] In November 2008, the DAB supported the LegCo to use its special power to summon the banking officials in a bid to investigate the mini-bonds scandal of Lehman Brothers because the bonds led to the financial loss of many ordinary citizens who bought them.[31]

On the issue of tax, the DAB usually advocates the government reduce the tax burden on citizens. But on the GST proposed by the government, Jasper Tsang, who was a member of the ExCo, had to support the government policy; however, his position was contrary to the DAB stance of opposing the GST.[32] Although the government later abandoned the idea due to widespread public opposition, including DAB legislators, Tsang's dilemma illustrated the DAB difficulties of supporting unpopular government policies.

In May 2009, when H1N1 erupted in the HKSAR, the DAB tried to win the hearts and minds of the populace by distributing masks to hawkers and citizens on the streets of the Wanchai district.[33] It urged the government to improve the hygiene problem of the corridors surrounding various private buildings and to allocate more financial resources to all 18 districts so that a clean-up campaign would be launched to prevent the spread of the H1N1 disease. In preparation for the Wanchai by-election, DAB member Chung Kar-man, who was also an appointed ad hoc member of the Wanchai District Board assisting the DAB work, went to distribute the masks with party chairman Tam Yiu-chung. Such visits illustrated the carefully orchestrated constituency work of the DAB. Chung was eventually elected in the by-election held for Wanchai in July 2009. Regardless of whether the DAB's top leaders are the hidden members of the CCP in the HKSAR, the party's rank-and-file members are mostly Hong Kong Chinese dedicated to articulating the interests of ordinary citizens at the grassroots level.

THE CHANGING ROLE AND POLITICAL VIEWS OF JASPER TSANG

Jasper Tsang, the former DAB chair from 1992 to 2003, shaped the DAB's development significantly. Persecuted by the British colonial rulers in the 1960s for his pro-PRC activities, Tsang was a long-time political loyalist of Beijing. Prior to the handover of Hong Kong, Tsang was a hardworking politician suffering from electoral defeat in LegCo direct elections. But he has been directly elected as a legislator since Hong Kong's return to China—a testimony to the changing political circumstances. During the Tung administration whose personnel appointments were explicitly biased in favor of the DAB elites, Tsang became a relatively arrogant politician who claimed that the half million citizens taking to the streets on July 1, 2003, were politically misled and instigated. His irresponsible remark showed that Tsang was out of touch with the reality of public sentiments in mid-2003, leading to his rapid public apology. Since then, Tsang has become more politically humble than before. In February 2009, Tsang admitted publicly that the Tiananmen incident was "clearly a mistake" made by the CCP, but the time was not yet ripe for Hong Kong people to request that the PRC should reverse its official verdict.[34] Instead, the PRC should be encouraged to learn from history and to "walk toward civilization and openness."[35] Tsang's changing political attitude is perhaps partly because of his deeper personal reflections on his own role in Hong Kong's political development, and partly because of his political conscience that the PRC government did make an error in the brutal military crackdown on student democrats in June 1989.

After Donald Tsang was selected as the chief executive replacing Tung Chee-hwa, who resigned in March 2005 for health reasons, rumors were rife that Jasper Tsang was at loggerheads with the new chief executive. However, the DAB was keen to dispel such rumors in March 2006, when Jasper Tsang opened his constituency office and when Donald Tsang attended its opening ceremony together with other principal officials. DAB member Chan Kam-lam criticized the mass media for falsifying and exaggerating the story of the personal problems among the two Tsangs.[36] Still, the early phase of Chief Executive Tsang was not easy because, as a former British-trained senior civil servant, he had to win the political support of the pro-Beijing DAB and its core leaders such as Jasper Tsang and Ma Lik, who perceived themselves as far more "patriotic" than the new Chief Executive. Jasper Tsang publicly clarified the rumors in March 2006, saying that he met Chief Executive Tsang every day and that "we both do not have any gap in terms of work and friend-ship."[37] He added that the DAB "is the government's closest partner," thus dispelling the "myth" of his strained relationships with Donald Tsang.[38] From the perspective of patron-client politics, Donald Tsang had to secure the DAB support for his election for the chief executive in March 2007, and his favoritism toward the DAB was understandable, especially as the DAB occupied one-eighth of the votes in the Election Committee that would select the chief executive.[39] Accompanied by the DAB deputy chair Tam Yiu-chung, Donald Tsang visited the Cheung Sha Wan district and chatted with ordinary citizens on the streets, show-ing that the chief executive could act like a party politician who under-stands public aspirations at the grassroots level.[40] As a new politician, Donald Tsang had little choice but to secure the friendship and support from Jasper Tsang, who can be regarded as an experienced political fox in the pro-Beijing camp.

Jasper Tsang knows that unless the DAB develops into the largest party capturing most seats in the legislature and becoming a ruling party in power, democratization in the HKSAR cannot easily adopt a Western-style system in which the whole LegCo is directly elected by citizens. As early as October 2004, Tsang said that the DAB would have to trans-form itself into a ruling party with governing capability.[41] Tsang's com-ment was made after he resigned from the DAB's unsatisfactory performance in the November 2003 DC elections. Seeing that the LP led by James Tien played a key role in becoming a "kingmaker" opposing the national security bill in the ExCo, Tsang went so far as to believe that the LP would be the only political party equipped with the governing capability in the HKSAR.[42] Tsang's judgment was partially accurate, for the LP led by James Tien performed well in the 2004 LegCo elections but it was quickly defeated in the 2008 LegCo direct elections. Tsang's com-ment showed that he became more modest after the July 1, 2003, protests that brought both the Tung regime and the DAB into disrepute. In Tsang's mind, political parties must develop further so as to groom leaders for the HKSAR. He thought that some "traditional leftists" in Hong Kong rejected the idea of developing parliamentary democracy because this would undermine the executive-led government. This argument, to Tsang, is invalid because the British parliamentary and American presi-dential systems can guarantee the stability of the executive-led administration.[43] In short, Tsang believes in the coexistence of governing efficiency with party politics under Western democracies—a view that can be seen as relatively liberal in the pro-Beijing camp.

On politically sensitive issues, Jasper Tsang remains a loyal supporter of Beijing. In April 2006, Wang Zhenmin, a legal expert at Tsinghua University and the former mainland member of the Hong Kong Basic Law Committee, mentioned that one of the preconditions for the HKSAR to have universal suffrage was to enact Article 23 of the Basic Law to outlaw subversion, treason, sedition, secession, and theft of state secrets. In response to Wang's comment, which created an outcry among some pro-democracy elites in Hong Kong, Jasper Tsang supported his view and reiterated that Hong Kong citizens not only enjoyed their rights but also had "the duties and responsibilities to safeguard national security." [44]

In September 2008 Jasper Tsang had the intention of running for the LegCo president, but he did not promise that he would refrain from voting and commenting on public affairs after being elected as the successor to Rita Fan.[45] Regina Ip, immediately after she was directly elected to the LegCo, believed that the president should not vote so as to project an image of impartiality. Frederick Fung of the ADPL and Albert Ho of the DP agreed with Ip. Tsang argued that Andrew Wong, a candidate running against Rita Fan for the LegCo president, did not state he would abandon his vote if he were elected. But the democrats at that time supported Wong. Tsang argued that, if he were elected as president, whether he would exercise his right to vote in the legislature would depend on the circumstances.[46]

After listening to public discussions on the proper role of the LegCo president, Tsang eventually modified his position. Before Tsang met the pan-democratic legislators, he said that if colleagues selected him as the president, he would not withdraw from the DAB, would not attend DAB caucus meetings, would not debate with legislators, would write on broader policy issues rather than touching on matters frequently examined by legislators, and would vote only if bills or debate motions concerned "important public interest" and would require his voting decision.[47] Tsang softened his stance and stressed that the LegCo's Standing Order did not say that the president could not vote. Hence, he made concessions to lobby for support from the legislators while maintaining his right to vote in case of "important public interest." He admitted for the first time that, if universal suffrage were implemented in the whole LegCo, the phenomenon of DAB legislator Wong Yung-kan, who was elected by obtaining only 100 votes in the fisheries and agricultural functional constituency, would definitely disappear. His more liberal position aimed at securing more votes from the legislators. During Tsang's meeting with the democrats, he reiterated his stance. In response, Ronny Tong of the CP said that he adopted "an open-minded" attitude toward Tsang's possibility of becoming the president, a remark that led to the immediate criticism from Li Wah-ming who would compete with Tsang for the president post.[48] Li thought that Tong should bear in mind the need for pan-democratic solidarity. Days before the election, some pan-democrats kept asking Tsang whether he was a member of the CCP in the HKSAR. Tsang dodged the question and repeated that "my neutrality would not be affected by any party interference," a remark that was interpreted by Leung Kwok-hung as tacitly admitting that Tsang himself was affiliated with the CCP.[49] On October 8 Tsang obtained 36 votes and defeated Li Wah-ming, who got 24 votes.[50] Tsang became the president, and he vowed to withdraw from his position as a member of the ExCo. He commented that "I do not see any relationships between the LegCo President who presides over the legislative meetings and the CCP's manifesto."[51] Although he avoided the question on his real and hidden party membership, the entire controversy over the proper role of Tsang as the president was significant because he had to moderate his originally rigid position.

After Tsang became the LegCo president, his expected neutrality has given him more autonomy to express his views independently from the pro-Beijing line. In February 2009, he admitted for the first time that the Tiananmen crackdown in June 1989 was "certainly a mistake," and that he had his "own ways of remembering the event without expressing political gestures by attending any remembrance activity."[52] He thought that in his lifetime he would perhaps be unable to see the phenomenon of Beijing reversing its official verdict on Tiananmen. But Tsang hoped the people of Hong Kong would promote the PRC to be more open. When asked whether he requested that Beijing should reverse the verdict on Tiananmen, Tsang replied he did not. One may see Tsang's answers as indicative of the hallmarks of a political fox, but his more open view toward the "mistake" made by the PRC government in the June 1989 tragedy was significant. As a former DAB leader and one of the most respected pro-Beijing politicians in the HKSAR, his unprecedented acknowledgment of the Tiananmen tragedy could be a rude awakening to many die-hard pro-Beijing loyalists in Hong Kong.

THE FEDERATION OF TRADE UNIONS

The pro-Beijing FTU developed its memberships from 20,000 in April 1948, when it was founded, to 300,000 in April 2008.[53] In 1982, the FTU managed to set up a school in Hong Kong for its members. It opened clinics for members' medical needs. The union is a *de facto* political party because it has traditionally nominated candidates to run in both LegCo direct elections and DC elections. In the 2000s, the FTU opened branch offices in Shenzhen, Dongguan, and Guangzhou to serve the needs of the Hong Kong people. The FTU not only lobbies the HKSAR government on various livelihood issues affecting the workers and lower-class citizens, but it also regularly sends delegations to Beijing to discuss issues like the occupational training for Hong Kong workers in the mainland and academic accreditations.

As with the DAB, the FTU has undergone a process of internal rejuvenation since the mid-2000s. In 2006, the FTU experienced internal reorganization in which two deputy directors were established. Moreover, the tenure of office of the FTU deputy chairpersons (Chan Yuen-han and Tam Yiu-chung since 2006) is restricted to 2 terms (six years) or at best 3 terms (nine years).[54] Younger members such as Yip Wai-ming and Lam Kam-yee are now deputy directors. Organizers of the FTU felt that its leaders served the union for too long and that there should be an institutionalization of their tenure of office. Former FTU chair Cheng Yiu-tong served for 13 years before the younger Wong Kwok-kin took over from his position. When Chan Yuen-han decided to be listed as the second candidate after Wong Kwok-kin in the FTU list running for the 2008 LegCo direct elections, it was clear that she intended to step down for the rejuvenation of FTU.

Traditionally, the FTU members have been keeping a certain distance from the HKSAR leadership because of class contradictions. Chan Yuen-han was well known for her critical attitude toward both the Tung and Tsang administrations for failing to do enough for the protection of working-class interests. When FTU members Chan, Wong Kwok-hing, and Kwong Chi-kin were elected to the LegCo in 2004, they were critical of Chief Executive Tsang's policies. Kwong criticized Tsang for failing to nominate an acting chief executive on the government gazette when Tsang went to the mainland for a four-day holiday.[55] When Tsang sought nominations for his election for chief executive, the three FTU members openly said they did not nominate him. When Tsang agreed to put the issues of minimum wage and working time into the agenda of the SDC, the three FTU activists then made a concession by agreeing to nominate him as the chief executive candidate.[56] Clearly, the FTU had class tensions with Tsang but made concessions on the condition that Tsang dealt with issues of working-class concerns.

Chan Yuen-han can be regarded as a critical left-wing trade unionist who often had opinion differences with the HKSAR government. Her father was a patriotic Hong Kong worker, and he passed away when Chan was 12 years old. Chan's family was poor and she studied in a patriotic school. After graduation Chan worked in the FTU loyally. Dubbed as "an open-minded leftist," Chan believed that it was naïve to think the working class would become the "master" in the HKSAR. Instead, the capitalist system in the HKSAR, to Chan, made the government biased against the workers. She said cynically: "We the working-class activists like to serve the people. But now this slogan of serving the people is put in the backburner and destined to be ostracized. If the old people see this situation, they must be suffocated to death."[57] When Chan was criticized by Andrew Cheng of the DP for "selling out" the interests of workers over the minimum wage issue, she was so upset that she immediately broke down in tears.[58] Sandwiched between the working-class interests and the need for the FTU to support the government, Chan was forced to allow the government to delay the process of preparing legislation on the minimum wage. Hence, the difficulties of being a critical trade unionist and a supporter of the government could be seen in Chan's political dilemmas.

Former FTU legislator Kwong Chi-kin once toyed with the idea of forming an independent labor party so as to fight for working-class interests and advocate for the election of the chief executive by universal suffrage in 2017. But FTU leaders did not really support his move. Kwong sighed that "legislators were merely focusing in elections and ignored Hong Kong's overall development." [59] His idea was not new; Chan Yuen-han in early 2005 revealed her intention of forming a labor party. Yet, FTU chair Cheng Yiu-tong said that the formation of a labor party might not solve all the problems—an implication that the FTU had internal opinion differences over whether it should turn into a political party, or whether some of its members would form a new labor party. Ultimately, as long as the DAB constitutes the most powerful and influential pro-Beijing party in direct elections, any move by the FTU to compete with the DAB can be seen as politically deviant or undesirable. As a result, the idea of forming a new labor party by some FTU members remains a castle in the air.

The DAB often has overlapping memberships with the FTU, which acts as the mobilization vehicle for the DAB in elections and its auxiliary force in nonelection time when the FTU organizes constituency services to maintain the rapport with voters. After the 2004 LegCo elections, FTU deputy director and DAB member Chan Yuen-han decided to withdraw gradually from the DAB affairs. Chan's decision was a personal one, but it was also prompted by her belief that the FTU would be able to nominate its own candidates to compete in future LegCo direct elections. However, some leaders of the FTU did not wish her to suddenly cut her affiliation with the DAB for fear that outsiders might view it as a political rift between the two organizations.[60] As a working-class champion, Chan might find the DAB increasingly "aristocratic" after the mid-2000s when the pro-business HKPA was incorporated and as more middle-class young professionals were recruited into the DAB. Her withdrawal from the DAB was a matter of time.

THE LIBERAL PARTY

The LP was formed in 1993 and its predecessor was a legislative clique named the Cooperative Resources Center. The LP is a pro-business party aiming at maintaining capitalism, achieving economic prosperity, protecting individual freedom, and supervising the government.[61] The party supports economic liberalism such as low tax and minimal government intervention in the economy, but it does not fully support political liberalism in the sense that its leaders have adopted a gradualist and cautious approach to the direct elections of both the chief executive through universal suffrage and the entire legislature. The LP is organized into several sections: party headquarters, election affairs committee, policy committee, and fund-raising committee. In 2009, the LP had 3 legislators and 32 DC members. The apex of the LP was in 2004 when party chair James Tien and executive committee member Selina Chow were directly elected to the LegCo. Both were defeated in the 2008 LegCo election, triggering Tien's resignation and then the party's internal power struggle. As a result of internal factional rivalry, three legislators left the party and weakened the LP. The membership of the party is small with about 300 members in late 2008.[62]

Tien rose to political prominence in mid-2003 when he opposed the national security bill, disagreed with the hard-liners in the ExCo, and abandoned Chief Executive Tung by resigning from his position in the ExCo. While the pro-democracy *Apple Daily* hailed him as a hero, the pro-Beijing forces and PRC officials saw Tien's action as a betrayal of Chief Executive Tung, whose popularity was then plunged into a nadir partly because of the controversy over the national security bill.

The period from 2005 to 2008 could be seen as the apex of LP's influence and profile. Because of the success of Tien and Chow in the 2004 direct elections, both were imbued with a sense of political empowerment from the people of Hong Kong. The media portrayed the LP as the second largest party in the LegCo and Tien had the ambition of increasing the party membership from 300 to 800.[63] He affirmed that the LP would try to have more members elected to the Election Committee selecting the chief executive and that it would nominate members to become the principal officials of the next administration.

Shortly after Chief Executive Tung resigned in March 2005 for health reasons, Tien toyed with the idea of competing in the chief executive election. In April he announced that he would not run for the election because of three factors.[64] First, public opinion polls showed that Donald Tsang's popularity was much higher than him. Second, he probed the views of Beijing, which, however, neither supported nor opposed his intention to run in the election. Tien felt that Beijing tended to favor Tsang as the chief executive. Third, he contacted many members of the 800-member Election Committee, and their support of him was unstable. It was speculated that Tien would not be able to secure 100 members' support for nominating him to be the candidate.[65] Under these circumstances, Tien decided not to run.

After Tsang was elected as the chief executive succeeding Tung, Allen Lee Peng-fei revealed that he heard a senior government official had asked the land developers whether there might be another businessman replacing Tien as the LP chair.[66] Lee added that the business support of Tien was solid and that the government's move would fail. Rumors were rife about the strained relationships between Donald Tsang and James Tien. But Tsang stressed that he and Tien had been friends for 21 years, while Tien remarked interestingly that the government should give the LP some space because having reservations about government policies did not necessarily mean that it was tantamount to political opposition.[67]

The LP acted as an influential force in the LegCo from 2005 to 2008, especially after the pan-democrats' rejection of the Tsang political reform plan. In January 2006, Tien said confidently that the government needed every vote of the pro-establishment camp, including the LP. But he criticized some principal officials for not cultivating closer relationships with his party, such as secretary for transport and public works Sarah Liao and secretary for health and food security York Chow.[68] He said the government should consult the LP more often, just as with the policy of banning smoking in all restaurants and entertainment centers. Tien added that due to insufficient consultation, the policy of banning smoking in restaurants, bars, and nightclubs led to severe opposition and the LP found it difficult to explain to its functional constituents.[69] According to Tien, public policies have to take into consideration public opinion in the first place. Clearly, he wished to maximize the LP's bargaining power vis-à-vis the government.

The LP has a competitive relationship with the DAB. While the LP opposed the national security bill in mid-2003, the DAB supported it. Both parties competed for the positions in the Election Committee that selected the chief executive in 2007. Ma Lik of the DAB appealed to the LP "not to cross the line" to compete with his party so that the beneficiaries would be the democrats.[70] After the 2008 LegCo elections, HYK chair Lau Wong-fat quit the LP because the LP put the blame of Selina Chow's defeat on the HYK's alliance with the DAB in the New Territories West.

Tien dislikes the label that there is "collusion between the HKSAR government and the business" because the government, to him, has made mistakes in granting land to developers and that such accusation merely damages the image of Hong Kong and frightens foreign investors.[71] His LP rejected the government's proposal of introducing the General Sales Tax so as to widen the tax base in Hong Kong.[72] Although the LP supports economic liberalism, it advocates more government intervention in providing jobs for the unemployed and subsidies for the small and medium enterprises during the global financial crisis that affected Hong Kong in 2008 and 2009.[73] During the global financial turmoil in late 2008, the LP urged the retail and restaurant sectors not to lay off their employees.[74] It proposed that the government should distribute to each citizen a consumption voucher of HK$1,000 so as to stimulate local consumption.[75] Fong Kwong and Tommy Cheung Yu-yan of the LP mobilized the retail services to support the proposal, which was, however, opposed by James Tien. The new LP chair, Miriam Lau, played down Tien's personal opinion difference.[76] After Michael Tien Pak-chun, the brother of James Tien, proposed a plan in which a citizen first would spend HK\$300 and then the government would subsidize each with HK\$700 while the business sector would offer a discount, Miriam Lau stressed that his plan was different from the LP's position that advocated the government to use HK\$200 billion to stimulate local consumption and economy.[77] The LP had lax internal discipline, and its core leaders failed to project an image of consensus on crucial economic remedies to the global financial tsunami.

On political reform, the LP in August 2006 proposed that the chief executive should be directly elected by universal suffrage in 2012, and that LegCo's functional constituencies would be abolished by stages.[78] It suggested that the franchise in functional constituencies could be expanded from corporate votes to the executive committee members of companies to cast their ballots. This was the most politically liberal position held by the LP, which became relatively silent on democratization shortly after the double defeat of Tien and Chow in the 2008 LegCo direct elections.

The LP has trained a number of prominent political elites apart from James Tien, notably Henry Tang and Michael Tien. Henry Tang was a former LP member, the financial secretary from 2003 to 2007, and chief secretary in the Tsang administration since 2007. Tang has been regarded as one of the hot contenders for the chief executive in the future. The party tried to groom young businesswoman Lily Chiang, but her involvement in an alleged corruption incident investigated by the ICAC undermined her political prospects in the short run.[79] On the other hand, Michael Tien has been groomed by the LP to be its leader in the future. Although Michael Tien joined the LP in April 2008 and was defeated in the 2008 LegCo direct elections in Kowloon West, his extensive public experiences pave the way for the possibility of climbing up the political ladder in the future. It was reported that Michael Tien would plan to run again in the LegCo's direct elections in Hong Kong Island. He has a vision of steering the LP toward the direction of a middle-right political party supportive of the corporate responsibility to avoid dismissing employees, of resource allocation to help the poor and the needy, and of the sanctity of market forces with proper government intervention under the circumstances of market failure.[80] Michael Tien's ideological vision of the LP is similar to Miriam Lau's public position,[81] which is actually much clearer and sharper than the party under the leadership of James Tien.

FACTIONALISM IN THE LP

Before Michael Tien becomes the target of the LP's cultivation and shortly after the party's defeat in the 2008 LegCo direct elections, factionalism emerged and three members eventually left the party. In the wake of Lau Wong-fat's withdrawal from the LP due to the row over why Selina Chow was defeated,[82] two factions in the LP were locked in a bitter power struggle. One faction urged James Tien to remain as the party chair. But the other faction led by Lam Kin-fung, Leung Kwan-yin, and Leung Lau Yau-fun reached a consensus with James Tien that Lam would be the new party chair while Leung would be the deputy chair in addition to another chairlady, Miriam Lau. Lau belonged to the pro–James Tien faction, and she was later supported by Tien to be the new chair. The faction led by Lam was dissatisfied with the way in which James Tien appeared to violate their original consensus. It criticized Tien of mobilizing LP members from the grassroots level to support Miriam Lau as the new party chair.

Compounding the power struggle was a businessman named Lee Tai-chong, who told other LP members not to retain Tien as the chair, and who argued that the LP should focus on functional constituency elections rather than LegCo's direct elections. Lee was reportedly close to the Liaison Office, fueling rumors that the PRC's representative agency in Hong Kong might try to penetrate into the LP and oust the pro–James Tien faction. James Tien himself accused the Liaison Office of meddling in his party affairs, but the Liaison Office's deputy director Wang Fengchao openly denied any interference with the LP's factional struggle. Wang said:

The transformations of the LP leadership are its internal affairs. We believe that the LP should deal with their affairs in accordance with the party constitution. We are pleased to see the LP to function actively in the various matters concerning Hong Kong.[83]

On September 29, the LP convened its Central Standing Committee meeting in which 11 members voted for the creation of an honorary chair for James Tien, but 6 members opposed.[84] Opponents included Leung Lau Yan-fun, who argued that the honorary post was unnecessary because the LP was a political party rather than a chamber of commerce.[85] Lee Tai-chong openly opposed the proposed honorary position.[86] James Tien publicly said that he would not be the honorary chair. However, he tried to strike a deal with Lam Kin-fung, securing Lam's support for Miriam Lau as the next party chair. In return, according to the deal, Lam would be nominated by the LP to be a member of the ExCo, but Leung Lau Yau-fun would no longer be the next deputy chair. Lam, Leung, and Leung Kwan-yin were angered by Tien's offer and "violation" of the earlier consensus under which Lam would be the party chair and Leung would be the deputy chair.[87] The three held a press conference and decided to withdraw from the LP. Clearly, James Tien tried to retain his control and influence on the party's leadership arrangement so that his supporter Miriam Lau would be the new chair while excluding the Lam Kin-fung faction from the political nucleus.[88] The LP's factional struggle was also characterized by the dispute over the proper direction of the party: whether it should focus on functional constituencies or whether it should cope with direct elections.[89] Although the pro–James Tien and pro-direct election faction won, it remains to be seen whether the LP will be able to perform better in the LegCo direct elections in the future.

The entire controversy dragged the Liaison Office into the LP's factional strife. Gao Siren, the director of the Liaison Office, met James Tien and stressed that Lee Tai-chong's action and remarks did not represent Beijing's position.[90] Gao added that the central government did not have any requests for the LP to focus on functional constituency elections rather than LegCo direct elections. At the same time, Lee openly said that what he did was not affected by the Liaison Office, that he only appealed to LP members to discuss the proper directions of the party, and that he would not withdraw from the LP.[91] Regardless of whether the Liaison Office interfered with the LP affairs indirectly, the entire controversy undermined the relationships between Beijing's representative agency and the LP.

In February 2009, the Liaison Office took the initiative to improve its relations and minimize any misunderstandings with the LP. Its director Gao Siren met three legislators and other party members. He expressed his wishes for the LP: "the need for solidarity, coordination, break-through, calm analysis, reorganization, reform, and renewal, and the necessity of improving the party's overall capability and standard of political participation, as well as enhancing the LP's social status and influence."[92] The LP chair, Miriam Lau, agreed that the communication with the Liaison Office was a positive step toward the development of their harmonious relationships.

THE BUSINESS ELITE

The HKSAR business elites are heterogeneous and cannot be represented by the LP alone. Some other businesspeople tend to be more pro-democracy, such as Jimmy Lai and George Cautherley. However, it can be said that most businesspeople in the HKSAR are politically conservative. Traditionally, they have been spoiled by the colonial political system that protected their vested interests through political appointments made to various policy-making and advisory bodies, such as the ExeCo and other consultative committees.

Yet, the business sector is not really as united as conventional wisdom may assume. A case in point was the surprising electoral victory of democrat Emily Lau, who ran for the chair position of the Finance Committee of the LegCo in October 2006. Before the election among all legislators, it was expected that she would lose to Chan Kam-lam of the DAB. Chan as a pro-Beijing businessman was expected to acquire the support from other businesspeople in the legislature, such as independent Li Kwok-po, James Tien and his colleagues in the LP, and the pan-coalition composed of several independent business legislators. Surprisingly, Chan got 25 votes instead of the expected 29 votes, while Emily Lau secured 25 votes rather than the expected 21 votes.[93] After drawing lots, Lau became the Finance Committee's chairperson. The "loss" of Chan's three votes was attributable to the possible "defection" of business elites, such as Li Kwok-po, James Tien, and Philip Wong, who voted for Emily Lau.[94] There was no evidence to show that James Tien voted for Lau, but Albert Cheng and Abraham Shek criticized Tien for his problematic and ambiguous position.[95] Occasionally the democrats in the LegCo benefit politically from the internal split of the business elite.

Some business elites did toy with the idea of forming another business party to protect the interests of the small and medium enterprises. The Chinese Chamber of Commerce's chairman Wan Tak-sing said in May 2008 that the business chambers would have to participate more in elections so as to defend their interests in the future, especially when the proportion of functional constituencies would perhaps be reduced. He said that the new party, if formed, would be different from the LP because it would focus on the small and medium enterprises, whereas the LP focused on the "second generation of the rich tycoons." [96] His remarks implied that while the LP belonged to the business party of upper classes, the new party composed of business chambers would target the small business people. Wan unveiled that his idea of forming a new party could be traced back to 2003, but the new party was not formed "due to various reasons." [97] By 2009, Wan's idea did not materialize. But given the upper-class nature of the LP, some business elites independent of the LP would likely entertain the idea of establishing another pro-business party in the future.

The business elites have at least five major channels of political influence in the HKSAR. First and foremost, they are appointed to various influential committees, including the ExCo and most importantly the Election Committee that selects the chief executive. Usually, they occupy some 200 seats in the Election Committee, as with the by-election held for the chief executive position vacated by Tung in 2005.[98] Sectors such as industry, commerce, tourism, monetary professionals, real estate, and construction are monopolized by the business elites. Second, they can directly lobby government officials through informal and formal meetings. Former director of planning Poon Kwok-shing openly admitted that land developers often visited his office to consult him on government views on urban planning and construction issues.[99] But legislators James To and Ronny Tong were concerned about the closeness of these interactions.

Third, the business elites participate in the elections held for the Hong Kong members to the NPC and can bypass the HKSAR government easily to express their views to Beijing. During the 2008 election of the Hong Kong NPC members, the second generation of tycoons, such as Bernard Chan, Michael Tien, and Fok Tsun-wan, participated in the competition for 36 positions.[100] Some business elites are appointed by the PRC as the Hong Kong members of the CPPCC, thus elevating their political status. The CPPCC members can freely express their views on not only mainland affairs but also the relations between the PRC and the HKSAR, especially after the CPPCC has opened the Hong Kong sector's meetings to the public since March 2008.[101] Although the Hong Kong NPC members are not expected to intervene in Hong Kong politics, they can also freely express their views on China and Hong Kong, enhance communications between the PRC and the HKSAR, help the Hong Kong people who encounter problems on the mainland, and enjoy a much higher political status than the CPPCC counterparts.[102] These channels of business participation make some business elites feel that local electoral politics in Hong Kong are less influential than their ability to have access to higher level officials in the PRC.

Fourth, the business elites set up think tanks such as the Bauhinia Foundation and submit policy recommendations to the HKSAR government. The Bauhinia Research Centre, for example, suggested that the government should reduce the profit tax from 16.5 percent to 15 percent so as to increase Hong Kong's economic competitiveness.[103] It recommended that the government establish a subcommittee under the treasury bureau to study tax reform.[104] Its chairman Anthony Wu has been a member of the CPPCC since 1998. Business tycoons such as Stanley Ho, Lee Shau-kei, and Cheng Yu-tung each donated about HK$3 million to the Bauhinia Foundation for research.[105]

Fifth, the business elites protect their interests through the LegCo functional constituency elections. As mentioned before, the anti–James Tien faction in the LP was keen to focus on the functional constituency elections held for the LegCo. Critics, such as Ronny Tong of the CP, challenged the traditional business view that functional constituencies must be maintained and that universal suffrage would undermine its interests. He wrote:

In fact, the business sector does not need functional constituencies to enter the LegCo. The business elites should realize that their representatives elected through direct elections are far more recognizable and influential than those elected through functional constituencies. The electoral victory of James Tien and Selina Chow in 2004 was a good example ... The business sector should understand that participation in the small circle election through functional constituencies only worsens the worries of the society about the collusion between officials and business people. It will exacerbate class contradictions and fail to convince the public that justice does exist, not to mention the fact that functional constituencies cannot coexist with direct elections . . . The view that universal suffrage would erode the social status of the business sector, would change the elite base to grassroots-based, and would shift the social capital to welfare has no foundation at all. The people of Hong Kong are enthusiastic toward success and respectful toward the elite. How can we change this culture?[106]

However, many business elites view direct elections as a means through which the pan-democrats would advocate more pro-welfare policies for the HKSAR. They see universal suffrage as the emergence of trade unionism and a serious challenge to the low tax regime and the relatively favorable investment environment in the HKSAR.

The older generation of Hong Kong's business elites is more politically cautious toward democratization. Stanley Ho, the chairman of the Chamber of Real Estate and Construction and the Macao casino tycoon, backed up Donald Tsang to be the successor of Tung Chee-hwa.[107] He supported the Tsang reform package in 2005 while appealing to Cardinal Zen to refrain from participating in politics.[108] When the HKSAR government was severely criticized by some legislators and community activists for inviting bidders to develop the entire Western Kowloon cultural and recreational district, Stanley Ho appealed to the government to separate the districts into subsections so that more tenders would be invited.[109] When asked about his view on universal suffrage, Ho remarked, "I am very satisfied with the current situation. Universal suffrage may not be good for Hong Kong. Take a look at Taiwan, Malaysia, and Indonesia where democratic development has been too fast. When the central government sees Hong Kong people as patriotic, it will tell us that we will have universal suffrage."[110]

As with Stanley Ho, business tycoon Li Ka-shing took the lead in supporting Donald Tsang to be reelected as the chief executive in March 2006. He praised Chief Executive Tsang's performance as "very good," and his open political posture was believed to trigger more solid support of Tsang from the business elites.[111] Similar to Stanley Ho, Li accepted the reality that the tendering process of the Western Kowloon cultural and recreational district had to be reviewed and be more strategic. Li Ka-shing has traditionally refrained from talking about politics. Instead, he has been focusing on economic issues, emphasizing during the global financial crisis that he was committed to investing in the HKSAR. He stressed that he has invested in Hong Kong since 1940, that the HKSAR government should provide more loans to the small and medium enterprises, and that the central government in Beijing implemented policies to benefit the HKSAR, such as the mainlanders' visit to Hong Kong.[112] It has been a tradition of an overwhelming majority of Hong Kong's business tycoons to support the HKSAR government and Beijing while avoiding the discussions on politically sensitive issues like democratization in Hong Kong and mainland China.

There are signs that some members of the new generation of business elites are more supportive of democracy than the older generation. Richard Li, the son of tycoon Li Ka-shing, was supportive of Donald Tsang in the nomination period of the 2007 chief executive election, but he openly called for the direct election of the chief executive as soon as possible.[113] Fok Kai-cheong, the son of Timothy Fok, remarked that he supported the direct elections for the chief executive in 2017 and for the entire LegCo in 2020. However, he stressed that it would take time for the people of Hong Kong to study the territory's political culture and development.[114] Bernard Chan, the former ExCo member, said that while Donald Tsang's policy of "distinguishing the relatives from those who are not" was natural in the world, he would like to reflect the views of the pro-democracy camp to Beijing because he was not just subservient to the central government.[115] It remains to be seen whether the new generation of the business elites will be more open-minded toward Hong Kong's democratic development in the future.

SUMMARY

The participation of the DAB in Hong Kong's electoral politics and its need to compete with other pro-democracy parties, which actually garner about 60 percent of the votes in direct elections, had positive implications for democratization in the HKSAR. Although the DAB's electoral participation checks the influence of the pro-democracy forces, it demonstrates to the CCP in the mainland that pluralistic politics entails open electoral contest with any political opposition. In other words, if the mainland opens up the political system, the ruling party will have to adopt a more open-minded acumen to allow a fair competition with any opposition forces, as with the HKSAR case. Moreover, elections cannot guarantee the absolute dominance of the ruling party in the PRC, even though the electoral system can be manipulated to favor the CCP. In Hong Kong, LegCo's functional constituencies have to be maintained for the sake of maintaining the executive-led polity and preventing the powerful democrats who get almost 60 percent of the votes from grasping the real political power. Although the DAB enjoys superior financial support from pro-Beijing organizations and the business elites, its performance in LegCo direct elections remains to be improved. As long as the DAB cannot really capture at least half of the votes in direct elections held for the LegCo, it will be unlikely that the PRC government would allow Hong Kong to have a wholly directly elected legislature. The need to maintain an executive-led administration and to prevent the democrats from capturing over half of the seats in the LegCo are critical to PRC authorities, who see democratization in the HKSAR as a real threat to its national interest.

The LP had made minimal contributions to Hong Kong's democratization. It did check the HKSAR government, won the direct elections held for the LegCo in 2004, and trained a few prominent political elites. However, its organizational problem, lack of district work, internal factional struggle, and inability to represent the interests of all the business elites hamper the LP's development in the long run. The LP is marked by personal rule in that James Tien and Miriam Lau play a crucial role in shaping the party development instead of institutionalizing the leadership succession. Unlike the DAB, which has a comprehensive plan of grooming young members in the process of leadership succession, the LP appears to be amateur and incremental in its leadership renewal and rejuvenation. Perhaps in a developing polity like Hong Kong, most political parties are still relying on the personal charisma of their leaders instead of relying on institutional mechanisms to train and groom their leaders internally.

CHAPTER 9

The Politics of Co-optation: Beijing, the HKSAR Government, and Democrats

Beijing's intervention in the HKSAR politics takes place formally and informally. Formally, the NPC Standing Committee interpreted the Basic Law three times—in 1999 over the right of abode of mainland Chinese in Hong Kong, in 2005 over the tenure of the chief executive, and in 2006 over the issue of direct elections—so as to impose its whims on how the HKSAR should be run.[1] It was inaccurate to claim that "during the first five years following Hong Kong's reunification with China, the mainland's general policy toward Hong Kong was rather *laissez faire*."[2] Beijing has long intervened in the HKSAR affairs since July 1, 1997. Informally, the PRC representative office in the HKSAR, the Liaison Office, has conducted extensive united front work to win the hearts and minds of the populace in the territory. It staff members are interacting with many Hong Kong people from all walks of life, including the capitalist, middle, and working classes so that the pro-Beijing forces continue to grow in Hong Kong.

Guoguang Wu and Benson Wong have offered perceptive insights on Beijing's utilization of patriotism, economic incentives, and the rewards of political followers as the means of co-opting the Hong Kong people.[3] In practice, the most powerful weapon employed by the PRC to co-opt the people of Hong Kong, to silence the critics, to buy off opportunists, to enforce a strong sense of public pragmatism, and to curb the demands for democracy is economic enticement. Economic enticement here refers to PRC policy measures designed and implemented to win the

Hong Kong people's support of Beijing. They include the Closer Economic Partnership Arrangement reached between Beijing and Hong Kong in 2003 so that Hong Kong companies, banks, and tertiary services would benefit from the preferential treatment they enjoy in the mainland. At the same time, many affluent mainland tourists have flocked to Hong Kong to buy luxurious apartments, consume luxurious goods, and stimulate the retail, jewelry, and real estate sectors remarkably.[4]

Economic enticement conferred by Beijing on the HKSAR is accompanied by the central government's policy of promoting the role and status of Shanghai as another monetary center in the PRC. As a result of this two-pronged policy, the HKSAR's economic status has been curbed, creating a constant sense of having economic crisis. In face of this crisis, the HKSAR leadership is destined to focus on economic revival and competitiveness, relegating democratization into an issue of secondary importance. In short, the economic dependency of the HKSAR is accompanied by an increase in the sense of being economically marginalized. Economics in command has been deeply entrenched in the psyches of the Hong Kong ruling elite, which prefers to adopt a model where economic prosperity is maintained with controlled democratization.

THE HETEROGENEITY AND CHAOS OF BEIJING'S INSTITUTIONS ON HONG KONG AFFAIRS

An article by the Liaison Office's researcher Cao Erbao in January 2008 about the coexistence of the two governing forces in Hong Kong—the establishment team of Hong Kong and the batch composed of central authorities—aroused the concern and criticisms from the Hong Kong democrats in April and May 2009.[5] The democrats held a forum to discuss whether the talk about the two teams might violate the Basic Law and constituted Beijing's explicit intervention in Hong Kong affairs.[6] Arguably, the team composed of the central government's various agencies, such as the NCNA (the predecessor of the Liaison Office) and the HKMAO, has long existed in Hong Kong before the handover.

Yet, Beijing's policies toward the HKSAR often come from various agencies whose power relations are confusing to the Hong Kong people, not to mention the democrats. These agencies include the Hong Kong Macao Work Coordination Committee led by Politburo member Xi Jinping since 2007 (the committee was set up in July 2003 to deal with the Article 23 crisis); the Hong Kong and Macao Work Committee headed by President Hu Jintao; the State Council's HKMAO led by Liao Hui; the State Council's Hong Kong and Macao Study Research Center led by the former Liaison Office deputy director Zhu Yucheng, and the Liaison Office in the HKSAR. There were reports on the opinion differences between the Liaison Office's former director Gao Siren (Peng Qinghua after May 2009) and the

HKMAO's Liao Hui during the Hong Kong and Macao Work Committee's meeting in 2004.[7] While the Liaison Office in the HKSAR is often portrayed negatively in the Hong Kong Chinese press as interventionist in Hong Kong politics and elections, the image of the HKMAO appears to be better as Liao Hui has been keeping a very low profile.[8] Many democrats tend to see the work of the Liaison Office quite negatively because it coordinates the candidates in the pro-Beijing camp in Hong Kong elections and is too close to the DAB.[9] What confuses the Hong Kong democrats is that many mainland provinces, like Guangdong, have their research agents collecting data from Hong Kong democrats.[10] Some claim that they have direct access to Beijing, but the democrats cannot simply verify their status and reliability.[11] Even when some mainland researchers claim that they come from Beijing, again the Hong Kong democrats cannot confirm their role. The chaotic nature of mainland agencies responsible for Hong Kong matters and the proliferation of provincial intelligence agents on the HKSAR exacerbate the chaotic picture of how the central government collects the views of Hong Kong people accurately.

Since the NPC Standing Committee's interpretation of the Basic Law in mid-1999, another mainland organ dealing with the HKSAR is the NPC's Legal Affairs Committee, and its secretary-general Qiao Xiaoyang has frequently consulted the views of the Hong Kong people prior to any interpretation of the Basic Law. The heterogeneity of the mainland agencies coping with Hong Kong matters, and the interest of provincial intelligence agencies in the HKSAR developments, have made the entire picture of the PRC policy making toward the HKSAR filled with mysteries and palace politics reminiscent of ancient China. Compounding this turbulent scenario is the occasional bureaucratic wrangling and opinion differences among these mainland agencies dealing with Hong Kong matters.[12] Even if the Hong Kong democrats engage Beijing's officials responsible for Hong Kong matters, the multiple agencies and diverse mainland authorities mean that such engagement and lobbying efforts are bound to be problematic, directionless, and doubtful in their political outcome and effectiveness. The heterogeneity of mainland agencies responsible for Hong Kong matters carries the implications of (1) worsening the sense of powerlessness on the part of Hong Kong democrats to lobby PRC officials, (2) complicating the understanding of top CCP leaders on Hong Kong's developments, and (3) generating perhaps unnecessary rivalries between mainland organs collecting public opinion and conducting united front work in the HKSAR.

BEIJING'S POLITICS OF CO-OPTATION

Beijing adopts both hard-line and soft-line tactics to co-opt the people of Hong Kong. Shortly after the July 1, 2004, protest in the HKSAR, PRC leaders realized that public discontent in Hong Kong was real as with the situation in mid-2003. Two weeks before the national day of the PRC in October 2004, the mainland authorities invited 10 Hong Kong democrats to Beijing to observe the ceremony celebrating the PRC's fifty-fifth anniversary—a move interpreted as a good sign of bridging the gap between Beijing and the Hong Kong democrats.[13] Not all the pan-democrats were invited. Beijing invited those democrats who were the target of immediate co-optation but excluded those "hard-line" democrats from the list of the delegation. Those who were invited included members of the Article 45 Concern Group, which played a pivotal role in leading the public opposition to the national security bill from early to mid-2003, such as lawyers Audrey Eu, Ronny Tong, Alan Leong, and Margaret Ng. The DP had only Sin Chung-kai who was invited to visit Beijing.[14] The other five democrats who were on the list embraced Frederick Fung of the ADPL, and independent democrats like Mandy Tam, Cheung Chiu-hung, Kwok Kar-kay, and Joseph Lee Kwok-lun. Obviously, PRC authorities divided those democrats who were previously involved in the Alliance from those relatively new and independent ones who successfully opposed the national security bill but who could perhaps be won over to the mainland side. Beijing was more relaxed after analyzing the results in the September 2004 LegCo elections in which the popular pan-democrats could not control so many seats as expected.[15] As a result, the tentacles of co-optation were extended to the newly elected democrats.

In response to public criticisms that the invited list deliberately excluded those "radical" democrats, deputy director of the Liaison Office Li Gang said that his office staff did have contacts with the DP members and that the invitation had quotas.[16] Although he answered diplomatically and politely, the explanation was indeed far-fetched. The newly elected pro-democracy legislator Audrey Eu did not believe that the PRC move would split the democrats. She remarked: "Will this invitation lead to a split within the democrats? I think that if we maintain our stance and solidarity, there will not be any problem of an internal split. We should not speculate on Beijing's motives."[17] The reaction of Eu illustrated the mind-set of many democrats who see dialogue and interactions with PRC authorities as necessary, but who try to maintain their principle of fighting for democracy without being compromised easily through the process of political co-optation.

Why does Beijing maintain an exclusionist policy toward some democrats? The root of the problem was the Tiananmen legacy in June 1989. The PRC Vice President Zeng Qinghong revealed the PRC official line in January 2005 when he was asked on the request of the Hong Kong democrats whether they would like to visit Beijing.[18] He said whether both sides would begin a dialogue depends on their viewpoints and requests. The "one country, two systems" is the basic principle. But if they call for the reversal of verdict of Tiananmen every day and shout for the termination of one-party rule, how can we communicate? If their action is subversive, both sides must have difficulties. This does not have any advantage to individuals and the society . . . This is not my own view. This is the message from the central government and the State Council. We also want Hong Kong to be better.[19]

The Tiananmen legacy presents the most baffling obstacle to the direct dialogue and interactions between the pan-democrats and Beijing. It is a thorn to PRC leaders and officials responsible for Hong Kong matters, while the pan-democrats regard it as an unforgettable tragedy whose official verdict will have to be reversed.

Another example of political co-optation is the ways in which Beijing dealt with the Hong Kong opposition to the NPC Standing Committee's interpretation of the Basic Law over the term of office of the chief executive who succeeded Tung Chee-hwa. Whether the term would be two or five years became a bone of contention in March and April 2005. The Hong Kong legal sector tended to view the term of office as having five years from what was written on Article 46 of the Basic Law, but the PRC interpretation tended to opt for the residual two years left by Chief Executive Tung. The NPC Standing Committee's interpretation was preceded by a carefully orchestrated consultation with the Hong Kong elites, including the visit of researchers, public security personnel, and military officers.[20] Widely criticized by the Hong Kong public for failing to tap local public opinion in mid-2003, the Liaison Office in 2005 dispatched a large number of officials to lobby and persuade the pro-Beijing elites to support the forthcoming NPC Standing Committee's interpretation. A special committee was set up by the central government to deal with the lobbying efforts, including officials from the Liaison Office, the Ministry of Public Security, the United Front Department, the HKMAO, and the NPC's Legal Affairs Committee.[21]

Incentives were given to some Hong Kong democrats prior to the NPC Standing Committee's interpretation. Democrats Lau Chin-shek and Li Wah-ming were invited to visit Beijing. Lau was the Alliance's executive committee member in 1989, and his home return permit expired in 1991. In May 2000, with help from Chief Executive Tung, Lau got his home return permit renewed so that he could visit his ailing mother in Guangzhou. Since then he could visit the mainland easily. In 2004, as a reciprocal move to Beijing's decision to allow him to visit the mainland, Lau decided to withdraw from the Alliance's executive committee. In early 2005, Lau was granted his home return permit, which would be valid for 10 years.[22] Lau did not even participate in the December 4, 2005, parade organized by the pan-democratic front to support direct elections for the chief executive and the LegCo in 2007 and 2008, respectively.[23] His fading role in Hong Kong's democracy movement in the mid-2000s was a testimony to the effectiveness of the co-optation policy adopted by Beijing to secure his support.

Another selective target of Beijing's soft-line policy in 2005 was Li Wah-ming. Li's home return permit was confiscated twice, the first time in June 1999 when he led a tour composed of *kaifongs* to visit the mainland. In November 2001 he got back his home return permit, but then it was confiscated again in July 2002 when he led another tour to mainland China. His ability to acquire the home return permit in 2005 could be interpreted as a deliberate move by Beijing to co-opt him prior to the NPC Standing Committee's interpretation of the replacement chief executive's term of office.

The PRC's boundary of political exclusion shifts over time. When the deputy secretary of the NPC Standing Committee, Qiao Xiaoyang, visited Shenzhen in April 2005 to consult the views of the Hong Kong people on the interpretation of the Basic Law, some democrats were included in the consultative list, but others were excluded. Those who were invited to go to the Shenzhen meeting included Sin Chung-kai, Li Wah-ming, Wong Wai-yin, Tik Chi-yuen, and Chow Yik-hei of the DP; Frederick Fung and Tam Kwok-kiu of the ADPL; and independent democrats Mandy Tam Heung-man, Kwok Kar-kay, and Lau Chin-shek.[24] Those democrats who were excluded from the consultative list included Martin Lee, Yeung Sum, Lee Wing-tat, Albert Ho, James To, Andrew Cheng, and Cheung Man-kwong of the DP; Margaret Ng, Audrey Eu, Alan Leong, and Ronny Tong of the CP; Lee Cheuk-yan of the Confederation of Trade Unions; Leung Yiu-chung of the Kaifong and Workers Service Center; and independent democrats such as Leung Kwok-hung, Chan Wai-yip, and Albert Cheng King-hon. The Liaison Office that arranged Qiao's consultation in Shenzhen was criticized for ignoring the transparency of the entire process because it only allowed the Hong Kong mass media to cover the outcome of the meeting.[25] In 2005, Beijing's umbrella of co-optation excluded the four CP members, who had been included in the invitation to observe the national day ceremony of the PRC in October 2004, but who later opposed the NPC Standing Committee's interpretation of the Basic Law in early 2005.

In September 2005, Chief Executive Tsang tried to mend the relations between the pan-democrats and Beijing by leading a delegation of legislators to visit Guangdong. All the 60 legislators submitted their names to the government for the visit, except for Chim Pui-chung and Miriam Lau Kin-yee.[26] Their visit to Guangdong was approved by the central government in Beijing, which allowed those Hong Kong legislators without home return permits to visit the mainland.[27] The DP requested a meeting with Guangdong's provincial secretary Zhang Dejiang.

Admitting that his party would not raise the issue of the June 4 tragedy during the meeting with Zhang, chairman Lee Wing-tat said that he had mailed a letter to Zhang before the visit, appealing to the mainland government to reverse the official verdict on Tiananmen.[28] The democrats moderated their "behavior" in exchange for their visit to Guangdong.

Yet, democrat Martin Lee expressed his worry that the improvement in the relationships between Hong Kong and the mainland would perhaps weaken the Hong Kong people's determination to call for a timetable for universal suffrage. But an editorial disagreed with his view and said:

Martin Lee, one of the DP's founders, is worried that such amicability (between Hong Kong and the mainland) may weaken Hong Kong people's determination to call for a timetable for introducing universal suffrage. We do not think such worry warranted, for it is certainly open to citizens and political parties fighting for the early introduction of universal suffrage to continue to strive to attain those goals. There is no need at all to link fighting for universal suffrage to communication or cooperation with the mainland . . . It is for two important reasons that Hong Kong people want pro-democracy legislators to communicate more with the mainland. One is that they hope Hong Kong democrats and the mainland government will overcome the political impasse consequent on the June 4 crackdown. Though neither would depart from its position on June 4, they hope the two sides will have normal contact and communication as they did before 1989. If that happens, the political atmosphere between Hong Kong and the mainland will be more amicable. The other is that Hong Kong-mainland ties are becoming closer and closer . . . It is incumbent on LegCo members, who represent Hong Kong people, to advance the Special Administrative Region's interests by representing its people's views on those matters to the mainland authorities.[29]

Because of the increasing interactions between Hong Kong people and the mainland, the democrats have to represent the interests of those Hong Kong people working, residing, and doing business in the PRC. In this aspect, the DAB enjoys an edge over the democrats because it can have easy access to mainland officials. The ability of the pan-democrats to enter the mainland and communicate with PRC officials is the *sine qua non* for their public support in Hong Kong and votes in local elections. However, as Martin Lee argues, as more democrats interact with the mainland, their danger of being co-opted is stronger than ever before, thus affecting the political will to fight for democracy in the long run. The dilemmas of communicating with mainland authorities and retaining both the spirit and will to struggle for democracy in the HKSAR remain a challenge to the democrats.

The Liaison Office tried to persuade the democrats to support the HKSAR government's political reform plan.[30] Lee Wing-tat of the DP admitted that the PRC officials contacted two DP legislators and other DC members for discussions. Ronny Tong acknowledged that some PRC officials contacted him to understand his view on political reform. Emily Lau argued that after Tsang became the chief executive, the intervention of PRC officials in Hong Kong affairs was prominent because they went to exert pressure on the legislators to support Tsang's reform plan.[31] In response to Lau's comment, the Liaison Office's deputy director Li Gang clarified that it did not go to the LegCo to lobby any legislator for supporting anything, and that it was his office's responsibility to gather Hong Kong's public opinion and to reflect the views to Beijing and the HKSAR government.[32] While hard-line democrats like Emily Lau viewed the lobbying and contacting activities of PRC officials in Hong Kong as more negative than positive, moderate democrats tend to perceive them as natural.

CAN THE LEGAL SECTOR BE CO-OPTED?

The PRC government attempts to divide some pro-democracy interest groups in the HKSAR so that the moderate elements are co-opted. A case in point was the Bar Association's chairman Rimsky Yuen Kwok-keung, who unprecedentedly accepted the appointment to be a member of the Guangdong People's Political Consultative Conference (GPPCC) in January 2008.[33] The Liaison Office grasped the opportunity that Yuen was the only candidate running for the Association's chairmanship and therefore invited him to be the GPPCC member. His appointment aroused the controversy over whether the Bar Association's chief should accept Beijing's united front work, which has been traditionally designed to win the hearts and minds of those who are political enemies. Yuen argued that if he did not accept the appointment, which provided him a golden opportunity to have dialogue with the mainland, Beijing would not be delighted. On the other hand, the Bar Association's past chairpersons, such as Martin Lee, hoped that Yuen would retain the Association's tradition of maintaining a certain degree of independence from the government. Lee cited the example of the Bar Association's support of the ICAC in 1974, when its creation triggered a police mutiny and protest. Yuen's move was supported by famous Senior Counsel Cheng Huan, who was defeated in the legal sector's election in 2006 for its representatives of the Election Committee that would select the chief executive in 2007.[34] Cheng recommended Clive Grossman to compete with Rimsky Yuen, who was supported by pro-democracy Ronny Tong in 2006. Grossman was defeated by Yuen, but the rift between the relatively conservative faction in the Bar Association and the pro-democracy faction became more serious than ever before. The conservatives complained that the CP attempted to dominate and influence the Bar Association, but Audrey Eu argued that it was impossible for the 300-member CP to "hijack" the 900-member Bar Association. It was reported that Cheng Huan has become the target of mainland co-optation, for he is a member of the Fujian People's Political Consultative Conference.[35] Although the PRC has made efforts at co-opting more barristers and solicitors in the legal sector, such co-optation has met resistance.

THE HONG KONG GOVERNMENT'S CO-OPTATION EFFORTS

As with Beijing, the HKSAR government has been trying to co-opt some democrats. In October 2005, when the SDC was expanded in its membership to co-opt some democrats and academics into the political reform discussions, some academics were hesitant to join the commission. As Sung Lap-kung said, he rejected the government's invitation to enter the SDC because it would be "inconvenient" for him to comment on political affairs after he was appointed into the body.[36] Although some democrats accepted the invitations to join the SDC's political reform committee, the gulf between the government and them was wide. The democrats who accepted the appointment felt that the SDC would like a "saliva meeting," meaning that there would be talks without meaningful compromise and progress.[37] In November 2005, although Chief Executive Tsang became the chairman of the political reform committee so that he could listen to the views of the democrats, the latter refused to make any concession on the grounds that the government failed to put forward any concrete timetable for Hong Kong to have double direct elections of both the chief executive and the entire legislature.[38]

In January 2009, Chief Executive Tsang reshuffled his ExCo by replacing five departing members with five new ones. The five new members included Anna Wu, an advisor of the Shantou University's Faculty of Law, and Lau Wong-fat, the chair of the rural advisory HYK, and a member of the LegCo. Critics of Anna Wu said that she no longer belongs to the pan-democratic camp, but Wu retorted by reminding the critics that she had played a crucial role in the fight for human rights and the formation of the Equal Opportunities Commission during the 1990s.[39] Wu belonged to the early generation of Hong Kong's democrats, whose profile and membership have been transformed greatly after the public opposition to the Tung regime's abortive attempt to legislate on Article 23 of the Basic Law in mid-2003. Some Hong Kong democrats easily see those moderates who are co-opted by Beijing or the HKSAR government as the pro-establishment elites. Arguably, moderate democrats who are co-opted by the administration can still fight for democratization within the establishment. Others, like Wu, try to work for mainland China's gradual democratization by promoting the development of Shantou University's legal training of lawyers, judges, and students. The zero-sum perception of the co-opted elites, who are seen as losing their impetus to fight for democracy, appears to be one-sided and simplistic.

This zero-sum view of the co-opted democrats has been strengthened by Tsang's policy of favoring his own friends and followers in the government's appointment policies, which exacerbate the mutual distrust between his regime and the pan-democrats. Tsang openly proclaims his policy of distinguishing those "who are relatives from those who are not." This patron-client proclivity was seen in the appointment of Lau Wong-fat into the ExCo.[40] Lau played a crucial role in the HKSAR government policy of introducing the double village heads elections, although his opponents vehemently resisted the electoral change that would minimize the power and influence of some indigenous village heads.[41] His appointment into the ExCo was seen as a government reward of how he dealt with the competition between the DAB and LP in the 2008 LegCo election. In February 2008, Lau announced his intention to run for the LegCo election through the DC.[42] Two months later, Ip Kwok-him of the DAB announced that his only choice of participating in the LegCo election would be through the functional constituency composed of DC. In June, James Tien, the leader of LP of which Lau was a member, claimed that Lau would participate in the 2008 LegCo election and that the LP reached a compromise with the DAB. However, Ip of the DAB was uncompromising. In July, Lau led the HYK delegation to visit Beijing, after which he was absent in the LP's campaign activity. Rumors were rife that Lau exchanged his decision not to run in the LegCo election through the DC constituency for the government appointment of him into the ExCo. In late July, Lau declared that he would participate in the LegCo election through the HYK constituency, while vice-chairman Lam Wai-keung would become an independent candidate running for the LegCo election through the DC constituency. After Chief Executive Tsang decided to appoint Lau into ExCo, Albert Ho of the DP and former government official (who then became a political commentator and university professor) Wong Wing-ping criticized the appointment. Ho wrote a letter to the ICAC, urging the agency to probe into the Lau matter.[43] An editorial referred to the governmental appointment of Lau as a "tragic" political reward.[44] The nature of the co-optees, especially those who are seen to engage in tacit bargaining with the ruling elites who favor their political friends and followers, has become a bone of contention.

The HKSAR government intentionally or unintentionally co-opts the democrats by providing more chances for them to interact with PRC officials. In June 2008, when Chief Executive Tsang visited Beijing, he raised the question of whether Hong Kong legislators would be allowed to visit the earthquake-plagued Sichuan province in the next month.[45] Two DP members were on the list: Andrew Cheng and chairman Lee Wing-tat, neither of whom had home return permits. The CP remained the target of co-optation. Its members Audrey Eu, Margaret Ng, and Cheung Chiu-hung were included in the delegation to Sichuan province. Independent democrats Lau Chin-shek and Albert Cheng were also invited. The delegation included six DAB members, including Jasper Tsang, Tam Yiu-chung, and Chan Kam-lam. The LP had six members in the visit. Hence, the tentacles of the HKSAR government's co-optation focused mainly on the two pro-establishment parties, the LP and the DAB, while the pan-democrats were of secondary importance.

The mass media remain a crucial target of political co-optation and control by both the HKSAR government and Beijing. While the HKSAR government has tried to control the future directions of the RTHK, Beijing's friendly business elites have been trying to buy into the shares of the two television stations—ATV and TVB—in the HKSAR. Since the early 2000s, the RTHK has been plagued by internal mismanagement, the problematic integrity of its leaders (such as the former director Chu Pui-hing who was found to hide behind a mainland woman who worked in karaoke bars in July 2007), and the outside criticisms that some of its current affairs programs were antigovernment.[46] The HKSAR government conducted a review of the RTHK's future in 2006 but has delayed the publication of the report, leading to the anxiety of many RTHK staff members, especially because those who were hired on a contractual basis could not change to civil service terms after several years.[47]

CAN THE PEOPLE OF HONG KONG BE CO-OPTED EASILY? THE CASE OF RICKY WONG WAI-KAY OF ATV

Although both the governments of Hong Kong and the PRC have made strenuous efforts to co-opt the media professionals, some of them cannot be co-opted easily, especially those who identify themselves strongly with Hong Kong. A case in point was the controversy over the remarks and action of Ricky Wong Wai-kay, who was a co-founder of the City Telecom and who in December 2008 joined Asia Television (ATV) as a chairman. Wong was a friend of Linus Cheung, the executive chairman of the ATV. Shortly after Ricky Wong joined the ATV in early December, he was determined to reform the station, saying that he would bring about substantial transformations by dismissing redundant staff members and reorganizing the news department. On December 4, Wong made a politically bold statement: "If ATV changes into a mainland station, I am not interested in it. The ATV remains the station of the Hong Kong people. I believe that the Hong Kong people should have dignity and they should not often ask for things from the northern grandfather. Even if the north supports, I do not need it."[48] He even maintained that "I do not have any mainland organizational background, except for being a CPPCC member in Zhejiang province. I even do not have any contacts or links with the Bank of China."[49] On December 12, Wong was criticized for making inappropriate remarks to one of the contestants for Miss ATV. On December 15,

Linus Cheung revealed that he accepted the resignation from Wong, but on the same night Wong announced that he did not resign. The confusion continued until December 17 when the Board of Directors of the ATV accepted Wong's "resignation" and then appointed him as an advisor. The entire saga appeared to focus on the alleged "harassment" of Wong's comment on the Miss ATV contestant, but the crux of the matter was actually Wong's determination to transform the news department and to "change ATV into a television station of the Hong Kong people." [50] His letter actually reiterated Wong's pro–Hong Kong stance, which was politically provocative to the pro-Beijing elites in the ATV. Wong asserted:

ATV is an institution with missions and social responsibilities. Regardless of whether we consider it from the perspective of Hong Kong people or from other factors, ATV remains the television station of the Hong Kong people. I think that this direction is correct. Hong Kong's productivity is tenfold that of the mainland. China is our country. When we have capability, we should think about how we can make contributions to China instead of excessively relying on the mainland. ATV remains a profit organization and it is expected to have its direction without long-term economic dependence ... Without boldness, we cannot do significant things. In the reform process, I have not thought about the need to acquire the consent of all the staff. In the reform process, we have to encounter the strong resistance from those who have vested interest ... All the people agree that ATV needs to establish new a culture and direction. My choice of stepping down should be the best move. [51]

Wong's audacious proposal was to revamp the ATV in such a way that it would be less economically dependent on the mainland. His policy, if implemented, would affect not only the political stance of ATV but also its advertisements and policy directions. From the perspective of media censorship, Wong was determined to de-mainlandize the ATV so that its programs, finances, and news coverage would be far less pro-Beijing than ever before. In the minds of the conservative and pro-Beijing elites in the ATV, Wong's visions were politically unacceptable and therefore he would have to be removed. Linus Cheung stressed in public that Ricky Wong's departure was not due to any pressure from the Liaison Office. Yet, Cheung's remark that the ATV would not "discriminate against mainland advertisements" proved that Wong's resignation was due to the abortive attempt at de-mainlandizing the ATV. [52] After Wong's resignation, a Taiwanese businessman named Tsai Eng-meng of the Want Want Group became one of the shareholders of the ATV, which is jointly owned by the pro-Beijing Alinery Group (47.58 percent), the Panfair Company (10.75 percent), the Kiu Kwong Group (14.81 percent), and a group composed of Phoenix director Liu Changle, and businessman Chan Wing-kei (26.85 percent). However, the mainlandization of ATV is inevitable. [53] The Cha family that dominates the ATV ownership remains pro-Beijing, and the television station's reliance on four hours of the mainland's China Central Television (CCTV) programs on the night of January 25, 2009, was severely criticized by some Hong Kong people in the blog's discussions. They argued that the ATV dependence on mainland programs aimed at saving money but it was "unfair" to the Hong Kong audience.[54]

The Hong Kong mass media are under tremendous pressure from the PRC efforts at controlling their ownership through patriotic businesspeople. A good example is the Hong Kong Television Broadcasting (TVB), whose news coverage that shunned the June 4 candlelight vigil was criticized by some Hong Kong people. In May 2006, pro-Beijing businessman Yeung Kwok-hung used HK$100 billion to buy 75 percent of the total shares owned by the Shaw Brothers in the TVB.[55] Yeung had earned a lot of money from his investment in the Guangzhou real estate market in the 1990s. Although his participation as one of the largest shareholders in the TVB would not change the already pro-Beijing line of the television station, his move could be seen as a consolidation of the pro-Beijing ownership of the TVB in the view of the aging Run Run Shaw. Since the return of Hong Kong to China, the TVB news reports on political issues have been gradually drifting toward self-censorship. While some Hong Kong people openly criticized the TVB news for downplaying the candlelight vigil on the night of June 4, 2009, the ATV that has been ridiculed as the "CCATV" broadcast a two-series program on the Tiananmen incident in late May.[56] Still, the occasional attempt at showing the existence of editorial independence cannot hide the fact that the overwhelming pro-Beijing ownership and advertisements are now making both the TVB and ATV news prone to self-caution and self-censorship.

PATRIOTISM AND CO-OPTATION

Since the handover, the PRC government has been co-opting many Hong Kong young people through the emphasis on patriotism. Many Hong Kong students at the secondary and tertiary levels have been visiting the mainland to understand the PRC system and culture. During their visits, the Hong Kong students were educated by mainland authorities and students on the achievements of the PRC, allowing them to understand the Chinese history and culture, letting them feel the patriotic fervor in the ceremony of hoisting the national flag, showing them the exercises of the PLA, and helping them appreciate the increasingly progressive and open aspects of the entire Chinese nation.[57]

Patriotism, to Beijing, can be utilized to directly shape the Hong Kong people's political attitude and indirectly assist the HKSAR government. In 2004, after the HKSAR recovered gradually from the SARS, Beijing decided to send the Olympic athletes who won gold medals to Hong Kong so as to encourage the people of Hong Kong and to boost their morale. The visit of the Olympic athletes at that time also aimed at enhancing the sense of patriotism among the Hong Kong people so that hopefully the pro-Beijing forces would acquire considerable patriotic votes in the September 2004 LegCo elections. Yet, no survey was conducted on whether the performance of the pro-Beijing forces in the 2004 LegCo elections was related to the higher degree of patriotism aroused by the visit of the Olympic athletes.

In April 2008, the HKSAR government prepared a list of local people who would participate in the relay of the Olympics torch in Hong Kong, but the list contained mostly pro-establishment elites and excluded all the democrats.[58] It was reported that the Liaison Office played a crucial role in nominating some Hong Kong people to the HKSAR government for the participation in the Olympics torch event.[59] At the same time, some foreigners who supported democracy and the Tibetan independence movement, such as Kate Woznow, Matt Whitticase, and Tsering Lama were barred from entering the HKSAR during the relay of the Olympic torch.[60] In late August 2008, the mainland Olympic athletes who won gold medals visited Hong Kong. The objectives were to share the fruits of the national glory with the Hong Kong people and to increase Hong Kong's patriotism toward the PRC.[61]

In April 2006, when Chief Executive Tsang released a list of 461 political appointees in 47 consultative bodies, the democrats were discriminated against. The DAB/FTU had 29 members appointed and the LP 20, but the DP had only 10, the CP 3, the ADPL 1, and the Frontier 1.[62] Although some democrats were politically appointed into these bodies, they were a minority. Anson Chan felt that the Tsang regime's policy of favoring its own friends and excluding those "who are not its relatives" was "too explicit," and she advocated that Chief Executive Tsang should communicate with the democrats in closed-door meetings.[63] Allen Lee, a Hong Kong NPC member, argued that "the government must abandon the policy of distinguishing the relatives from those who are not" and that "it must absorb the opposing voice." [64] In January 2009, it was reported that while the DAB had 23 members appointed to various committees, the LP had 15 members appointed to advisory groups, the DP 10 members, the CP 6 members, the FTU 6 members, the pro-democracy Confederation of Trade Unions 1 member, and the ADPL only 1 member.[65] Hence, the Tsang administration continued to favor its political friends and followers while giving symbolic representation to some democrats.

The way in which PRC officials excluded Cardinal Joseph Zen showed that the traditional Chinese concept of dividing those who are enemies from those who are friends remains influential in Hong Kong politics. Frequently criticizing Beijing for its internally repressive religious policy toward the mainland Catholics and staunchly supporting the Hong Kong democrats, Cardinal Zen had a huge communication gap with PRC authorities.[66] The Liaison Office's officials did not attend a local function celebrating Zen to be the cardinal appointed by the pope in March 2006.[67] Zen appealed to Chief Executive Tsang to urge PRC leaders to reverse the official verdict on Tiananmen.[68] After Zen's retirement, Bishop John Tong Hon of the Hong Kong Diocese supported the idea of reversing the official verdict on Tiananmen and the direct elections of the chief executive and the entire legislature, but Tong adopted a low public profile and avoided appealing to citizens to take to the streets.[69]

BEIJING'S HARD-LINE AND SOFT-LINE POLICIES TOWARD THE DEMOCRATS

The core leaders of the pan-democratic camp have been consistently deprived of their opportunity to visit the mainland, but, on the other hand, the PRC occasionally allows them to do so after the lobbying effort of the HKSAR government. The soft-line change aims at creating an image that the HKSAR government has fought for the interests of the democrats. A case in point was the visit of 36 LegCo members to Guangdong in May 2009. Among the democrats who were allowed by the PRC to visit Guangdong included six who did not have their home return permits renewed by PRC authorities, namely Albert Ho, Emily Lau, Lee Wing-tat, Andrew Cheng, James To, and Cyd Ho. Cheng could not visit Guangdong due to family reasons.[70] However, "radical" democrat Leung Kwok-hung was screened out from the visit.[71] The delegation was led by LegCo President Jasper Tsang, a symbolic gesture showing that it was the patriotic elite who led the legislators, including the democrats, to visit the mainland.

Prior to the visit, Tsang revealed his stance on the Tiananmen tragedy. He said that the time was not ripe in 2009 to request that the PRC government should reverse the official verdict on the Tiananmen incident. Tsang thought that the top Chinese leader who ordered the military to tackle the students in 1989 was Deng Xiaoping, who proposed the idea of using "one country, two systems" to solve the problem of Hong Kong's political future. Therefore, Tsang thought that any attempt at pushing the PRC government to reverse the official verdict would be tantamount to a move to alter Deng's policy toward Hong Kong.[72] Critics of Tsang, such as Lee Cheuk-yan, quickly retorted that the attempt to reverse the official verdict is different from any move to change Deng's policy toward Hong Kong, and that his remarks were misleading.

During the visit to Guangdong, the pan-democrats seized the opportunity to raise the issue of whether the Tiananmen verdict would be reversed in the future, but Guangdong deputy governor Wan Qiangliang avoided the question and said that their meeting time was over.[73] Although democrats such as Chan Wai-yip and Albert Ho were disappointed with Wan's reaction, they both agreed that the deputy governor flexibly and skillfully responded to their sensitive question. Ho later informally asked Wan whether those democrats without the home return permits would be granted the documents or would have them renewed. Wan replied that Hong Kong's legislators who did not have the home return permits could not enter the PRC. Ho pursued Wan by asking whether name cards of the Hong Kong democratic legislators concerned could be used to enter the mainland. Wan reiterated that they would need the home return permits and that he would invite any legislator who visited China to lunch and dinner.[74] If the response of governmental officials to sensitive political questions is an indicator of tolerance, Wan's diplomatic responses to the questions from the pan-democratic legislators from Hong Kong could be seen as a small amount of progress in the mainland's policy toward the pro-democracy camp in the HKSAR.

The Guangdong visit in 2009 did contribute to a better relationship between the democrats and PRC authorities. The democrats themselves admitted that the visit opened their horizon to the new changes and progressive development in the PRC, such as Shenzhen's environmental protection work and hygiene improvement measures.[75] Chan Wai-yip acknowledged that he now understood the difficult predicament of the Hong Kong businesspeople in the mainland and that he would consider this aspect when discussing the government's new policy of enhancing the provision of bank loans and subsidies to Hong Kong's small and medium enterprises.

ECONOMIC ENTICEMENT AS A MEANS OF CO-OPTATION AND ECONOMIC COMPETITION AS DEPOLITICIZATION

In order to delay the pace and curbing the scope of democratic reforms, Beijing often utilizes economic benefits, which can buy the political support from many pragmatic Hong Kong people. From 2004 to 2009, 2,100 Hong Kong service providers benefited from the Closer Economic Partnership Arrangement implemented by Beijing to help the HKSAR after the governing crisis in mid-2003.[76] About 38 billion mainlanders visited Hong Kong from July 2003 to June 2009 so as to stimulate the Hong Kong economy. In Table 9.1, the number of mainland tourists to Hong Kong rose drastically from 2003 onwards, generating a strong impression that the mainlanders are not only big spenders contributing to Hong Kong's economic recovery but also modern comrades who can no longer be looked down upon by the Hong Kong people. Moreover, the status of Shanghai as an emerging mainland monetary center constitutes such a serious threat to Hong Kong that the HKSAR ruling elite tends to adopt an economics-in-command mentality. Consequently, democratic reform is bound to be put on the back burner.

Table 9.1

The Number of Mainland Tourists Visiting the HKSAR Since Mid-2003

Year	Individual Mainlanders Freely Visiting Hong Kong (% increase from past year)	Total Number of Mainland Tourists (% increase from past year)
2008	9,619,280 (11.9% increase)	16,862,003 (8.9% increase)
2007	8,593,141 (28.8% increase)	15,485,789 (13.9% increase)
2006	6,673,283 (20.2% increase)	13,591,342 (8.4% increase)
2005	5,550,255 (30.3% increase)	12,541,400 (2.4% increase)
2004	4,259,601	12,245,862
2003 July to December	667,271	5,231,851

Source: Sing Tao Daily, January 29, 2009, p. B3.

Beijing adopts the tactic of increasing the economic alarm of Hong Kong's ruling and business elites so that their focus is shifted to economic competitiveness rather than political democratization. This depoliticization strategy works well in the Hong Kong case where many elites regard themselves as economic rather than political animals. In April 2009, Premier Wen Jiabao warned the people of Hong Kong that the HKSAR's financial and monetary status would be endangered if they are complacent.[77] He added that Hong Kong must face competition from other places and that it must work hard to maintain its laurels. Wen reiterated that Beijing was going to promote several mainland cities as the focal centers for Reminbi exchange in the international trade—a policy that would be beneficial to Hong Kong. In response, the Hong Kong government's Central Policy Unit principal advisor Lau Siu-kai remarked that Hong Kong would have to compete with other countries in East and Southeast Asia and that it would encounter the danger of being marginalized. Clearly, the impact of Beijing's policy of promoting other mainland cities to a level on par with Hong Kong has created a crisis consciousness among the top policy-making elites, who tend to emphasize economic development rather than democratic reforms.

The crisis of economic decline in the HKSAR has prompted some business elites to criticize the senior civil servants for not understanding the PRC sufficiently and for lagging behind the process of economic integration with the mainland. Ronnie Chan of the Hang Lung Group has said that while many Hong Kong people in the past looked down upon the mainlanders, the situation has been reversed. He has maintained that some Hong Kong officials still lag behind in their understanding of the PRC's developments.[78] The former Chief Executive Tung has appealed to the people of Hong Kong to understand mainland China in a deeper way in the era of globalization, which demands that the HKSAR should contribute more to the co-prosperity between Hong Kong and its motherland.[79] Tung asks the Hong Kong professionals in accountancy, law, and monetary services to make their contributions to China's economic development. In view of the competitiveness of mainland students who study in Hong Kong's universities, who can stay working in the HKSAR, and whose salaries are in general higher than Hong Kong graduates, an editorial appealed to the Hong Kong students to change their attitudes, to be more diligent, to develop the mastery of several languages, and to broaden their international horizon.[80] Stephen Bradley, the former British consul general, pointed to the low English standard of some young people in Hong Kong, a phenomenon that in his opinion would affect the territory's economic competitiveness.[81] The American Chamber of Commerce's chair, Steven DeKrey, expressed his concern about whether the HKSAR would have sufficient local talent.[82] One mainland academic even went so far as to argue that the Hong Kong currency would disappear in 20 years while the *Reminbi* would replace it in the long run.[83] His remark prompted a rebuttal from treasury secretary Chan Ka-keung who maintains that the Hong Kong currency will remain in the region in accordance with the Basic Law. Overall, Hong Kong's crisis of economic decline has diverted the elite's attention to the question of how to develop the enclave's economic competitiveness and whether the HKSAR can really catch up with its giant neighbor and fast-growing motherland.

In May 2009, the governor of the People's Bank of China, Zhou Xiaochuan, said explicitly that the PRC would need only "one international monetary center," namely Shanghai, and that this would be the "long-term strategic objective."[84] He asserted that Shanghai's new role in the future would not threaten the HKSAR. Zhou thinks that the formation of international monetary centers has two routes: the accumulation of monetary business through talents and institutions, and the emergence of a new market of monetary business through the Internet. He believes that Hong Kong's monetary center belongs to the first type, whereas Shanghai will be the second one. Zhou appealed to the need for the HKSAR to facilitate Shanghai's development of the new monetary center. The two cities, to him, will complement each other. Under the long-term plan of Beijing, Hong Kong is going to be the offshore *Renminbi* exchange center, and this would facilitate the internationalization of *Renminbi*. Arguably, Hong Kong remains an economic window for the PRC as long as *Renminbi* remains a domestic rather than an international currency. From this perspective, the elites in Hong Kong perhaps need not overworry about the marginalization of the HKSAR. Understandably, many Hong Kong people perceive China's rapid rise in the 2000s, including Shanghai as the new monetary center in the future, as a substantial threat eroding the HKSAR status to a certain extent.

The increase in the migration of mainlanders into the HKSAR since July 1, 1997, is producing a silent revolution in Hong Kong's social profile. Many of the mainlanders, who have been educated in the PRC, generally have a more patriotic political outlook than the Hong Kong-born citizens. They tend to be more interested in issues like economic prosperity and social stability than political reform in Hong Kong. Indeed, some of them may change their political orientations if they are exposed continuously to Hong Kong's civil liberties, rule of law, and open society. The political orientations of mainland Chinese who have migrated to the HKSAR remain an important but under-researched topic in the study of the evolving political culture in the HKSAR.

More Hong Kong people are now residing in the mainland than ever before, triggering a two-way process of integration leading to much closer economic entity between the HKSAR and the mainland in 2047. The number of Hong Kong people residing in the PRC increased from 41,300 in 2001 to 61,800 in 2003, to 91,800 in 2005, and then to 155,400 in 2007.[85] In early 2009, the PRC State Council published its blueprint on how to integrate Hong Kong and Macao closer with the Pearl River Delta (PRD) region. The blueprint can be seen as a top-down initiative made by Beijing to foster regional coordination and cooperation in South China rather than encouraging competition among Hong Kong, Macao, Zhuhai, Shenzhen, Guangzhou, and other PRD regions.[86] Indeed, internal rivalries persist, such as the competition between Guangzhou and Shenzhen as the regional urban centers in Guangdong province, but the idea of fostering economic coordination and cooperation in such areas as trade, logistics, infrastructure, environmental protection, education, and even governance means that the HKSAR will sooner or later be fully economically integrated into Guangdong's and Beijing's long-term economic planning in the future. In the midst of accelerated economic integration, Hong Kong's pragmatic ruling and business elites are far more concerned about how to maintain the HKSAR's economic competitiveness rather than being interested in political democratization along any Western line advocated by the local democrats.

LIMITATIONS OF BEIJING'S UNITED FRONT WORK: SOCIAL MOVEMENT AND THE HONG KONG STYLE OF DEMOCRACY

The PRC united front work on the HKSAR is not often smooth. When Du Qinglin, the PRC United Front Work Department chief and a member of the Hong Kong Work Committee, visited the HKSAR in July 2009, he presided over the founding ceremony of the Association for the Promotion of Peaceful Reunification of China in the territory. The Association is a united front organization uniting the pro-Beijing business elites in the HKSAR and propagating the "success" of the "one country, two systems" in Hong Kong.[87] But the Association's activities did not reach out to the democrats who were excluded from participation in the opening ceremony. It represented a small circle co-optation in which the pro-Beijing loyalists simply harped the same theme of the success of "one country, two systems" without any independent viewpoints. Some CPPCC members complained to Du that the Hong Kong LegCo was "too powerful" and "obstructive" to the policy implementation of the HKSAR government.[88] The narrow nature of Du's united front work failed to lure both the Hong Kong democrats and the Taiwan Chinese to accept the PRC's political appeals easily.

Although the HKSAR is by no means a full-fledged Western-style democracy where the chief executive is elected by citizens through universal suffrage and where the legislature is fully directly elected, its semidemocratic system is characterized by the persistent activities of environmental, human rights, and social groups to make their voices heard, to check public maladministration, to force the government to respond to criticisms, and to inject an element of democratic accountability into the polity. This vibrant social movement remains weak in the PRC where social groups independent of the state's control should arguably be encouraged, tolerated, and promoted so that the accountability of both the ruling CCP and the bureaucracy will be improved significantly.

In June 2009, a campaign launched by the staff members of the RTHK made a declaration in response to the criticism of Cheung Chi-kong, who is the director of the pro-Beijing One Country Two Systems Economic Research Institute, and who said that a RTHK program host was "anti-communist." [89] The program host, Lee Siu-mei, used the collapse of the communist regimes in Eastern Europe to express her disappointment that the June 4 student movement in the PRC failed.[90] Cheung questioned whether the RTHK should have such a stance and whether Lee's comment represented the HKSAR government. What he implied was that the RTHK as a radio station funded by the HKSAR government should not make such comments on the Tiananmen incident. In response, the RTHK spokesman said Lee's remarks were already made known to the program director and that she did not intend to bring out any "anti-communist" position. The campaign in support of the RTHK argued that Cheung's remarks tried to mainlandize the RTHK and to turn it into another mainland television station.[91] The arguments between Cheung and the RTHK campaign group showed that the HKSAR as a pluralistic society easily generates opposing political viewpoints. The pro-RTHK group is resistant to any political effort at revamping the RTHK or changing it into a pro-government mouthpiece. Neither the HKSAR government nor Beijing can co-opt the vociferous civil society groups in Hong Kong.

The political institutions of the HKSAR often impose significant checks and balances on the administration. A case in point is the row over the government's attempt at relocating Christian Zheng Sheng College, which is a school for the rehabilitation of students who have drug addiction problems, to Mui Wo Island. The Island residents complained that there should be more local schools for their children rather than integrating the Zheng Sheng College into the Southern District Secondary School in Mui Wo.[92] The row became emotional as residents were criticized by government officials, including Chief Executive Tsang and chief secretary Henry Tang, for being intolerant of the young people who had drug addiction problems. The residents and District Council members in Mui Wo insisted that the HKSAR government had failed to solicit their opinions earlier. The HYK tried to propose various solutions, but they were not favored by the government.[93] The whole saga illustrated not only the strong opposition of local residents to the relocation plan but also the government's failure to request their opinions.

The media and LegCo play a crucial role in checking public maladministration. In 2009, the former permanent secretary for housing, planning, and lands, Leung Chin-man, testified about his role in his employment in the New World China Land after retirement. The hearings not only brought to light whether Leung might have conflicts of interest by joining the company so quickly after he handled a housing project involving the New World, but it also revealed the close relationships between senior civil servants and the business elites. Leung admitted in the LegCo hearings that he had accepted the New World offer for the Hunghom Peninsula housing project in 2004 even though it was 25 percent below the ExCo's bottom line.[94] Leung said: "I was involved in the issue but I did not have much knowledge in land premiums and I was not involved in the negotiations." [95] He even blamed the lands department officials for shifting the responsibility of making decisions to him. Moreover, Leung said he had consulted his former supervisor Michael Suen, who talked to the chief executive without the need to request the opinion of the ExCo. Leung also admitted that his postretirement employment application did not mention the Hunghom Peninsula, and he felt that the application's approval should have gone to Suen. The entire hearings demonstrated the discretion of senior officials, including both Leung and Suen, in dealing with the land developers. The postretirement application of Leung appeared to show the loopholes in the approval process during which both the civil service bureau and the committee, which approved the employment applications of former civil servants, were not aware of the political sensitivity and controversy in the Leung case.

Although the Chinese televisions in the HKSAR are under tremendous pressure toward self-censorship and self-caution, the local Chinese press remains critical of public maladministration in Hong Kong.

The Hong Kong Chinese press coverage of the June 4 tragedy in 1989 has remained constant since July 1, 1997. It has been playing a crucial role in checking public maladministration, such as the revelation of the Deputy Commissioner Lam Wing-hong of the Privacy Commission for misusing public money and squeezing HK$120,000 for personal gains and visits from 2001 and 2005.[96] The Chinese press also severely criticized the government for incompetence and the absence of departmental coordination after a rotten tree neglected by the fisheries department and the department of recreation and culture collapsed and killed a young girl in 2009.[97]

Although the democrats are destined to be a minority in the LegCo, the legislature does constitute an effective check against public maladministration. A case in point was the activation of the special power of LegCo (Power and Privilege) to hear the testimony of officials and authorities related to the mini-bonds of the Lehman Brothers. In each of the two sectors, namely functional constituencies and direct elections, 20 of the 27 legislators (3 voted against and 4 abstained) returned from functional constituencies voted for the use of the special power to investigate the incident, while 27 of the 28 councilors returned from direct elections (only Regina Ip voted against it) supported the proposed move.[98] Supporters of the move argued that the legislature must look into any maladministration on the part of the banks and monetary authorities so that the victims of mini-bonds would be financially compensated. Opponents, such as banker Li Kwok-po, contended that the use of the special power would undermine the status of Hong Kong as a financial center and that the victims themselves were private investors who should be responsible for their own action and investment decisions.

The Hong Kong style of democracy is characterized not only by active social groups, the vibrant press, and the assertive legislature, but also by a relatively respectable and clean civil service, the existence of the ICAC, the persistence of the Office of the Ombudsman to check public maladministration, and the usefulness of the Audit Commission to expose excessive expenditure in government agencies. Moreover, the persistence of civil liberties and the rule of law are the features of the Hong Kong style of democracy. Hong Kong does not have a Western-style democratic system, but it is semidemocratic in the sense that the chief executive is elected by a small electoral college and the legislature includes a powerful opposition with almost 60 percent of the votes in direct elections.

Thanks to the efforts of the ICAC, the Hong Kong civil service is in general clean, although a minority of corrupt bureaucrats taking bribes and abusing their powers is often reported by the press. Before her retirement from the head of the ombudsman office, Alice Tai criticized the HKSAR government's POAS, which refers to the political appointees made by the chief executive to be responsible for various ministerial portfolios since mid-2002, for (1) failing to check public administration; (2) lacking coordination among the secretaries; (3) ignoring internal division of labor and vertical communications between the superiors and subordinates; and (4) implementing policies at an inappropriate time.[99] She also criticized the government for losing talents and reducing bureaucratic efficiency, contracting out excessive services to companies outside the civil service, and undermining the morals of bureaucrats. Meanwhile, the Audit Commission regularly checks the budgets of government departments. The consolidation of the anticorruption and auditing work can be seen in the PRC, which, however, has to learn more from the Hong Kong style of democracy in terms of allowing more political space to social groups, giving more autonomy to the mainland press, empowering the NPC, and enhancing the integrity and administrative propriety of civil servants.

CAN MYSTERIOUS INTIMIDATION THREATEN THE HONG KONG DEMOCRATS?

Quite often some Hong Kong democrats encounter mysterious intimidations of a political nature. Li Wah-ming said that in 1999 when he supported a rehabilitation center to be built in Kwung Tong, his remarks and action antagonized some residents and he eventually received the ghost papers used by citizens to mourn the dead relatives.[100] Moreover, the door of his home was full of red paint—another warning sign that triads threatened him. In August 2006, democrat and lawyer Albert Ho of the DP was attacked by a gangster at the McDonald's restaurant in the Central district. At that time, Ho was the solicitor for Winnie Ho Yuen-ki during a legal battle with her brother and Macao casino tycoon Stanley Ho. Albert Ho had received threatening letters during the litigation, and Winnie Ho's first solicitor, C. K. Mok, resigned after being attacked on two occasions.[101] After Anson Chan was elected as a legislator in December 2007, she received a letter inside which there was a razor with the note saying that Chan "should turn over a new leaf" and stop being a "traitor."[102] The note also said that without the help of "traitors" Martin Lee and Leung Kwok-hung, Chan could not have been directly elected. Chan's office worker received the razor and the note and then reported the incident to the police. The ultimate origins of these intimidations targeted at the democrats were unknown.

In July 2009, a 50-year-old man involved in a plot by 13 suspects to teach the DP founder Martin Lee a lesson was imprisoned for three years.[103] Five of them were Hong Kong persons and the rest were mainlanders.[104] Ho Wai-kan pleaded guilty in April to the possession of a gun and ammunition. His mainland accomplice, Huang Nanhua, alias Wong Siu-man, was imprisoned for 16 years. Huang was arrested at a police roadblock on August 14, 2008, and he was found to carry a pistol and five rounds of ammunition. He carried a note with Lee's addresses and places where Lee often dined with Jimmy Lai, the chairman of the Next Media Group and the supporter of Hong Kong's democracy movement. Martin Lee repeatedly said he did not believe that the CCP was behind the conspiracy. It was reported that the mastermind behind the plot on Lee and Lai was a Hong Kong businessperson residing in Taiwan, that the Hong Kong media were "too free and so the two might antagonize some people," that the mainland assassins were paid HK$3.3 million to HK$5 million if the two targets were assassinated, and that all the 10 Hong Kong men participating in the plot were members of the triad Shui Fong.[105] When the Shui Fong heads heard of the assassination plot, they were shocked and persuaded the subordinates "to injure the two only because 10 lives would not be able to compensate the two lives if the target were killed."[106] Another report revealed that a senior official of Shui Fong was involved, but it was unclear who had asked him to "injure" the two targets.[107] His order was passed onto the subordinates, who recruited mainland assassins but the original intention of "injuring" Lee and Lai was distorted to the objective of assassinating the two.[108] While Martin Lee insisted that the plot on Lai and him "had no relations with politics,"[109] the entire issue was shrouded in secrecy.

Lawsuits and legal charges can be another type of intimidation challenging the future of some democrats who are economically less well-off. A notable example is Chu Hoi-dick who took political and legal action to challenge the government on the demotion of the Queen's Pier, which was demolished by the government without sufficient public consultations.[110] Although the government would rebuild the Queen's Pier in the newly reclaimed harbor front in the Central District, its legal department sought Chu to pay the legal costs amounting to HK$270,000. As a grassroots-level resident, Chu had no choice but to raise funds from Facebook, and he collected donations of HK$30,000 from 241 citizens within three days.[111] Chu got the support of some angry residents, who believed that Chu was an activist yearning for a better Hong Kong with a strong sense of "collective memory" and that the HKSAR government went perhaps too far to pursue him for the legal costs incurred in the lawsuit.[112]

While the democrats are not afraid of being intimidated, the thrust of pro-democracy views is sometimes so strong that minority views supportive of the PRC suppression of student democrats can be politically ostracized and marginalized. This phenomenon could be seen in the controversial remarks made by the former chair of the University of Hong Kong Student Union, Ayo Chan Yi-ngor, who said in a public forum that the PRC suppression of the student democrats in June 1989 "might have some problems," and that Chai Ling evaded her responsibility to escape from China.[113] His provocative remarks became so controversial that some angry university students, notably Christina Chan who supported publicly the Tibetan independence movement and who complained about the police's abuse of power in dealing with her pro-Tibetan activities in the HKSAR, decided to impeach Chan.[114] Ayo Chan was eventually removed from his union chair position as 1,592 votes impeached him, 949 opposed such impeachment, and 114 abstained.[115] The unprecedented removal of a university student union leader from office through impeachment because of his pro-PRC views on Tiananmen showed that the pro-democracy sentiments in the HKSAR remain strong. Indeed, the fate of Ayo Chan was decided in a democratic mechanism in accordance with the constitution of the Student Union at the University of Hong Kong, but those democrats who were mysteriously intimidated could have their lives endangered.

SUMMARY

Although Beijing has been using economic enticement, integration, and political rewards to co-opt the people of Hong Kong, most democrats remain politically defiant and independent of its influence. The reason is that many Hong Kong democrats are idealists and by no means opportunists who can yield to the politics of co-optation easily. Still, Beijing's assumption of co-optation is that by using economic penetration and enticement, many pragmatic Hong Kong people will become far more patriotic than ever before. Patriotism is therefore built on economic benefits and incentives. It is combining the cultural identity of the Hong Kong Chinese hopefully with their political identification with the CCP. However, many Hong Kong democrats, especially those who support the reversal of the official verdict on Tiananmen, cannot be easily lured to transform their cultural identity as Chinese into the political recognition and unconditional acceptance of the ruling party in the mainland. Hence, the path toward politically absorbing all the democrats in the HKSAR is destined to be difficult and perhaps impossible unless the PRC regime is going to liberalize and democratize its political system in the future, or unless the official Chinese verdict on Tiananmen could be reversed.

Similarly, the HKSAR government encounters enormous hurdles in co-opting the local democrats mainly because of its favoritism toward friends and its exclusionist policy on enemies. Donald Tsang's policy of "distinguishing the relatives from those who are not" confers official tone explicitly upon such exclusionist tactics. It has the unintended consequence of solidifying the resistance and vigilance from the democrats to their appointment by the government to various consultative committees. The outcome is a vicious circle in which both sides distrust each other to the extent that communications and political bargaining can be difficult.

Finally, many Hong Kong democrats are bold idealists yearning for a democratic HKSAR and China. They do not easily succumb to triad intimidations or threats from mysterious forces. Their idealism is parallel to the Chinese revolutionary hero Sun Yat-sen who desired a democratic China. Although their democratic vision may be even more Westernized than Sun's ideas, they are all tenacious idealists and patriots believing that democracy is the best form of government.

Conclusion

The vision of democracy held by most Hong Kong people is far more Westernized than that held by the mainland's political elites. Most Hong Kong people, especially the democrats, are hoping for an idealistic political system in which the chief executive is elected by citizens through universal suffrage and the whole legislature is also directly elected. However, the mainland's political elites are not imbued with such an ideal for both the PRC and Hong Kong.

The mainland Chinese democracy remains very Chinese in that political power remains to be vested with the central authorities; opposition needs to be loyal and pro-establishment; the line of political tolerance is to accept the verdict of the ruling party in power; civil society and its groups independent of the central authorities have to be tamed; and severe criticisms of the leadership are seen as undermining its legitimacy and being disrespectful of the traditional concept of face. The PRC's political system has witnessed progressive transformations since the early 2000s: the emphasis on supervising the government's performance at both central and local levels; the consolidation of anticorruption and internal auditing work; the granting of some political space for groups and citizens to articulate their interests and check public maladministration; the resurgence of the NPC to monitor government work; the introduction of village elections to enhance cadre and official accountability to the public; the stress on the development of the rule of law; and the development of a more open-minded attitude of government officials toward public criticisms, especially through the Internet. Still, these progressive transformations in the PRC are no match for the civil liberties, the rule of law, and the political space enjoyed by the people of Hong Kong. If Hong Kong remains the freest society on the Chinese soil, its vision of democracy also represents an ideal type of political development for the PRC.

The two competing Chinese visions of democracy include the issues of the 1989 Tiananmen tragedy, universal suffrage, referendum, electoral competition, and patriotism. Most Hong Kong people are actually yearning for the day when the mainland Chinese leaders would at least admit the mistakes in violently suppressing the student democrats on the Tiananmen Square in June 1989, if not totally reversing the official verdict. The PRC leaders so far have been dodging this issue until their future generations. But many Hong Kong democrats are hopeful that generational changes in the PRC would sooner or later lead to a gradual reversal of the official verdict on Tiananmen. By that time, democratization in both the mainland and Hong Kong would hopefully enter a new era.

While universal suffrage is the demand of most Hong Kong people regarding the election of the chief executive and the whole legislature, the PRC leaders and officials responsible for Hong Kong see it as potentially subversive. Allowing Hong Kong to be fully democratic would run the risk of allowing "unpatriotic" Hong Kong people to be directly elected, just like the case of Taiwan under the former pro-independence and now disgraced President Chen Shui-bian. As most Hong Kong people believe that they would not directly elect an unpatriotic Hong Kong leader, PRC authorities distrust them mainly due to the clashes in their political cultures. The political culture of the Hong Kong people tends to be pro-liberal values, such as freedom of speech and of press, and to favor substantial checks and balances as with Western democracies. Yet, the PRC ruling elites remain traditional in their Chinese political culture, and they view Western-style democracy as not only alien but also eroding the political center's power so seriously that other regions such as Xinjiang and the Tibetan Autonomous Region may demand separatism and self-determination. As long as the mainland's ruling elite culture sees Western-style democracy as potentially generating the fragmentation of China, Hong Kong's demand for double direct elections will continue to encounter the politico-cultural obstacles.

While the Hong Kong democrats see any referendum as an impartial and a scientific means to gauge public opinions on democratic reform, PRC authorities view it as politically undesirable and entailing the assumption that the people of Hong Kong can constitute a separate entity with the right of self-determination. The mainland Chinese hardline authorities reject any right of self-determination on the part of the Hong Kong people. In the mainland Chinese democratic tradition, rights are conferred by the paternalistic state on the citizens and groups. The Hong Kong vision of democracy is arguably un-Chinese in that the rights possessed by citizens, groups, and political parties can subvert the political center and seriously challenge the authority of the paternalistic state.

Electoral competition in the HKSAR, to the local democrats, should allow for the likelihood of the pan-democrats grasping political power, but PRC authorities fear that the 60 percent vote garnered by the democrats in direct elections would lead to a lopsided executive-legislative relationship in favor of legislative supremacy. Legislative supremacy, to the PRC tradition, should come from the NPC Standing Committee that can exercise its legal power and political discretion to interpret the Hong Kong Basic Law and to veto the directions of political reform in the HKSAR. Legislative supremacy in the form of the democrats capturing over half of all the seats in the LegCo is politically unacceptable to PRC authorities, because it would paralyze the executive branch of the government and bring about a serious legitimacy problem of the chief executive, who would be checked more by the legislature than by the central government in Beijing.

Dividing the two competing political visions is the ingredient and meanings of patriotism. To the Hong Kong democrats, patriotism and Western-style democracy are compatible. Martin Lee, Szeto Wah, and Anson Chan all believe that patriotic Hong Kong people should strive for democracy in the HKSAR, which will then become an ideal model for mainland China to develop its political system. To PRC authorities, especially hard-liners, patriotism means accepting the political bottom line of the ruling party in power. Patriotism to them also refers to the adoption of a non-Western political system without any influence and intervention from foreign countries. After the Tiananmen crackdown, the rescue of mainland Chinese dissidents by the Hong Kong triads, by democrats, and above all by foreign countries prove to PRC hard-liners that foreigners have attempted to subvert the CCP. Hence, the PRC vision of patriotism has a strong xenophobic sentiment, unlike the patriotism of most Hong Kong democrats who tend to be far more receptive of foreign ideas and foreigners. The rise of China and the perceived China threat by the West worsen the worries of PRC hard-liners that foreign countries would like to use Hong Kong's democratization as a means to transform the PRC regime in the long run. Arguably, the PRC vision of Chinese democracy has strong antiforeign sentiment that underscores the ongoing debate over democratization in the HKSAR.

Indeed, the HKSAR government has since July 1, 1997, loyally followed the PRC vision of Chinese democracy, for it is legally bound by the Basic Law to accept the central government as the supreme power holder. Yet, it does not mean that progress toward democratic reform cannot be made. The lesson of the abortive Tsang reform plan is that the HKSAR government would have to dissect any reform package into various components so that the democratic rejection of one item would not automatically affect others. Moreover, the HKSAR authorities need to engage the soft-liners within the democratic camp, making compromises and carving out a potentially acceptable formula. The radical democrats may have to be politically sidelined, but this would perhaps be necessary if political bargaining would lead to a gradual development of Hong Kong's democratization. The crux of the problem is whether the key leaders and core architects of Hong Kong's democracy movement would be willing to make sufficient concessions to allow for a political breakthrough. If not, Hong Kong's democratic path would likely be stuck in a stagnant *cul-de-sac*. The political cost is that public aspirations for a more democratic system would be frustrated and the democrats would run the risk of being labeled as unconstructive oppositionists reluctant to bargain creatively with the HKSAR government. The prospects of a bargaining agreement on Hong Kong's democratization will depend on a number of crucial factors: the determination of the HKSAR government to make significant concessions, Beijing's approval of such political breakthrough, the ability of democratic soft-liners to persuade the hard-liners of the need to make compromises, and the willingness of the DAB and the business elites to abandon their vested interests and change the political *status quo*.

THE HONG KONG MODEL OF DEMOCRACY AND DEMOCRATIZATION

Although Hong Kong's popular vision of democracy is very different from the mainland ruling elite's, the Hong Kong model of democracy and democratization entails implications for the PRC political development. These implications include participatory, institutional, constitutional, attitudinal, or cultural dimensions.

From a participatory perspective, Hong Kong's democrats actively participated in the rescue of mainland democrats after the June 1989 Tiananmen tragedy. Hong Kong remains the only place in the PRC that can hold the annual candlelight vigil in commemoration of the victims of Tiananmen. This annual event has tremendous educative impact on both the Hong Kong people and many mainland visitors to the HKSAR. It provides the necessary participatory channel for the Hong Kong and mainland Chinese. Yang Jianli, a Chinese dissident in the United States, believes that many young Chinese citizens do not know what happened in June 1989 because they have been "brainwashed and indoctrinated with nationalistic sentiments."[1] If so, Hong Kong's annual candlelight vigil as widely reported in the HKSAR and overseas can have hidden impacts on the political culture and attitude of many young Chinese who have been politically indoctrinated in the mainland.

Another aspect of participation is that the Hong Kong democrats remain aggressively active in influencing the PRC policy toward the HKSAR, especially their struggle for the direct elections of the chief executive through universal suffrage and of the entire LegCo. As a result of public pressure, the PRC government has to admit that the end point would be universal suffrage in Hong Kong, although it has not really spelled out a concrete timetable. This responsiveness of PRC officials responsible for Hong Kong matters has often been neglected by critics. If governmental responsiveness is an indicator of democracy, such responsiveness on the part of PRC elites can be seen as a democratizing phenomenon resulting from persistent public pressure and demands from Hong Kong. The HKSAR has already acted like a political actor continuously lobbying the political center in Beijing for concessions. The minimal concessions from Beijing do show that the mainland's ruling elite culture has to be adaptive to Hong Kong's ceaseless political pressure and demands. To put it in another way, Hong Kong can politically modernize the PRC.

Institutionally speaking, the HKSAR model of democracy offers institutional experiences for the PRC to emulate. The Hong Kong model of democracy embraces its respectable anticorruption work, the relatively clean and efficient civil service, the solid rule of law, the media scrutiny of public maladministration, electoral competition among pluralistic political parties, and the legislative supervision on government policies. Pan Wei believed that the PRC can establish a "consultative rule of law" regime like Hong Kong where the legal system remains vibrant and independent and where the government constantly consults public opinion on government policies.[2] Arguably, institutionalization in the PRC in the form of peacefully managing leadership succession is an insufficient condition for democratization. A much fuller scale of institutionalization in the PRC must entail the invigoration of its anticorruption work, including the expanded role of the anticorruption CDIC, the increased autonomy given to the mass media to check public maladministration, more electoral competition at various levels of government, and the empowerment of the NPC to supervise the government. If "democracy is a good thing" as admitted by more mainland ruling elites than ever before, and if the Chinese themselves can design their democracy with Chinese features, then the current Hong Kong model of democracy can be humbly learned by PRC leaders at the national, provincial, and local levels.

Constitutionally and culturally, the HKSAR can be seen as an experiment in Chinese federalism in which the central government has delegated considerable autonomy, especially financial and economic, to the territory. This experiment in Chinese federalism constitutes a gradual and silent revolution in the mainland Chinese political culture, which according to the late Lucian Pye develops "the fear of local kingdoms." In other words, the PRC has distrusted independent kingdoms defying the central government's policy directives. Hence, if the PRC is increasingly getting used to dealing with the Hong Kong model where small political parties persist, where opposition forces thrive, where legislative and district-level elections remain competitive without deliberate manipulation by the regime, and where citizen protests are commonplace, the mainland's ruling elites in Beijing would hopefully also develop a political culture of tolerating pluralism. The four aspects of Hong Kong's democratizing impacts on the mainland—participatory, institutional, constitutional, and cultural—cannot be neglected in the PRC's political interactions with the HKSAR.

The Hong Kong model of democratization is characterized by the rational behavior and peaceful nature of the participants. The Hong Kong people are rational political animals and the majority of them do not resort to any violence to make their demands and grievances heard. The orderly nature of the annual July 1st parade organized by the democrats is a testimony to their political maturity and moderate inclinations. The Hong Kong model also shows that the HKSAR as an economically vibrant city entails a lot of law-abiding citizens whose identities include not simply a strong sense of Hong Kong belonging but also calmness and rationality in their struggle for democracy in both the HKSAR and the mainland.

This rationality could be discerned in the case of triad members who were determined to rescue the mainland democrats after the Tiananmen crackdown. They ventured into the mainland and saw patriotism as the love of the lives of Chinese citizens rather than the love of the ruling party in power. Patriotism, to some Hong Kong triads involved in Operation Yellowbird, is humanistic instead of the brutal retaliation and violent bloodshed that often characterize the triads on the streets of Hong Kong, mainland China, and Taiwan. Triad elements are not interested in the vision of democracy held by the Hong Kong democrats, but some of them had already demonstrated a very strong sense of humanistic patriotism as with most Hong Kong Chinese who were saddened and shocked by the Tiananmen crackdown immediately after June 4, 1989. Indeed, some Hong Kong triad members can be seen as the heroes of the Tiananmen rescue, but other triads have also played a mysterious role in intimidating the Hong Kong democrats. The dialectical role of Hong Kong triads in promoting democratization in the PRC and yet threatening some democratic idealists in the HKSAR can be seen.

REVISITING VARIOUS PERSPECTIVES ON DEMOCRATIZATION IN HONG KONG

There are at least six major perspectives for us to comprehend the dynamics of democratization: elite, class, cleavage, geopolitics, political culture, and social movement. The competing Chinese political visions on democracy, as discussed above, have been largely shaped by the varying political cultures between the Hong Kong democrats and the mainland's ruling elites. The huge differences in their political visions reflect the fundamental gap between the liberal-pluralistic political culture of the Hong Kong democrats and the paternalistic-centralist psyche of the PRC ruling elites.

From the elite perspective, PRC leaders remain relatively hard-line toward Hong Kong's democratization, while the Hong Kong democrats are led by hard-liners without the urgency of bargaining for a more moderate solution for democratic development in the HKSAR. The rejection of the Tsang reform package by the hard-line democrats in 2005 has an important lesson: any breakthrough in democratization would require a moderate faction prevailing over hard-liners within the democratic camp, while PRC authorities dealing with Hong Kong would have to be more moderate or soft-line. This convergence of moderate elites in both the democratic camp and PRC leadership would perhaps force the HKSAR government, which has basically toed the official line of Beijing, to be more soft-line and more willing to make concessions to the democrats. The complexity of the HKSAR government is that any soft-line position it intends to adopt, as the three stages in the reduction of appointed DC members in the 2005 Tsang reform package showed, can be opposed by the hard-line DAB and LP. Hence, Larry Diamond's hope for a bargaining solution for Hong Kong's democratization depends on the changing configurations between the soft-liners and hard-liners in each of three camps: the Beijing leadership, the Hong Kong democrats, and the HKSAR establishment.

From the class perspective, Hong Kong as a capitalist city-state remains to be ruled by Beijing's political loyalists in collaboration with the powerful local capitalist class. The liberal-minded middle-class professionals and intellectuals are the pillars of Hong Kong's democracy movement, but their demands are frustrated by the triple alliance between Beijing's hard-line leaders, Hong Kong's capitalist class, and those conservative middle-class professionals co-opted by the HKSAR government. The split within the middle-class professionals is prolonged by the persistence of the LegCo's functional constituencies, which protect the interests of the middle-class conservatives without their need to run in direct elections. The co-optation of the conservative segment of the middle class in the HKSAR means that the middle class as a whole is not forceful enough to propel political reform along the path of Western-style democracy. On the other hand, the working-class members remain ideologically divided: those who ally with the pro-government and pro-Beijing FTU tend to be far more moderate and anti-democratization than those who are pro-democracy. Although the working class relies on labor movement and strikes to force their employers to make concessions and compensate for the absence of any formal right of collective bargaining, overall it remains politically subordinated to the ruling coalition of the capitalist class, Beijing, and the HKSAR government.

In terms of cleavages, identity and ideology are intertwined in the struggle for Hong Kong's democratization. While the pan-democrats tend to have a much stronger sense of Hong Kong's identity and liberal values, the pro-Beijing and pro-government residents not only are identifying themselves as more Chinese than the democrats but they also reject liberalism as the panacea for the political future of both Hong Kong and mainland China. Those Hong Kong people who identify themselves as culturally Chinese are more likely to accept the mainland Chinese political vision; namely, the Chinese democracy is unique and different from the separation of powers and universal suffrage of Western democracies.

Ideology is also mingled with class in Hong Kong's democratization. The capitalist class is imbued with a politically conservative ideology. It views democratization as a threat to business interests and influence, opening the door to welfarism, trade unionism, and working-class collective bargaining. The capitalists believe that democratization would lead to higher profit tax and a deterioration of investment environment in Hong Kong. Hence, they fiercely oppose democratization and delay it as long as possible. Moreover, the working-class representatives who are pro-welfare but who have been co-opted by Beijing, like Chan Yuen-han of the DAB, understand that the capitalist class in Hong Kong is structurally destined to be dominant and powerful. Yet, the pro-Beijing unionists are expected to be politically supportive of the HKSAR government, thus constraining their ability to fully articulate the interests of the local workers. On the other hand, FTU leaders such as Cheng Yiu-tong have been politically co-opted to such an extent that they can be seen as the "labor aristocrats" in the HKSAR without any real bargaining power vis-à-vis the influential and conservative capitalist class. In short, the pro-Beijing working-class leaders have little choice but to reluctantly accept the political dominance of the capitalist class in the HKSAR. Nor do they have the boldness to advocate a faster pace of democratic reform to the detriment of the national security concerns of Beijing.

Geopolitically speaking, the HKSAR is a very small city economically dependent on the PRC, but its political influence on the mainland, as this book argues, is perhaps disproportionate to its tiny location on the map of China. Although the PRC's intervention in the HKSAR has been pervasive through the NPC Standing Committee's interpretation of the Basic Law and the Liaison Office's constant coordination and support of pro-Beijing candidates in local elections, Hong Kong's pluralistic political system has demonstration effects on the mainland government at the national, provincial, and local levels. Its clean government, moderate opposition, fair elections, rule of law, and civil liberties provide a yardstick for measuring the PRC's political progress and democratization.

Meanwhile, as a former British colony for 155 years, the HKSAR provides a strategic location for Western democracies, notably the United States, to promote and encourage democratic development in mainland China. As a result, the United States has replaced Britain to be the most prominent pro-democracy foreign country. Yet, under the context of Sino-American power struggle, the PRC sees the United States as having the sinister motive of using Hong Kong's democratization as a means to contain China politically and subvert the CCP. Beijing's opposition to Hong Kong's democratization is understandable because it perceives the Hong Kong democrats as being politically utilized by the United States as a chess game to transform the PRC political system.

Social movement includes labor, environmental, and human rights activists in Hong Kong. Social movement in the HKSAR cannot really influence the PRC due to the mainland's authoritarian system that suppresses social groups and movement independent of the state. But it does buttress civil liberties, check the Hong Kong government, and consolidate the momentum of democratization in the HKSAR. In brief, all these multiple perspectives can be applied and combined to comprehend Hong Kong's difficult path of democratization.

DRIVERS OF THE DEMOCRACY MOVEMENT IN HONG KONG AND CHINA: MINI-POLITICAL PARTIES AND PARTICIPANTS

The mini-political parties in Hong Kong's democratic camp, especially the DP, CP, LSD, and ADPL, are playing a critical role in sustaining the momentum of democratization in the HKSAR. Their struggle and mass mobilization of citizens to participate in the June 4 candlelight vigil have been contributing to the PRC's long but difficult process of democratization. Critics can easily point to the lack of organization and leadership of the pan-democratic camp. To be fair to the Hong Kong democrats, however, they do have organization although it cannot be compared to the DAB/FTU alliance of mobilizing the Hong Kong patriots in elections and of interacting with constituents on a daily basis. Organizers of the Hong Kong democrats are numerically inferior to the pro-Beijing forces because they are volunteers rather than well-paid employees. Yet, they do have leadership. Despite the persistence of internal debates, opinion differences, and personality conflicts, the pan-democratic camp in Hong Kong remains cohesive in its ideology of liberalism and its consensus of reversing the official Chinese verdict on Tiananmen in the future.

The mini-political parties in Hong Kong's democratic front are arguably a formidable force to the pro-Beijing front, the HKSAR government, and Beijing. Garnering almost 58 to 60 percent of the total votes in direct elections, the pan-democrats could have easily become a ruling party under a truly Western-style democracy. The artificially created functional constituencies in Hong Kong's LegCo check their power and curb their ability of becoming any ruling party. Beijing understands that unless the pro-Beijing DAB/FTU coalition can substantially improve their electoral performance in such a way that it can really capture at least half of the seats in the legislature, the democratic ideal of having a fully directly elected legislature will remain a castle in the air.

The pro-business LP remains a political baby learning how to participate more effectively in direct elections held for the legislature. Unless the glorious victory of James Tien and Selina Chow in the 2004 legislative direct election can be repeated, most business elites will see democracy as definitely detrimental to their vested economic interests and entrenched political influence in Hong Kong. The Hong Kong capitalist class has been traditionally spoiled by both the colonial and postcolonial regimes in such a way that it remains reluctant to participate in electoral politics aggressively, organizationally, and positively.

The participants of the democracy movement in Hong Kong are intentionally or unintentionally contributing to China's democratization. Early leaders such as Szeto Wah and Martin Lee, latecomers such as Anson Chan, behind-the-scene coordinators such as George Cautherley, grassroots-level politicians like Albert Ho and Li Wah-ming, social activists such as Lee Cheuk-yan and Chu Hoi-dick, and many ordinary citizens participating in parades and protests are all sustaining the momentum of democracy movement in Hong Kong. The core leaders of Hong Kong's democracy movement cannot be easily intimidated by any mysterious forces. Nor do they abandon their long-term struggle in the HKSAR. Their democratic idealism, liberal values, and Western definition of democracy are constantly testing the political bottom line of PRC leaders to the utmost limit. Contrary to the traditional Chinese ruling elite's political culture that rejects Western liberalism and universal suffrage in the quest for a better political structure, the Hong Kong democrats are firm believers of the positive impacts of universal suffrage on regime legitimacy and governance. They hold the view that, without the direct election of the chief executive by universal suffrage and of the entire legislature, regime legitimacy remains weak and its authority is bound to be challenged. Their political vision of using the people's vote to check executive power is in conflict with mainland Chinese leaders, who see such direct democracy as undermining the harmony between the rulers and the ruled. Yet, it is in the HKSAR where a majority of Chinese believes in the virtue of direct democracy, namely, effective checks and balances against executive power and public maladministration. Historians and political scientists should reassess the tremendous contribution of the Hong Kong democrats to maintain the momentum of democracy movement in both Hong Kong and the PRC in a far more positive way than some critics have pessimistically portrayed.

The future scenarios of Hong Kong's democratization ultimately depend on the PRC's political transformations. If the PRC leaders decide to dilute the official verdict on Tiananmen, the Hong Kong democrats and their supporters will likely continue to strive for the total reversal of official PRC judgment on the Tiananmen incident. On the other hand, they will persist in their fight for democracy in the HKSAR. In the event that the PRC leaders democratize the mainland Chinese political system and take a bold step in reversing the verdict on Tiananmen, the Hong Kong democrats will adopt a two-pronged strategy, promoting further democratization in the mainland and accelerating the push for double direct elections in the HKSAR. If so, the clash between the liberal-minded Hong Kong democrats and the conservative business elites would likely be inevitable. At this juncture, the opposition to democratic reforms in Hong Kong will likely stem from the coalition between the business elites and the DAB/FTU forces, especially if the DAB is keen to maintain its political influence without the ability to capture at least 50 percent of the votes in direct elections. It can be anticipated that the class contradictions between the DAB and FTU, on the one hand, and the DAB/FTU and LP, on the other, will be increasingly acute in the debate over democratization in the HKSAR.

In both scenarios, the HKSAR will unlikely move toward the Western-style democratic system in the foreseeable future, but the democratic idealists will continue to fight for the achievement of their political visions of having the direct elections of the chief executive through universal suffrage and the entire legislature. In short, the democratic idealism of many Hong Kong people will continue to enshrine the democracy movement in both the HKSAR and mainland China.

Notes

INTRODUCTION

1. Guillermo O' Donnell and Philippe Schmitter, *Transitions from Authoritarian Rule: Tentative Conclusions about Uncertain Democracies* (Baltimore: Johns Hopkins University Press, 1986).

2. Samuel P. Huntington, *The Third Wave of Democratization in the Late Twentieth Century* (Norman: University of Oklahoma Press), pp. 290–295.

3. For a comprehensive overview of the Patten years and the Tung era, see Ming Chan, "Introduction," in Ming K. Chan and Shiu-Hing Lo, *Historical Dictionary of the Hong Kong SAR and the Macao SAR* (Lanham, MD: Scarecrow Press, 2006), pp. 39–55.

4. Shiu-Hing Lo and Wing-yat Yu, "The Politics of Electoral Reform in Hong Kong," *Journal of Commonwealth & Comparative Politics*, vol. 39, no. 1 (July 2001).

5. Personal discussion with Alan Lung, the Chairman of the Hong Kong Democratic Foundation, December 2008.

6. Leo F. Goodstadt, *Uneasy Partners: The Conflict Between Public Interest and Private Profits in Hong Kong* (Hong Kong: Hong Kong University Press, 2005), pp. 216–217.

7. Ibid., p. 217.

8. Ibid., p. 227.

9. Ray Yep, "Accommodating Business Interests in China and Hong Kong: Two systems, one way out," in Ka Ho Mok and Ray Forrest, *Changing Governance and Public Policy in East Asia* (London: Routledge, 2009), p. 192.

10. Ibid., p. 186.

11. For the arguments between Li Peng and Zhao Ziyang over whether students on the Tiananmen Square had a conspiracy against the Chinese Communist Party during the Politburo Standing Committee meeting on May 16, 1989, see "The Politburo Standing Committee Holds an Emergency Meeting," in

Zhang Liang, Perry Link, and Andrew J. Nathan, eds., *The Tiananmen Papers: The Chinese Leadership's Decision to Use Force Against Their Own People—In Their Own Words* (New York: Public Affairs, 2001), pp. 177–181. Also see hard-liner Li Peng's speech in "Li Peng Delivers Important Speech on Behalf of Party Central Committee and State Council," in Michel Oksenberg, Lawrence R. Sullivan, and Marc Lambert, eds., *Beijing Spring, 1989: Confrontation and Conflict The Basic Documents* (New York: M. E. Sharpe, 1990), pp. 309–315.

12. David Potter, "Democratization in Asia," in David Potter, ed., *Prospects for Democracy* (Oxford: Polity Press, 1994), p. 357.

13. Ibid.

14. Ibid., p. 358.

15. Shiu-Hing Lo, *The Politics of Democratization in Hong Kong* (London: Macmillan, 1997), pp. 302–324.

16. Tai-lok Lui, "Under Fire: Hong Kong's Middle Class After 1997," in Joseph Y. S. Cheng, ed., *The July 1 Protest Rally: Interpreting a Historic Event* (Hong Kong: City University of Hong Kong Press, 2005), pp. 298–299.

17. Alvin Y. So, "The Making of the Cadre-Capitalist Class in China," in Joseph Y. S. Cheng, ed., *China's Challenges in the Twenty-first Century* (Hong Kong: City University of Hong Kong Press, 2003), pp. 475–501.

18. Maurice Meisner, *The Deng Xiaoping Era: An Enquiry into the Fate of Chinese Socialism, 1978–1994* (New York: Hill and Wang, 1996), p. 503.

19. For the hegemony of the state vis-à-vis the working class, see Marc J. Blecher, "Hegemony and Workers' Politics in China," Lowell Dittmer and Guoli Liu, eds., *China's Deep Reform* (Lanham, MD: Rowman & Littlefield Publishers, Inc., 2006), pp. 405–427.

20. On the earlier application of the cleavage approach to study Hong Kong's political development, see the discussion on the division between reformers and conservatives in Lynn T. White, "The Political Appeals of Conservatives and Reformers," in Lee Pui-tak, ed., *Hong Kong Reintegrating with China: Political, Cultural and Social Dimensions* (Hong Kong: Hong Kong University Press, 2001), pp. 3–38. Also see Li Pang-kwong, *Hong Kong from Britain to China: Political Cleavages, Electoral Dynamics, and Institutional Changes* (Aldershot: Ashgate, 2000).

21. Nicholas Thomas, *Democracy Denied: Identity, Civil Society and Illiberal Democracy in Hong Kong* (London: Ashgate, 1999), p. viii.

22. Ibid., p. ix.

23. For identity politics in Hong Kong, see Sonny Shiu-Hing Lo, *The Dynamics of Hong Kong-Beijing Relations: A Model for Taiwan?* (Hong Kong: Hong Kong University Press, 2008), Chapter 6, pp. 151–183.

24. Barry Sautman and June Teufel Dreyer, eds., *Contemporary Tibet: Politics, Development, and Society in a Disputed Region* (New York: M. E. Sharpe, 2006); and Colin Mackerras, "China's Ethnic Minorities: Policy and Challenges under the Fourth-generation Leadership," in Joseph Y. S. Cheng, ed., *Challenges and Policy Programmes of China's New Leadership* (Hong Kong: City University of Hong Kong Press, 2007), pp. 457–493. Also see a very perceptive work on the origins of the inequalities of ethnic minorities by Hsieh Jiann, "A Preliminary Study on the Inequalities of China's Minorities at the Starting Point of Modernization Process," *Asian Studies Periodical* (published in both English and Chinese by Hong Kong Chu Hai College), no. 57 (September 1, 2008), pp. 3–24.

25. On crime and the weak state in the PRC, see Sonny Shiu-Hing Lo, *The Politics of Cross-Border Crime in Greater China: Case Studies of Mainland China, Hong Kong and Macao* (New York: M. E. Sharpe, 2009).

26. Political space for citizen protests persists due to the discrepancies between the central government and local governments on their policy priorities. For details, see Cai Yongshun, "Managing Social Unrest," in John Wong and Lai Hongyi, eds., *China Into the Hu-Wen Era: Policy Initiatives and Challenges* (Hackensack, NJ: World Scientific, 2006), pp. 379–403.

27. Meisner, *The Deng Xiaoping Era: An Enquiry into the Fate of Chinese Socialism, 1978–1994*, p. 508.

28. On Hong Kong's rule of law and judicial independence, see Steve Tsang, "Commitment to the Rule of Law and Judicial Independence," in Steve Tsang, ed., *Judicial Independence and the Rule of Law in Hong Kong* (Hong Kong: Hong Kong University Press, 2001), pp. 1–18.

29. Two mainland scholars believed that the United States, after the collapse of the Soviet Union, has been trying to use the strategy of "peaceful evolution" to topple socialism in the world. For this argument, see Wang Keqian and Wu Zhongying, *Values and the Cohesion of the Chinese Nation (Jianzhiguan Yu Zhonghuaminzu Ningjuli)* (Shanghai: Century Publication, 2001), pp. 244–246.

30. For the harmony of interests between the rules and the people, see Andrew J. Nathan, *Chinese Democracy* (New York: Alfred A. Knopf, 1985), p. 228–229. On elections, see Joseph Y. S. Cheng, "Elections at the Village and Town/Township Levels and Political Reform in China," in Joseph Cheng, ed., *China's Challenges in the Twenty-first Century*, pp. 783–802. On the rule of law and anticorruption, see Zou Keyuan, "Rule of Law and Governance," in John Wong and Lai Hongyi, eds., *China into the Hu-Wen Era* (Hackensack, NJ: World Scientific 2006), pp. 191–216.

31. Daniel A. Bell and Kanishka Jayasuriya, "Understanding Illiberal Democracy: A Framework," in Daniel Bell, David Brown, Kanishka Jayasuriya, and David Martin Jones, eds., *Towards Illiberal Democracy in Pacific Asia* (London: St. Martin's Press, 1995), pp. 15–16.

32. Herbert Yee and Zhu Feng, "Chinese Perspectives of the China Threat," in Herbert Yee and Ian Storey, eds., *The China Threat: Perceptions, Myths and Reality* (London: RoutledgeCurzon, 2002), p. 34.

33. Lucian W. Pye, *The Spirit of Chinese Politics* (Cambridge, MA: Harvard University Press, 1992); and Richard Solomon, *Mao's Revolution and the Chinese Political Culture* (Berkeley: University of California Press, 1971).

34. Pye, *The Spirit of Chinese Politics*, pp. 197–232.

35. Lucian Pye, *Asian Power and Politics: The Cultural Dimensions of Authority* (Cambridge, MA: The Belknap Press of Harvard University Press, 1985), pp. 320–344.

36. Geir Helgesen and Li Xing, "Good Governance—Democracy or *Minzhu?*" in Hans Antlov and Tak-wing Ngo, eds., *The Cultural Construction of Politics in Asia* (New York: St. Martin's Press, 2000), pp. 175–202.

37. Ibid., p. 199.

38. Samuel P. Huntington, *The Clash of Civilizations and the Remaking of World Order* (New York: Simon & Schuster, 1996), p. 228.

39. Siu-kai Lau, *Society and Politics in Hong Kong* (Hong Kong: The Chinese University Press, 1983); Siu-kai Lau and Hsin-chi Kuan, *The Ethos of Hong Kong Chinese*

(Hong Kong: The Chinese University Press, 1988); and Hsin-chi Kuan and Siu-kai Lau, "Intermediation Environment and Election in Hong Kong," *Democratization*, vol. 7, no. 2 (Summer 2000), p. 83.

40. S. N. G. Davies, "Bureaucracy and People in Hong Kong . . . Like a Horse and Carriage?" *Asian Journal of Public Administration*, vol. 5, no. 1 (June 1983); Ross Grainger, "From Anti-Foreignism to Democratization: Hong Kong as a Deviant Case of Political Development," unpublished PhD thesis, School of Political Science, Faculty of Arts and Social Sciences, University of New South Wales, July 2000; and Wai-man Lam, *Understanding the Political Culture of Hong Kong: The Paradox of Activism and Politicization* (New York: M. E. Sharpe, 2004).

41. See the important report by Michael DeGolyer, "Birdcage or Framework? Considering What Comes Next in Constitutional Reform," a report for the National Democratic Institute for International Affairs and Community Development Initiative Foundation by the Hong Kong Transition Project, July 2009, p. 54.

42. Ibid., p. 29.

43. Philip Stalley and Dongning Yang, "An Emerging Environmental Movement in China," *China Quarterly* (June 2006), pp. 333–356; Ronald C. Keith and Zhiqui Lin, "The 'Falun Gong Problem': Politics and the Struggle for Rule of Law in China," *China Quarterly* (September 2003), pp. 623–642; David Kelley, "Citizen Movements and China's Public Intellectuals in the Hu-Wen Era," *Pacific Affairs*, vol. 79, no. 2 (Summer 2006), pp. 183–204.

44. For some of these movements like environment, community, and student as well as women, see Stephen Wing-kai Chiu and Tai-lok Lui, eds., *The Dynamics of Social Movement in Hong Kong* (Hong Kong: Hong Kong University Press, 2000).

45. Joseph Y. S. Cheng, "Hong Kong Since Its Return to China: A Lost Decade?" in Joseph Y. S. Cheng, ed., *The Hong Kong Special Administrative Region in Its First Decade* (Hong Kong: City University of Hong Kong Press, 2007), p. 48.

46. Joseph Y. S. Cheng, "Hong Kong's Democrats Stumble," *Journal of Democracy*, vol. 16, no. 1 (January 2005), p. 141.

47. Ibid., p. 152.

48. Joseph Y. S. Cheng, "Confucian Values and Democratic Governance in Hong Kong," *The International Journal of the Humanities,* vol. 6, no. 1 (2008), pp. 30–31.

49. Joseph Man Chan and Francis L. F. Lee, "Political Opportunities, Social Mobilization and Collective Action: The Re-invigorated Pro-Democracy Movement in Hong Kong," *The China Review*, vol. 7, no. 2 (Fall 2007), pp. 116–117.

50. Sing Ming, *Hong Kong's Tortuous Democratization: A Comparative Analysis* (London: RoutledgeCurzon, 2004), pp. 204–205.

51. Ibid., p. 204.

52. Ibid., p. 223.

53. Suzanne Pepper, *Keeping Democracy at Bay: Hong Kong and the Challenge of Chinese Political Reform* (Lantham, MD: Rowman & Littlefield Publishers, Inc., 2008), pp. 394–395.

54. Margaret Ng, "Democratization of the Hong Kong SAR: A Pro-democracy View," in Ming K. Chan, ed., *China's Hong Kong Transformed: Retrospect and Prospects Beyond the First Decade* (Hong Kong: City University of Hong Kong Press, 2008), p. 84.

55. Ibid., p. 85.

56. Ibid., p. 85.

57. Bob Beatty, *Democracy, Asian Values, and Hong Kong* (Westport, CT: Praeger, 2003), pp. 187–188.

58. Alvin Y. So, *Hong Kong's Embattled Democracy: A Societal Analysis* (Baltimore, MD: The Johns Hopkins University Press, 1999), pp. 273–274.

59. Ma Ngok, "Democratic Development in Hong Kong: A Decade of Lost Opportunities," in Joseph Cheng, ed., *The Hong Kong Special Administrative Region in Its First Decade* (Hong Kong: City University of Hong Kong Press, 2007), pp. 73–74.

60. Ma Ngok, *Political Development in Hong Kong: State, Political Society, and Civil Society* (Hong Kong: Hong Kong University Press, 2007), pp. 230–231. Ma's "institutional incongruity" thesis is similar to Ian Scott's "disarticulation of Hong Kong's post-handover political system." See Ian Scott, "The Disarticulation of Hong Kong's Post-Handover Political System," *China Journal*, no. 43 (January 2000).

61. Larry Diamond, "A Comparative Perspective on Hong Kong's Democratization: Prospects Toward 2017/2020," in Chan, ed., *China's Hong Kong Transformed: Retrospect and Prospects Beyond the First Decade*, p. 328.

62. Bruce Gilley, *China's Democratic Future: How It Will Happen and Where It Will Lead* (New York: Columbia University Press, 2004), pp. 97–147.

63. Ibid., pp. 199–200.

64. Ibid., p. 200.

65. Minxin Pei, *China's Trapped Transition: The Limits of Developmental Autocracy* (Cambridge, MA: Harvard University Press, 2006), pp. 206–207.

66. Ibid., p. 208.

67. Ibid., p. 210.

68. Ibid., p. 211.

69. Ibid., p. 212.

70. For a positive view, see Larry Diamond, "The Rule of Law as Transition to Democracy in China," *Journal of Contemporary China*, vol. 12, no. 35 (2003), pp. 319–331. For a negative view, see Jacques Delisle, "Legalization Without Democratization in China under Hu Jintao," in Cheng Li, ed., *China's Changing Political Landscape: Prospects for Democracy* (Washington: Brookings Institution Press, 2008), pp. 185–211.

71. For a more positive view, see Yongshun Cai, "China's Moderate Middle Class: The Case of Homeowners' Resistance," *Asian Survey*, vol. 45, no. 5 (September/October 2005), pp. 777–799; and He Li, "Emergence of the Chinese Middle Class and Its Implications," *Asian Affairs* (Washington), vol. 33, no. 2 (Summer 2006), pp. 67–83. For a negative view on the role of middle class in pushing for political changes and democracy, see David S. G. Goodman, "Why China has no new middle class: cadres, managers and entrepreneurs," in David S. G. Goodman, ed., *The New Rich in China* (London: Routledge, 2008), pp. 23–37. Kellee Tsai even asserts that the private entrepreneurs in China are by no means pro-democracy. See Kellee S. Tsai, *Capitalism Without Democracy: The Private Sector in Contemporary China* (Ithaca, NY: Cornell University Press, 2007).

72. For the first view, see Guobin Yang, "The Co-Evolution of the Internet and Civil Society in China," *Asian Survey*, vol. 43, no. 3 (2003), pp. 405–422. For the second view, see Yongnian Zheng and Guoguang Wu, "Information Technology,

Public Space, and Collective Action in China," *Comparative Political Studies*, vol. 38, no. 5 (June 2005), pp. 507–536.

73. For the first view, see Kathleen Hartford, "Dear Mayor: Online Communication with Local Governments in Hangzhou and Nanjing," *China Information*, vol. XIX, no. 2 (2005), pp. 217–260. For the second view, see Beatrice Leung, "China's Religious Freedom Policy: The Art of Managing Religious Freedom," *China Quarterly* (December 2005), pp. 894–913.

74. Jonathan Hassid, "Controlling the Chinese Media: An Uncertain Business," *Asian Survey*, vol. 48, no. 3 (2008), pp. 414–430; and Teresa Wright, "The Chinese Democratic Party and the Politics of Protest in the 1980s-1990s," *China Quarterly* (December 2002), pp. 906–926.

75. For the first point, see Kevin J. O'Brien and Liangjiang Li, "Suing the Local State: Administrative Litigation in Rural China," *The China Journal*, no. 51 (January 2004), pp. 75–96. For the second point, see Yongshun Cai and Songcai Yang, "State Power and Unbalanced Legal Development in China," *Journal of Contemporary China*, vol. 14, no. 42 (February 2005), pp. 117–134.

76. For the first view, see Baogang He, *Rural Democracy in China: The Role of Village Elections* (New York: Palgrave Macmillan, 2007). For the second view, see Zhenglin Guo and Thomas Bernstein, "The Impact of Election on the Village Structure of Power: The Relations between the Village Committees and the Party Branches," *Journal of Contemporary China*, vol. 13, no. 39 (May 2004), pp. 257–275.

77. Feng Chen, "Between the State and Labor: The Conflicts of Chinese Trade Unions: Double Identity in Market Reforms," *China Quarterly* (December 2003), pp. 1006–1028; and Feng Chen, "Individual Rights and Collective Rights: Labor's Predicament in China," *Communist and Post-Communist Studies*, 40 (2007), pp. 59–79.

78. Yunxiang Yan, "Little Emperors or Frail Pragmatists? China's '80ers Generation,'" *Current History* (September 2006), pp. 255–262.

79. Larry Diamond, "Why China's Democratic Transition Will Differ from Taiwan's," in Bruce Gilley and Larry Diamond, eds., *Political Change in China: Comparisons with Taiwan* (Boulder: Lynne Rienner, 2008), p. 256.

80. For a similar view, see Yanlai Wang, *China's Economic Development and Democratization* (Aldershot: Ashgate, 2003), pp. 225–230.

81. Pan Wei, "Toward a Consultative Rule of Law Regime in China," *Journal of Contemporary China*, vol. 12, no. 35 (2003), pp. 319–331.

82. For the institutionalization of leadership succession in the PRC, see Andrew Nathan and Bruce Gilley, eds., *China's New Rulers: The Secret Files* (London: Granta Books, 2003), pp. 230–232.

83. Keping Yu, *Democracy Is a Good Thing: Essays on Politics, Society, and Culture in Contemporary China* (Washington: Brookings Institution Press, 2009), pp. 3–5.

84. Pye, *Asian Power and Politics: The Cultural Dimensions of Authority*, p. 189.

85. Ibid., p. 190.

CHAPTER 1

1. June-Fang Tsai, *Hong Kong in Chinese History: Community and Social Unrest in the British Colony, 1842–1913* (New York: Columbia University Press, 1995), pp. 164–166.

2. *Ming Pao* (hereafter *MP*), June 5, 2009, p. A19.

3. Ibid.

4. *Chinese Exploration* (Toronto Chinese magazine, the Toronto version of *Asia-week*), no. 188 (June 12, 2009), pp. 15–16.

5. Ibid.

6. Ibid., p. 16.

7. Ibid., p. 18.

8. Ibid, p. 18.

9. Ibid., p. 18.

10. Ibid., p. 19.

11. *Sing Tao Daily* (hereafter *STD*), June 10, 2009, p. B1.

12. *Chinese Exploration*, no. 188 (June 12, 2009), p. 20.

13. Sonny Shiu-Hing Lo, *The Politics of Cross-Border Crime in Greater China: Case Studies of the Mainland, Hong Kong and Macao* (Armonk, NY: M. E. Sharpe, 2009).

14. Mark Perry unveiled that the CIA provided sophisticated technology in the rescue operation. See Mark Perry, *Eclipse: The Last Days of the CIA* (New York: William Morrow, 1992), p. 249.

15. *MP*, May 31, 2009, p. A3.

16. Ibid., p. A3.

17. Ibid., p. A3.

18. Ibid., p. A3.

19. *Chinese Exploration*, pp. 16–17.

20. For the 600,000 to 1 million estimates, see *Sing Tao Daily*, June 9, 2009, p. B10.

21. *MP*, May 22, 2009, p. A21. One of the editors in *Wen Wei Po* who decided to deviate from Beijing's line was Kam Yiu-yu, who was later forced to leave the news organization and who eventually decided to go to the United States. In 2009, the Hong Kong media professionals set up a Kam Yiu-yu Foundation to support Hong Kong's press freedom and encourage the Hong Kong reporters in their work.

22. *MP*, June 2, 2009, p. A24.

23. *MP*, May 4, 2009, p. A18.

24. *STD*, June 9, 2009, p. B10.

25. *MP*, May 4, 2009, p. A18.

26. *MP*, May 4, 2009, p. A19. Gary Cheng and Wong Wai-hung withdrew from the executive committee in July 1989. A few other pro-Beijing groups such as the Federation of Education Workers also withdrew from the Alliance.

27. Ibid.

28. *World Journal* (hereafter *WJ*), June 3, 2009, p. C9.

29. Ibid.

30. *MP*, June 1, 2009, p. A15.

31. *MP*, June 1, 2009, p. A15.

32. Chu's discussion with Professor Ming Chan of Stanford University and the author in March 2005.

33. *MP*, May 18, 2009, p. A20.

34. *MP*, May 18, 2009, p. A20.

35. *MP*, May 25, 2009, p. A19.

36. *MP*, May 25, 2009, p. A19.

37. *MP*, May 31, 2009, p. A18.

38. *MP*, June 1, 2009, p. A18. In July 2009, the author could not access the Web site: http://neticle23.net/6420bt/torrent.php.

39. Ibid.

40. In 2009, the public examination in Chinese history at form five level had a question on Tiananmen, but it merely asked students who the Chinese Premier was at that time. Critics also said that the question gave inaccurate background information to students, such as mentioning the price problem and bureaucratic corruption without touching upon the desire of students for more democracy in the PRC. See *Ming Pao*, May 5, 2009, p. A20.

41. *MP*, May 4, 2009, p. A24.

42. Ibid.

43. *MP*, May 31, 2009, p. A23.

44. For *Sing Tao Daily*'s coverage, see May 29, 2009, p. B11; May 30, 2009, pp. B12–B13; and May 31, 2009, p. B10.

45. *MP*, May 30, 2009, p. A18. Also see its coverage of individual figures such as Feng Congde, Zhou Fengsuo, Deng Xiaoping, and Sheng Xue, June 5, 2009, p. B1 and June 3, 2009, pp. B8–B11.

46. *MP*, June 3, 2009, p. A18.

47. Ibid.

48. *Apple Daily* (hereafter *AD*), May 12, 2009, p. A15.

49. Ibid.

50. Ibid.

51. *STD*, May 28, 2009.

52. *MP*, May 28, 2009, p. A21.

53. *STD*, May 28, 2009.

54. *MP*, June 4, 2009, p. A21.

55. *MP*, May 15, 2009, p. A23.

56. "Raping public opinion" was uttered by Leung Kwok-hung. See *Ming Pao*, May 15, 2009, p. A23. Also see *STD*, May 15, 2009, p. A1.

57. The strong reaction of some democrats, such as Leung Kwok-hung and James To, appeared to add fuel to the fire ignited by Tsang. See *MP*, May 15, 2009, p. A29.

58. *MP*, May 15, 2009, p. A31.

59. *MP*, May 17, 2009, p. A1.

60. Editorial, "June 4th Candlelight, the Light for China," *MP*, June 5, 2009, p. A22.

61. *STD*, June 5, 2009, p. A2.

62. *MP*, June 5, 2009, p. A22.

63. *MP*, June 6, 2009, p. A18.

64. *MP*, June 2, 2009, p. A18.

65. *MP*, June 5, 2009, p. A19.

66. "In Open Letter, Tiananmen Mothers Urged China's Leaders to Investigate June 4," at http://www.hrichina.org/public/contents/press?revision% 5fid=135276&item%5fid=135136 (accessed July 25, 2009).

67. *MP*, May 30, 2009, p. A19.

68. "China: Tiananmen's Unhealed Wounds," at http://www.hrw.org/en/news/2009/05/12/china-tiananmen-s-unhealed-wounds (accessed July 25, 2009).

69. *MP*, May 27, 2009, p. A16. Also see Famil Anderlini, "Tanks Were Roaring and Bullets Flying," *Financial Times*, May 30/31, 2009, p. A3.

70. *MP*, June 3, 2009, p. A20.

71. For details, see "Du Daozheng on the Zhao Ziyang Memoirs," *MP*, May 27, 2009, translated at http://www.zonaeuropa.com/200905c.brief.htm (accessed July 25, 2009).

72. *MP*, May 24, 2009, p. A21.

73. Ibid.

74. Ibid.

75. Samuel P. Huntington, *The Third Wave: Democratization in the Late Twentieth Century* (Norman: University of Oklahoma Press, 1991), pp. 46–58.

76. Editorial, "The 20-year Interpretation of June 4th Is Different between the Overseas Chinese on the One Hand and Beijing and Overseas Chinese Dissidents on the Other," *WJ*, June 4, 2009, p. A5.

77. *STD*, June 1, 2009, p. B13. After the Tiananmen crackdown, Wang escaped from Beijing to Harbin, and then he went to Shanghai and Anhui. Wang later sneaked to Beijing and met a Taiwan reporter, but Wang's whereabouts were discovered and arrested in Beijing. See *STD*, June 10, 2009, p. B1.

78. *STD*, June 1, 2009, p. A5.

79. *MP*, June 1, 2009, p. A14.

80. *WJ*, June 4, 2009, p. A2.

81. *MP*, June 3, 2009, p. A21.

82. *WJ*, June 4, 2009, p. A2.

83. *MP*, June 3, 2009, p. A21.

84. James Wang, "Thousands March in Hong Kong to Remember Tiananmen," at http://www.asianews.it/index.php?l=en&art=15393 (accessed July 25, 2009).

85. *MP*, June 4, 2009, p. A20.

86. Bill Schiller, "A Day China Wants You to Forget," *Toronto Star*, June 5, 2009, p. A14.

87. *MP*, June 4, 2009, p. A16.

88. *World Journal*, June 5, 2009, p. C9.

89. Sonny Shiu-Hing Lo, *The Dynamics of Beijing-Hong Kong Relations: A Model for Taiwan?* (Hong Kong: Hong Kong University Press, 2008).

90. Shiu-Hing Lo, "Hong Kong's Political Influence on South China," *Problems of Post-Communism*, vol. 46, no. 4 (July/August 1999), pp. 33–41.

CHAPTER 2

1. The ethnically instigated Xinjiang unrest was reported in *China Exploration* (*Zhonghua Tanshuo*, a weekly Chinese magazine attached to *Ming Pao* in Toronto, and it carries reports and commentaries from the Chinese version of the *Asiaweek* or *Yazhou Zhoukan*), no. 193, July 17, 2009, pp. 14–22. The Western media's inaccurate and biased coverage of the Xinjiang unrest was similar to their understanding of the 2008 Tibetan unrest. Objectively speaking, the anti-China sentiment has been accompanying the rise of the PRC since the early 2000s.

2. Hong Kong TVB News, March 2008.

3. Interview with two mainland officials responsible for Hong Kong matters, June 30, 2009, and July 4, 2009.

4. Shiu-hing Lo, "The Politics of Policing the Anti-WTO Protests in Hong Kong," *Asian Journal of Political Science*, vol. 14, no. 2 (December 2006).

5. *Apple Daily* (hereafter *AD*), July 1, 2009, p. A1.

6. Ibid.

7. *AD*, July 1, 2009, p. A2.

8. *AD*, July 1, 2009, p. A27.

9. Ng Chi-sum, "Not Enough Reasons for Us to Take to the Streets?" *AD*, July 1, 2009, p. A20.

10. *AD*, June 28, 2009, p. A6.

11. Ibid.

12. Ibid.

13. Ibid.

14. Chan Kin-man, "Taking to the Streets on July 1?" *MP*, July 1, 2009, p. B12.

15. Anthony Cheung Bing-leung, "July 1 Should Not Become a Political Burden," *MP*, July 1, 2009, p. B12.

16. Ibid.

17. *AD*, July 1, 2009, p. A1.

18. *MP*, June 13, 2009, p. A22.

19. *AD*, July 1, 2009, p. A6.

20. Joseph Wong, "Wrestling with Pay," *South China Morning Post* (hereafter *SCMP*), July 1, 2009, p. A11.

21. Jolene Chan, "Surely This Is a Special Case," Letter to the Editor, *SCMP*, July 1, 2009, p. A10.

22. Wilson Lo, "Police Officers Do Difficult Job," Letter to the Editor, *SCMP*, July 1, 2009, p. A10.

23. Chris Yeung, "Police Chief's Stand Puts Tsang on Spot," *Sunday Morning Post*, June 28, 2009, p. 10.

24. Ibid.

25. Stephen Vines, "Police Chief Crosses the Establishment Line," *SCMP*, July 3, 2009, p. A11.

26. *AD*, June 30, 2009, p. A6.

27. Hong Kong TVB News, July 1, 2009, at 10:15 am.

28. Adele Wong, Bonnie Chen, and Beatrice Siu, "40,000 Cheer the Handover," *The Standard*, July 2, 2009, p. 3.

29. *Headline Daily*, www.hkheadline.com, July 2, 2009, p. 8.

30. Ibid.

31. *Hong Kong Economic Journal* (hereafter *HKEJ*), July 2, 2009, p. 6.

32. *MP*, June 29, 2005, p. A17.

33. Ibid.

34. Ibid.

35. Martin Regg Cohn, "Fewer Rally for Democracy in Hong Kong," *Toronto Star*, July 2, 2005, p. A14.

36. *MP*, June 29, 2005, p. A17.

37. Gary Cheung, "Policy Chief Expects March to Reflect Increasing Civil Discontent," *SCMP*, July 1, 2009, p. A2.

38. Editorial, "A Mystery on the Number of Participants in the March, the Demand for Universal Suffrage Is Not Met," *HKEJ*, July 2, 2009, p. 1.

39. Personal discussion with a police officer, July 6, 2009.

40. Personal estimate of the number of participants on July 1, 2009. I stood in Wanchai and began to calculate roughly every group of 10 marchers crossing my line of observation. Sometimes a group of 10 crossed my line, sometimes 20, sometimes 30 and 40, depending on the tightness of the entire group. I observed for two and a half hours and estimated 58,000 marchers, excluding perhaps a thousand workers along the streets. It must be noted that a few marchers who were older or who took a rest used the pedestrian walk. Dr. Bruce Kwong and Dr. Suzanne Pepper who also observed the march agreed that both the police and Chung figures were underestimated. Also see "How Did Two Universities Estimate the Number," *Hong Kong Economic Times* (hereafter *HKET*), July 2, 2009, p. A22.

41. "Nation as the Shield, Hong Kong People Have Confidence," Editorial, *Ta Kung Pao*, July 2, 2009, p. A2.

42. "The Opposition Wrongly Assess the Hearts and Minds of the People," *Wen Wei Po* (hereafter *WWP*), July 2, 2009, p. 2.

43. *Sun*, July 2, 2009, p. A1; and *Oriental Daily* (hereafter *OD*), July 2, 2009, p. A1.

44. *OD*, July 2, 2009, p. A2.

45. *Sun*, July 2, 2009, p. A1.

46. "Twelve Years of Winds and Rainfall, Grievances Pouring over Hong Kong," *OD*, July 2, 2009, p. A27.

47. Ibid.

48. "The Democratic Grandmother Was Dried and Fried," *Sun*, July 2, 2009, p. A18.

49. *AD*, July 2, 2009, p. A2.

50. Ibid.

51. Ibid.

52. Ibid., p. A6.

53. Ibid., p. A8.

54. "Confronting the July 1 Parade Positively, Improving Policies and Performance," *HKET*, July 2, 2009, p. A3.

55. "Grasping the Chance, Creating an Atmosphere of Rational Political Discussion," *STD*, July 2, 2009, p. A19.

56. "The Politics of Extraction Is Hollowing out Hong Kong and There Should Be a Responsible System of Power Relations," *MP*, July 2, 2009, p. A22.

57. Fung Kwong-ning, "I Admire the Right of the People of Hong Kong to Take to the Street," *AD*, June 30, 2009, p. A20.

58. Personal email correspondence with a mainland student in the HKSAR, July 10, 2009.

59. *AD*, July 2, 2009, p. A9.

60. Personal discussion with two mainland officials responsible for Hong Kong matters, June 30, 2009.

61. *AD*, July 4, 2009, p. A17.

62. The Executive Council members also followed the principal officials to have their salaries cut. The pay cut of the principal officials amounted to

5.38 percent of their monthly salaries. *Today Daily News* (hereafter *TDN*), June 16, 2009, p. 2.

63. *MP*, May 16, 2009, p. A22.

64. Sonny Lo, "Casino Capitalism and Its Legitimacy Impact on the Politico-administrative State in Macao," *Journal of Current Chinese Affairs: China Aktuell*, vol. 38, no. 1 (2009), pp. 19–47.

65. *AD*, July 4, 2009, p. A2.

66. *STD*, May 31, 2009, p. A1.

67. *AD*, July 3, 2009, p. A4.

68. *STD*, July 2, 2009, p. B6.

69. *AD*, July 4, 2009, p. A8.

70. *AD*, July 3, 2009, p. A2.

71. Fanny W. Y. Fung, "We Did What Had to Be Done, Police Say in Face of Complaints from Demonstrators," *SCMP*, July 3, 2009, p. A3.

72. Editorial, "Police Action of Clearing the Site Was Rational, Those Who Violate the Law Should Be Pursued," *WWP*, July 3, 2009, p. A3.

73. "Parade Has Become a Chaotic Show, Citizens Reprimand the Radical Action of the Civil Human Rights Front," *WWP*, July 3, 2009, p. A11. Also see the commentaries by Ma Yin, "The Opposition Exaggerates the Number Again," and Ku Wan, "What Was the Purpose of Violently Trespassing the Government Headquarters?" *WWP*, July 3, 2009, p. A28.

74. Mary Ma, "Beijing Ties Also a Matter of Concern," *The Standard*, July 2, 2009, p. 2.

CHAPTER 3

1. *MP*, October 26, 2004, p. A14.

2. Editorial, "Referendum Proposal Does Not Seem Productive," *MP*, October 25, 2004, p. D16.

3. *MP*, October 21, 2004, p. A16.

4. Ibid.

5. Ibid.

6. Ibid.

7. Ibid.

8. *MP*, October 23, 2004, p. A16.

9. *MP*, October 22, 2004, p. A21.

10. *STD*, October 21, 2004, p. B1.

11. *MP*, October 30, 2004, p. A17.

12. Ibid.

13. *STD*, November 2, 2004, p. B1.

14. Ibid.

15. *STD*, November 2, 2004, p. B1.

16. Ibid.

17. *MP*, November 30, 2004, p. A18.

18. Ibid.

19. Ibid.

20. *MP*, November 28, 2004, p. A15.

21. Ibid.

22. *MP*, January 13, 2005, p. A20.

23. *WJ*, September 23, 2005, p. A21.

24. *STD*, October 20, 2005, p. B1.

25. *STD*, October 20, 2005, p. B1.

26. *MP*, October 20, 2005, p. A19.

27. Ibid.

28. *MP*, October 20, 2005, p. A1.

29. Ibid.

30. Ibid.

31. *STD*, October 10, 2005, p. B3.

32. Ibid.

33. Ibid.

34. *MP*, October 28, 2005, p. A17.

35. *MP*, October 30, 2005, p. A13.

36. Ibid.

37. *MP*, November 4, 2005, p. A16. The academics included Chan Kin-man, Joseph Man Chan, Clement So, Thomas Wong, and Ivan Choy.

38. Ibid.

39. Ibid.

40. Ibid.

41. *TDN*, November 8, 2005, p. B5.

42. Tong's softer tone could be traced back to January 2005 when he said he was willing to abandon double direct elections in 2007 and 2008 if the government proposed a reform model close to the wishes of pan-democrats. See *MP*, January 31, 2005, p. A14.

43. *MP*, November 24, 2005, p. A20.

44. Ibid.

45. Ibid.

46. *MP*, November 22, 2005, p. A20.

47. Ibid.

48. *STD*, December 3, 2005, p. B4.

49. Ibid.

50. *STD*, December 5, 2005, p. A1.

51. *MP*, December 5, 2005, p. A13.

52. *STD*, December 4, 2005, p. B1.

53. *MP*, December 7, 2005, p. A20.

54. *MP*, December 5, 2005, p. A12.

55. Ibid.

56. *MP*, December 6, 2005, p. A20.

57. *STD*, December 4 2005, p. A1.

58. *MP*, December 7, 2005, p. A20.

59. *STD*, December 7, 2005, p. B1.

60. Personal discussion with a Beijing official who mentioned that Chan was "used" by the foreigners, April 2009.

61. *STD*, December 7, 2005, p. B1.

62. Ibid.

63. Ibid.

64. Ibid.

65. Ibid.

66. *WJ*, December 5, 2005, p. A3.

67. *STD*, December 6, 2005, p. B1.

68. *MP*, December 7, 2005, p. A20.

69. *WJ*, December 8, 2005, p. A21.

70. *STD*, October 7, 2004, p. A19.

71. *WJ*, December 7, 2005, p. A5.

72. *STD*, December 9, 2005, p. B1.

73. Philip Pan and K. C. Ng, "Hong Kong Rejects Modest Proposals," *The Washington Post*, December 22, 2005, p. A20.

74. Teddy Ng, "Hong Kong Opposition Reject Election Reform Package," *China Daily*, December 22, 2005.

75. *STD*, June 29, 2009, p. B1.

76. *STD*, July 3, 2009, p. B5.

77. Ibid.

78. Jimmy Cheung and Gary Cheung, "Beijing's Trust Will Be Hurt, Warns Tsang," *SCMP*, December 23, 2005, p. A1.

79. *MP*, November 16, 2005, p. A18.

80. *MP*, November 12, 2005, p. A19.

81. Ibid.

82. *STD*, November 1, 2005, p. A15.

83. Anita Lam and Jimmy Leung, "Bishop, Martin Lee Shrug Off Criticism," *SCMP*, December 23, 2005, p. A2.

84. *STD*, November 5, 2005, p. B4.

85. Ibid.

86. Ibid.

87. *MP*, November 8, 2005, p. A16.

88. *MP*, December 10, 2005, p. A18.

89. Ibid.

90. *WJ*, December 30, 2005, p. A21.

91. Ibid.

92. "A Victory of the People, A Victory for Democracy," *SCMP*, December 23, 2005, p. A8.

93. *MP*, January 24, 2006, p. A18.

94. *STD*, January 24, 2006, p. B3. *WJ*, January 24, 2006, p. A21.

95. *WJ*, December 30, 2005, p. A21.

96. Ng Hong-man, "The Opposition Faction Vetoes and Changes Its Course," *MP*, April 21, 2006, p. A18.

97. *TDN*, June 24, 2006, p. B9. Wang told the author that the Hong Kong media misinterpreted his views.

98. *MP*, August 17, 2006, p. A15.

99. *AD*, December 1, 2007, p. A10.

100. *STD*, December 13, 2007, p. B1.

101. Editorial, "The Pace of Political Reform Reaches a Critical Stage, Whether It Will Be Successful Depends on Practical Compromise," *MP*, December 13, 2007, p. A11.

102. *MP*, December 30, 2007, p. A1.

103. *STD*, January 10, 2008, p. B4.

104. *MP*, January 10, 2008, p. A14.

105. Personal discussion with a Beijing official, April 2009.

106. Ibid.

107. *TDN*, January 7, 2008, p. C9.

108. Martin Lee, "It Is the Strategic Development Commission Stepping Across the Line, Not the Legislative Council," *MP*, March 1, 2006, p. D8.

109. *WJ*, November 26, 2005, p. A21.

110. An editorial was critical of Tsang's handling of the timetable issue. Editorial, "The SDC Document Lacks Sincerity and Honesty," *MP*, November 26, 2005, p. A14.

111. Lo Chi-kin, "The Political Space of the Opposition Faction," *MP*, April 14, 2006, p. A20.

112. *STD*, November 6, 2005, p. B7.

113. *MP*, November 26, 2005, p. A20.

114. Ibid.

115. *MP*, November 6, 2005, p. A20.

116. *STD*, November 7, 2005, p. B5.

117. *MP*, November 26, 2005, p. A20.

118. Ibid.

119. Ibid.

120. *STD*, March 23, 2006, p. B6.

121. Ibid.

122. *TDN*, February 22, 2008, p. C7.

123. Ibid.

124. *STD*, March 23, 2006, p. B6.

125. *TDN*, April 26, 2008, p. C8.

126. Ibid.

127. "Is Commission on Strategic Development Swan or Goose?" *MP*, November 18, 2005, p. D19.

128. *STD*, January 16, 2009, p. B1.

129. "The Reasons and Opportunities Behind the Delay in Public Consultation on Political Reform in Hong Kong," *STD*, January 16, 2009, p. A20.

130. For details on the crisis of legitimacy in the HKSAR under the Tung regime before the July 2003 protests, see Shiu-hing Lo, *Governing Hong Kong: Legitimacy, Communication and Political Decay* (New York: Nova Science, 2001).

131. *STD*, September 13, 2008, p. B6.

132. Ibid.

133. *WJ*, February 18, 2009, p. B16.

134. *STD*, June 10, 2009, p. B6.

135. Toronto's Fairchild Radio, FM1430, August 6, 2009, at 11:15 am. Also see *Star Magazine*, vol. 395 (August 16, 2009), pp. 28–30. The magazine report argued that Szeto Wah saw Anson Chan as a "democratic opportunist," meaning that she joined the Hong Kong democracy movement late and opportunistically.

136. Toronto's Fairchild Radio, FM1430, August 6, 2009, at 11:15 am.

137. *Consultation Document on the Methods for Selecting the Chief Executive and for Forming the Legislative Council in 2012* (Hong Kong: HKSAR Government,

November 2009), at http://www.cmab-cd2012.gov.hk/doc/consultation
_document_en.pdf (accessed November 27, 2009).

CHAPTER 4

1. Richard Tsoi's Interview by the Toronto Fairchild Television on June 3, 2009.

2. Personal discussion with a mainland official responsible for Hong Kong matters, July 4, 2009.

3. Kristine Kwok, "Hu Urges Improved Democracy within the Communist Party," *SCMP*, July 1, 2009, p. A5.

4. Ibid.

5. Phoenix TV commentary, March 2009.

6. *TDN*, March 29, 2008, p. C3.

7. "Biography of Martin C. M. Lee," provided by Martin Lee and his assistant Tiffany Kwok to the author in March 2009.

8. Lo, *Governing Hong Kong: Legitimacy, Communication and Political Decay*, pp. 161–165.

9. "Biography of Martin C. M. Lee," March 2009.

10. Erica Cheong, "Father of Democracy Retires," *MP*, April 10, 2008, p. D17.

11. *WJ*, March 28, 2008, p. A21.

12. *MP*, March 29, 2008, p. A20.

13. Ibid.

14. Face is extremely important in the spirit and operation of Chinese politics. See Lucian W. Pye, *The Spirit of Chinese Politics* (Cambridge, MA: Harvard University Press, 1992), p. 213.

15. *STD*, March 29, 2008, p. B1.

16. *TDN*, March 30, 2008, p. C7.

17. *WJ*, March 30, 2008, p. A22.

18. *STD*, March 30, 2008, p. B3.

19. *MP*, March 29, 2008, p. A20.

20. Ong Yew Kim, "Please Note That Martin Lee Praises Premier Wen," *TDN*, May 29, 2008, p. C9.

21. Gary Cheng Kai-nam, "The End of an Era," *TDN*, March 31, 2008, p. C9.

22. Ann Yu, "Twenty Years of Not Following Timing and Opportunism," *MP*, March 30, 2008, p. C4.

23. Ibid.

24. Ibid.

25. Ibid.

26. Martin Lee, "Democracy with Chinese Characteristics," a manuscript given to the author in March 2009, p. 6.

27. Ibid., p. 8.

28. Ibid., p. 10.

29. Ibid., p. 10.

30. *Star Magazine* (a magazine attached to Toronto's *Sing Tao Daily* every Sunday), vol. 337 (July, 6, 2008), pp. 19–25. Lai's *Apple Daily* in Taiwan has a wide circulation.

31. Interview with Martin Lee, *Hong Kong University Magazine*, May 2007, p. 23.

32. Ibid.

33. Ibid.

34. *MP*, March 28, 2008, p. A20.

35. Ibid.

36. *STD*, March 29, 2008, p. B1.

37. *Ming Pao Saturday Magazine* (Toronto edition), May 24, 2008, p. 51.

38. Ibid.

39. Szeto Wah, "Patriotism and the Love for Democracy Are Not Incompatible," in Ming Pao, ed., *Discussions and Disputes on Patriotism* (Hong Kong: Ming Pao, April 2004), pp. 174–178.

40. Ibid., pp. 174–175.

41. Ibid., p. 176.

42. Ibid., p. 176.

43. Ibid., p. 177.

44. Ibid., p. 178.

45. Szeto Wah, "20 Years of Difficult Democratic Path, Will My Students See Universal Suffrage?" *MP*, December 4, 2005, p. C8.

46. Ibid.

47. Ibid.

48. *MP*, April 21, 2009, p. A3.

49. *WJ*, September 14, 2005, p. A21.

50. Ibid.

51. See George Cautherley, Honorary Doctor of Business Administration, Edinburgh Napier University, at http://www.napier.ac.uk/ALUMNI/NEWS/HONGRADS/Pages/GeorgeCautherley.aspx (accessed July 20, 2009).

52. Personal interview with George Cautherley, July 4, 2009.

53. Ibid.

54. Ibid.

55. Ibid.

56. Ibid.

57. Ibid.

58. Ibid.

59. Ibid.

60. Ibid.

61. George Cautherley, "Constitutional Development, 2011–2020: Possible Scenarios for Discussion," given to the author on July 4, 2009, pp. 1–2.

62. Ibid., p. 2.

63. *MP*, June 9, 2009, p. A24.

64. *Next Magazine*, no. 567 (January 18, 2001), p. 47.

65. *WJ*, December 6, 2005, p. A21.

66. *MP*, December 3, 2007, p. A1.

67. It was reported that while the Liaison Office fully supported Ip, the DAB might not fully mobilize its supporters to vote and work for Ip. See *AD*, December 1, 2007, p. A21.

68. *MP*, December 3, 2007, p. A1.

69. The voter turnout in the Legislative Council's direct elections on the Hong Kong Island was 57.62 percent in 2004, 33.27 percent in 2000, 42.03 percent in 2000, and 51.96 percent in 1998. See *TDN*, December 1, 2007, p. C6.

70. *STD*, December 3, 2007, p. B1.

71. *MP*, December 4, 2007, p. A15.

72. Editorial, "A Different By-election," *MP*, December 2, 2007, p. A10.

73. Personal observations on election day, December 2, 2007.

74. See the commentaries on *AD*, December 1, 2007, p. A20.

75. *AD*, December 1, 2007, p. A2.

76. *STD*, December 2, 2007, p. B1.

77. *TDN*, November 16, 2007, p. C6.

78. *STD*, April 22, 2008, p. B1.

79. *TDN*, January 30, 2008, p. C7. Also see *The Sun*, December 4, 2007, p. A4.

80. *MP*, July 6, 2008, p. A16.

81. Bonnie Chen, "Chan Turns Up Reform Heat as Polls Fight Set," *The Standard*, June 18, 2008. Also see *TDN*, June 18, 2008, p. C8.

82. "Mrs. Anson Chan and Her Core Group," at http://www.yourchoice yourvoice.org/CoreGroup/profile.org.htm (accessed August 4, 2009).

83. *TDN*, June 18, 2008, p. C8.

84. *MP*, February 5, 2008, p. A16.

85. For this view, see Editorial, "Whether Mrs. Chan Can Leave Her Name in Hong Kong's Democracy Movement Depends on the Success or Failure of the Promotion of Civil Society," *MP*, July 21, 2008, p. A8. Also see a perhaps premature and unfair commentary from Ma Ka-fai, who said her "contributions were not much," in Ma Ka-fai, "Choosing the Wrong Time, Selecting the Right Conclusion," *MP*, July 8, 2008, p. A16.

86. Cheung Man-yee, "The Meanings of Anson Chan's Participation in the By-election of the Legislative Council," *China Exploration* (Toronto's version of *Asiaweek* in Chinese), no. 107 (November 23, 2007), p. 33.

87. Ibid.

88. "Interview with Anson Chan: Looking for a Larger Political Arena," *Asiaweek* (*Yazhou Zhoukan* in Chinese), July 20, 2008, p. 33.

89. Ibid.

90. Ibid.

91. *MP*, January 30, 2009, p. A20.

92. "Interview with Anson Chan: Looking for a Larger Political Arena," *Asiaweek* (*Yazhou Zhoukan* in Chinese), July 20, 2008, p. 33.

93. Ibid.

94. *STD*, September 25, 2007, p. B4.

95. Tam Tin-mei, "Hong Kong Election Result Revealed, Beijing's Reaction Exposed," *China Exploration*, no. 110 (December 14, 2007), p. 13.

96. *MP*, October 20, 2008, p. A11.

97. *MP*, January 14, 2009, p. A24.

CHAPTER 5

1. Macao has competitive legislative elections. See Sonny Shiu-Hing Lo, *Political Change in Macao* (London: Routledge, 2008).

2. *HKEJ*, November 21, 2007.

3. *MP*, November 20, 2007, p. A15.

4. Johnny Lau Yui-siu, "Election Is a Full-scale Engineering Work," *MP*, November 22, 2007, p. E4.

5. *TDN*, November 4, 2007, p. C9.

6. Shiu-Hing Lo, Wing-yat Yu, and Kwok-fai Wan, "The 1999 District Councils Elections," in Ming K. Chan and Alvin Y. So, eds., *Crisis and Transformation in China's Hong Kong* (New York: M. E. Sharpe, 2002).

7. *STD*, April 24, 2006, p. B5.

8. For an insightful analysis of the DAB's election strategy, see Sit Kwan, "Why Did the DAB Win the District Councils Elections?" *Wide Angle*, no. 423 (December 16, 2007–January 15, 2008), pp. 38–41.

9. *MP*, November 20, 2007, p. A14.

10. *STD*, November 20, 2007, p. B4.

11. *TDN*, November 15, 2007, p. C8.

12. Ibid.

13. *STD*, November 20, 2007, p. B4.

14. Editorial, "No Mind and No Energy to Expand New Sources of Votes, the Pan-democratic Camp Should Learn from Ip Kwok-him," *MP*, November 20, 2007, p. A12.

15. Editorial, "Happy to See the 40s Generation to Begin Its Journey, the Democratic Party Needs to Renew and Rejuvenate," *MP*, November 22, 2007, p. A12.

16. *TDN*, December 9, 2007, p. C7.

17. *WJ*, December 9, 2007, p. A22.

18. *MP*, November 19, 2007, p. A14.

19. Alan Leong, "An Evaluation," *MP*, December 4, 2007, p. D23.

20. *TDN*, November 19, 2007, p. C4.

21. Li Wah-ming was defeated in a by-election held for the Kwun Tong District Council in October 2005, when DAB-backed candidate Cheung Shun-wah won with 1,491 votes. Li got 1,249 votes. It is by no means easy for any legislator to contest DC elections because the constituencies are smaller and the candidates need to demonstrate district work to the voters. *STD*, October 24, 2005, p. B4.

22. *MP*, November 19, 2007, p. A14.

23. Personal discussion with Cyd Ho in March 2008.

24. *MP*, November 19, 2007, p. A14.

25. *MP*, November 20, 2007, p. A14.

26. *TDN*, November 21, 2007, p. C2.

27. Ibid.

28. Triad is a criminal organization with hierarchy, membership, and rankings. It engages in criminal activities such as smuggling, prostitution, drug trafficking, money laundering, and extortion. In recent years, Hong Kong triads have penetrated deep into South China. See Sonny Shiu-Hing Lo, *The Politics of Cross-Border Crime in Greater China: Case Studies of the Mainland, Hong Kong and Macao* (New York: M. E. Sharpe, 2009).

29. *MP*, November 17, 2007, p. A24.

30. *TDN*, November 18, 2007, p. C1.

31. *WJ*, November 18, 2007, p. A22.

32. Ibid.

33. *TDN*, November 18, 2007, p. C1.

34. *STD*, December 3, 2007, p. A14.

35. Editorial, "Active Voters Facing Powerless Councils," *MP*, November 21, 2007, p. A20.

36. Ibid.

37. Ronny Tong, "Non-mainstream Political Reform Model," *STD*, March 28, 2008, p. B6.

38. *TDN*, January 11, 2008, p. C4.

39. *STD*, April 28, 2006, p. B1.

40. Personal discussion with former DP member Fung King-man, who was arrested for "deceiving rental subsidies," in December 2008. For the reports on her case, see *MP*, January 11, 2006, p. A11.

41. *MP*, January 11, 2006, p. A11.

42. *STD*, March 17, 2005, p. B9.

43. *STD*, December 15, 2007, p. B1.

44. *MP*, January 11, 2008, p. A15.

45. *TDN*, January 11, 2008, p. C4.

46. *WJ*, January 11, 2008, p. A21.

47. *WWP*, September 9, 2008.

48. "Decision of the Standing Committee of the National People's Congress on Issues Relating to the Methods for Selecting the Chief Executive of the Hong Kong Special Administrative Region in the Year 2007 and for Forming the Legislative Council of the Hong Kong Special Administrative Region in the Year 2008: Adopted by the Standing Committee of the Tenth National People's Congress at its Ninth Session on 26 April 2004," S.S. No. 5 to Gazette Extraordinary No. 8/ 2004, in http://www.info.gov.hk/cab/cab-review/eng/basic/pdf/ es5200408081.pdf (accessed December 29, 2004).

49. *TDN*, August 23, 2008, p. 56.

50. *STD*, August 23, 2008, p. B6.

51. *MP*, May 19, 2008, p. A16.

52. *MP*, August 12, 2008, p. A11.

53. *A Bicameral System for Hong Kong* (Hong Kong: Business and Professionals Federation of Hong Kong, January 2006).

54. Ibid., p. 37.

55. *MP*, July 26, 2008, p. A14.

56. Editorial, "The Liaison Office Should Not Intervene in Hong Kong's Elections, the Centre Should Better Solve the Political Deadlock through Political Party Politics," *MP*, September 15, 2008, p. A9.

57. For this argument, see Sonny Shiu-hing Lo, *The Dynamics of Beijing-Hong Kong Relations: A Model for Taiwan?* (Hong Kong: Hong Kong University Press, 2008), pp. 137–138.

58. *WJ*, March 20, 2008, p. A21. My personal observations of the by-election held for the LegCo in 2008 confirmed the mobilization of many school students by pro-Beijing groups to conduct exit polls outside many voting stations.

59. *TDN*, March 26, 2008, p. C7.

60. *MP*, August 30, 2008, p. A16.

61. Ivan Choy of the Chinese University of Hong Kong and Sung Lap-kung of City University of Hong Kong immediately criticized Chung. See Ibid.

62. *STD*, September 3, 2008, p. B3.

63. *MP*, September 3, 2008, p. A13.

64. *TDN*, September 3, 2008, p. 50.

65. Editorial, "Robert Chung Ting-yiu Competes to Be a Rotten Apple, But This Devalues His Own Image," *MP*, September 3, 2008, p. A10. A letter to the editor from the Neighborhood and Worker's Service Center also criticized Chung for failing to protect academic freedom and providing opportunities for media organizations to leak the polls data to political groups and candidates. See "An Open Letter to Robert Chung Ting-yiu: When Exit Polls Cannot Represent Public Opinion," *STD*, September 5, 2008, p. B6.

66. *TDN*, September 5, 2008, p. 51.

67. *MP*, September 4, 2008, p. A13. Also see *Sing Tao Daily*, September 4, 2008, p. B3.

68. For the inaccuracy of polls results and the refusal of many citizens to respond to the research, see *STD*, September 5, 2008, p. B1.

69. Ibid.

70. Editorial, "The Functions of Exit Polls Are Abolished and the Electoral Affairs Commission Should Shoulder the Greatest Responsibility," *MP*, September 5, 2008, p. A11.

71. Ronny Tong, "Human Rights, Elections and Exit Polls," *STD*, March 14, 2008, p. B5.

72. Personal discussion with Professor Kuan Hsin-chi of the Civic Party, December 2008.

CHAPTER 6

1. Pok Fu Lam, "The Functional Deficiencies of Hong Kong's Political Parties," *TDN*, June 18, 2009, p. 19.

2. Samuel Huntington, *The Third Wave: Democratization in the Late Twentieth Century* (Norman: University of Oklahoma Press, 1991).

3. "DP Basic Information," at http://www.dphk.org/e_site/index_e.htm (accessed July 28, 2009).

4. *TDN*, April 15, 2006, p. B6.

5. *MP*, October 21, 2004, p. A16.

6. *STD*, April 1, 2008, p. B1.

7. *TDN*, April 1, 2008, p. C8.

8. Ibid.

9. "The Fading Away of Charismatic Leaders, the Democratic Party Is in Transition and Has New Opportunities," *MP*, March 29, 2008, p. A12.

10. *TDN*, May 5, 2008, p. C7. *STD*, May 5, 2008, p. B2.

11. *MP*, April 21, 2008, p. A12.

12. *MP*, May 5, 2008, p. A9.

13. *STD*, May 4, 2009, p. B3.

14. *MP*, December 15, 2008, p. A18.

15. *TDN*, December 15, 2008, p. 25.

16. Ibid.

17. *MP*, December 15, 2008, p. A18.

18. *MP*, September 12, 2008, p. A22.

19. *MP*, February 7, 2005, p. A3.

20. *WJ*, February 5, 2005, p. A21.

21. Ibid.

22. *STD*, February 5, 2005, p. B2. *Ming Pao*, February 4, 2005, p. A23.

23. See Editorial, "Ho Wai-to Dishonest, Detention Center Inhuman," *MP*, February 5, 2005, p. A23.

24. *MP*, February 14, 2005, p. A1.

25. Personal discussion with Fung, December 2008.

26. *TDN*, April 9, 2009, p. 22.

27. *MP*, April 10, 2008, p. A20.

28. *STD*, March 23, 2006, p. B6.

29. Ibid.

30. *STD*, March 26, 2006, p. B4.

31. Ibid.

32. *STD*, March 22, 2006, p. B8.

33. *MP*, March 18, 2006, p. A13.

34. *MP*, April 21, 2006, p. A23.

35. *STD*, June 3, 2006, p. B5.

36. *MP*, June 3, 2006, p. A24.

37. *MP*, June 2, 2006, p. A20.

38. *TDN*, June 3, 2006, p. B4.

39. See Tam Ching-chi, "A Moral Crisis Resulting From the Resistance to Open the Membership Record," *TDN*, July 15, 2006, p. D12. Tam Ching-chi, "Knowing the Law But Violating the Law by Not Disclosing the Membership List," *TDN*, June 11, 2006, p. D12.

40. *STD*, October 29, 2004, p. B3; and *World Journal*, August 24, 2005, p. A21.

41. *MP*, February 23, 2008, p. A14.

42. *TDN*, February 5, 2009, p. 23.

43. *STD*, July 24, 2008, p. B4.

44. Ibid.

45. *MP*, June 3, 2006, p. A24.

46. *WJ*, August 5, 2007, p. A22.

47. Ibid.

48. Ibid.

49. *HKET*, November 3, 2004, p. A28.

50. *STD*, October 27, 2004, p. B3.

51. *MP*, November 21, 2004, p. A17.

52. Ibid.

53. *MP*, November 22, 2004, p. A15.

54. *MP*, November 24, 2004, p. A19.

55. Ibid.

56. *MP*, November 22, 2004, p. A15.

57. *STD*, December 15, 2004, p. B4.

58. Ibid.

59. *MP*, February 2, 2006, p. A16.

60. *WJ*, January 25, 2006, p. A21.

61. Ibid.

62. Ibid.

63. *TDN*, March 11, 2006, p. B9.

64. *WJ*, April 9, 2006, p. A22.

65. *STD*, August 14, 2006, p. B3.

66. Yeung Sum of the DP initiated the motion in opposition to the GST plan and 40 legislators supported it, 4 voted against, and 5 abstained. Even DAB legislators opposed GST although most of them did not openly speak against it. See *STD*, October 20, 2006, p. B4.

67. Kwok Chung-hang, "The Role of Emily Lau in the DP," *TDN*, August 13, 2009, p. 19.

68. *TDN*, November 24, 2008, p. 22.

69. *MP*, November 24, 2008, p. A20.

70. *TDN*, November 24, 2008, p. 22.

71. For the plan before the name of Alan Leong was revealed, see *STD*, April 13, 2006, p. B5.

72. *MP*, May 7, 2005, p. A22.

73. *MP*, March 30, 2008, p. A20.

74. Ibid.

75. Ibid.

76. *STD*, February 21, 2009, p. B3.

77. For a classic work on the DP adaptability, see Yu Wing-yat, "Organizational Adaptation of the Hong Kong Democratic Party: Centralization and Decentralization," *Issues & Studies*, vol. 33, no. 1 (January 1997), pp. 87–115.

CHAPTER 7

1. *MP*, December 3, 2005, p. A17.

2. Editorial, "Article 45 Concern Group Will Become a Party," *MP*, November 3, 2005, p. D19.

3. Criticism made by Tam Chun-yin, a representative of the Coalition of Public Supervision on World Trade Organization, see *MP*, March 16, 2006, p. A18.

4. *MP*, March 28, 2006, p. A15.

5. Ibid.

6. *STD*, June 27, 2006, p. B4.

7. *Star Magazine* (a weekly Chinese magazine attached to Toronto's *Sing Tao Daily*), no. 224 (May 7, 2006), p. 24.

8. *MP*, May 24, 2006, p. A19.

9. *MP*, February 20, 2009, p. A25.

10. *Star Magazine*, no. 368 (January 18, 2009), p. 24.

11. *Star Magazine*, no. 224 (May 7, 2006), p. 24.

12. For details, see Lo, *The Dynamics of Hong Kong-Beijing Relations: A Model for Taiwan?*, Chapter 3, pp. 81–108.

13. *WJ*, May 27, 2006, p. A21.

14. *MP*, May 27, 2006, p. A20.

15. *MP*, November 10, 2008, p. A23.

16. *STD*, June 7, 2009, p. B1.

17. *MP*, June 8, 2009, p. A20.

18. *MP*, June 8, 2009, p. A20.

19. *STD*, May 4, 2009, p. B3.

20. *MP*, November 19, 2008, p. A21.

21. "Move on from June 4, Says Civic Chief," *STD*, April 12, 2006, p. D30.

22. Ibid.

23. Alan Leong, "Is the Civic Party Right or Left," *MP*, March 31, 2006, p. D8.

24. *STD*, March 6, 2006, p. B4.

25. *STD*, March 23, 2006, p. B6.

26. *STD*, October 31, 2006, p. B4.

27. *MP*, November 9, 2006, p. A23.

28. During his childhood, Alan Leong studied in La Salle primary school and then Wah Yan College in his secondary school years. He revealed that his experience in democratic elections could be traced back to 1976, when Wah Yan College had already instituted elections among class representatives to select their student union leader. See "Alan Leong Met Universal Suffrage in 1976," *MP*, November 28, 2005, p. D2. Leong himself has often been a moderate democrat. The Tung Chee-hwa government once toyed with the idea of appointing him to the ExCo in October 2004, but the Article 45 Concern Group at that time had internal opinion differences over whether Leong should join the top policy-making body. Ronny Tong questioned whether Leong's participation in the ExCo would be a greater contribution than his work in the Legislative Council. Tong was also concerned that the principle of confidentiality in the ExCo might be a political liability to Leong if the latter entered the policy-making organ. See *MP*, October 9, 2004, p. A14; and *STD*, October 6, 2004, p. B4.

29. *STD*, October 4, 2006, p. B4.

30. *STD*, June 27, 2006, p. B7; and *MP*, June 17, 2006, p. A18.

31. *MP*, May 2, 2006, p. A14.

32. *MP*, May 2, 2006, p. A14.

33. *WJ*, November 16, 2008, p. B12.

34. See www.lsd.org.hk (accessed August 13, 2009).

35. *HKEJ*, November 23, 2007.

36. Chung was supported also by the Federation of Trade Unions and independent legislator Regina Ip. See *MP*, June 9, 2009, p. A24.

37. *TDN*, June 9, 2009, p. 24.

38. *The Legend*, vol. 43 (May 2009), p. 4.

39. Ibid.

40. Ibid.

41. Ibid., p. 5.

42. Ibid., p. 6.

43. Ibid., p. 6.

44. Ibid., p. 7.

45. *STD*, October 16, 2008, p. B3.

46. *The Legend*, vol. 43 (May 2009), p. 7.

47. Ibid., p. 7.

48. *STD*, September 12, 2005, p. B3.

49. Ibid.

50. Editorial, "Hong Kong Legislator Raising His Finger and Setting a Bad Example," *STD*, October 7, 2004, p. A19.

51. *STD*, October 9, 2004, p. B3.
52. Ibid.
53. Ibid.
54. Ibid.
55. *MP*, October 6, 2004, p. A17.
56. Ibid.
57. Ibid.
58. *MP*, October 7, 2004, p. A20.
59. Ibid.
60. *MP*, August 17, 2005, p. A20.
61. *MP*, August 16, 2005, p. A15.
62. *MP*, September 14, 2008, p. A20.
63. *MP*, January 17, 2009, p. A19.
64. *TDN*, July 5, 2008, p. C7.
65. *MP*, July 5, 2008, p. A19.
66. *STD*, February 26, 2009, p. B1.
67. Ibid.
68. Ibid.
69. Ibid.
70. Ibid.
71. *TDN*, February 28, 2009, p. 27.
72. *STD*, February 28, 2009, p. B4.
73. *STD*, March 27, 2009, p. B5.
74. Ibid.
75. Ibid.
76. Ibid.
77. *TDN*, May 1, 2009, p. 26.
78. Lowell Dittmer, "Political Culture and Political Symbolism: Toward a Theoretical Synthesis," *World Politics*, vol. 79, no. 4 (July 1977), p. 557. For an insightful analysis of political symbolism in Taiwan's presidential elections, see Benson Wong, "Localization in the 2004 Presidential Election Campaign in Taiwan: An Iconographic Approach," *China Perspectives*, no. 55 (September/October 2004), pp. 49–56.
79. *MP*, April 14, 2005, p. A18.
80. Priscilla Leung, "Public Figures Should Pay Attention to the Consequences of Their Words and Action," *TDN*, April 16, p. 19. Also see Chan King-sun, "Taiwanization of Legislators Questioning the Government, the Politicians Criticize Them, But Public Opinion Supports Them," *WJ*, April 14, 2009, p. B9.
81. *STD*, November 21, 2007, p. B4.
82. *MP*, February 18, 2008, p. A16.
83. Ibid.
84. Lau Wan-lung, "The ADPL Plan of Rescuing the Party," *WJ*, February 19, 2008, p. A21.
85. Ibid.
86. Wong On-yin, "Lau Chin-shek Should Not Follow the Example of the ADPL!" *TDN*, March 10, 2008, p. C8.
87. Ibid.

CHAPTER 8

1. See www.dab.org.hk (accessed August 13, 2009).

2. Ma Lik died of cancer in August 2007. He had graduated from the pro-Beijing Pui Kiu primary and secondary schools. Later he taught at Pui Kiu and became the deputy secretary-general of the Basic Law Consultative Committee from 1985 to 1990. From 1991 to 1997 he worked in the editorial section of the pro-Beijing *Hong Kong Commercial Daily*. In 1988 he was selected as the Hong Kong member of the NPC. In 2004, he was directly elected as a legislator in the HKSAR. See *TDN*, August 9, 2007, p. A16.

3. See www.dab.org.hk (accessed August 13, 2009).

4. *STD*, February 17, 2005, p. B1.

5. *MP*, January 6, 2009, p. A15.

6. *MP*, February 14, 2005, p. A11.

7. *STD*, February 15, 2005, p. B1.

8. *MP*, October 21, 2004, p. A16.

9. *STD*, October 25, 2004, p. B3.

10. *MP*, September 19, 2005, p. A13.

11. *TDN*, June 15, 2008, p. C5; and *STD*, February 1, 2006, p. B5.

12. *MP*, January 31, 2006, p. A19.

13. *STD*, April 5, 2008, p. B4.

14. *TDN*, March 18, 2008, p. C1.

15. *TDN*, March 31, 2008, p. C6.

16. *TDN*, March 29, 2008, p. C1.

17. *TDN*, April 6, 2009, p. 22.

18. *STD*, March 15, 2008, p. B5.

19. *STD*, January 21, 2006, p. B8.

20. *STD*, July 23, 2008, p. B4.

21. *MP*, July 23, 2008, p. A9.

22. *MP*, September 15, 2008, p. A13.

23. *WJ*, January 8, 2008, p. A21.

24. Jasper Tsang, "The Third Wave of Party Development," *STD*, February 1, 2008, p. B8.

25. A good example was the government's request for the LegCo to approve a scheme of constructing the government headquarters near the Tamar military base. The DAB supported the government in the legislature's Finance Committee, but the democrats opposed it. See *MP*, April 8, 2006, p. A18.

26. *TDN*, November 9, 2007, p. C8.

27. *TDN*, January 7, 2008, p. C7.

28. *MP*, December 1, 2008, p. A18.

29. *WJ*, May 22, 2008, p. A21.

30. *TDN*, June 23, 2008, p. C6.

31. *MP*, November 8, 2008, p. A22.

32. *MP*, August 24, 2006, p. A18. Also see *MP*, August 11, 2006, p. A18.

33. *TDN*, May 3, 2009, p. 28.

34. *MP*, February 25, 2009, p. A20.

35. Ibid.

36. *TDN*, March 18, 2006, p. B2.

37. Ibid.

38. *TDN*, March 19, 2006, p. B3.

39. *STD*, May 31, 2005, p. B7. For patron-client politics, see Bruce Kwong, *Elections and Patron-Client Politics in Hong Kong* (London: Routledge, 2009).

40. *STD*, June 30, 2005, p. B1.

41. *HKET*, October 25, 2004, p. A25.

42. Ibid.

43. Ibid.

44. *MP*, April 29, 2006, p. A16.

45. *MP*, September 22, 2008, p. A10.

46. *TDN*, September 21, 2008, p. 55.

47. *TDN*, October 3, 2008, p. 53.

48. *TDN*, October 4, 2008, p. 50.

49. *MP*, October 7, 2008, p. A11.

50. *STD*, October 9, 2008, p. B3.

51. Ibid.

52. *MP*, February 25, 2009, p. A20.

53. *TDN*, April 16, 2008, p. A13.

54. *WJ*, August 22, 2005, p. A21.

55. *MP*, September 8, 2005, p. A13.

56. Ibid.

57. *MP*, October 1, 2006, p. A14.

58. *STD*, October 27, 2006, p. B3.

59. *MP*, February 17, 2006, p. A19.

60. *WJ*, November 1, 2004, p. A21.

61. See www.liberal.org.hk (accessed August 14, 2009).

62. Its Web site in August 2009 did not even update the number of its party members.

63. *STD*, February 18, 2005, p. B1.

64. Editorial, "James Tien Abandons to Run for the Election, Revealing Again the Problems of Small Circle Election," *MP*, April 14, 2005, p. A20.

65. *MP*, April 13, 2005, p. A18.

66. *MP*, September 7, 2005, p. A16. That official was reportedly Chief Secretary Rafael Hui Si-yan. See *STD*, September 7, 2005, p. B4.

67. *MP*, April 13, 2005, p. A18.

68. *MP*, January 23, 2006, p. A17.

69. *STD*, May 24, 2006, p. B4.

70. *MP*, April 25, 2006, p. A17.

71. *MP*, February 7, 2005, p. A14.

72. *MP*, August 16, 2006, p. A19.

73. *TDN*, February 16, 2009, p. 19.

74. *STD*, November 22, 2008, p. B3.

75. *WJ*, November 22, 2008, p. B12.

76. *MP*, November 22, 2008, p. A22.

77. *MP*, November 25, 2008, p. A22; and *Ming Pao*, November 24, 2008, p. A21.

78. *MP*, August 8, 2006, p. A14.

79. *MP*, January 8, 2008, p. A16.

80. For details, see *MP*, February 7, 2009, p. A22.

81. Miriam Lau also said the LP would adopt four principles: marketization, minimal government intervention, the distribution of social resources to help the minorities and the needy, and corporate responsibility. See *MP*, January 12, 2009, p. A22.

82. *MP*, September 12, 2008, p. A20.

83. *STD*, September 20, 2008, p. B4.

84. *STD*, October 10, 2008, p. B1.

85. *STD*, September 30, 2008, p. B5.

86. *TDN*, September 18, 2008, p. 52.

87. *STD*, October 10, 2008, p. B1.

88. For details, see *Star Magazine*, vol. 352 (October 19, 2008), pp. 50–52.

89. *MP*, September 19, 2008, p. A13.

90. *STD*, September 26, 2008, p. B5.

91. *MP*, October 21, 2008, p. A12.

92. *MP*, February 4, 2009, p. A27.

93. *STD*, October 7, 2006, p. B5.

94. *MP*, October 7, 2006, p. A17.

95. *MP*, October 20, 2006, p. A24.

96. *STD*, May 6, 2008, p. B5.

97. *STD*, May 6, 2008, p. B5.

98. *MP*, June 1, 2005, p. A12.

99. *MP*, February 4, 2005, p. A18.

100. *WJ*, January 4, 2008, p. A21.

101. *TDN*, February 21, 2008, p. B7. One CPPCC member and Hong Kong actress Lisa Wang initiated a motion calling for the PRC government to reissue the home return permits to Hong Kong democrats, but her motion was received coolly by other CPPCC members. *MP*, March 10, 2008, p. A14.

102. Editorial, "Not Being the Second Power Center, Not Representing They Are the Rubber-stamp," *MP*, January 14, 2008, p. A9.

103. *TDN*, May 15, 2008, p. C6.

104. See its Web site www.bauhinia.org (accessed August 15, 2009).

105. *WJ*, March 5, 2006, p. A22.

106. Ronny Tong, "Is the Business Sector Afraid of Democracy?" *STD*, April 11, 2008, p. B5.

107. *STD*, May 2, 2005, p. B3.

108. *STD*, November 27, 2005, p. B14; and *STD*, October 7, 2005, p. B3.

109. *MP*, January 8, 2005, p. A19.

110. *TDN*, September 21, 2007, p. C6.

111. *STD*, March 24, 2006, p. B4.

112. *STD*, October 31, 2008, p. B1.

113. *MP*, February 5, 2007, p. A14.

114. *MP*, January 13, 2008, p. A13.

115. *MP*, February 6, 2008, p. A20; and *STD*, May 26, 2006, p. B1.

CHAPTER 9

1. Ming Chan, "Transforming China's Hong Kong: Toward 2047 Merger-Convergence?" in Ming Chan, ed., *China's Hong Kong Transformed: Retrospect and*

Prospects Beyond the First Decade (Hong Kong: City University of Hong Kong Press, 2008), p. 6.

2. For this inaccurate claim, see Jie Cheng, "The Story of a New Policy," *Hong Kong Journal* (Fall 2009), p. 2, at www.hkjournal.org/PDF/2009_fall.pdf (accessed August 18, 2009).

3. Guoguang Wu, "Identity, Sovereignty and Economic Penetration: Beijing's Responses to Offshore Chinese Democracies," *Journal of Contemporary China*, vol. 10, no. 51 (May 2007), pp. 295–313; and Benson Wong, "Can Co-optation Win Over the Hong Kong People?" *Issues & Studies*, vol. 33, no. 5 (May 1997).

4. *TDN*, August 2, 2009, p. 14.

5. Editorial, "The Concept of 'Hong Kong Team' Leads to Worries and 'Two Teams' Theory Needs Clarification," *MP*, April 27, 2009, p. A22.

6. Hong Kong Democratic Foundation's Forum, "The 'One Country, Two Systems' and Hong Kong's Governing Forces," held at the United Center, Hong Kong, May 9, 2009. Commentators such as Joseph Lian and Ching Cheong and academics like Johannes Chan, Ma Ngok, Ray Yep, and Benny Tai attended the forum.

7. *Dongxiang* (*The Trend Magazine*), no. 235 (March 2005), p. 17.

8. Liao's predecessor Lu Ping often argued in public with Governor Christopher Patten from 1993 to 1997, when the last Hong Kong governor pushed forward his political reform plan.

9. Personal discussion with two moderate democrats who said they had contacts with the HKMAO rather than the Liaison Office, December 2008.

10. The author communicated with two mainland researchers from Guangdong province twice shortly after the July 1, 2003, protests in the HKSAR.

11. Two of the Beijing researchers chatted with the author after the July 1, 2003, protest. One of them revealed to the author in March 2008 that Beijing's hard-line leaders originally did not think that the HKSAR government under Tung had serious problems. He managed to persuade these leaders in December 2003 that Hong Kong's governance problems were not due to outsiders or foreign influence, but they stemmed from internal matters.

12. For the elite conflicts in the PRC and how they affected mainland agencies dealing with Hong Kong, see Shiu-hing Lo, "The Chinese Communist Party Elite's Conflicts over Hong Kong, 1983–1990," *China Information*, vol. VIII, no. 4 (Spring 1994), pp. 1–14.

13. *STD*, October 10, 2004, p. A17.

14. *STD*, September 24, 2004, p. B1.

15. Ibid.

16. *STD*, September 25, 2004, p. B1.

17. Ibid.

18. *STD*, January 31, 2005, p. B4.

19. Ibid.

20. *MP*, April 15, 2005, p. A23.

21. Ibid.

22. *MP*, August 31, 2005, p. A14.

23. *MP*, December 5, 2005, p. A1.

24. *MP*, April 15, 2005, p. A23.

25. *WJ*, April 13, 2005, p. A21.

26. *MP*, September 24, 2005, p. A23.

27. *MP*, September 17, 2005, p. A20.

28. *MP*, September 24, 2005, p. A23.

29. Editorial, "Fruit of Legislative Council Members' Guangdong Visit," *MP*, October 4, 2005, p. D19.

30. *STD*, October 31, 2005, p. B4.

31. Ibid.

32. Ibid.

33. *Next Magazine*, January 24, 2008, pp. 56–58.

34. Ibid.

35. Ibid.

36. *MP*, October 22, 2005, p. A19.

37. Editorial, "The Strategic Development Commission Cannot Become a Saliva Meeting and There Should Be Compromises and Concrete Reform Models," *MP*, October 30, 2005, p. A13.

38. *STD*, November 5, 2005, p. B4.

39. *MP*, February 2, 2009, p. A18. Albert Ho of the Democratic Party said that the pan-democrats' relations with Wu "are not so intimate." See *STD*, January 21, 2009, p. B3.

40. Bruce Kwong, *Elections and Patron-Client Politics in Hong Kong* (London: Routledge, 2009).

41. For details, see Nicholas Cheung Yat-fung, *Modernization of Village Politics in Hong Kong*, unpublished MPhil thesis, Department of Politics and Public Administration, University of Hong Kong, 2003.

42. *MP*, January 24, 2009, p. A27.

43. Ibid.

44. Editorial, "Lau Wong-fat Whose Performance Is Poor Can Even Enter the Executive Council, It Is a Tragic That the Body Has Become a Place for Political Rewards," *MP*, January 21, 2009, p. A22.

45. *STD*, June 29, 2008, p. B1.

46. Editorial, "RTHK's Poor Governance," *MP*, May 1, 2006, p. D20; and Editorial, "Review of RTHK Should Be Focused," *MP*, November 7, 2005, p. D20.

47. *MP*, July 28, 2009, p. A18.

48. *MP*, December 16, 2009, p. A21.

49. *STD*, December 16, 2008, p. B1.

50. See Wong's resignation letter in *MP*, December 18, 2009, p. A2.

51. *MP*, December 18, 2009, p. A2.

52. *MP*, December 20, 2008, p. A21.

53. *STD*, January 30, 2009, p. B1.

54. *MP*, January 27, 2009, p. A26.

55. *STD*, May 28, 2008, p. B10; and *TDN*, May 28, 2008, p. C2. Also see *Star Magazine*, May 25, 2008, pp. 28–34.

56. *MP*, May 23, 2009, p. A23.

57. See the Beijing visit of Hong Kong students in journalism, in *WWP*, July 3, 2009, pp. 32–33.

58. *TDN*, May 1, 2008, p. C9; and *TDN*, April 30, 2008, p. C4.

59. *MP*, April 30, 2008, pp. A19–A20.

60. *MP*, May 1, 2008, p. A20.

61. *TDN*, August 30, 2008, p. 52.

62. *MP*, April 18, 2006, p. A14.

63. *TDN*, January 27, 2008, p. C7.

64. Quoted in Editorial, "Donald Tsang Claims That 'Distinguishing Relatives from Those Who Are Distant' as Rational. Regretful!" *MP*, July 18, 2008, p. A11.

65. *MP*, January 5, 2009, p. A20.

66. Zen said, "China needs real religious freedom." See *MP*, March 24, 2006, p. A15.

67. *MP*, April 1, 2006, p. A19.

68. *MP*, April 2, 2006, p. A16.

69. *MP*, April 17, 2009, p. A24.

70. *MP*, April 30, 2009, p. A27.

71. *STD*, April 30, 2009, p. B4.

72. *MP*, April 28, 2009, p. A26.

73. *MP*, May 18, 2009, p. A20.

74. Ibid.

75. *TDN*, May 16, 2009, p. 26.

76. *TDN*, July 2, 2009, p. 25.

77. *STD*, April 11, 2009.

78. *MP*, December 5, 2008, p. A23.

79. Ibid.

80. Editorial, "Mainland Students' Competitiveness Is Increasing, They Are Forcing the Hong Kong Counterparts to Make Progress," *MP*, July 22, 2008, p. A10.

81. *MP*, March 14, 2008, p. A20.

82. *WJ*, February 9, 2008, p. A21.

83. *MP*, May 24, 2009, p. B1.

84. *TDN*, May 16, 2009, p. 12.

85. *TDN*, April 15, 2009, p. 24.

86. Personal discussions with three academics at the Shenzhen Social Science Academy, March 18, 2009.

87. *TDN*, July 31, 2009, pp. 28–29.

88. *MP*, July 30, 2009, p. A22.

89. *STD*, June 18, 2009, p. B5.

90. *STD*, June 17, 2009, p. B1.

91. *STD*, June 18, 2009, p. B5.

92. *MP*, June 16, 2009, p. A19.

93. *MP*, June 17, 2009, p. A20.

94. Bonnie Chen, "Leung Admits Pushing New World Deal," *The Standard*, July 21, 2009.

95. Ibid.

96. *MP*, August 17, 2006, p. A20.

97. *Sun*, March 28, 2009, p. A6.

98. *STD*, November 13, 2008, p. B4.

99. *HKET*, March 26, 2009, p. A18.

100. *MP*, June 17, 2009, p. A23.

101. Peter Brieger, Barclay Crawford, and Ambrose Leung, "Martin Lee Case: Who, Why and What Now?" *SCMP*, July 5, 2009, p. 3.

102. *WJ*, December 8, 2007, p. A21.

103. Diana Lee, "Martin Lee Plotter Gets Three Years," *The Standard*, July 7, 2009, p. 7.

104. *MP*, July 23, 2009, p. A22.

105. *TDN*, July 23, 2009, p. 30.

106. *MP*, July 23, 2009, p. A22.

107. *Next Magazine*, July 23, 2009, pp. 38–44.

108. Ibid.

109. *STD*, June 23, 2009, p. B7.

110. "Pier Vigil Comes to Dramatic End," *The Standard*, August 10, 2007; and "Death Knell on Pier," *The Standard*, August 6, 2007. The activities of Chu and other young people fighting for Hong Kong's collective memory and retaining the Queen's Pier were internationally reported. Geoffrey York, "Hong Kong Suddenly Seeks Its Soul," *Globe and Mail* (Canada), March 31, 2007, pp. F4–F5.

111. *MP*, August 4, 2009, p. A24.

112. Ibid.

113. *STD*, April 17, 2009, p. B6.

114. Christina Chan publicly advocated that the Tibetans should have their right of self-determination. See *Star Magazine*, vol. 329 (May 11, 2008), pp. 24–28; and *MP*, August 10, 2008, p. A19.

115. *WJ*, April 25, 2009, p. B9.

CONCLUSION

1. Yang brought the American donations to Beijing prior to the June 4 incident in 1989. After June 4, he returned to the United States. In 2002, he tried to enter the PRC with another person's passport to observe the labor protests in the northwest of China, but he was arrested when he entered the mainland. In 2004, he was on trial and charged with illegal entry and espionage. Yang received a sentence of five years' imprisonment. In 2007 he was released from prison and allowed to return to the United States. See *Sing Tao Daily*, June 14, 2009, p. B6.

2. Pan Wei, "Toward a Consultative Rule of Law Regime in China," *Journal of Contemporary China*, vol. 12, no. 35 (2003), pp. 319–331.

Glossary

Chinese democracy: The Chinese concept of democracy is unique in that it emphasizes the harmony between the rulers and the ruled, de-emphasizes the notion of individual rights, assumes that the rights possessed by individuals and groups are granted by the state, and regards the power of the central government as far more important than that of the localities. The Chinese democracy as envisioned by the Chinese Communist Party is different from the Western-style democracy. It refers to the need to strengthen anticorruption work, the auditing of government departments, the internal supervision on the ruling party, and the use of elections to enhance the accountability of Party and government officials.

Co-optation: It refers to the political process of absorbing friends and enemies of the state into the existing political institutions. Quite often co-optation cannot absorb the enemies and critics of the state completely and easily, for some of them are resistant to being appointed to various policy-making, advisory, and consultative bodies.

Democracy: It refers to the Western-style political system where political leaders have to struggle for the people's votes in national elections and where a rotation of political party in power takes place. Hong Kong is not a Western-style democracy, but it can be regarded as a semidemocracy where the chief executive is elected by a small group of people, where the legislature embraces a vibrant opposition directly elected by the ordinary citizens, and where civil liberties and the rule of law persist.

Democracy movement: It means a movement initiated by various social and political groups to defend their rights and clamor for a more democratic political system. Such movement is sustained by civil society groups involving, for example, the human rights activists, lawyers, intellectuals, teachers, religious priests, and social workers.

Democratization: It is a long process of political transformations that may take several generations. Usually it is triggered by political liberalizations when the ruling elites open up the political system and allow more space for civil liberties. Democratization can begin with a split of the ruling elites between soft-liners who favor political reform and the hard-liners who oppose it. When the soft-liners prevail over the hard-liners, democratization is triggered, followed by the push from civil society groups and then by the holding of a national election whereby the opposition has the golden opportunity of grasping political power.

Hong Kong style of democracy: The Hong Kong style of democracy is characterized by active social groups, a vibrant press, an assertive legislature, a relatively respectable and clean civil service, the existence of the Independent Commission Against Corruption (ICAC), the persistence of the Office of the Ombudsman to check public maladministration, and the usefulness of the Audit Commission to expose excessive expenditure in government agencies. Moreover, the persistence of civil liberties and the rule of law are the features of the Hong Kong style of democracy. Hong Kong does not have a Western-style democratic system, but it is semidemocratic in the sense that the chief executive is elected by a small electoral college and the legislature includes a powerful opposition with almost 60 percent of the votes in direct elections.

Operation Yellowbird: It was a term used by John Shum Kin-fun, an actor in the Hong Kong entertainment circle, to refer to the rescue of mainland Chinese democrats who were suppressed and under the arrest warrant of the mainland Chinese police and security agents shortly after the June 4 Tiananmen tragedy in 1989. The operation was composed of a loosely organized group without hierarchy and fixed memberships. It lasted from June 1989 to June 1997. Rescuing altogether about 300 mainland democrats from China, Operation Yellowbird clandestinely transported all the related documents and records to overseas countries. Triads and triad members were involved in the rescue operation, using speedboats to save the lives of mainland Chinese democrats.

United front work: It is a concept used by the Chinese Communist Party to unite the people, including friends and enemies. The Party utilizes patriotism, economic incentives, and the rewards of political followers as the means of winning the hearts and minds of the Hong Kong people. The most powerful weapon employed by the Chinese government to co-opt the people of Hong Kong, to silence the critics, to buy off opportunists, to enforce a strong sense of public pragmatism, and to curb the demands for democracy is economic enticement. Economic enticement includes the policy measures designed and implemented to win the Hong Kong people's support of Beijing, such as the Closer Economic Partnership Arrangement and the scheme of allowing mainlanders to visit Hong Kong.

Bibliography

NEWSPAPERS AND MAGAZINES

Apple Daily (Hong Kong).
Asiaweek (*Yazhou Zhoukan* in Chinese).
China Daily.
Chinese Exploration (Toronto Chinese magazine, the Toronto version of *Asiaweek*).
Dongxiang (*The Trend Magazine*, Hong Kong).
Globe and Mail (Canada).
Headline Daily (Hong Kong).
Hong Kong Economic Journal.
Hong Kong Economic Times.
Ming Pao (Hong Kong and Toronto).
Ming Pao Saturday Magazine (Toronto edition).
Next Magazine (Hong Kong).
Oriental Daily (Hong Kong).
Sing Tao Daily (Hong Kong and Toronto).
South China Morning Post (Hong Kong).
Star Magazine (a magazine attached to Toronto's *Sing Tao Daily* every Sunday).
Sun (Hong Kong Chinese newspaper).
Sunday Morning Post (Hong Kong).
Ta Kung Pao (Hong Kong).
The Legend (Hong Kong).
The Standard (Hong Kong).
The Washington Post.
Today Daily News (Toronto Chinese newspaper that includes news reports from Hong Kong's *Sun* and *Wen Wei Po*).
Toronto Star.
Wen Wei Po (Hong Kong).

Wide Angel (Hong Kong).
World Journal (Toronto Chinese newspaper).

BOOKS AND ARTICLES

A Bicameral System for Hong Kong (Hong Kong: Business and Professionals Federation of Hong Kong, January 2006).

Beatty, Bob, *Democracy, Asian Values, and Hong Kong* (Westport, CT: Praeger, 2003).

Bell, Daniel A., and Jayasuriya, Kanishka, "Understanding Illiberal Democracy: A Framework," in Bell, Daniel; Brown, David; Jayasuriya, Kanishka; and Jones, David Martin, eds., *Towards Illiberal Democracy in Pacific Asia* (London: St. Martin's Press, 1995).

Blecher, Marc J., "Hegemony and Workers' Politics in China," Dittmer, Lowell, and Liu, Guoli, eds., *China's Deep Reform* (Lanham, MD: Rowman & Littlefield Publishers, Inc., 2006).

Cai, Yongshun, and Yang, Songcai, "State Power and Unbalanced Legal Development in China," *Journal of Contemporary China*, vol. 14, no. 42 (February 2005).

Cai, Yongshun, "China's Moderate Middle Class: The Case of Homeowners' Resistance," *Asian Survey*, vol. 45, no. 5 (September/October 2005).

Cai, Yongshun, "Managing Social Unrest," Wong, John, and Lai, Hongyi, eds., *China into the Hu-Wen Era: Policy Initiatives and Challenges* (Hackensack, NJ: World Scientific, 2006).

Cautherley, George, "Constitutional Development, 2011–2020: Possible Scenarios for Discussion," a paper given to the author on July 4, 2009.

Chan, Joseph Man, and Lee, Francis L. F., "Political Opportunities, Social Mobilization and Collective Action: The Re-invigorated Pro-Democracy Movement in Hong Kong," *The China Review*, vol. 7, no. 2 (Fall 2007).

Chan, Ming, "Introduction," in Ming K. Chan and Shiu-Hing Lo, *Historical Dictionary of the Hong Kong SAR and the Macao SAR* (Lanham, MD: Scarecrow Press, 2006).

Chan, Ming, "Transforming China's Hong Kong: Toward 2047 Merger-Convergence?" in Chan, Ming ed., *China's Hong Kong Transformed: Retrospect and Prospects Beyond the First Decade* (Hong Kong: City University of Hong Kong Press, 2008).

Chen, Feng, "Between the State and Labor: The Conflicts of Chinese Trade Unions: Double Identity in Market Reforms," *China Quarterly* (December 2003).

Chen, Feng, "Individual Rights and Collective Rights: Labor's Predicament in China," *Communist and Post-Communist Studies*, 40 (2007).

Cheng, Jie, "The Story of a New Policy," *Hong Kong Journal* (Fall 2009), p. 2, at www.hkjournal.org/PDF/2009_fall.pdf (accessed August 18, 2009).

Cheng, Joseph Y. S., "Hong Kong's Democrats Stumble," *Journal of Democracy*, vol. 16, no. 1 (January 2005).

Cheng, Joseph Y. S., "Hong Kong Since Its Return to China: A Lost Decade?" in Cheng, Joseph Y. S., ed., *The Hong Kong Special Administrative Region in Its First Decade* (Hong Kong: City University of Hong Kong Press, 2007).

Cheng, Joseph Y. S., "Confucian Values and Democratic Governance in Hong Kong," *The International Journal of the Humanities*, vol. 6, no. 1 (2008).

Cheung, Nicholas Yat-fung, *Modernization of Village Politics in Hong Kong*, unpublished MPhil thesis, Department of Politics and Public Administration, University of Hong Kong, 2003.

Chiu, Stephen Wing-kai, and Lui, Tai-lok, eds., *The Dynamics of Social Movement in Hong Kong* (Hong Kong: Hong Kong University Press, 2000).

Davies, S. N. G., "Bureaucracy and People in Hong Kong . . . Like a Horse and Carriage?" *Asian Journal of Public Administration*, vol. 5, no. 1 (June 1983).

"Decision of the Standing Committee of the National People's Congress on Issues Relating to the Methods for Selecting the Chief Executive of the Hong Kong Special Administrative Region in the Year 2007 and for Forming the Legislative Council of the Hong Kong Special Administrative Region in the Year 2008: Adopted by the Standing Committee of the Tenth National People's Congress at its Ninth Session on 26 April 2004," S. S. No. 5 to Gazette Extraordinary No. 8/2004, at http://www.info.gov.hk/cab/cab-review/eng/basic/pdf/es5200408081.pdf (accessed December 29, 2004).

DeGolyer, Michael, "Birdcage or Framework? Considering What Comes Next in Constitutional Reform," a report for the National Democratic Institute for International Affairs and Community Development Initiative Foundation by the Hong Kong Transition Project, July 2009.

Delisle, Jacques, "Legalization Without Democratization in China under Hu Jintao," in Li, Cheng, ed., *China's Changing Political Landscape: Prospects for Democracy* (Washington: Brookings Institution Press, 2008).

Diamond, Larry, "The Rule of Law as Transition to Democracy in China," *Journal of Contemporary China*, vol. 12, no. 35 (2003).

Diamond, Larry, "A Comparative Perspective on Hong Kong's Democratization: Prospects Toward 2017/2020," in Chan, Ming, ed., *China's Hong Kong Transformed: Retrospect and Prospects Beyond the First Decade* (Hong Kong: City University of Hong Kong Press, 2008).

Diamond, Larry, "Why China's Democratic Transition Will Differ from Taiwan's," in Gilley, Bruce, and Diamond, Larry, eds., *Political Change in China: Comparisons with Taiwan* (Boulder: Lynne Rienner, 2008).

Dittmer, Lowell, "Political Culture and Political Symbolism: Toward a Theoretical Synthesis," *World Politics*, vol. 79, no. 4 (July 1977).

Gilley, Bruce, *China's Democratic Future: How It Will Happen and Where It Will Lead* (New York: Columbia University Press, 2004).

Goodman, David S. G., "Why China Has No New Middle Class: Cadres, Managers and Entrepreneurs," in Goodman, David S. G., ed., *The New Rich in China* (London: Routledge, 2008).

Goodstadt, Leo F., *Uneasy Partners: The Conflict Between Public Interest and Private Profits in Hong Kong* (Hong Kong: Hong Kong University Press, 2005).

Grainger, Ross, "From Anti-Foreignism to Democratization: Hong Kong as a Deviant Case of Political Development," unpublished PhD thesis, School of Political Science, Faculty of Arts and Social Sciences, University of New South Wales, July 2000.

Guo, Zhenglin, and Bernstein, Thomas, "The Impact of Election on the Village Structure of Power: The Relations between the Village Committees and the Party Branches," *Journal of Contemporary China*, vol. 13, no. 39 (May 2004).

Hartford, Kathleen, "Dear Mayor: Online Communication with Local Governments in Hangzhou and Nanjing," *China Information*, vol. XIX, no. 2 (2005).

Hassid, Jonathan, "Controlling the Chinese Media: An Uncertain Business," *Asian Survey*, vol. 48, no. 3 (2008).

He, Baogang, *Rural Democracy in China: The Role of Village Elections* (New York: Palgrave Macmillan, 2007).

He, Li, "Emergence of the Chinese Middle Class and Its Implications," *Asian Affairs* (Washington), vol. 33, no. 2 (Summer 2006).

Helgesen, Geir, and Li, Xing, "Good Governance—Democracy or *Minzhu*?" in Antlov, Hans, and Ngo, Tak-wing, eds., *The Cultural Construction of Politics in Asia* (New York: St. Martin's Press, 2000).

Hsieh, Jiann, "A Preliminary Study on the Inequalities of China's Minorities at the Starting Point of Modernization Process," *Asian Studies Periodical* (published in both English and Chinese by Hong Kong Chu Hai College), no. 57 (September 1, 2008).

Huntington, Samuel P., *The Third Wave of Democratization in the Late Twentieth Century* (Norman: University of Oklahoma Press, 1991).

Huntington, Samuel P., *The Clash of Civilizations and the Remaking of World Order* (New York: Simon & Schuster, 1996).

Keith, Ronald C., and Lin, Zhiqui, "The 'Falun Gong Problem': Politics and the Struggle for Rule of Law in China," *China Quarterly* (September 2003).

Kelley, David, "Citizen Movements and China's Public Intellectuals in the Hu-Wen Era," *Pacific Affairs*, vol. 79, no. 2 (Summer 2006).

Kuan, Hsin-chi, and Lau, Siu-kai, "Intermediation Environment and Election in Hong Kong," *Democratization*, vol. 7, no. 2 (Summer 2000).

Kwong, Bruce, *Elections and Patron-Client Politics in Hong Kong* (London: Routledge, 2009).

Lam, Wai-man, *Understanding the Political Culture of Hong Kong: The Paradox of Activism and Politicization* (New York: M. E. Sharpe, 2004).

Lau, Siu-kai, *Society and Politics in Hong Kong* (Hong Kong: The Chinese University Press, 1983).

Lau, Siu-kai, and Kuan, Hsin-chi, *The Ethos of Hong Kong Chinese* (Hong Kong: The Chinese University Press, 1988).

Lee, Martin, "Biography of Martin C. M. Lee," provided by Martin Lee and his assistant Tiffany Kwok to the author in March 2009.

Leung, Beatrice, "China's Religious Freedom Policy: The Art of Managing Religious Freedom," *China Quarterly* (December 2005).

Li, Pang-kwong, *Hong Kong from Britain to China: Political Cleavages, Electoral Dynamics, and Institutional Changes* (Aldershot: Ashgate, 2000).

Lo, Shiu-hing, "The Chinese Communist Party Elite's Conflicts over Hong Kong, 1983–1990," *China Information*, vol. VIII, no. 4 (Spring 1994).

Lo, Shiu-Hing, *The Politics of Democratization in Hong Kong* (London: Macmillan, 1997).

Lo, Shiu-Hing, "Hong Kong's Political Influence on South China," *Problems of Post-Communism*, vol. 46, no. 4 (July/August 1999).

Lo, Shiu-hing, *Governing Hong Kong: Legitimacy, Communication and Political Decay* (New York: Nova Science, 2001).

Lo, Shiu-hing, "The Politics of Policing the Anti-WTO Protests in Hong Kong," *Asian Journal of Political Science*, vol. 14, no. 2 (December 2006).

Lo, Shiu-Hing, and Yu, Wing-yat, "The Politics of Electoral Reform in Hong Kong," *Journal of Commonwealth & Comparative Politics*, vol. 39, no. 1 (July 2001).

Lo, Shiu-Hing; Yu, Wing-yat; and Wan, Kwok-fai, "The 1999 District Councils Elections," in Ming K. Chan and Alvin Y. So, eds., *Crisis and Transformation in China's Hong Kong* (New York: M. E. Sharpe, 2002).

Lo, Sonny, "Casino Capitalism and Its Legitimacy Impact on the Politico-administrative State in Macao," *Journal of Current Chinese Affairs: China Aktuell*, vol. 38, no. 1 (2009).

Lo, Sonny Shiu-Hing, *The Dynamics of Hong Kong-Beijing Relations: A Model for Taiwan?* (Hong Kong: Hong Kong University Press, 2008).

Lo, Sonny Shiu-Hing, *The Politics of Cross-Border Crime in Greater China: Case Studies of Mainland China, Hong Kong and Macao* (New York: M. E. Sharpe, 2009).

Lui, Tai-lok, "Under Fire: Hong Kong's Middle Class After 1997," in Cheng, Joseph Y. S., ed., *The July 1 Protest Rally: Interpreting a Historic Event* (Hong Kong: City University of Hong Kong Press, 2005).

Ma, Ngok, "Democratic Development in Hong Kong: A Decade of Lost Opportunities," in Cheng, Joseph, ed., *The Hong Kong Special Administrative Region in Its First Decade* (Hong Kong: City University of Hong Kong Press, 2007).

Ma, Ngok, *Political Development in Hong Kong: State, Political Society, and Civil Society* (Hong Kong: Hong Kong University Press, 2007).

Mackerras, Colin, "China's Ethnic Minorities: Policy and Challenges under the Fourth-generation Leadership," in Cheng, Joseph Y. S., ed., *Challenges and Policy Programmes of China's New Leadership* (Hong Kong: City University of Hong Kong Press, 2007).

Meisner, Maurice, *The Deng Xiaoping Era: An Enquiry into the Fate of Chinese Socialism, 1978–1994* (New York: Hill and Wang, 1996).

"Mrs. Anson Chan and Her Core Group," at http://www.yourchoiceyourvoice.org/CoreGroup/profile.org.htm (accessed August 4, 2009).

Nathan, Andrew J., *Chinese Democracy* (New York: Alfred A. Knopf, 1985).

Nathan, Andrew, and Gilley, Bruce, eds., *China's New Rulers: The Secret Files* (London: Granta Books, 2003).

Ng, Margaret, "Democratization of the Hong Kong SAR: A Pro-democracy View," in Ming K. Chan, ed., *China's Hong Kong Transformed: Retrospect and Prospects Beyond the First Decade* (Hong Kong: City University of Hong Kong Press, 2008).

O'Brien, Kevin J., and Li, Liangjiang, "Suing the Local State: Administrative Litigation in Rural China," *The China Journal*, no. 51 (January 2004).

O'Donnell, Guillermo, and Schmitter, Philippe, *Transitions from Authoritarian Rule: Tentative Conclusions about Uncertain Democracies* (Baltimore, MD: Johns Hopkins University Press, 1986).

Oksenberg, Michel, Sullivan, Lawrence R., and Lambert, Marc, eds., *Beijing Spring, 1989: Confrontation and Conflict The Basic Documents* (New York: M. E. Sharpe, 1990).

Pan, Wei, "Toward a Consultative Rule of Law Regime in China," *Journal of Contemporary China*, vol. 12, no. 35 (2003).

Pei, Minxin, *China's Trapped Transition: The Limits of Developmental Autocracy* (Cambridge, MA: Harvard University Press, 2006).

Pepper, Suzanne, *Keeping Democracy at Bay: Hong Kong and the Challenge of Chinese Political Reform* (Lantham, MD: Rowman & Littlefield Publishers, Inc., 2008).

Perry, Mark, *Eclipse: The Last Days of the CIA* (New York: William Morrow, 1992).

Potter, David, "Democratization in Asia," in Potter, David, ed., *Prospects for Democracy* (Oxford: Polity Press, 1994).

Pye, Lucian, *Asian Power and Politics: The Cultural Dimensions of Authority* (Cambridge, MA: The Belknap Press of Harvard University Press, 1985).

Pye, Lucian W., *The Spirit of Chinese Politics* (Cambridge, MA: Harvard University Press, 1992).

Sautman, Barry, and Dreyer, June Teufel, eds., *Contemporary Tibet: Politics, Development, and Society in a Disputed Region* (New York: M. E. Sharpe, 2006).

Scott, Ian, "The Disarticulation of Hong Kong's Post-Handover Political System," *China Journal*, no. 43 (January 2000).

Sing, Ming, *Hong Kong's Tortuous Democratization: A Comparative Analysis* (London: RoutledgeCurzon, 2004).

Sit, Kwan, "Why Did the DAB Win the District Councils Elections?" *Wide Angle*, no. 423 (December 16, 2007–January 15, 2008).

So, Alvin Y., *Hong Kong's Embattled Democracy: A Societal Analysis* (Baltimore, MD: The Johns Hopkins University Press, 1999).

So, Alvin Y., "The Making of the Cadre-Capitalist Class in China," in Cheng, Joseph Y. S., ed., *China's Challenges in the Twenty-first Century* (Hong Kong: City University of Hong Kong Press, 2003).

Solomon, Richard, *Mao's Revolution and the Chinese Political Culture* (Berkeley: University of California Press, 1971).

Stalley, Philip, and Yang, Dongning, "An Emerging Environmental Movement in China," *China Quarterly* (June 2006).

Szeto, Wah, "Patriotism and the love for democracy are not incompatible," in Ming Pao, ed., *Discussions and Disputes on Patriotism* (Hong Kong: Ming Pao, April 2004).

Thomas, Nicholas, *Democracy Denied: Identity, Civil Society and Illiberal Democracy in Hong Kong* (London: Ashgate, 1999).

Tsai, June-Fang, *Hong Kong in Chinese History: Community and Social Unrest in the British Colony, 1842–1913* (New York: Columbia University Press, 1995).

Tsai, Kellee S., *Capitalism Without Democracy: The Private Sector in Contemporary China* (Ithaca, NY: Cornell University Press, 2007).

Tsang, Steve, "Commitment to the Rule of Law and Judicial Independence," in Tsang, Steve, ed., *Judicial Independence and the Rule of Law in Hong Kong* (Hong Kong: Hong Kong University Press, 2001).

Wang, Keqian, and Wu, Zhongying, *Values and the Cohesion of the Chinese Nation* (*Jianzhiguan Yu Zhonghuaminzu Ningjuli*) (Shanghai: Century Publication, 2001).

Wang, Yanlai, *China's Economic Development and Democratization* (Aldershot: Ashgate, 2003).

White, Lynn T., "The Political Appeals of Conservatives and Reformers," in Lee, Pui-tak, ed., *Hong Kong Reintegrating with China: Political, Cultural and Social Dimensions* (Hong Kong: Hong Kong University Press, 2001).

Wong, Benson, "Can Co-optation Win Over the Hong Kong People?" *Issues & Studies*, vol. 33, no. 5 (May 1997).

Wong, Benson, "Localization in the 2004 Presidential Election Campaign in Taiwan: An Iconographic Approach," *China Perspectives*, no. 55 (September/October 2004).

Wright, Teresa, "The Chinese Democratic Party and the Politics of Protest in the 1980s–1990s," *China Quarterly* (December 2002).

Wu, Guoguang, "Identity, Sovereignty and Economic Penetration: Beijing's responses to offshore Chinese democracies," *Journal of Contemporary China*, vol. 10, no. 51 (May 2007).

Yan, Yunxiang, "Little Emperors or Frail Pragmatists? China's '80ers Generation,'" *Current History* (September 2006).

Yang, Guobin, "The Co-Evolution of the Internet and Civil Society in China," *Asian Survey*, vol. 43, no. 3 (2003).

Yee, Herbert, and Zhu, Feng, "Chinese Perspectives of the China Threat," in Yee, Herbert, and Storey, Ian, eds., *The China Threat: Perceptions, Myths and Reality* (London: RoutledgeCurzon, 2002).

Yep, Ray, "Accommodating Business Interests in China and Hong Kong: Two Systems, One Way Out," in Mok, Ka Ho, and Forrest, Ray, eds., *Changing Governance and Public Policy in East Asia* (London: Routledge, 2009).

Yu, Keping, *Democracy Is a Good Thing: Essays on Politics, Society, and Culture in Contemporary China* (Washington: Brookings Institution Press, 2009).

Yu, Wing-yat, "Organizational Adaptation of the Hong Kong Democratic Party: Centralization and Decentralization," *Issues & Studies*, vol. 33, no. 1 (January 1997).

Zhang, Liang; Link, Perry; and Nathan, Andrew J., eds., *The Tiananmen Papers: The Chinese Leadership's Decision to Use Force Against Their Own People—In Their Own Words* (New York: Public Affairs, 2001).

Zheng, Yongnian, and Wu, Guoguang, "Information Technology, Public Space, and Collective Action in China," *Comparative Political Studies*, vol. 38, no. 5 (June 2005).

Zou, Keyuan, "Rule of Law and Governance," in Wong, John, and Lai, Hongyi, eds., *China into the Hu-Wen Era* (Hackensack, NJ: World Scientific 2006).

Index

American Ambassador to China: 25. *See also* Lilley, James

American Chamber of Commerce: 219

American Consul General in Hong Kong: 67. *See also* Cunningham, James

Anarchist: 169, 172

Annual June 4 candlelight vigil: 35–41

Anti-China: 97, 152, 247

Anti-communist: 25, 27, 97, 166, 221

Anti-corruption: 8, 21–22, 93, 224, 228, 232, 241, 271

Anti-democratic: 6, 51

Anti-foreign (see also xenophobic): 27, 230, 242, 275

Article 23 of the Basic Law: and Bishop Zen, 77; and the Chinese Politburo, 203; and Liaison Office, 52; and "people's power," 33; and political opposition, 159, 210; and public fears of the freedom of speech, 51; content, 47; its impact on DAB, 180; its legislation delayed, 77–78; its relations with double direct elections, 79, 88

Article 45 Concern Group: 78, 108, 131; and the Civic Party, 158–159, 162–

163; and the "Long Hair" Leung Kwok-hung, 168; co-optation by Beijing, 205

Asia Television (ATV): 40–41, 165–66, 212–14

Asian values: 8, 15, 243

Assassination attempt at Martin Lee: 57, 225

Association for Democracy and People's Livelihood: 158; and its decline, 174–76

Audit Commission 8, 105, 223–24, 272; its work, 228, 271

Australia: 137

Autonomy: given to the Legislative Council President, 189; given to the mainland press, 224, 232; in Hong Kong, 22, 76; of the Democratic Alliance for the Betterment and Progress of Hong Kong vis-à-vis Beijing, 184; of the workers from the state control, 6

Beatty, Bob: 15, 20, 243

Bao, Tong: 40

Bar Association: American, 95; Hong Kong, 94, 209

Bargaining: 69, 211, 231, 234–35; between democrats and Hong Kong government, 76–77, 87, 226; between Liberal Party and the Hong Kong government, 193

Basic Law Committee: 62, 71, 79, 84, 86, 188

Beijing's concern about American influence on Hong Kong: 74

Beijing's institutions responsible for Hong Kong matters: 203–4

Beijing's united front work on the Hong Kong democrats: 220–24

Bicameral system: 66, 83–84, 135, 258, 274

Bradley, Stephen: 67, 219. *See also* British Consul General in Hong Kong

Bribe: 147, 223

Britain: 1, 236, 240

British Consul General in Hong Kong: 67, 219. *See also* Bradley, Stephen

Business and Professionals Federation: 66–67, 258, 274

Canada: 137–38, 270

Canada–Hong Kong Link: 80

Candlelight vigil: and DAB, 185; and July 1 parade, 34, 44; and mass mobilization, 236; and political parties, 105; and Tiananmen commemoration, 33; and Xiong Yan, 42; avoided by the TVB coverage, 214; its impact on mainland comrades, 56, 60; its significance, 35–41

Cao, Erbao: 203

Capitalist class: 6, 18, 234–35, 237, 240, 278

Casino: 250, 277; tycoon, 199, 224

Cautherley, George: 104–7

Censorship: 28; of the media, 106, 213–14, 222

Central Discipline Inspection Commission: 22, 93, 232

Chai, Ling: 30, 42, 225

Chan, Anson: 108–14

Chan, Ayo Yi-ngor: 225–26

Chan, Christina Hau-man: 58, 226, 270

Chan, Kenneth Ka-lok: 65, 106, 159–60, 163

Chan, Tat-ching: 23–27; and Ministry of Public Security, 26; and triads, 26–27

Chan, Wai-yip: and double direct election, 81; and the 2009 resignation plan, 90; his view on the policy line of the Democratic Party, 151; lobbied by Hong Kong government, 67, 75; withdrew from the Democratic Party, 148

Chang, Denis: 79

Chen, Albert: 84, 86

Chen, Shui-bian: 73, 229

Chen, Yizhe: 24–25

Chen, Ziming: 25, 40

Cheng, Albert King-hon: and ATV talk show, 166; and Qiao Xiaoyang's consultation meeting, 207; and the 2005 referendum debate, 63; criticized James Tien, 197; harassed by triads, 166; invited to visit Sichuan, 211–12; lobbied by the government, 67

Cheng, Andrew: 102, 143–44, 149–50, 190, 207, 211, 216

Cheng, Gary Kai-nam: 28–29, 97, 245, 254

Cheng, Joseph Yu-shek: 11, 14, 16, 160, 163, 241, 243

Cheng, Yiu-tong: 50, 85, 190–91, 235

Cheng, Yu-tung: 198

Cheung, Chiu-hung: 61, 63–65, 159, 161, 205

Cheung, Man-kwong: 29, 70, 102, 142, 155, 207

Chim, Pui-chung: 65, 207

Chinese Communist Party: and elite conflict over Hong Kong, 267; and Hans domination in China, 7; and hard-liners, 6, 10; and Tiananmen, 239; and Zhao Ziyang, 4, 10; controls the mass media, 19; its liberal forces, 18; suppresses criminal groups, 26; utilizes socialism, 7; views democracy, 271; views the United States, 8

Chinese federalism: 22, 232

Chinese People's Political Consultative Conference (CPPCC): 28–29, 107, 179, 198, 212, 221, 266

Chow, Selina: 76, 134–35, 192–93, 195, 198, 237

Chu, Yiu-ming: 30–31; and his opposition to the Tsang reform plan, 77–78

Chu Hai College: 166, 240, 276

Chung, Robert: 52–53, 65, 136–37, 259

Citizens' Commission on Constitutional Development: 105, 110–12

Civic Party: 158; its emergence, 158–64

Civil Human Rights Front: 48, 52, 65, 71, 93, 121, 250

Civil liberties: and Article 23, 51; and books deemed as "subversive" in mainland China, 32; and Civic Party, 162; and Hong Kong style of democracy, 223, 235; and July 1 protest, 59; and mainland students, 38, 56, 220; and Martin Lee, 99; and Szeto Wah, 30; and the PRC, 228; and Tiananmen, 32; became the concern of Hong Kong people after 1997, 36, 182; cherished by Hong Kong people, 43

Civil society: and co-optation by Beijing and Hong Kong government, 221; and democracy movement, 271; and democratization, 272; and July 1st parade, 55; and the Internet, 19; groups, 2

Class contradictions: 85, 190, 199, 238

Commemoration of June 4: 41; and Chai Ling, 42; and overseas Chinese democrats, 42–43; and Wu'er Kaixi, 42

Competing Chinese visions of democracy: 229

Confucianism: 12

Co-optation: 202–3; and economic enticement, 217–20; and patriotism, 214–16; and intimidation of the democrats, 224–226; and Ricky Wong of the Asia Television, 212–14; of democrats by Beijing, 204–9, 216–17; of democrats by the Hong Kong

government, 210–12; of the legal sector, 209–10

Corruption: 7, 18, 45, 93–94, 170, 173, 194, 246

Court: and Andrew Cheng's speeding, 149; and Chan Wai-yip, 172; and Civic Party, 160; and Leung Kwok-hung, 168–69; and overseas Chinese democrats, 31; and public maladministration, 19; and the assassin of Martin Lee, 57; and the Fung King-man case, 145; and the Ng Chung-tak case, 127; and the 1999 right of abode case, 160

Crime: and Ho Wai-to, 123; and the League of Social Democrats, 166; organized, 7, 26

Crisis of governance: 10, 16

Cultural Revolution: 23

Cunningham, James: 67. *See also* American Consul General in Hong Kong

Dalai Lama: 46

Democracy: deficit, 10; definition, 1; Chinese vision of, 1, 8; Western vision of, 1

Democracy movement: and Anson Chan, 111, 253, 256; and China's democratization, 237; and George Cautherley, 104; and generational change, 106; and idealism of Hong Kong people, 238; and Lau Chin-shek, 206–7; and Martin Lee, 95, 100; and middle-class professionals, 55, 234; and mini-political parties, 236–37; and pact making, 16; and Szeto Wah, 101; and the Alliance, 29; and the League of Social Democrats, 172, 177; and the role of Democratic Party and Civic Party, 155–56, 163; and the veto power of democratic legislators, 90; and triads, 26–27; defined, 271–72; its architects, 237; its contributions to Hong Kong and China, 14; its organizational and leadership problems, 14

Democratic Alliance for the Betterment and Progress of Hong Kong: 178; and Jasper Tsang, 186–89; and the Federation of Trade Unions, 189–91; fighting for the people's livelihood, 185–86; its electoral performance and merger with the Hong Kong Progressive Alliance, 179–80; its succession planning, 181–85

Democratic idealism: 237–38

Democratization: bargaining perspective on Hong Kong, 16–17; class perspective, 4–6, 234; cleavage perspective, 6–7, 235; definition, 2; elite perspective, 3–4, 234; geopolitical perspective, 7–8, 235; ideological perspective, 235; in China, 17–20; optimistic perspective on Hong Kong, 15–16; pessimistic perspective on Hong Kong, 13–14; political culture perspective, 9–10, 234; prospects and scenarios, 238; social movement perspective, 10–11, 236

Deng, Xiaoping: 4, 6, 94, 99, 216, 240–41, 246, 277

Diamond, Larry: 16, 20, 234, 243–44

Direct election: of the chief executive, 10, 21, 200, 237; of the Legislative Council, 57, 111, 229

Dissidents: and Tiananmen, 21, 26, 29, 40; and foreign countries, 45; and Nancy Pelosi, 43; and the Alliance, 29; and triads, 26, 230

District Councils: 126–27; and internal rivalries, 127–28

District Councils elections in 2007: 116–25; and triads, 125–26

Distrust: between Beijing and independent kingdoms, 22, 232; between business elite and ordinary people, 3; between China and Anson Chan, 72–73; between China and most Hong Kong people, 229; between democrats and Donald Tsang, 226; between democrats and the Chinese Communist Party, 77–78, 147; between democrats and the Hong Kong government, 5, 211

Dongguan: 79, 123, 145, 152, 189

Drug trafficking: 25, 257

Educative: function, 80; impact, 21, 31–32, 55, 112, 231; tool, 32

Electoral Affairs Commission: 136–38, 259

Enemies of the state: 4, 271

Environmental protection: 11, 164, 217, 220

Espionage: 270

Eu, Audrey: and elections, 109, 122, 133; and Leung Kwok-hung, 168; and the Article 45 Concern Group, 205; and the Bar Association, 209; and the Civic Party, 101, 156, 158, 161; and referendum, 63; as a target of political co-optation, 211; criticized the Tsang reform plan, 68, 77; her views on communications with Beijing, 163; her views on exit polls, 136

European Union: 70

Executive-legislative relationship: 230

Factionalism: 194–95

Falun Gong: 10, 242, 276

Federation of Trade Unions (FTU): and alliance with DAB, 120, 133–35, 191, 236–38; and electoral alliance, 123; and Regina Ip, 108; and the May 1989 parade, 28; and the pro-Beijing parade on July 1, 50; and trade unionism, 85; competes with the democratic camp, 139; criticized by Raymond Wong, 164; its ideology compared with the League of Social Democrats, 173; its leaders as labor aristocrats, 235; its membership and internal rejuvenation, 189–90; its political opportunism, 33; its tendency of being more anti-democratic, 234; penetrates the ADPL power base, 174

Feng, Chongde: 30

Fok, Kai-cheong: 200

Fok, Timothy: 200
Foreign: aggression, 8; diplomats, 182; influence, 267; investors, 193; media, 155
Foreigners: and Anson Chan, 72–73; and DAB interactions, 182; and Tibetan independence movement, 215; in the eyes of mainland Chinese leaders and officials, 27, 30, 45, 111–12, 230; participated in the July 1 protest in 2009, 58
Foreign Ministry: 50, 74
France: 45, 72, 137–38
Freedom of press: 170
Freedom of speech: 42, 51, 96, 229
French Consul General: 24
Fujian: 50, 210
Functional constituencies: and democratic majority, 129, 132, 135; and executive-led polity, 200; and political reform, 86; and the Lehman Brothers case, 223; and the Liberal Party, 196–97; and their franchise expansion, 106–7; and Tiananmen-related motions, 33; check the democrats, 133; favor pro-establishment elites, 11; in the bicameral system, 67, 83–84; in the eyes of Beijing and Hong Kong government, 133; in the eyes of Ronny Tong, 198–99; in the 2005 Tsang reform plan, 66; protect middle-class conservatives, 234; restricted franchise of, 2; their arrangement in 2012, 81; the abolition of, 10, 57, 194
Fung, Frederick: and elections, 124–25, 158, 174–76; and political reform, 70, 75, 81; as a target of co-optation, 207; as welfarist, 7; his view on the role of the Legislative Council president, 188; lobbied by the Hong Kong government, 67
Fung, King-man: 127, 145, 153, 258

Gilley, Bruce: 17, 20, 243–44
Guangdong province: 94–95, 204, 207–9, 216–17, 220, 267–68
Guangzhou: 18, 25, 189, 206, 214, 220

Guanxi: 25–26, 150
Guevara, Che: 169, 172

Hainan: 24, 26
Hard-liners: 2, 272; in China, 4, 8–10, 27, 29–30, 91, 109, 112, 230; in Hong Kong's democratic camp, 12, 19, 97–98, 100, 231, 234; in Hong Kong's Executive Council, 192
Heung, Chin: 166
Heung Yee Kuk (HYK): 50, 134, 183, 193, 210–11, 222
Ho, Albert: and architects of democracy movement, 92; and Democratic Party, 148, 150–51, 153; and elections, 121–22, 142, 144–45; and Martin Lee, 96; and Szeto Wah, 102; and the Alliance, 29, 162; and the referendum debate, 65; and the reform proposals in 2012, 89; and the Tsang reform plan, 84; attacked by gangster, 224; his view on the Lau Wong-fat's appointment to Executive Council, 211; his view on the League of Social Democrats, 171; his visit to Guangdong in 2009, 216
Ho, Cyd: and election, 96, 124, 133–34, 152; and lunch box meeting, 57; and the Frontier, 154; and the League of Social Democrats, 171; and the resignation plan, 90; view on July 1 protest, 57
Ho, Stanley: 198–99, 224
Ho, Wai-to: 123, 152, 260
Hong Kong Alliance in Support of the Patriotic and Democratic Movement in China: 24–26, 33, 35–37, 40, 162, 167, 205–6, 245; its leaders, 27–31, 101–2, 114
Hong Kong and Macao Affairs Office: 51, 72–73, 76, 203–4, 206, 267
Hong Kong Democratic Party: 140–41; cooperate with other democratic parties, 154–56; infiltration by mysterious forces, 146–49; internal selection mechanism and party strife, 149–51; managing internal disputes, 151–54; members'

integrity and persecution, 145–46;
   merger with the Frontier, 154–56;
   succession planning, 141–45;
Hong Kong's influence on China's
   democratic development: 15, 20–22,
   93–94
Hong Kong's model of democracy and
   democratization: 231–33
Hu, Jintao: 66, 78, 93, 203, 243, 275
Hui, Rafael: 67, 76–77, 79, 265
Human rights: activists, 5, 272;
   American concern about, 43; and
   Anna Wu, 210; and Hong Kong civil
   servants, 111; and Leung
   Kwok-hung, 168; and Liu Xiaobo,
   47; and Martin Lee, 96, 99–100; and
   social movement, 236; and Szeto
   Wah, 102; and the bourgeoisie and
   middle class, 6; award, 95; organi-
   zations in America and Canada, 80
Huntington, Samuel: 9, 41, 140, 259

Identity: and Hong Kong's
   democratization, 235; and political
   cleavage, 6; cards, 125; Chinese, 28,
   105; cultural, 226; Democratic Party
   and secret, 148; Hong Kong, 106; of
   Martin Lee, 99
Ideology: 6–7
Imprison: and Chan Tat-ching's sub-
   ordinate, 25; and Gary Cheng
   Kai-nam, 97; and Leung Kwok-
   hung, 169; and Martin Lee's
   assassin, 57, 224; and Ng Chung-tak,
   127; and Wang Juntao, 33
Independent Commission Against
   Corruption (ICAC): 127, 146, 153,
   194, 209, 211, 223, 272
Independent kingdoms: 22, 232
India: 106, 137
Indians: 119
Infiltration: 146–48, 182
Intellectuals: 5, 12, 20, 106, 234, 242,
   272, 276
Interest groups: 19, 47–48, 209
Internal struggle: 142, 146, 149
International Covenant on Civil and
   Political Rights: 31

Internet: 19, 39, 51, 219, 228, 243, 279
Intra-party democracy: 93
Ip, Regina: 262, 108–9, 118, 128, 134,
   184, 188, 223

Japan: 8
Japanese: 94, 104
Jiandu: 93
Judicial independence: 162, 241, 278
July 1 March: 44; and its dynamics,
   46–51; and the coverage of the Hong
   Kong Chinese newspapers, 53–55;
   Beijing concern, 56–58; prediction on
   the number of participants, 51–56

Kam, Nai-wai: 133, 142, 149–50
Kidnap: 27
Ku, Si-yiu: 167
Kuan, Hsin-chi: 159, 162–63, 259, 276
Kwok, Ka-kay: 65

Lai, Chi-keung: 142–43, 149
Lai, Jimmy: 54, 79, 90, 99, 196, 225
Lau, Chin-shek: 65, 133, 154, 175–76,
   263; and Article 23 of the Basic Law,
   77–79; and Operation Yellowbird,
   24; and the Democratic Party, 148,
   151; and the Tsang reform plan, 67,
   75; became target of co-optation,
   206–7, 212
Lau, Emily: and Chinese officials, 69;
   and elections, 154; and Robert
   Chung, 136; and the Frontier, 68,
   155; and the League of Social
   Democrats, 172; and the Legislative
   Council, 196–97; and the resignation
   plan, 89; her focus, 7; her view on
   the Chinese officials, 209; her view
   on universal suffrage, 64; joined the
   Democratic Party, 143–44; visited
   Guangdong, 216
Lau, Miriam Kin-yee: 207
Lau, Siu-kai: 66, 218, 276
Lau, Wong-fat: 129, 183–84, 193, 195,
   210–11, 268
Lawyers: and Andrew Cheng, 149;
   and Martin Lee, 114; and the Civic
   Party, 100, 159–60; and their

opposition to the national security bill, 205; in China, 19, 154, 210; in democracy movement, 5, 272

Leach, James: 68

Leadership succession: in China, 22, 232, 244; in the Hong Kong Democratic Party, 141; in the Hong Kong Liberal Party, 201

League of Social Democrats: 158; and Leung Kwok-hung, 167–70; and political symbolism, 170–73; and Raymond Wong, 165–67; its emergence, 164–65

Lee, Allen: 65, 79, 90, 94, 105, 110, 112, 215; and the Anson Chan core group, 73; and the Democratic Party, 145; and the Liberal Party, 192; as a middleman to deal with the Alliance, 29

Lee, Martin: and Cardinal Zen, 77–78, 100; and double direct elections, 81, 122; and foreigners, 155; and July 1 march, 47; and justice, 98; and Legislative Council elections, 96, 116; and Leung Kwok-hung, 224; and Szeto Wah, 27, 101–3, 147; and the 2009 political reform plan, 90; and the Alliance, 29; and the attempt to assassinate him, 57, 225; and the Bar Association, 209; and the Basic Law drafting process, 63; and the member list of the Democratic Party, 148; as a target of political exclusion, 207; as architects of democracy movement, 114; his background, 94; his classical liberalism, 99; his contribution to China's democratization, 237; his friendship with Jimmy Lai, 99; his legacy, 100; his patriotism, 97, 230; his view on the democracy movement, 156; his view on the dialogue with Beijing, 81; his view on the Liaison Office, 146; his view on the Strategic Development Commission, 82–83, 87; his view on the Tsang reform plan, 68, 79; lobbied for international support of democracy in Hong Kong, 70; recruited

young people into the Democratic Party, 145; stepped down from legislative elections, 101, 133, 141; visited the United States, 71

Lee, Shau-kei: 198

Lee, Wing-tat: and District Councils elections, 121; and legislative elections, 142, 150; and political reform, 69, 75; and the Alliance, 29; and the Democratic Party, 68, 144, 147–48; and the Strategic Development Commission, 85–86; as a target of political co-optation, 211; as a target of political exclusion, 207; his view on bicameral system, 84; his view on the government's appointees in District Councils, 208; his view on the mass media in exposing the Democratic Party's internal problems, 208; his view on Tiananmen, 208

Lee Cheuk-yan: and elections, 131, 154; and referendum, 62; and the Alliance, 102; and the Confederation of Trade Unions, 81; and the Mandatory Provident Fund, 156; and the Strategic Development Commission, 84; and the Tsang reform plan, 68, 75; as a social activist, 237; as a target of political exclusion, 207; as welfarist, 7; his role in the Tiananmen Incident, 28–29; his view on Donald Tsang's comment on the Tiananmen Incident, 216; his view on Leung Kwok-hung, 168; his view on the bicameral system, 84

Legislative Council elections in 2008: 128–38; and public opinion polls, 136–38

Legislative supremacy: 230

Leong, Alan: 81, 89, 101, 122, 155, 207, 257, 261–62; and Article 23 of the Basic Law, 47, 205; and the Civic Party, 158, 162–64; competed with Donald Tsang in the 2007 Chief Executive election, 106, 155

Leung, Chun-ying: 171

Leung, Kwok-hung: and opposition to

the Tung regime in 2003, 47; and
political symbolism, 170; and the
League of Social Democrats, 164–65;
and the People's Radio, 80; and the
referendum debate, 64; and the resignation plan in 2009, 90; as a target
of political exclusion, 207, 216; his
action and language in the Legislative Council, 51, 171; his contribution to Hong Kong's democracy
movement, 177; his ideology, 167;
his popularity, 172; his view on Jasper Tsang, 167, 189; in the eyes of
Szeto Wah, 104
Li, Ka-shing: 199–200
Li, Peng: 28
Li, Richard: 200
Li, Wah-ming: 79, 123, 144, 150–51,
188–89, 206–207, 224, 237
Liaison Office: and business people,
140; and Cao Erbao, 203; and
Cardinal Zen, 216; and DAB, 120,
139, 182; and dialogue with
democrats, 81, 205; and Hong
Kong's elections, 235; and political
reform, 76; and Regina Ip, 108, 255;
and the Liberal Party, 135, 195–96;
and the Olympics torch event, 215;
and the pro-Beijing parade on July 1,
50; and the Ricky Wong incident,
213; and *Wen Wei Po*, 58; arranged
Qiao Xiaoyang's consultation with
Hong Kong people, 207; as Beijing's
representative office in Hong Kong,
28, 42; clarified Beijing's stance on
universal suffrage in 2017, 74; lobbied pro-Beijing elites, 206; in the
eyes of Martin Lee, 146; in the eyes
of Yeung Sum, 152; its concern about
July 1 march, 44; its negative image
in the Hong Kong Chinese press,
204; its responsibility to reflect the
views of Hong Kong people to Beijing, 77, 209; its united front work,
152, 202; its view on Leung
Kwok-hung, 168; its view on referendum, 62; its work on the legal
sector, 209; misread Hong Kong's

public opinion in 2003, 51; per-
suaded democrats to support politi-
cal reform plans, 208
Liang, Xiang: 24, 26
Liao, Hui: 76, 108
Liberalism: 7–8, 96, 191–93, 235–37
Liberal Party: 178–79, 191–94; and its
factionalism, 194–96; and the
business elite, 196–200
Lilley, James: 25. *See also* American
Ambassador to China
Liu, Xiaobo: 47, 54
Lo, Chi-kin: 83, 151, 253
London: 36, 94, 101
Lu, Ping: 267

Ma, Ngok: 15, 267
Ma, Ying-jeou: 43
Macao: and Wu'er Kaixi, 42; casino
tycoon, 199, 224; Chief Executive
Edmund Ho, 56; China's concern
about foreign political influence on,
27; Chinese Club in Boston, 80;
integration with the Pearl River
Delta region, 220; style of politics in
Hong Kong, 54
Mad Dog Daily: 166
Mainland Chinese democracy: 228–29
Mainland Chinese democratization:
93–94
Mainland democrats: and Hong Kong
democrats, 21, 29, 231; and Hong
Kong's pro-Beijing elites, 34; and
Hong Kong triads, 27, 166, 233; and
James Lilley, 25; and Operation
Yellowbird, 24, 272; and Reverend
Chu Yiu-ming, 30; and Szeto Wah,
101, 114; and the Alliance, 28;
escaped from China, 4, 23, 43; in the
eyes of Chan Tat-ching, 26
Mainland immigrants: 10, 124
Mainland policing: 44–45; its learning
from Hong Kong, 46
Mainland tourists: 32, 55–56, 203,
217–18
Marxism: 173, 177
Marxist: 6, 172–73
Middle class: agent for political

activism, 19; and Democratic Party, 151, 159; and democratization, 5; and modernization theory, 9; and the Civic Party, 156, 163, 173; and the League of Social Democrats, 172; and universal suffrage, 76; co-opted by the mainland Chinese state, 6; educated, 18; in South China, 9; professionals, 5, 16, 176, 191, 234; split, 5; values democracy, 12
Mini-political parties: 154, 236
Ministry of Public Security: 25–26, 206
Montagne, Jean Pierre: 24

National People's Congress: and Annex 2 of the Basic Law, 132; and chair Wu Bangguo, 93; and the business elites, 198; and Tiananmen mothers, 40; annual meeting, 94; checks government performance, 8, 22, 228, 232; empowered, 224; its Legal Affairs Committee, 204, 206; member Allen Lee, 73, 79, 90, 105, 112, 145, 215; members, 28, 65, 107, 179, 264
National security: 27, 45, 166, 188; agency, 169; agents, 177; bill, 47, 59, 91, 109, 187, 192–93, 205; concerns, 235; interest, 4; legislation, 78; threat, 59
Ng, Margaret: 34, 70, 101, 207, 242; and Article 45 Concern Group, 205; and the Civic Party, 106, 158, 211; her remark cited by Bishop Zen, 77; view on democracy movement, 14–15; view on referendum, 64
Non-Governmental Organizations: 106

Operation Yellowbird: 23–27, 233, 272
Organized crime: 7, 26
Overseas Chinese: 28, 31–32, 36, 40–43, 47, 80, 98, 247

Parade: an ideal model for mainland police to learn how to cope with, 45; and Anson Chan, 72, 114; and Cardinal Zen, 71; and democracy movement, 14; and mainland tourists, 56; and overseas Chinese democrats, 41; and political maturity, 233; annually before June 4, 30, 35; in May 1989, 28; in support of political reform, 73, 87, 103, 206, 237; on July 1, 34, 48, 50, 53, 55, 59; orderly, 46; participants, 35–36, 69; pro-Beijing, 50;
Patten, Christopher: 2, 72, 161, 267
Patriotism: 230
Peaceful evolution: 241
People's Liberation Army: 27, 50
People's Radio: 80
Pepper, Suzanne: 14, 132, 242, 249
Pistol: 25, 225
Police: and Anson Chan, 224; and Bao Tong, 40; and Chan Tat-ching's colleagues, 27; and Lee Cheuk-yan, 29; and Lehman Brothers victims, 58; and Leung Kwok-hung, 167, 173; and mainland protests, 44–45; and Operation Yellowbird, 26, 272; and rubber bullets, 46; and salary dispute, 55; and social protests in Hong Kong, 46; and the assassins of Martin Lee, 224–25; and triad harassment of Albert Cheng and Raymond Wong, 166; arrest warrant on Chinese democrats, 23; checkpoint, 24; commissioner in Hong Kong, 50, 126; discretion, 45; Dongguan, 123, 145; estimates on the number of participants in the annual candlelight vigil, 37; estimates on the number of participants on the annual July 1 march, 52–53; figures on participants in the annual parade commemorating June 4, 35–36; grievances in Hong Kong, 49; in Yuen Long's electoral violence, 126; intelligence shared between China and Hong Kong, 169; mainland police learn from Hong Kong, 59; modernization in the mainland, 94; mutiny in 1974, 209; penetrated working-class meetings in Hong Kong under British rule, 97; power,

170, 226; protected Szeto Wah and
Martin Lee, 27

Police Commissioner Tang
King-shing: 126

Policing: 248, 277; social unrest, 44–46

Policy implementation: 221

Political culture: and democratization,
2, 9; Chinese paternalistic, 9; clashes
between mainland Chinese and
Hong Kong, 229; Confucian, 9; of
familism and pragmatism in Hong
Kong, 9; in the eyes of the sons of
Hong Kong tycoons, 200; its fear of
localism in China, 22; its transformation in Hong Kong, 10, 220; mass,
172; of Hong Kong shaping mainland political culture, 43, 231; of
Hong Kong shaping mainland
visitors, 60; of Hong Kong students,
38; of mainland students, 38; of
tolerating pluralism on the part of
mainland ruling elites, 233; pro-
democracy, 38; silent revolution in
the mainland, 232

Political opposition: 138, 173, 193, 200

Political reform proposals in 2005: 66;
and Anson Chan, 72–73; and Chief
Executive Donald Tsang, 68; and
public opinion, 67, 69, 78; and the
American Consul General, 67; and
the concessions made by the Hong
Kong government, 74–75; and the
two houses model, 66; factors explaining the Legislative Council's
vote, 75–77; mobilization of the
public to oppose, 70–71; opportunities for bargaining between
democrats and Beijing, 69; rejected
by the Legislative Council, 75; the
reaction of democrats to, 67

Political show: 33, 64, 104, 114, 168

Political space: 11, 33, 82–83, 86, 155,
229, 253; for China, 39, 139, 224, 228,
241

Pro-Beijing groups: 110, 245, 258

Pro-independence (Taiwan): 229

Proportional representation: 2, 150

Prostitution: 123, 145, 257

Public maladministration: 21–22, 221–
23, 228, 232, 237, 272; in China, 19,
93, 232

Public opinion: and Anson Chan's
participation in the legislative
by-election, 112; and Liaison Office,
52; and mainland agencies responsible for Hong Kong, 204; and
Michael DeGolyer's findings, 10;
and referendum, 62–63, 229; and the
democrats, 65; and the Hong Kong
government, 81; and the Liberal
Party, 193; and the Tsang reform
plan, 68; divided on universal suffrage's timing, 69; Hong Kong
government consults, 21, 61, 232;
Liaison Office failed to tap, 206; on
the League of Social Democrats, 172;
polls on Donald Tsang's popularity,
192; polls on legislative elections,
136; "raping," 34; reflected to Beijing, 209; support of Martin Lee and
Szeto Wah, 141

Pye, Lucian: 9, 22, 232, 241

Qiao, Xiaoyang: 64, 70–72, 81, 168, 170,
204, 207

Radicalism: 13, 167, 169, 177

Radio Television Hong Kong (RTHK):
57–58, 112, 212, 221, 268

Referendum debate in 2004: 60; Allen
Lee's view, 65; and Article 74 of the
Basic Law, 64; and private member's
bill, 64; and Stephen Lam, 64; and
Tung Chee-hwa, 64; Cheung
Chiu-hung's view, 61–65; debate in
Legislative Council, 61–62; Martin
Lee's view, 63; Qiao Xiaoyang's
view, 64; Ronny Tong's view, 62;
voting result in Legislative Council
on referendum, 65; Wang Zhenmin's
view, 62–63; Xiao Weiyun's view, 65;
Zhu Yucheng's view, 63

Revolutionary: 37, 172, 227; base, 23,
29, 36; hero, 169, 227; party, 26

Rice, Condoleezza: 67

Right of self-determination: 229

Rule by law: 19
Rule of law: and Hong Kong's
   semidemocracy, 271; and Hong
   Kong style of democracy, 223, 272;
   and Leung Kwok-hung, 168; and
   Martin Lee, 95; and Western values
   of liberalism and capitalism, 8; as a
   yardstick for measuring China's
   political progress, 235; changes the
   political orientations of mainlanders
   migrating to Hong Kong, 220; Chinese leaders' fear of, 99; development in China, 8, 228; Hong Kong
   people's support of, 12, 43; Hong
   Kong's respectable, 8; in Hong Kong
   being challenged by mainland
   China, 18; its absence in China, 18;
   resolves politically sensitive issues,
   33; solid in Hong Kong, 21, 36, 232;
   taken more seriously by Beijing, 56

Secret societies: 26
Security agents: 23, 42, 166, 177, 272
Shanghai: 18, 58, 203, 217, 219, 241, 247
Shenzhen: 41, 70, 189, 207, 217, 220, 269
Shum, John Kin-fun: 23–27; and CIA,
   25; and Operation Yellowbird, 26–27
Sichuan: 44–45, 97, 170, 185, 211
Silent revolution: 38–39, 60, 220, 232
Sin, Chung-kai: and Kam Nai-wai, 142,
   143; and Lai Chi-keung, 142; and
   Martin Lee, 143; and the Democratic
   Party, 143–44, 149, 153; as a target of
   political co-optation, 207; as archi-
   tect of democracy movement, 114;
   criticized the Electoral Affairs Com-
   mission, 136; his view on Leung
   Kwok-hung, 168; visited Beijing,
   205; visited foreign countries to
   lobby for international support of
   Hong Kong's democratization, 70
Sing, Ming: 13, 83, 242, 278
Sino-American power struggle: 236
Smuggle: 24
Smuggling: 25–26, 257
Snakeheads: 25
So, Alvin: 15
Social movement: 2, 10–11, 220–24, 275

Social unrest: 7, 45–46, 94, 241, 244,
   274, 278
Soft-liners: 2, 19, 234, 272; in Hong
   Kong's democratic camp, 231; in
   Hong Kong's government, 4
Sovereignty: 1–2, 65–66, 70, 83, 175,
   267, 279
Sovereignty visions between Beijing
   and Hong Kong democrats: 65–66,
   70
Speedboat: 25–26, 272
Spy: 161
Standing Committee of the National
   People's Congress: and Bishop Zen,
   77; and China's intervention in
   Hong Kong matters, 235; and the
   Article 45 Concern Group, 159;
   decision in April 2004 on the procedures of voting on bills and
   motions, 133; decision in mid-1999
   on the right of abode of mainland
   Chinese, 161; decision on the tenure
   of the Chief Executive in 2005, 202,
   207; Hong Kong democrats reacted
   to the decision of, 80–81; its deputy
   secretary Qiao Xiaoyang went to
   Shenzhen, 70; its elites control
   China's policy toward Hong Kong,
   72; veto in April 2004 over double
   direct elections in 2007 and 2008,
   61–62, 64, 74, 184
Strategic Development Commission:
   66, 82–89
Sun, Yat-sen: 23, 36, 100, 227
Suppression of student democrats: 26,
   97, 225
Szeto, Wah: and double direct
   elections, 31; and infiltration into the
   Democratic Party, 147; and the
   Alliance, 27, 29–30, 162; and the
   Basic Law Drafting Committee, 97;
   and the People's Radio program, 80;
   and the resignation plan, 89–90; and
   the unfinished democracy
   movement, 101; as architect of
   democracy movement, 92, 114; as
   party whip in the Democratic Party,
   153; cherishes diversity, 104;

contributes to China's democratization, 237; contributes to Hong
Kong's democracy movement, 114;
criticized by *Ming Pao*, 141; fights for
justice in both Hong Kong and
China, 98; his background, 101; his
view on Anson Chan, 253; his view
on Donald Tsang, 141; his view on
the compatibility between
patriotism and democracy, 230

Taiwan: and Heung Chin, 166; and
Hong Kong's democratization, 76;
and Jimmy Lai, 225; and
Kuomintang flags on Hong Kong's
July 1 march, 58; and Martin Lee's
father, 94; and referendum in Hong
Kong, 63–64; and the League of
Social Democrats, 164, 173; and
triads, 233; and Wang Dan, 41; and
Wu'er Kaixi, 42; businessman Tsai
Eng-meng and ATV, 213; change of
political culture in, 9; Chinese as
targets of Beijing's co-optation, 221;
compared with Hong Kong and
South Korea's democratization, 13,
16; in the eyes of Stanley Ho, 199; its
opposition Democratic Progressive
Party, 138; its President Chen Shui-
bian, 229; its President Ma Ying-
jeou, 43; its Western-style polity, 73,
91; presidential elections, 96, 263;
reunification with China seen as
being obstructed by the United
States, 8; the possibility of China
following its model of democratization, 20
Taiwanization of Hong Kong: 91, 173,
263
Tam, Mandy: 65, 67, 75, 120, 161, 205,
207
Tam, Yiu-chung: 63, 69, 134, 179, 183–
85, 187, 190, 212
Tang, Henry: 171, 194, 222
Television Broadcasting (TVB): 45, 55,
212, 214, 248
Tiananmen Incident: and Operation
Yellowbird, 23–27; impact on the

young people of Hong Kong, 31–34
Tiananmen Square: and hard-liners of
the CCP Politburo, 4, 10; and the
arguments between Li Peng and
Zhao Ziyang, 239–40; and the ATV
coverage, 41; and the Hong Kong
people in 1989, 29; and the military
crackdown of student democrats,
23; and the tight security, 36; in the
eyes of most Hong Kong people,
229; in the eyes of the League of
Social Democrats, 165–66; in the
minds of Szeto Wah and Martin
Lee, 97
Tibetan: Autonomous Region, 229;
independence movement, 215, 226;
issue and Christina Chan, 58, 270;
monks, 45; protests, 45; struggle for
the right of self-determination, 7;
unrest, 45–46, 247; Youth Congress,
46
Tien, James: and Lau Wong-fat, 211;
and legislative elections, 134, 187,
192, 237; and the Liaison Office, 135;
and the Liberal Party, 194–97, 201;
appealed to the democrats, 81; his
relationship with Donald Tsang,
193; his view on political reform, 69;
opposed the national security bill,
187
Tien, Michael: 194, 198
To, James: 117, 121, 144, 148, 150, 152,
197, 207, 216, 246
Tong, Ronny: 48, 62, 64; and his view
on the 2005 political reform plan,
69–70; contact with Beijing, 74
Triad: boss, 166; members, 24, 27, 126,
166, 233, 272
Triads: 26–27, 103, 125–26, 272;
harassment of Albert Cheng and
Raymond Wong, 166; Hong Kong
triad 14K, 126; Hong Kong triad
Shui Fong, 225
Tsang, Donald: 34, 112, 186; and Li
Ka-shing, 199; and Richard Li, 200;
and Stanley Ho, 199; and the
accountability system, 113; and the
dispute over police salary, 49; and

the Liaison Office, 50; and universal suffrage in 2017, 74; competed with Alan Leong in the 2007 Chief Executive election, 106, 163; criticized by Anson Chan, 48; criticized by Martin Lee, 71; criticized by Raymond Wong, 167; his political reform package, 61, 84; his popularity, 120, 192; his relations with DAB, 187; his relations with James Tien, 193; his view on the Tiananmen incident, 34, 36; policy of favoring friends and followers, 200, 226

Tsang, Jasper: 186–89; his possible membership of the underground CCP, 167, 189

Tsoi, Richard: 93

Tung, Chee-hwa: 172, 199; and Alan Leong, 262; and the crisis of governance, 10; and the Hong Kong Macao Affairs Office, 51; and the Liaison Office, 51; his popularity, 184; his successor's term of office, 206; implicitly criticized Martin Lee, 96; met Szeto Wah on the Alliance activities, 29–30; resigned in March 2005, 186; the July 1 protest in 2003 against his administration, 44

Tycoon: 99, 160, 197–200, 224

United Front Department: 206

United Kingdom: 25, 45, 72, 100, 104, 137–38

United States: and Chai Ling, 42; and Chan Tat-ching, 25; and China's democratic development, 236; and Kam Yiu-yu, 245; and Martin Lee, 71; and the Chinese Foreign Ministry, 74; and the Hong Kong democrats, 70; and the pro-democracy overseas Chinese organizations, 80; and Wang Dan, 41; and Wang Juntao, 33; and Yan Jianli, 231, 270; Donald Tsang's visit in 2005 to, 68; in the eyes of mainland Chinese hard-liners, 9; interested in Hong Kong's democratic development, 8; its view on the Tiananmen incident,

32; seen as using "peaceful evolution" to topple socialism in the world, 241; superpower struggle with China, 8; support of student democrats, 45

Universal suffrage: 16, 46, 48; and a roadmap, 87; and a timetable, 68–71, 73–74, 77–78; and Article 23 of the Basic Law, 188; and Beijing's leadership, 3, 232; and mass mobilization, 57; and party development, 174; and the ADPL, 174; and the Basic Law, 15; and the CCP, 54; and the Civic Party, 198; and the competing Chinese visions of democracy, 229, 237–38; and the Democratic Party, 89; and the International Covenant on Civil and Political Rights, 31; and the Liberal Party, 192, 194; and the middle class, 76; and the resignation plan initiated in 2009, 89–90; and trade unionism, 199; and triads, 103; and welfarism, 84–85; in the eyes of *Ta Kung Pao*, 53; in the mind of Anson Chan, 113; in the mind of business elites, 7, 134–35, 199; in the mind of George Cautherley, 107; in the mind of Leung Kwok-hung, 169; in the mind of Martin Lee, 102, 208; in the mind of Regina Ip, 109; in the mind of Szeto Wah, 103; in the mind of Xu Chongde, 71–72; its future from 2017 onwards, 17; of the chief executive, 1, 10, 43, 61, 80, 82, 99; of the entire legislature, 1, 61, 79, 81, 228; ruled out in 2007 and 2008, 62, 64; supported by *Apple Daily*, 47; supported by most Hong Kong people, 21, 229

Uygurs: 7, 45

Voter turnout: 117, 119, 255

Wang, Dan: 40–41, 45, 47

Wang, Juntao: 33

Wang, Weilin: 41

Wang, Zhenmin: 62–63, 79, 188

Washington: 44, 80, 243–44, 252, 273, 275–76, 279
Wen, Jiabao: 32, 72, 79, 218
Wen Wei Po: 79
Western-style democracy: and mainland China, 93; and the Chinese political culture, 9, 229; and the Hong Kong democrats, 230, 236; and the United States, 8; different from Chinese democracy, 271; in Taiwan, 91; in the eyes of the middle class, 5; its absence in Hong Kong, 221, 271; the Hong Kong middle class is not forceful enough to push for, 234
Wilson, David: 24, 29
Wong, Raymond: 7, 51, 89–90, 114, 133, 155, 165–67; and the League of Social Democrats, 164–71, 177
Wong, Ricky Wai-kay: 212–14
Wilson, David: 24, 29
Wu, Bangguo: 93

Xenophobic (see also anti-foreign): 95, 109, 111, 230
Xi, Jinping: 203
Xiao, Weiyun: 65

Xinjiang: 45–46, 94, 229, 247
Xu, Chongde: 71

Yan, Jiaqi: 32
Yang, Wenchang: 65
Yeung, Sum: and legislative elections, 95, 109; and the Alliance, 29; and the Democratic Party, 144, 148, 151–153; and the Donald Tsang reform plan, 79–80; and the GST plan, 261; as a target of political exclusion, 207; as principal in the Democratic Party's Party School, 143; criticized appointments to District Councils, 127

Zen, Cardinal Joseph: 71, 77–79, 100, 199, 215
Zeng, Qinghong: 104, 167, 205
Zhang, Xiaoming: 62
Zhao Ziyang: 4, 10, 26, 32, 40, 239, 247; his son, 24
Zhejiang province: 212
Zhu, Yucheng: 63, 76, 203
Zhuhai: 220

About the Author

SONNY SHIU-HING LO is Professor in the Department of Political Science at the University of Waterloo, Ontario, Canada. His single-authored books include *Political Development in Macau* (1995), *The Politics of Democratization in Hong Kong* (1997), *Governing Hong Kong* (2001), *Political Change in Macao* (2008), *The Dynamics of Beijing-Hong Kong Relations: A Model for Taiwan?* (2008), and *The Politics of Cross-Border Crime in Greater China: Case Studies of Mainland China, Hong Kong and Macao* (2009).